GOD SPEAKS

MEHER BABA, 1956

GOD SPEAKS

*The Theme of Creation
and Its Purpose*

BY MEHER BABA

*Second Edition,
Revised and Enlarged*

DODD, MEAD & COMPANY
New York   1973

Second Printing 1967
Third Printing 1968
Fourth Printing 1970

Second Edition 1973
Second Printing 1975

Library of Congress Catalog Card Number: 72-13984
Printed in the United States of America
by Vail-Ballou Press, Inc., Binghamton, N. Y.

Address of Sufism Reoriented, Inc.:
1290 Sutter Street, San Francisco, Calif. 94109

DEDICATION

To the Universe—
the Illusion that sustains Reality

Preface to First Edition

A NUMBER of factors have entered into the writing and editing of this volume which require some word of explanation.

Through the medium of his alphabet board, Meher Baba has dictated in its entirety the present contents of the major portion of this work, consisting of parts I through VIII.

Parts IX and X, "The Ten States of God" and the "Conclusion," were written by Eruch B. Jessawala in elaboration of notes dictated to him by Meher Baba, and are a recapitulation of the previous sections dictated directly by Meher Baba.

Certain footnotes have been added by the editors using both previously published and unpublished statements by Meher Baba, as well as illustrative quotations rendered in free form from the great mystic poets of the East. In addition, several footnotes and the Supplement to this work include notes taken down by some disciples of Meher Baba, including the Sufi disciple of more than twenty-five years' standing, the late Dr. Abdul Ghani Munsiff, and are based on Baba's explanations and used with his permission. The translation of the Persian poem "The Ascending Soul" on page 33 is reprinted from Reynold A. Nicholson's *Rumi, Poet And Mystic* published by George Allen & Unwin Ltd. The quotation from the Bhagavad Gita found on page xviii of the Introduction is reprinted from Sir Edwin Arnold's *The Song Celestial* published by Routledge & Kegan Paul Ltd. For permission to reprint these translations grateful thanks are due to the above publishers. The complete contents of *God Speaks* have been carefully corrected and approved by Meher Baba.

The function of the present editors has been one primarily of handling certain mechanical details necessary in rendering any work into final form for publication. They would hardly have undertaken even this minor function in relation to so fundamental a document had they not been specifically requested to do so by the author.

Their own relationship to Sufism Reoriented should not be misconstrued by those few persons who are aware of the connection. Meher Baba's pronouncements have always been without sectarian purpose or bias. He has often made direct statements to the effect that he appreciates all "isms" (Sufism, Vedantism, Christianity, Zoroastrianism, Buddhism, etc.), religious and political parties for the many good things that they seek to achieve, but does not and cannot belong to any of them. He regards Absolute Truth as including and transcending them all, and his function as being detached from all these divine paths, awakening the followers of these divine paths to their real meaning and true spirit. "The unity of all life is integral and indivisible. It remains unassailable and inviolable in spite of all ideological differences."

The reader will soon become aware of the fact that numerous passages of *God Speaks* are distinctly repetitive. If this work were intended to clarify or restate some reasonably well-known theorem of current culture it would perhaps be desirable to arrange the work in simple logical sequence and allow the thesis to unfold in brief finality. However, *God Speaks* not only picks up the fragments of many previous concepts of spiritual truth and arranges them in orderly and mutually compatible fashion, but it takes the entire subject several steps further than it has historically existed and establishes several new and detailed thought patterns.

To do this effectively it seems necessary to look at the subject matter again and again from a number of angles and with increasing conceptual proliferation. Illustrations and anecdotes are often repeated in these various circumstances in order that each portion may be self-contained, thus obviating the necessity of the reader's referring back to earlier passages for details which might be omitted in a later context.

The net result is not unlike the effect achieved musically in the constantly elaborating theme of a Ravel's "Bolero" or a Bach Fugue from the "Well-Tempered Clavichord."

Although it would seem at first a minor item, one of the most troublesome issues in undertaking the editing of this work has been the establishing of a consistent policy for capitalization of words. The normal procedure of reserving such usage for proper names, the Deity and His immediate attributes is brought to a sorry dilemma in a work which has as its major thesis the divinity of all creation. To establish such a connotation in strict literality would result in a flood of capital letters which not only would not aid in emphasizing such a thesis but would obstruct the progress of the reader.

This matter is made even more puzzling by the subtle fashion in which Meher Baba gradually draws the consciousness of the reader from the concept of God in His unmanifest states to those stages of development in which the individualized soul is apparently furthest from realizing his essential eternal oneness with God. A strictly rational policy on capitalizations during such a progression of development, ending in a final return to full union with the Father, is apparently unobtainable, and therefore the editors have adopted the more feasible usage of capitalizing the Deity and His immediate attributes, and thereafter have used capitals primarily for the sake of emphasis and helping the reader to distinguish readily between conditions associated with the higher as contrasted with the more gross planes (*i.e.*, Energy of the subtle planes compared to nuclear energy).

Similar problems were encountered in as mechanical a process as punctuation. In the complex issues which Meher Baba sorts out for meticulous elucidation, strict adherence to classic rules of punctuation would result in an almost unendurable jumble of commas, colons, dashes and semicolons. Here again the editors have adopted an arbitrary policy of deliberately avoiding meticulous usage of punctuation within a sentence as long as the thought flowed readily.

In many instances Meher Baba has coined terms to express a specific concept. It has seemed preferable to insure exact understanding of his intent rather than to render the work more conventional by substitution of well-seasoned terminology which **almost** expresses the content of the coined phrase. Inverted and complex sentence structure has also been left in numberless instances where possible ambiguity or a breaking of the flow of thought seemed to result from reinversion of structure or shortening of sentences.

In brief, the function of editor is to render a work into conventional usage and for ready assimilation. Wherever the present editors have found this inconsistent with the major purpose of the work, conventional usage and simplicity of style have been happily sacrificed for specificity of intent.

It would not do to leave the mechanical phase without cautioning the reader that most writers differentiate between the terms "knowledge" and "wisdom," assigning a more valued or spiritual function to the latter. Meher Baba makes no such differentiation and uses "knowledge" rather in the sense of "true knowledge."

After intense concentration on this volume some readers may wish to broaden their knowledge of Meher Baba's viewpoint on the subject of the finite and the infinite. Additional valuable material is contained in his *Discourses* in five volumes, published by Meher Publications, Ahmednagar, India,* as well as in Meher Baba's foreword to Dr. William Donkin's *The Wayfarers,* † and also Chapter I of that work.

Washington, D.C.   Ivy O. Duce
January 23, 1955   Don E. Stevens

---

* Republished in three volumes by Sufism Reoriented, Inc., 1967.
† Reprinted by Sufism Reoriented, Inc., 1969.

Introduction to First Edition

GOD has never spoken in my presence, but I am sure that I have seen Him act in human form. That is the only manner in which I can explain the incredible sensitivity of action and reaction which characterized Meher Baba during those brief periods on a Saturday afternoon in New York when I first saw him in action.

He was telling a story of a seeker after Truth who was called upon to bear acts of arbitrariness and harshness of an extreme degree before his teacher would accept him. As Meher Baba's fingers flew over the alphabet board which he uses for communication, and as his hands raised occasionally in brief gesticulation, I found myself rapt even more in the teller and manner of telling than in the story.

Sitting off to the side and outside his line of vision I raised my hand almost involuntarily with thumb to forefinger to inscribe the age-old circle of perfection. Even as I started to do so I was warmed to see Meher Baba turn his gaze full upon me and lift his own hand in the identical gesture. Human beings are not too often aware of the feelings of their fellows, let alone minutely responsive to them, and it surprised me to be in the presence of someone who possessed such sensitivity of feeling.

I forgot the episode until he was en route to the elevator late in the day, and as I stood among a knot of people at the side of his passageway I again raised my hand in a similar gesture, now deliberately wondering if he would catch it in the even less probable position in which I was placed. Again as I started the gesture he turned until he looked me full in the face and repeated his response. This time I was even more surprised than delighted at what now began to assume the proportions of an unexplainable phenomenon. As he progressed on out into the hall and finally proceeded through the door of the elevator I raised my hand quickly a third time to make the gesture of the circle of perfection. This time he turned his entire body and with deliberation repeated his acknowledgement.

I do not feel that this is a trivial incident to introduce as important a topic as the basic purpose and mechanics of Creation, and the author of that treatise. Meher Baba is memorable and eminently satisfying not because of his undoubted genius in the realm of philosophy and universal mechanics, but because he has the capacity to warm the cockles of one's heart as perhaps no other living being is able to do.

In the long run each one of us is searching for a deep inner sense of satisfaction and peace, a feeling of being contained in some presence which is trustworthy and loving, for a spontaneous understanding and response to our innermost needs. Above all we need to be ourselves and to be accepted completely for ourselves. The deep response which Meher Baba elicits from so many people is due to that undreamed-of sensitivity to one's most profound self.

There are many things of a much more astounding nature which I might recount from the vast lore which has accumulated around this figure in the four decades since he achieved his present spiritual stature. But all of them would obscure the one central issue, his complete ability not only to understand but, in some manner, to be one's own self. Don't ask me to describe such a phenomenon nor to explain it. It must be experienced to be believed.

Even so, one would expect such a feeling of well-being to fade gradually after its source had been removed. Even the most ecstatic experience normally fades and becomes a memory, as does a nightmare as well. However, therein lies another of the unexplainable mysteries of contact with such a being. As I sat in the plane en route home after a jammed eventful week-end I started to re-sort back into my usual context of reality. Turning over one or two of my pet worries in my mind I realized suddenly that they no longer worried me.

Not being easily panicked into rash conclusions, I sampled several more troubles and was completely puzzled to find that in some instances I could see answers where I had seen none before, and in others I could recapture no sense of agitation. Frankly, I thoroughly expected to renew my usual troubled relation with these difficult subjects as soon as I settled down at home again, but as the days and weeks and months and finally years rolled by I began to realize that even a short week-end in the company of such a man had performed a major surgery on my emotional anatomy and had removed my ability to worry.

I describe these incidents in no sense of pride nor of beating a tom-tom. They are two events which occurred in my own life and I would be remiss to omit them from the small frame which I have been entrusted to construct around the masterly painting created in the following pages. I am sure that I have not knowingly heard God speak, but I am sure that in my lifetime I have seen Him act.

In the choice of a title for his book *God Speaks* Meher Baba has succinctly stated both the major thesis which he is to elaborate, as well as his right to speak authoritatively on subjects which may be treated by only the most advanced of our era. Before discussing the right of the author to imply such a sublime source for his work, it might be well to complete the complexity of the issue by stating quite simply that the greatest proportion of Meher Baba's disciples and followers from all over the world regard him as the *Avatar* of the Age. Put in western terminology, they consider him as the Christ of our times, the successor to the tradition of Muhammad, Jesus, Buddha, Krishna, Rama, Zoroaster, and so on back into the dusky past, and as the identical nature which reincarnated in those specific and successive personalities.

If Meher Baba occupies such a crowning position in the spiritual structure of our civilization, then there would be no question of his right to speak positively and with authority on the deepest mechanics of Creation. But the simpler issue of his Divine Source then becomes the much greater one of the legitimacy of his function in the key role of a religious hierarchy which in turn is doubted or frankly disbelieved by many people.

In two paragraphs we have stated a tremendous and a challenging problem. But it is one which must be worked out in actuality by means other than the written words of an Introduction. In the long run there are only two reliable answers to the fundamental question of whether a given man is the Messiah. The personal answer can be personal contact. At this writing this is still physically possible, and many have already availed themselves of this direct attack on the issue. Many have concluded their question in the affirmative, a surprisingly small proportion have reached a definite negative, and another portion have confessed a deep bemusement in which pleasure and delight are two major ingredients, but still with an apparent inability to reach an ultimate conclusion on the ultimate question.

The broad and long-term answer must be the net assessment which society makes over the generations to come of the forces set in motion. If the words spoken and the concepts advanced seem to grow in vitality and reality, then the man is automatically recognized by hindsight to have been the great sculptor of the divine shape for his age.

But no amount of advance argument nor demonstration can convince society. It is as if the concepts carry their own vitality and become the property and the watchword of the race regardless of the efforts to conjoin or defeat their purpose.

For many, however, there will be no opportunity for personal contact nor for acceptance or rejection in the flesh. And as these events are occurring in our age, none of us can rely on the consensus of evaluation that society will have made over the generations that are to come. For these, then, who are in such a position, it is required to peruse, and to think and to mull with an open mind, for here may well be a great storehouse of the Truth and Reality for which each of us searches throughout a lifetime. It is not necessary to make a crisis of acceptance or rejection, but to allow the concepts described to simmer in one's own mental stew-pot. Gradually one's own deep sense of the sufficient, as well as the sheer factuality of life itself, will corroborate or refute the outlines described.

During the five years which elapsed between the time I first became aware of the fact that there was someone in existence named Meher Baba, and my meeting him for the first time in New York, I had ample opportunity to question and rebel and come back to the neutral point of "I just don't know" on any number of the controversial issues of Meher Baba's life. He is not an easy man either to accept or to reject.

That one week-end with its several opportunities to see him in action was sufficient to convince me that he was hands-down the best story teller with gentle humor (even via the handicap of an alphabet board) I had ever encountered, the best business mind I had known in a life spent working in big business, the best philosopher I had met, and the most sensitively human and loving individual I had ever enjoyed.

These are certainly a sufficiently formidable collection of qualities, but you immediately object that the addition of finite quantities can never produce infinity. Had I decided that he was really the *Avatar* of the Age?

Frankly I haven't the foggiest notion, and to me the question is irrelevant. I'm sure I would have no means of judging the qualifications and achievements of Avatarhood, and further I had found Meher Baba surpassing all of my previous standards of excellence in areas in which I felt competent to judge. Once the rocket has left my terrestrial sphere I have no concrete means of identifying its position in stellar space. But this I can say, my own intuition tells me that I shall never again meet an individual with those profound capabilities and that uncanny ability to satisfy me internally which I found in Meher Baba.

I cannot help but think back to a statement which one of

my research fellows made some years ago after hearing a brilliant discussion of the real Christ given by a director of the Mormon church. "I have an idea," he said, "that if Christ were on earth today, almost none of us would recognize or accept Him."

Those words have peculiar meaning to me now because they have a content much deeper than the apparent cynicism shown on their surface. Almost none of us would recognize Him not only because of our ingrained prejudices, but because almost none of us has developed the inner standards of measurement capable of estimating the true size of such a being. His capacity and stature soar off into realms where we are incapable of following and so we admit our frustration in sizing, even if we have not already succumbed to the virtually insuperable temptation to reject.

One of our most frequent crutches in estimating the probable spiritual calibre of a man is to look for miracles accredited to him. "What miracles has Meher Baba done to corroborate his stature?" you ask. There are many stories of such, and I have personally witnessed events which startled my staid notions of the normalcy of events. However, to start evaluating miracles would fall far short of the actuality and would becloud the reality with trivia. The importance of the advent of a spiritually advanced soul lies not in what he apparently does outside of natural law, but what he is and does within it. Such an individual does not come as some sort of glorified showman, to astound by performing feats of incredibility. This would only leave humanity gaping for a short while in amazement, rather than affecting the basic pattern of their lives and giving them a gauge by which they might measure their own accomplishments, as well as reaffirming the ability of any human to achieve such a way of life.

These key figures in the history of the spiritual life take on a superhuman job of providing a living example of perfection, demonstrated amid all the restrictions and limitations with which we more usual human beings are faced. To provide such an example by drawing on forces outside our scope, or unhampered by many of the restrictions with which we wrestle, would clearly not be just and we would have every right to dissociate ourselves from such an unrealistic scheme.

When the example is provided, however, in a rugged world of harsh realities, subject to all the conditions of those realities, and still turns out incredibly fine, then there is indeed reason to take hope and strive for the same thing. This is one of the functions of such individuals. One of the best established principles of effective teaching is to provide a practical demonstration of the subject matter either through a bench experiment or by field experience. The fact that God Himself should use the identical technique in the demonstration of His realities should astound no one.

These are tremendous things which we encounter and we must not be hasty in our assessment of them.

One might ask at this point the circumstances under which a God-Man manifests. This seems to follow a basic natural law of need similar to the economic law of supply and demand. When the thread of recognition of spiritual truth begins to fray, this aspect of God responds to the need and the great Awakener is born who will reawaken mankind. As a consequence the advent of great spiritual teachers has always been associated with crisis in world affairs and has been followed by a resurgence of human development in some field which previously had lain almost fallow.

It is good to know that when the *Avatar* comes he comes to show us the reality of our own selves, through laws and techniques which are inherent in nature. It is good to know that these things are hearty, spontaneous and at least three-dimensional, rather than removed, other-worldly, pale and two-dimensional. It is good to know that when a legitimate spiritual teacher assigns a task or a discipline, it is effective because it is based on profound insight into the mechanics by which nature produces change and the needs of the individual nature. Spirituality then becomes a challenging matter of robust day-to-day living rather than a restrictive discipline acquired on Sundays and progressively lost through the week.

It would not be fair to touch on various of the highlights of the history of Meher Baba without discussing several controversial aspects of his nature. For instance, he often changes his plans in midstream, or says he intends to do something at a certain time and then delays or seemingly never does it. Isn't this irresponsible and shortsighted, coming from so great a personage?

Meher Baba's process of sudden reversal is indeed rugged, but it does produce valuable results. Those who have lived long with Baba are almost universally notable for their resiliency and adaptability, but in addition to this there are undoubtedly more basic reasons which have to do with the sheer indeterminacy of the average human being's free will as well as the functioning of a Perfect Master on levels of existence other than our own.

I cannot help but speculate that there is a direct carry-over from the lessons learned in the world of material affairs into the realm of spiritual development. Isn't it true that the individual who has never ossified into a set physical routine, but is rather alert and adaptable, will have a similar adaptability to the multitudinous changes to be made in inner development?

The fact that Meher Baba fasts quite frequently is incomprehensible to many people unacquainted with his way of working. Baba has always fasted intermittently for short and long periods, and this phase appears consistently and importantly in his work. This has sometimes been misconstrued as a good and holy act for himself, or for penance or spiritual benefit. But it is not for himself, but rather for his work on earth. As Krishna said to Arjuna in the Bhagavad Gita:—

> "Thou Son of Pritha! in the three wide worlds
> I am not bound to any toil, no height
> Awaits to scale, no gift remains to gain,
> Yet I act here!"   *Canto 3–22*

Meher Baba's silence of almost three decades and substitution of an alphabet board as a means of communication are equally puzzling. Many people may regard it as unproductive to use an alphabet board, and some even label it a subterfuge.

There have been a number of discussions by Meher Baba and others on the reasons for this prolonged silence. I do not wish to go into the various potential explanations here, but rather to call attention to the most astounding fact of all. Despite such a severe handicap, the equivalent of having one hand tied behind one's back, Meher Baba has planned minutely and personally the most complex undertakings, taught hundreds and blessed thousands, directed undertakings and given words of cheer to persons at far distant points, and "dictated" in a relatively brief period of time as monumental an enterprise as this book.

Meher Baba's methods are often productive of exasperation. There are many things which he does which defy understanding, and he blithely goes on about his business without bothering to proffer an explanation. For myself I admire greatly someone who does not sit down at every other step to justify himself, but there are apparently quite sound reasons for such behaviour in that there just is not time for constant explanation, nor is there probably in us the comprehension to encompass an explanation of the more abstruse phases if given.

On February 25, 1894, Meher Baba was born of Persian parents in Poona, India, and was given by them the name Merwan Sheriar, the family name being Irani. In 1914 he became God-realized * through a kiss on the forehead bestowed by the great Sufi Master, Hazrat Babajan. In 1915 he met his second master, Upasni Maharaj. In 1921 he became a Perfect Master. In 1925 he commenced his silence, using as a means of communication a small rectangular board on which are painted the letters of the alphabet. Baba forms words quickly by pointing successively to the letters on this board. By this time he had

---

* The *Avatar* is in reality one with God, but comes into the physical world with a veil which must be removed by a Perfect Master when the time is ripe. Hazrat Babajan performed this function for Baba.

collected a small group of disciples who called him "Meher Baba." In 1931 he went to the western world and made his first contacts with the West. In 1932 he was feted by many of those whom you and I would perhaps consider Hollywood's greatest. At fifty-eight he broke a leg and an arm in a severe automobile accident in Oklahoma. Now, at the age of sixty-one, Meher Baba is dynamic, active, acutely aware of all that goes on about him.

I have not tried to give in any detail the events of Baba's earlier life because they have been ably described in C. B. Purdom's *The Perfect Master,** followed more recently by Jean Adriel's *The Avatar.*† The biographical outline given here is intended as nothing more than a point of orientation so that we may go on to discuss several of the key issues associated with Baba's life which are inherently complex and perhaps impossible of interpretation in the long run.

There has been much speculation concerning the reason for many of Baba's actions and journeys, but the greater proportion continue to be shrouded in some degree of mystery. In such a situation the usual procedure is to declare the individual irrational and to write off his actions as delusion. This is not done with Baba for the simple reason that a goodly number of his efforts and suggestions are seen to be based on an insight into the shape of things utterly beyond the average human ken. Often such an outcome results within hours. Sometimes the verdict of events is not given for weeks or months or even years.

However, this uncanny insight causes those who have invested more than a few moments of casual criticism, to hold their peace and be prepared to find the desirable long-term answer back of any of Baba's actions regardless of how imponderable they may appear at the time.

There is further reason to regard Baba's deeds and suggestions with credence. One would be hard put to find one single

---

* C. B. Purdom, *The Perfect Master*, Williams & Norgate, 1937, (now out of print).

† Jean Adriel, *The Avatar*, J. F. Rowny, 1947.

situation in which his influence has resulted in harm to the individual concerned. He will often push a person to the point of exhaustion or even desperation in order to increase the capacity of that individual. But there is a fine line of the possible which he never transgresses.

One of the periods in Baba's life which has both drama and pathos in it * is that covering the establishment of his school for boys of all sects and castes. Established in the summer of 1927, it contained at one point a total of 102 boys, of whom 49 were Hindus, 20 Moslems, 32 Zoroastrians and 1 Christian.

One of Baba's favorites among the students, Ali, was removed from the school by his father when he became alarmed by reports that many of the boys in the school had periodic fits of uncontrolled weeping. These were apparently related in some fashion to the daily meditations which the boys carried out.

Three times Ali's father removed the boy from the school and carried him off to his home in Bombay. Three times the boy escaped from the most careful surveillance and made his way back, mostly on foot, to the school, so deep was his loyalty to Baba. Shortly after the occasion of Ali's fourth withdrawal, the school boys were all sent home temporarily by Meher Baba and early in 1929 the school was permanently closed. Soon after this Baba's period of extended world tours began and in seven short years he made seven trips to the West and two around the world.

Attendant on these was some favorable publicity and much that was critical or even scurrilous. Baba has never attempted to develop a favorable "press." He persistently maintains that those who attack him do his work equally with those who praise him. His consistency in his attitude of refusing to defend himself or to correct errors in quoting his "remarks" or even simple misunderstandings is a phenomenon in this day when the world has become convinced of the need for vindication of oneself in the eyes of society. Such absolute indifference might well be

---

* Beautifully described in a book entitled *Sobs and Throbs* by Ramjoo Abdulla.

attributed to failure to realize practicality, but one ends up with the sense that Baba acts according to deep internal knowledge and is satisfied that the results will occur regardless of interpretation. Great receptions were held for him in Europe and in America, and the publicity which rocketed back and forth on his introduction to Hollywood created a flood of statements which will never be completely integrated.

These trips to the West produced their own treasury of incidents rich in human emotion. One that has always interested me deeply has been the account of Baba's meeting with a Russian lady who was profoundly disturbed because of her inability to form any sense of warm relatedness to her daughter, who at that time was in her twenties. Baba stroked her hand and told her that he would help her, and several days later when she awakened in the morning she was suffused by a deep and warm sense of love for the daughter such as she had never known. She asked forgiveness at once of her daughter for her treatment of her in the past and forthwith there was established a profound and trusting relationship.

Another instance which savours of the magic lamp of human emotions was Baba's meeting in Italy with a disturbed and brilliant university professor who unpacked his own knowledge of esoteric philosophy before Baba. After arriving at complete frustration in his efforts to piece together the components of his life's wisdom in spite of Baba's patience in listening, he finally threw up his hands in despair and asked Baba just to sit quietly with him in meditation.

Baba smiled and laid his hand over that of the professor, and those present in the room comment on the rapt sense of peace which suffused the room and gradually erased the appearance of desperation from the face of the man. After a few moments of silence he suddenly exclaimed, "I know now that Truth is Love."

There are miraculous tales of Baba's stay in the cave in which St. Francis of Assisi had once meditated, of a meeting of the hierarchy atop a mountain in the Swiss Alps and of the violent storm which raged as Baba stood untouched in a shaft of light which pierced the disgorging clouds, while those who attended him were drenched as they stood waiting for him a few feet down the slope.

There followed some years spent in dealing with the mad and then the spiritually intoxicated. A so-called "mad ashram" was established at Rahuri in 1936 to which Baba and his disciples brought a number of truly mad individuals. Later Baba's work was increasingly with the "spiritually intoxicated," those who had lost their normal conscious contact with their surroundings as a result of the intoxication of their divine love.

The difference between conventional madness and loss of normal consciousness as a result of spiritual ecstasy is recognized in India, and as a tradition the people care for these latter *"masts"* as they are termed. Baba's work in this field is reminiscent of the function performed for him over the course of seven years by Upasni Maharaj, the Perfect Master who gradually brought him back to full consciousness of his surroundings after the kiss on his forehead by the Sufi Master Babajan, had torn away the veil. Both of these Perfect Masters selected Meher Baba as their spiritual chargeman (spiritual heir), a unique function uniting the highest flowering of both Hindu and Islamic traditions.

Meher Baba's work with the *masts* in his ashram at Rahuri branched out increasingly and over the course of the ensuing years he made more and more trips into the heart and to the far corners of India, contacting even if for a brief instant all the available *masts* and saints. The story of these journeys is replete with instances of severe hardship and the expenditure of great effort on the part of all who participated.*

Once again one can only speculate on the inference of such contacts. If I were to hazard a guess I would suppose that a dual function had been fulfilled. Such spiritually advanced souls

---

* For details see William Donkin, *The Wayfarers,* Meher Publications, Ahmednagar, India. (Reprinted 1969 by Sufism Reoriented, Inc.)

certainly control or have available some type of basic psychic or cosmic energy, term it what one may. As a whole, they act something like the worker bee, and India functions somewhat as the honey-comb.

Baba, as the royal patriarch of the hive, was setting up his liaison to draw upon this vast store of energy, and in return no doubt gave each individual *mast* or saint a further push in his spiritual on-going. This contacting of the *masts* reached a climax in the period of 1946–1948, and was followed by two years of what Baba has called his "New Life" phase starting on October 16, 1949. This is doubtless the most imponderable of all the imponderables with which the student has to deal. Preceding the New Life Baba broke up all the ashrams maintained for the *masts* and for the more or less permanent close disciples, as well as for the constant flow of people whose stays range all the way from a brief interview to a period of weeks, months or years.

Provision was made for the care of those who were dependent, and then Baba asked for volunteers to follow him on a series of journeys, often on foot and involving the most severe hardships. Rigid rules of discipline and renunciation were set up before the disciples were asked for volunteers to follow Baba into this new phase of his New Life, which was one of exile, helplessness and renunciation. Twenty were finally selected and set out with Baba.

The travels and spiritual disciplines of those two years were among the most difficult which Baba's disciples have ever undergone. Those who participated in the journeys were tired, thin and drawn as they emerged in late 1951. The detailing of the events and their significance must await a more extensive work, but the onlooker cannot help but conclude that in this obscure phase there was established a major blueprint for the future individual and social development of the race. On October 16, 1950 Baba had stated at Mahabaleshwar, "My old life places me on the altar of Godhood and divine perfection. My New Life makes me take the stand of an humble servant of God and His people. In my New Life I am the seeker, the lover and the friend. Both these aspects—perfect divinity and perfect humility—have been God's will and both are everlastingly linked with God's eternal life."

On February 13, 1951 Baba had gone into seclusion at Mahabaleshwar for about 100 days, at the end of which he stated that on October 16 it would be necessary for him to enter another phase of his work. This latter came to be known as the *"manonash"* (annihilation of the mind) period. This work lasted four months, ending February 16, 1952.

Baba then announced that he and a few disciples would leave shortly for the United States and that he would lead from March 21 to July 10, 1952, a "complicated-free" life in which weakness would predominate over strength, from July 10 to November 15 a "full-free" life in which strength would predominate over weakness, and from November 15 on a "fiery-free" life in which both strength and weakness would be consumed in the fire of divinity.

On April 20, 1952 Baba arrived in New York with six men and six women disciples of both eastern and western origins. They went directly to Myrtle Beach, South Carolina, where a property had been dedicated to Baba, and after a period of several weeks, Baba received many old and new followers, particularly on May 17 when a vast crowd congregated from all over the United States to see him.

The group then set out by car for California and another projected series of interviews. While crossing Oklahoma the car carrying Baba was struck and four of the five occupants seriously injured in one of the heartbreaking incidents so common to our highways.

In the nearby little town of Prague, Oklahoma, there existed by great good fortune a small private hospital operated by Dr. Burleson. The efforts of this man and his tiny staff, confronted with a mass of bloody flesh and stained clothing in which were entangled a silent master and his injured companions, is certainly an epic in the constant drama of the medical world in its ceaseless battle to alleviate misery and prolong life. As the tangle of misery was gradually sorted out it became clear that no one was in immediate danger, but the number of broken bones and the areas of skinless and abraded flesh were formidable. For days the dull and dreary routine of setting, cleaning, bandaging and pumping in of new life went on. Baba's broken left leg and arm and severe contusions of the face were not the most severe of the injuries, but among the most painful. After two weeks the party returned by ambulance to South Carolina and a period of recuperation.

How could a great spiritual leader allow such an accident to happen to himself and his followers? Surely he could foresee and prevent it? I wonder how many times these questions have been asked. Actually Baba had predicted as long ago as 1928 such an accident to himself and the necessity for it. He had even mentioned on occasion that it would be necessary to "spill" his blood in America. But such a declaration on my part of "he knew it all the time" falls wide of the central issue. The great spiritual leaders of the ages have never avoided the mishaps of a reckless and unheeding civilization. In fact they have embraced their portion of human catastrophe and have lived it through without recourse to the arbitrary usage of the cosmic power at their finger tips. The supreme function of the spiritually great is not what they do outside the law of our physical world, but what they do within it.

In 1937 * Baba had explained this function of the Perfect Masters. "A Perfect Master, who has to take upon himself the burdens of the world, to absorb them, must necessarily have physical reactions, and consequently must suffer physically, like ordinary human beings.

"By submitting themselves to the law of action and reaction, the Perfect Masters establish that law, and are selflessly and

---

* [At that time Baba had as yet made no public statement regarding his Avatarhood and he was generally regarded as a Perfect Master (*Sadguru*). However, in Supplement 30 Baba explains the difference between the roles of *Avatar* and Perfect Master. Ed.]

willingly subject to it. But in spite of subjecting themselves to this law, they stand above the law, and could rid themselves from physical reactions. What then would be the meaning and purpose of 'action and reaction'?

"Perfect Masters absorb the dual effect of the 'universal illusion' by taking humanity out of the illusion, through liberating mankind from the bonds of action and reaction.

"The Perfect Master absorbs duality in his true existence, in order to sublimate it."

After additional days of interviews with people in New York Baba set out by air for a visit with followers old and new in Europe, returning to India in late August, 1952. Almost at once he set out on further journeys in that country to contact a few more *masts,* but now his activities focalized more on giving spiritual blessing to the great masses who thronged to the locations announced for his public appearances. These mass *darshans* culminated in September, 1954 when he called on his male followers throughout the world to congregate at his ashram in Ahmednagar for a "last" spiritual conclave. About a thousand collected from the various corners of India and the far reaches of Asia, Europe and America. Those who arrived early witnessed on September 12 the congregration of sixty thousand souls from the countryside surrounding Ahmednagar to receive Baba's blessing in the form of *prasad.*

Following this colorful and moving occasion each afternoon Baba personally instructed the travellers. On September 29 Baba addressed the thousand who had collected at his call, blessed them and sent them on their way. On October 7 he abandoned the use of even his alphabet board, depending now only on gestures for communication. (It is interesting to note that the gestures Baba uses for communication are not the alphabetical A B C D—the formation of fingers a silent person is apt to make use of, nor a sign language as used by the deaf and dumb, but free and easy and somewhat exaggerated gestures uniquely his own that describe most vividly what he wishes to convey.)

Once again Baba announced that the breaking of his silence, his manifestation and his death were all near. Baba has said that when he breaks his silence he will speak only one word, the Word of words, which will penetrate the hearts of men.

Thus, in collaboration with Murshida Duce, I have tried to bring up to date once again the eventful life of *Avatar* Meher Baba. It is left to history to sort out and weigh in the perspective of accumulating events the significance of his life and actions. We who participate in the immediacy of the now can only offer the measure of our love and human allegiance and declare our gratitude for the great thing that has come into our lives.

DON E. STEVENS

Introduction to Second Edition

IN THE eighteen years that have passed since publication of the first edition of *God Speaks,* the flood tide of Meher Baba's presence has spread around the world and his name has become a symbol of hope and faith to millions. At the end of January four years ago he himself dropped the body, which now lies interred in the tomb prepared many years ago under his own careful instructions at Meherabad, near Ahmednagar, India.

In this period it has been possible to witness the impact of the universality of Meher Baba's approach to the problems of the world, and the uniformity of response of the peoples of all faiths and sects to his love. From the earliest days, Meher Baba had pointed out that he belonged to no particular religious group; rather that it was his objective to breathe vitality into the words of truth handed down in all the great world faiths. In repeated, clear, concise statements he has underlined his independence of action and universality of approach:

"I have no connection with politics. All religions are equal to me. And all castes and creeds are dear to me. But though I appreciate all 'isms', religions and political parties for the many good things that they seek to achieve, I do not and cannot belong to any of these 'isms', religions or political parties, for the absolute Truth, while equally including them, transcends all of them and leaves no room for separative divisions which are all equally false. The unity of all life is integral and indivisible. It remains unassailable and inviolable in spite of all conceivable ideological differences.

"I am equally approachable to one and all, big and small,
To saints who rise and sinners who fall,
Through all the various Paths that give the Divine Call.
I am approachable alike to saint whom I adore
And to sinner whom I am for,
And equally through Sufism, Vedantism, Christianity,
Or Zoroastrianism and Buddhism, and other 'isms' of any kind
And also directly through no medium of 'isms' at all . . ." *

The thorny subject of Meher Baba's Avatarhood (Christ, Messiah status) has also clarified greatly in these intervening years. When the first edition of *God Speaks* was placed before the public in 1955, the fact of Baba's *Avataric* function had been described to those other than his closest disciples for only a few years. Before that time most people had regarded him as a great saint or a Perfect Master, without guessing the further significance of his mission.

In 1954, however, Baba stated clearly and for the first time publicly that he was the *Avatar* of the Age. Already having recognized him as a Perfect Master, the devotee had no problem making allowance for this extension of universal responsibility.

To the outsider, intrigued by the calibre of Meher Baba but lacking the opportunity to become absorbed into his being through personal surrender, it was still early to try to judge the external activities and results of the *Avataric* role. Surprisingly, very few people took strong public difference with the statement that Baba was the *Avatar* of the Age. Many, through reading *God Speaks* itself, were convinced that such a work could come only from one who had attained to the highest spiritual status and therefore it would be better to wait and observe before making any judgment.

Oddly enough, of those who had not encountered Baba in the flesh, it was not the traditionally spiritually inclined who first began to accept him as the Ancient One. It was the young, the

---

* From messages given out during the "Fiery Free Life," 1952.

rebels, the experimentalists, questing for the clues to meaning in a life of confusion and frustration, who suddenly began to recognize the image and the words of this silent Master. Their instincts, sharpened by need and stretched by repeated failures of approach, suddenly found the answer in a photo of Baba, a book of his discourses, a pithy statement about life printed on a small card.

As Baba had so often stated in the decades preceding, the advent of the *Avatar* and the acceptance of his word is precipitated by the needs of Creation. When the need is great, the *Avatar* comes. And his word is accepted because it is the only thing which can satisfy. Mankind's search for worthy and dependable goals has been growing for generations. In our day it has become so insistent that it has lashed out in wave after wave of social turbulence.

Into this social ferment steps Meher Baba with a clear statement of the purpose of Creation and an all-embracing love so powerful that the raw abrasions of need are soothed so abruptly as to lead to silence and tears of relief. Repeatedly Baba describes Creation as the vehicle by which God's impulse to know His own divinity consciously is brought to fruition. In careful statements in *God Speaks* he describes the manner in which the mechanism for the generation of consciousness is developed. The reality of infinite unity and the consciousness evolved through resolving the infinite challenges posed within the duality of Creation is traced in the most minute detail. The physical form that acts as the medium for experiencing the opposites of Creation is shown to be an increasingly complex by-product of this will of God to know Himself consciously. The very force of evolution of form becomes, not a random selection of the fittest, but a result of the necessity of the residues of experience to express themselves through increasingly more complex instruments. The evolution and perfecting of consciousness is itself described as the entire purpose of Creation:

> "And, in regard to the evolutionary process, it is well to remember always that the beginning is a beginning in consciousness, the evolution is an evolution in conscious-

ness, the end, if there be an end, is an end in consciousness . . ." *

These, as well as the host of balanced, practical insights into
daily life given out by Meher Baba over the decades, have been
what the young have cried out for. They recognize Baba em-
pirically for what he is: the answer to the dilemma of modern
life. This is exactly what Baba had stated that the *Avatar* must
be. Thus the hand and the glove fit exactly. In looking at the
match, one can have no doubt that Baba is precisely what he
has said he is, the *Avatar* of the Age.

But what about Meher Baba's more personal life during
this period? Despite his long-predicted serious automobile accident near Prague, Oklahoma, in 1952, and a later, even graver
one near Satara in India in December, 1956, in which his hip
joint was smashed and Dr. Nilu killed outright, nevertheless the
fifteen years encompassed much intensive inner and outer work.
With reference to these two accidents, one must keep in mind
that it is a world of systematic balances in which we live, with
none of the magic of the fairy wand. The *Avatar* himself trues
the balance by the very process of the suffering which he willingly undergoes. On these two occasions he has spilled his blood
on two continents for the sake of what he has known must be
done.

In 1956 he made a trip to Europe and America and on
around the world, visiting Australia for the first time. This
twelfth visit to the West is amply chronicled in *The Awakener*
(vol. IV, no. 1 and vol. V, no. 2) and other works.

His thirteenth trip to the West in 1958, including this time
only Australia and America, produced an intense atmosphere of
the reciprocal play of love between lovers and beloved (*The
Awakener,* vol. V, nos. 3 and 4). On this occasion it was clear
that Baba was to be for those who knew the song of their own
hearts. The public was not discouraged from seeking the presence
of this intriguing being, but no publicity was given to the visit.
It was a true living in the presence of the Beloved. In retrospect,

---

* *The Awakener*, vol. VIII, no. 4, 1962.

one understands that Baba knew that for many this would be the last personal contact. In fact he stated as much, but we did not hear him.

In 1962 Meher Baba again performed the magic of drawing the close ones to him, but in a significantly new pattern this time. In the past there had been only the most limited mixing of his followers from the East and the West. In 1962, however, the mixing was deliberate and on a grand scale.

Hundreds poured into Poona, India, the site of the meeting, from Europe, America and Australia. Other thousands came from Iran, Pakistan and India. The 1962 "East-West Gathering" at the beautiful residence of Guruprasad in Poona was an epic of the joining of streams of love from widely different natural springs of culture. For five days Meher Baba sat with this closed invitational group of some thousands and mixed together the elements of disparity within the solvent that produces the only true unity: supreme love.

One wonders how this incredible being was able to draw from a body seriously hampered by long, hard use and crippling accidents, the physical resource to greet and bless the multitude for long hours each day and well into the night. On the sixth day he went even further. The gates of Guruprasad were thrown open and the masses were allowed to come before him for the coveted spiritual blessing. From sunup to sunset the living stream passed before him, and when finally the gates were closed at dark, a long ribbon of humanity four abreast still stretched far into the distance, hoping against hope for the glance or the touch.

From this time, with brief exceptions in 1963 and 1965 for his Indian devotees, Meher Baba went into increasingly restricted seclusion. Finally, in August, 1966, he issued instructions that no one would be allowed to see him except at his own specific invitation. There were very, very few invitations given, and even fewer exceptions made. He let all know that he was in the crowning phases of his universal work, and then finally, that that work had been achieved to his 100 percent satisfaction. This should have been the signal to his devoted followers.

But one never conceives of the day when the beloved will not be physically at hand. On February 1, 1969, the news spread quickly around the world via the network of deep devotion that Meher Baba had dropped his body shortly after noon of the previous day. For seven days the shell lay garlanded and strewn with fragrant rose petals in the tomb long prepared for the occasion, head propped up on a light pillow, "so that I may give my lovers *darshan* without having to rise." He had seen what would be necessary and, as always, had prepared for it. His devotees recognized "the passing away of the Infinite as Infinite, in its own Infinitude." The entombment was followed in April, May and June by visits of large groups from the East and the West to Guruprasad, to Meherazad—the residence—and to Meherabad—the tomb. We do not know how one can describe what happened. The only way it can be done is for you to sit down with one who was there. Francis Brabazon has related this great event most beautifully in a pamphlet entitled "Three Talks" published by Meher House Publications, Sydney, Australia, in 1969.

In this revised edition of *God Speaks* certain new points and corrections indicated by Meher Baba have been made. There are also some additions to the Supplement. Various of the charts have received minor but necessary changes and five more charts have been included. One chart was done as a labor of love by Ludwig Dimpfl and concerns "Mystic, Sufi and Vedantic Terms Related to the Planes of Consciousness as Used in *God Speaks*." This chart was sent to Meher Baba several years before he dropped the body. Eruch B. Jessawala tells us that Baba went over it meticulously, making two or three corrections, and expressed complete satisfaction with it, approving its usage for *God Speaks*. It was so large it has been enclosed separately. Further footnotes have been added in the text from separate information Meher Baba gave from time to time.

It should also be noted at this time that some terms used under headings denoting Sufi, Vedantic and mystic terminology are in certain instances not classic terms employed in those three disciplines. Rather are they terms employed to allow comparative study and better understanding of the theme by the reader. A complete glossary compiled by Ludwig Dimpfl was approved by Meher Baba before he dropped his body.

In closing, we cannot avoid suggesting an inevitable corollary of the life and words of Meher Baba. While he lived for the inner man, that he might break through the shackles of the delusions of reality by which he had bound himself, still the clarifications given by Meher Baba have great import for the physical disciplines as well. As one reads the various works given out by "The Highest of the High" of our times, the implications for all manner of physical sciences are seen to be basic and revolutionary. As those trained in the fields of physics, chemistry, geology, psychology and many other disciplines study the life and statements of Meher Baba, they will quite rightfully apply them first to the needs of their own inner natures. However, as his words accomplish the first task of establishing a sense of vital purpose and assured support, a second phase of significance will inevitably begin to assert itself. Life begins to move. And it moves both internally and externally. The quick, successive recognitions of truths that bore inwards are followed by matching insights into the functioning of the external.

The simple, almost self-evident statements of Meher Baba are seen to ramify into a kaleidoscope of fundamental and exciting implications. He was sparing of words. He did not elaborate. He laid down only a vital reinterpretation of basic truth. Out of that flows the multitude of inevitable conclusions. The physicist, once he has set the wheels in motion to rediscover his essential self, will also begin to discover the impact of Meher Baba on his own field of physics.

Meher Baba is like that. He flows quietly through all aspects of life, and before one knows it, all of life has become nothing but the fascinating game of watching Meher Baba deal with Meher Baba. Certainly this is the ultimate in universality.

Ivy O. Duce
Don E. Stevens

San Francisco, California
April, 1973

"I am not come to establish any cult, society or organization; nor even to establish a new religion. The religion that I shall give teaches the Knowledge of the One behind the many. The book that I shall make people read is the book of the heart that holds the key to the mystery of life. I shall bring about a happy blending of the head and the heart. I shall revitalize all religions and cults, and bring them together like beads on one string."

MEHER BABA

Contents

Charts

GOD SPEAKS

States of Consciousness

ALL souls (*atmas*) were, are and will be in the Over-Soul
(*Paramatma*).
Souls (*atmas*) are all One.
All souls are infinite and eternal. They are formless.
All souls are One; there is no difference in souls or in their being
and existence as souls.

There is a difference in the consciousness of souls;
there is a difference in the planes of consciousness of souls;
there is a difference in the experience of souls and thus
there is a difference in the state of souls.

Most souls are conscious of the **gross** body (*sthul sharir*);
some souls are conscious of the **subtle** body (*pran*);
a few souls are conscious of the **mental** body (mind or *mana*);
and
a very few souls are conscious of Self.

Most souls have experience of the gross sphere (world);
some souls have experience of the subtle sphere (world);
a few souls have experience of the mental sphere (world); and
a very few souls have experience of the Over-Soul.

Most souls are on the gross plane (*anna bhumika*);
some souls are on the subtle plane (*pran bhumika*);
a few souls are on the mental plane (*mano bhumika*); and
a very few souls are on the plane beyond the mental plane
(*vidnyan*).

Most souls have great binding; some souls have little binding; a few souls have very little binding; and a very few souls have absolutely no binding.

All these souls (*atmas*) of different consciousness, of different experiences, of different states are in the Over-Soul (*Paramatma*).

If, now, all souls are in the Over-Soul and are all One, then why is there any difference in the consciousness, in the planes, in the experiences and in the states?

The cause of this difference is that the souls have different and diverse impressions (*sanskaras*).*

Most souls have **gross** impressions; some souls have **subtle** impressions; a few souls have **mental** impressions; and a very few souls have **no** impressions at all.

Souls having gross impressions, souls having subtle impressions, souls having mental impressions and souls having no impressions, are all souls in the Over-Soul and all are One.

Souls with gross impressions have consciousness of the gross body (*sthul sharir*) and have experience of the gross sphere.

Souls with subtle impressions have consciousness of the subtle body (*pran*) and have experience of the subtle sphere.

Souls with mental impressions have consciousness of the mental body (*mana* or mind) and have the experience of the mental sphere.†

---

* [See also: Meher Baba, "The Formation and Function of *Sanskaras*," *Discourses*, 6th ed., 3 vols. (San Francisco: Sufism Reoriented, Inc., 1967), 1: 54–64. Ed.]

†	SPHERE	BODY		
	MYSTIC	MYSTIC	SUFI	VEDANTIC
	Gross Sphere (World)	Gross Body	*Jism-e-Kasif*	*Sthul Sharir*
	Subtle Sphere (World)	Subtle Body	*Jism-e-Latif*	*Sukshma Sharir* (*Pran*)
	Mental Sphere (World)	Mental Body	*Jism-e-Altaf*	*Karan Sharir* (*Manas*)

Souls with no impressions have consciousness of Self (soul, *atma*) and have the experience of the Over-Soul (*Paramatma*).

Thus souls with gross impressions experience the gross sphere through the gross body; that is, they experience different and diverse experiences such as seeing, hearing, smelling, eating, sleeping, clearing the bowels and urinating. All these are experiences of the gross sphere.

Souls with subtle impressions experience successively three planes of the subtle sphere through the subtle body, and in these three planes they have only the experiences of seeing, smelling and hearing.

Souls with mental impressions, through the mental body or **mind,** in the mental sphere experience only seeing, and this seeing is the seeing of God.

Souls having no impressions, through the Self experience the infinite power, infinite knowledge and infinite bliss of the Over-Soul.

The soul that is conscious of the gross body is **not** conscious of the subtle body, **not** conscious of the mental body, and **not** conscious of Self.

The soul that is conscious of the subtle body is **not** conscious of the gross body, **not** conscious of the mental body, and **not** conscious of Self.

The soul that is conscious of the mental body is **not** conscious of the gross body, **not** conscious of the subtle body, and **not** conscious of Self.

The soul that is conscious of Self is **not** conscious of the gross body, **not** conscious of the subtle body, and **not** conscious of the mental body.

The soul that has experience of the gross world does not have experience of the subtle world, nor experience of the mental world, nor does it have experience of the Over-Soul.

The soul that has experience of the subtle world does not experience the gross world, nor does it have experience of the mental world, nor does it have experience of the Over-Soul.

The soul that has experience of the mental world does not experience the gross world, nor does it experience the subtle world, nor does it have experience of the Over-Soul.

The soul that has experience of the Over-Soul does not experience the gross world, nor does it experience the subtle world, nor does it experience the mental world. That is, the soul that is conscious of Self and has experience of the Over-Soul is not conscious of the gross body, subtle body and mental body and does not experience the gross, subtle and mental spheres (worlds).

This means that in order to have consciousness of Self and to have the experience of the Over-Soul, the soul must lose consciousness of the gross, subtle and mental bodies. But as long as the soul is impressioned either by the gross, subtle or mental impressions, the soul consistently and respectively has consciousness of the gross body, subtle body or mental body, and the gross, subtle and mental experiences are persistently and necessarily undergone.

The obvious reason for this is that as long as the consciousness of the soul is impressed by gross impressions, there is no way out except to experience these gross impressions through the gross body.

Similarly, as long as the consciousness of the soul is impressed by subtle impressions, there is no way out but to experience these subtle impressions through the subtle body.

Similarly, as long as the consciousness of the soul is impressed by mental impressions, there is no escape but to experience these mental impressions through the mental body.

As impressions of the gross, subtle and mental vanish or completely disappear, the consciousness of the soul is automatically and obviously directed and focussed towards itself, and this soul then necessarily has no alternative but to absorb experience of the Over-Soul.

Now, gross, subtle and mental bodies are nothing but the **shadows of the soul.** The gross, subtle and mental spheres (worlds) are nothing but the **shadows of the Over-Soul.**

Gross, subtle and mental bodies are finite, have forms and are changeable and destructible. The gross, subtle and mental worlds are false; they are zero, imagination and vacant dreams. The only reality is the Over-Soul (*Paramatma*).

Therefore when the soul with its gross, subtle and mental bodies experiences the gross, subtle and mental worlds, the soul actually experiences in reality the shadows of the Over-Soul with the help of its own shadows.

In other words, the soul with its finite and destructible form experiences falsity, zero, imagination and a vacant dream.

Only when the soul experiences the Over-Soul with its Self does it experience the Real with reality.

When the soul is conscious of its gross body, then this soul identifies itself with the gross body and takes itself as the gross body.

This means that the infinite, eternal, formless soul finds itself as finite, mortal and having form.

Impressions (*sanskaras*) are the cause of this ignorance. In the beginning the soul, which is eternally in the Over-Soul, at first acquires ignorance through impressions rather than acquiring Knowledge.

When the soul acquires a particular form (body or *sharir*) according to particular impressions, it feels and experiences itself as being that particular form.

Soul in its stone-form experiences itself as stone. Accordingly, in due course, the soul experiences and feels that it is metal, vegetable, worm, fish, bird, animal, man or woman. Whatever be the type of gross form and whatever be the shape of the form, the soul spontaneously associates itself with that form, figure and shape, and experiences that it is itself that form, figure and shape.

When the soul is conscious of the subtle body, then this soul experiences that it is the subtle body.

When the soul becomes conscious of the mental body, then this soul experiences that it is the mental body.

It is only because of impressions (*nuqush-e-amal* or *sanskaras*) that the soul without form, the Infinite Soul, experiences that it is veritably a gross body (*sthul sharir*), or a subtle body (*pran*) or a mental body (*mana* or mind).

The soul, while experiencing the gross world through gross forms, associates with and dissociates from innumerable gross forms. The association with and dissociation from gross forms are termed **birth** and **death** respectively.

It is only because of impressions that the eternal, immortal soul, existing in reality without births and without deaths, has to experience births and deaths innumerable times.

While the soul has to undergo this experience of innumerable births and deaths because of impressions, it has not only to experience the gross world, which is a shadow of the Over-Soul and which is false, but together with it the soul has also to experience the happiness and misery, virtue and vice of the gross world.

It is only because of impressions that the soul, which is beyond and free from happiness and misery, virtue and vice, has necessarily to undergo experiences of misery and happiness, vice and virtue.

Now this much is established, that the experiences of births and deaths, happiness and misery, virtue and vice are experienced only by the gross form of the soul while experiencing the gross world; but the gross form of the soul is a shadow of the soul and the gross world is a shadow of the Over-Soul.

Thus all the experiences of births and deaths, virtue and vice, happiness and misery experienced by the soul are nothing but the experiences of the shadow. Hence all that is thus experienced is false.

Atma in Reality is *Paramatma*

In order to clarify the relationship of *"atma-Paramatma"* we compare *Paramatma* with an infinite ocean, a limitless ocean, and the *atma* as a drop in this ocean. The *atma* is never out of this limitless ocean (*Paramatma*).

The *atma* can never be out of *Paramatma* because *Paramatma* is infinite and unlimited. How can the *atma* come out of, or have a place beyond, the limitlessness of the limitless? Therefore the *atma* is in *Paramatma.*

After establishing the primary fact that the *atma* is **in** *Paramatma* we go a step further and say that *atma* **is** *Paramatma.* How?

For example, let us imagine an unlimited ocean. Let us also imagine that we separate or take out one iota of ocean from the limitless expanse of this unlimited ocean. It follows then that this iota of ocean, while in the limitless ocean, before separation is ocean itself, and is not there in the shoreless ocean as an iota of the ocean, because every iota of ocean, when not limited by the limitations of a drop, is unlimited ocean.

It is only when an iota of ocean is separated from the unlimited ocean, or is taken out of the unlimited ocean as a drop, that this iota of ocean obtains its separate existence as a drop of the shoreless ocean, and that this iota of ocean begins to be looked upon as a drop of the unlimited ocean.

In other words, the infinite, unlimited and limitless ocean itself is now looked upon as merely a drop of that infinite, unlimited and limitless ocean. And in comparison to that infinite, unlimited and limitless ocean this iota of ocean, or this drop of the iota of ocean, is most finite and most limited with infinite limitations. That is, the infinitely free iota finds itself infinitely bound.

Similarly, the *atma,* which we have compared with a drop of the infinite ocean, obtains a seeming separate existence, though in reality it can never be out of the limitlessness of the limitless, infinite *Paramatma* which we have compared with the infinite, unlimited and limitless ocean.

But just as the iota of ocean acquires its limitation as a drop through being in the form of a bubble on the surface of the ocean, and the bubble bestows upon the iota of ocean an apparently separative existence from the infinite ocean, likewise the *atma,* which is **in** *Paramatma* and **is** *Paramatma,* apparently experiences separative existence from the infinite *Paramatma* through the limitations of a bubble (of ignorance) with which the *atma* shrouds itself. No sooner does the bubble of ignorance burst, than the *atma* not only finds itself **in** *Paramatma* but experiences itself **as** *Paramatma.*

Through this limitation, formed by the bubble of ignorance, self-created by the *atma,* the *atma* apparently inherits a separative existence from *Paramatma.* And because of this self-created separativeness from infinite *Paramatma,* the *atma,* which is itself infinite, unlimited and limitless, apparently experiences itself as most finite with infinite limitations.

The Initial Urge and the Journey of Evolving Consciousness

LET us now think of one unconscious soul.

In the beginning the soul had no impressions (*sanskaras*) and no consciousness.

Therefore at this stage or in this state, the soul had no gross form or body, subtle body or mental body, **because only the existence of gross, subtle and mental impressions (*sanskaras*) can give existence to gross, subtle and mental bodies,** and only the existence of these bodies can make possible the existence of gross, subtle and mental worlds.

Hence in the beginning the soul had no consciousness of gross, subtle and mental bodies and was also unconscious of its own self, and the soul then naturally had no experience of the gross, subtle and mental worlds and also had no experience of the Over-Soul (*Paramatma*).

This infinite, impressionless, unconscious tranquil state of the soul reverberated with an impulse which we call THE FIRST URGE (the first urge to know Itself).

The first urge was latent in *Paramatma*.

When we compare *Paramatma* to an infinite, unlimited ocean and when we say that *Paramatma* got the first urge, it could also be said in terms of comparison that the infinite, unlimited ocean got the first urge or THE WHIM.*

In the Infinite, both finite and infinite are included.

Now was this first urge infinite or finite, and was it at first finite and then infinite or vice versa?

The first urge was most finite, but this first urge was of the Infinite.

This most finite first urge was of the infinite Ocean-*Paramatma,* and the manifestation of this latent most finite first urge of the Infinite was restricted to a most finite point in the infinite, unlimited Ocean.

But as this most finite point of manifestation of the latent first urge, which was most finite too, was in the infinite, unlimited Ocean, this most finite point of manifestation of the first urge was also unlimited.

Through this most finite point of manifestation of the first urge (also most finite), the shadow of the Infinite (which shadow, when of Reality, is infinite) gradually appeared † and went on expanding.

This most finite point of manifestation of the latent first urge is called the *"Om"* **Point** or **Creation Point** and this point is unlimited.

Simultaneously with reverberations of the first urge, the most gross first impression emerged, objectifying the soul as the most absolute opposite and most finite gross counterpart of the Infinite.

Because of this most gross first impression of the first urge, the infinite Soul **experienced** for the first time. This first experience of the infinite Soul was that it (the Soul) experienced a contrariety in its identity with its infinite, impressionless, unconscious state.

This experience of contrariety effected changeableness in

---

* [See also: Meher Baba, "The Whim from the Beyond," *Beams from Meher Baba on the Spiritual Panorama* (San Francisco: Sufism Reoriented, Inc., 1958), pp. 7–11. Ed.]

† The sense to be conveyed is that the shadow of the Infinite seeped through or oozed out of the most finite point.

the eternal, indivisible stability of the infinite Soul, and spontaneously there occurred a sort of eruption, disrupting the indivisible poise and the unconscious tranquility of the infinite Soul with a **recoil or tremendous shock** which impregnated the unconsciousness of the unconscious Soul with first consciousness of its apparent separateness from the indivisible state of *Paramatma*. But the Soul being infinite, the first consciousness that it derived from the recoil or shock of an absolutely opposite and most gross first impression of its apparent separateness was naturally and necessarily **finite** first consciousness.

This first consciousness derived by the Soul is obviously most, most-finite in proportion to the experience of the absolute opposites of its own original infinite state.

It then means that in the beginning, when the impressionless infinite Soul was first impressioned, it got as its first impression an absolutely gross impression. And the first consciousness it (the Soul) derived was most, most-finite.

Simultaneously at that instant, the unconsciousness of the infinite Soul actually experienced most, most-finite first consciousness of the most-gross first impression.

This infinite and eternal Soul did get consciousness, but this consciousness by impression, was not of its **eternal** state or its infinite Self but was of the most-finite, by the most-gross impression.

Now as will be explained later, if the soul is conscious of impressions (*sanskaras*) then the soul **must necessarily experience these impressions,** and in order to experience the impressions, the consciousness of the soul must experience them through proper media.

As the impressions are, so are the experiences of impressions and so must be the media to experience the impressions. That is, the impressions give rise to experiences, and to experience the impressions the use of appropriate media is necessitated.

Therefore as the infinite, eternal and formless Soul now has the most, most-finite first consciousness of the most, most-gross first impression, quite obviously and necessarily this most, most-finite first consciousness of the soul must utilize the most, most-finite and most, most-gross **first** medium to experience the most, most-gross first impression.

At this stage it suffices to mention here for the limited human understanding that the most, most-finite first consciousness of the soul, while experiencing the most, most-gross first impression, centred itself in an appropriate most, most-finite and most, most-gross medium, imperceptibly tending the Soul (without form) to associate and identify its very infinite, eternal Self with this most, most-gross and most, most-finite limited form as its first medium.

The first consciousness of the indivisible Soul, experiencing the first impression through the first medium, creates a tendency in the soul to associate and identify its eternal, infinite Self with the first form, the most-finite and most-gross, which was as the seed of the contrariety, spontaneously sown by the reverberations of the first urge, imperceptibly germinated and manifested, for the first time, in the shape of duality. When it is made to associate and identify itself, by its newly gained consciousness, with the finite, gross form or medium, the consciousness of the soul actually makes the infinite, eternal, indivisible Soul without form experience that it is that finite, gross form.

Thus the consciousness gained by the unconscious soul, instead of experiencing **reality** through unity and identity with the Over-Soul, experiences **illusion** through duality and identity with the gross form, multiplying diverse, innumerable impressions in a series of experiences while associating with the gross form and gradually gaining or evolving more and more consciousness.

In order to understand more clearly and concretely how the consciousness gained by the soul gradually develops through the process of evolution, let us examine that state of the conscious soul where the consciousness of the soul associates itself with stone-form as the most-finite and most-gross medium, and the soul thus begins to identify itself as stone.

Actually the consciousness of the soul utilizes the stone-form only after innumerable cycles and ages of diverse experiences through diverse species of forms, of which there are **seven major** different kinds of most, most-finite and most, most-gross gaseous forms, which cannot even be concretely grasped nor imagined by ordinary human beings.

It is for convenience that we begin with that state of conscious soul when it just begins to associate and identify itself with stone-form.

In stone-form, too, there are varied species, and the consciousness of the soul has to utilize each and all of these species as appropriate media, one after the other, in accordance with the diversity of impressions of the soul, to experience varied and countless impressions gathered one after the other in stone-form.

If we take stone as a medium for most-gross impressions, it follows that the soul, which is eternally in the Over-Soul, now with most-finite consciousness experiences most-gross impressions through the medium of stone-form.

It is thus that the infinite, indivisible, eternal soul (without form) which is eternally in the Over-Soul, while experiencing the most-finite gross impressions through its own most-finite consciousness, utilizes the most-finite gross medium of the first-most species of stone ("first-most" meaning the very, very first), and the soul is thus imperceptibly, though spontaneously, made to identify itself as stone.

After ages and cycles the most-finite gross consciousness is gradually much more evolved in the soul by innumerable and varied experiences of the most-gross finite impressions through the identification of the soul with the first-most species of stone. Eventually, when a limit to having experiences is reached, the identification of the soul with the first-most species of stone is gradually dissociated and that stone-form is dropped.

The soul remains now for a period without any medium, though the most-finite consciousness which has been evolved remains together with the most-gross finite impressions of the most-first species of stone-form just shed.

Thus the soul, now without any medium or form, is conscious of the most-finite impressions (*sanskaras*). But as long as consciousness is centred in impressions, the soul must necessarily experience those impressions.

Therefore, in order to experience the impressions of the most-first species of stone-form dropped, the consciousness of the soul centred in the impressions of the dropped stone-form begins to associate with the most-next species of stone-form. The soul identifies itself with this species of stone, and the consciousness of the soul begins to experience, through association with the new medium of the most-next species of stone-form, the impressions of the most-first species of stone-form.

The most important point to be understood here is that when the consciousness of the soul dissociates its identification from one form or medium and retains only the impressions of the form so dissociated, these impressions are experienced through another appropriate medium when the consciousness of the soul associates with the next medium or form. But this next medium or form is always created and moulded of the consolidated impressions of the last species of form with which the soul associated and identified itself and which (impressions) were retained by the consciousness of the soul even when dissociated from the form.

Thus, innumerable diverse experiences of countless impressions experienced by the consciousness of the soul through diverse species of stone-forms, one after the other, lead to the greater evolution of consciousness of the soul.

Ultimately a stage is reached after ages and cycles of experiences where the consciousness of the soul has a tendency to dissociate the soul even from the most-last species of stone-form; and, although the most-last species of stone-form is dissociated or dropped by the soul, the most-finite consciousness evolved thus far remains together with the most-finite gross impressions of the most-last species of stone-form dropped.

The soul, now without any medium or form, is conscious of the most-finite gross impressions (*sanskaras*) of the most-last species of stone-form. The soul must necessarily experience these impressions.

Now, in order to experience the impressions of the most-last stone-form, the soul associates and identifies with another medium—the metal-form. This medium of metal-form is but the mould of the impressions of the most-last species of stone-form. In other words, the most-first species of metal-form is created and moulded of the most-last species of stone-form impressions.

It is thus that the infinite, eternal soul without form, which is eternally in the Over-Soul, experiences through evolved consciousness the most-gross finite impressions of the most-last species of stone-form while associating and identifying itself with the most-first species of metal-form.

There are diverse species of metal-form just as there are of stone-form, and the consciousness of the soul utilizes these diverse innumerable species of metal-form as media through which to experience the diverse and innumerable impressions gathered. Thus the evolution of the consciousness of the soul gains and gathers momentum in proportion to the diverse and multiple experiences of varied and innumerable impressions, through different media or species of forms.

This is how the cycles of evolution of consciousness of the soul go on evolving further and greater consciousness with evolution of forms of higher and higher species, while experiencing and exhausting the impressions of the dissociated forms of the lower and lower species.

The consciousness of the soul experiences and exhausts all the impressions of the most-last species of stone-form through the medium of the most-first species of metal-form. When all the impressions of the most-last species of stone-form are exhausted, the consciousness of the soul dissociates itself from the most-first species of metal-form, and drops that form. But the consciousness now retains the impressions of the most-first species of the metal-form.*

---

* [The reader should not think the oft-appearing "mosts," such as most-first, most-next, most-finite, are superfluous or redundant, because each species

These impressions of the most-first species of the metal-form are now experienced by the conscious soul through its association and identification with the most-next species of metal-form. This form is but the consolidated mould of the impressions of the most-first species of metal-form which was dropped or dissociated by the conscious soul. A chain of varied species of metal-forms is thus created and the soul (or to be more precise, the consciousness of the soul) associates with and dissociates from every species of the metal-form, exhausting and gaining diverse impressions. While experiencing these impressions, the soul evolves more and more consciousness simultaneously with the evolution of the higher and higher species of forms. After ages and cycles, at last the consciousness of the soul associates and identifies itself with the most-last species of metal-form to experience the impressions of the most-last but one species of metal-form that the soul has just dropped or dissociated.

This soul, eternally in the Over-Soul, though being infinite and without form, finds itself as metal.

While identifying itself with diverse species of metal-form the soul begins to experience simultaneously the gross world in accordance with and in proportion to the soul's experiences of the stone-form and the metal-form.

The metal-form, which includes a series of diverse species of metal, is as inorganic, inanimate and solid as the stone-form, which includes a series of diverse species of stone.

The soul, or more precisely, the consciousness of the soul, while identifying itself with the species of stone- and metal-forms, finds itself as one with the stone- or metal-form and thus realizes itself as inorganic, inanimate and solid, and experiences these inorganic, inanimate and solid states throughout the entire evolution of the stone- and metal-forms in the gross world.

The solid, inanimate state of the soul is one in which life

---

of a certain form—stone, for instance—has numerous repetitions with slight variations before going on to the most-next species of that same form, and it seemed necessary to differentiate. "Most-last" is used to mean the form most recently encountered, i.e., the highest and latest evolutionary form of the species, and should not be construed as the form furthest down the scale. Ed.]

and energy are still dormant in spite of greater evolution of consciousness. Hence the forms in this solid state cannot of their own accord move about by themselves (*i.e.,* they cannot have voluntary motion), and therefore the consciousness of the soul, associating with these solid forms which are inanimate and inorganic and with life and energy still dormant in them, tends to assert recumbent, horizontal positions rather than to assert vertical, upright stands or erect positions in the gross world.

After ages and cycles of varied innumerable gross experiences of diverse and innumerable impressions through a variety of species of metal-forms, the consciousness of the soul eventually dissociates itself even from the most-last species of metalform. Thus the identity of the soul with the most-last species of metal-form is dropped and as usual the conscious soul now is once again temporarily unidentified with any form (*i.e.,* the soul is now without any form).

In this state of the conscious soul, when there is no form with which to be associated, the consciousness of the soul is centred only in the impressions of the most-last species of metalform, which has now been dropped.

Thus the conscious soul in this state—of having no form for identification—is conscious only of the impressions of the most- last species of metal-form.

The conscious soul must exhaust these impressions of the most-last species of the metal-form by the consciousness of the soul experiencing these impressions through some appropriate medium. And the appropriate medium to spend or exhaust these impressions of the most-last species of metal-form is the most-first species of vegetable-form. This species of vegetable-form is nothing but the consolidated mould of the impressions of the most-last species of the metal-form.

When the consciousness of the soul associates now with the most-first species of vegetable-form, the soul, thus conscious, tends to identify itself with that form and actually finds itself as that species of vegetable-form, quite oblivious of the reality that it (soul) is infinite, eternal and without form—eternally in the Over-Soul (*Paramatma*).

In this state of the most-first species of the vegetable-form the consciousness of the soul experiences the gross world, in accordance with and in proportion to the impressions it experienced and experiences of the stone-forms, metal-forms and vegetable-form respectively.

While thus experiencing the gross world, this consciousness of the soul, identified with the vegetable-form, realizes now that it is vegetable and has half inanimate and half animate attributes. The conscious soul now asserts in the gross world through this vegetable-form an upright, erect stand. Although this form cannot stand independently by itself, it uses the support of other media to assert an upright stand. This form is still not capable, however, of giving the experience of voluntary movement to the consciousness of the soul.

After the impressions of the last-most species of the metal-form are exhausted by the consciousness of the soul through the most-first species of vegetable-form, this most-first species of vegetable-form is dropped (*i.e.,* the consciousness of the soul dissociates itself from this most-first species of vegetable-form).

Again the conscious soul realizes that it is without a form although the evolved consciousness is there. This evolved consciousness of the soul is now centred in the impressions of the most-first species of the vegetable-form just dropped or dissociated.

To experience these impressions of the most-first species of vegetable-form, the consciousness of the soul, now without any form, utilizes an appropriate medium, which is the most-next species of the vegetable-form. This most-next species of the vegetable-form is nothing but the consolidated mould of the impressions of the most-first species of vegetable-form.

By association with the medium of the most-next species of vegetable-form, the consciousness of the soul experiences in the gross world the impressions of that last species of the vegetable-form just dropped. When these impressions are exhausted through diverse experiences, the consciousness of the soul relinquishes its association with the most-next species of vegetable-form and again experiences that it (the soul) is without gross form and that its consciousness is centred only in the impressions of that species of form last dropped. Again, to experience these impressions the consciousness of the soul tends the soul to identify with the next species of vegetable-form. This chain of impressions, experiences and species of form, from one form to another, is so linked that it is apparently endless; and the consciousness of the soul, in order to evolve itself fully and completely, has no other course but to become entangled in this vicious circle until, perforce, the consciousness of the soul thus gained, makes the soul realize that it is infinite, eternal and eternally in the Over-Soul, and makes the soul experience infinite power, knowledge and bliss.

The point that is important and which is to be carefully noted is that, as the cycle of evolution of consciousness of the soul rolls on and on, and further and greater consciousness is evolved through experiences of further and greater impressions, this evolution of consciousness inadvertently evolves a series of forms of higher and higher species while exhausting the impressions of the lower and lower species that get dissociated or dropped or shed.

Thus the gap between the beginning and the end of a series of species of one particular form, such as stone-form or metal-form or vegetable-form or other forms, beginning with the lowest or crude most-first species of a form of particular kind and ending with the highest or sublime most-last species of form of that particular kind, is progressively filled in by the evolution of forms of higher and higher types suitable to the impressions and aiding the consciousness of the soul to gain higher and higher consciousness. In short, in between the most-first and most-last **species** of form of a particular form, there are diverse species of forms of that particular form, evolved to suit the requirements of the evolving consciousness of the soul.

Coming to the point, when the consciousness of the soul associates itself with the most-last species of vegetable-form, the

conscious soul identifies itself with this most-last species of vegetable-form and experiences the impressions of the most-last
but one species of the vegetable-form that was last shed.

When all the impressions of this most-last but one species
of vegetable-form are exhausted, the conscious soul no longer
identifies itself with the most-last species of vegetable-form because the consciousness of the soul has dissociated itself from
that most-last species of vegetable-form. This most-last species
of vegetable-form is also eventually shed by the conscious soul
after ages and cycles of experience of the whole vegetable kingdom through the gross world, on the earth and in the waters.

Although the most-last species of vegetable-form is shed
by the conscious soul and the soul is now without any form, yet
the conciousness evolved is there, and through this consciousness
the soul (though without form) is conscious of the impressions
of the most-last species of the vegetable-form just shed.

These impressions must necessarily be spent or exhausted.

In order to experience these impressions the consciousness
of the soul now associates with an appropriate medium to experience these impressions of the most-last species of the vegetable-
form. Therefore, the consciousness of the soul thus tends the
soul to identify itself with the most-first species of the worm-
form. It must be remembered that this form of the most-first
species of worm-form is nothing other than the consolidated
mould of the impressions of the most-last species of vegetable-
form.

While the conscious soul thus identifies itself with this most-
first species of worm-form, the soul realizes that it is actually a
worm and becomes worm-conscious.

Despite all of the consciousness so far evolved, the soul is
still not conscious of its reality, its original, infinite, eternal state,
eternally in the Over-Soul. Although the soul is eternally in the
Over-Soul and is infinite and without form, this partially conscious soul actually experiences itself as a worm in the gross
world. This is ignorance. This ignorance persists as long as the
consciousness of the soul is not fully evolved, but even when the

soul has come to full consciousness, it is still said to be enveloped by ignorance because this fully evolved consciousness does not make the soul Self-conscious instantaneously. On the contrary, when the consciousness of the soul is fully evolved the soul begins to identify itself as a human being.

While the consciousness of the soul associates itself with the most-first species of worm-form it experiences and exhausts the impressions of the most-last species of the vegetable-form. When all the impressions of the most-last species of vegetable-form are completely exhausted or spent through the diverse experiences had by the soul while identified with the most-first species of worm-form, then this most-first species of worm-form is dropped or dissociated and the soul is once again without any form although it is conscious of the impressions of the most-first species of worm-form.

These impressions of the most-first species of worm-form must be experienced and exhausted. Therefore the consciousness of the soul associates itself with another appropriate medium and tends the soul to identify with the most-next species of worm-form. This medium of the most-next species of worm-form is nothing other than the consolidated mould of the impressions of the most-first species of worm-form.

Species after species of worm-form are thus moulded and dropped while the consciousness of the soul rapidly evolves through experiencing the varied impressions of worm-forms through diverse species of worm-forms.

When the conscious soul is worm-conscious and experiences itself as a worm in the gross world, the consciousness of the soul also has for the first time the experience of voluntary movement, and also experiences that it is an animate creature. This worm-conscious soul in its travail to gain more and greater consciousness also experiences itself in the gross world as an invertebrate, and at a later stage in other states of vertebrate, limbless, creeping worm-forms of diverse species. In other diverse species of worm-form the consciousness of the soul undergoes further varied experiences of voluntary movement through crawling, through pairs of legs and sometimes through multiple pairs of legs, and sometimes through pairs of legs and pairs of wings. Sometimes the worm-conscious soul in varied species of worm-form realizes itself as possessing a hairy surface, sometimes a smooth and silky and sometimes a rough or scaly surface (hide). The worm-conscious soul also realizes more acutely that it has to struggle for its sustenance and also for its survival, and that it is endowed with sensation and life.

This worm-conscious soul, with further evolution of consciousness through greater and varied innumerable experiences of varied and multiple impressions of varied species of worm-form, also experiences and realizes that it is an amphibian—that it has not only voluntary movement on earth but also freedom and mobility in water.

For our own convenience in understanding the evolution of consciousness more clearly, we include in the worm-form the varied species of worms, varied species of insects, varied species of reptiles and varied species of amphibia. In short, we include in the worm-form all species that tend to crawl or that crawl in spite of having limbs, legs and wings, or that are otherwise distinct from birds and quadrupeds.

The stone- and metal-forms had no upright or erect stand. They were recumbent forms. Their posture was flat and horizontal. The vegetable-form had an upright, erect stand. Now the worm-form is again of the recumbent type of form which has no upright or erect stand but is prone to have a prostrate posture.

When the consciousness of the soul associates itself with the most-last species of worm-form after experiencing all the impressions of the varied species of worm-form, and when the conscious soul eventually drops or sheds this most-last species of worm-form after ages and cycles of multiple diverse experiences in the gross world, the conscious soul again finds itself without any association or identification with forms. But the consciousness of the soul is now centred in the impressions of the most-last species of worm-form just shed. These impressions must necessarily be exhausted through experience, and to get experience a suitable medium is necessary.

Therefore the consciousness of the soul, being centred in the impressions of the most-last species of worm-form, associates with an appropriate medium and tends the soul to identify itself with the most-first species of fish-form in order to experience and exhaust the impressions of the most-last species of worm-form. This most-first species of fish-form is nothing other than the consolidated mould of the impressions of the most-last species of worm-form.

As soon as the impressions of the most-last species of the worm-form are exhausted through experiences, the most-first species of fish-form is dropped or shed because the consciousness of the soul dissociates from this most-first species and the conscious soul no longer identifies itself with that species.

Although the conscious soul is now once again temporarily without form, yet the consciousness of the soul is centred in the impressions of the most-first species of fish-form.

In order to experience these impressions of the most-first species of fish-form, the consciousness of the soul associates itself with a suitable medium and tends the conscious soul to identify itself as the most-next species of fish-form. This species is nothing but the consolidated mould of the impressions of the most-first species of fish-form.

After ages and cycles, and after innumerable varied impressions of diverse species of fish-forms are experienced and exhausted, the consciousness of the soul eventually associates itself with the most-last species of fish-form in order to experience and exhaust all the impressions of the most-last but one species of fish-form.

Thus the fish-conscious soul, identifying with varied species of the fish-form, experiences in the gross world that it is a living creature in water; a vertebrate endowed with life, sensation and voluntary motion; an animate creature with limbs (if any) modified into fins; and that it has to struggle for sustenance and for survival. The fish-conscious soul does not experience an upright, erect stand but it experiences itself as a recumbent that can never hold its head high and erect and assert an upright stand in the gross world.

The fish-conscious soul eventually sheds or drops its identity with the most-last species of fish-form as soon as the consciousness of the soul has experienced and exhausted all the impressions of the most-last but one species of fish-form. Thus the conscious soul once again finds itself without identification with any form. But the consciousness of the soul is conscious of impressions of the most-last species of fish-form.

These impressions of the most-last species of fish-form must be experienced and exhausted, and therefore the consciousness of the soul now associates with another suitable medium and thus tends the soul to identify itself with the most-first species of bird-form, which is but the consolidated mould of the impressions of the most-last species of fish-form.

In the most-first species of bird-form the consciousness of the soul experiences and exhausts the impressions of the most-last species of fish-form.

When all the impressions are thus exhausted the consciousness of the soul dissociates itself from the most-first species of bird-form, and the conscious soul drops or sheds its identity with the most-first species of bird-form (*i.e.,* the most-first species of bird-form is dropped).

The conscious soul is once again without form but it has consciousness centred in the impressions of the most-first species of bird-form just dropped.

These impressions must be experienced and exhausted, and therefore the consciousness of the soul automatically associates itself with the most-next species of bird-form and tends the conscious soul to identify itself with the most-next species of bird-form, which species is but the consolidated mould of the impressions of the most-first species of bird-form.

On and on, ages after ages and cycles after cycles, this chain of successive associations and dissociations with varied species of a particular form moves onwards steadily and progressively, and gives out innumerable different impressions to be experienced by the conscious soul. Directly and indirectly, these associations and dissociations of the consciousness of the soul are absolutely essential to keep the wheel of evolution of consciousness revolving. The evolution of gross forms is but a by-product in the universal factory of evolution of consciousness.

The bird-conscious soul identifies with one species, then with the next, and then the next species of bird-form, one after the other, in regular succession until all the species of bird-form are associated and dissociated alternately by the consciousness of the soul while experiencing multifarious impressions in the gross world, and thus the evolved consciousness of the conscious soul tends the soul to realize itself as bird in every species of the bird-form. Though the soul is eternally without form and in the Over-Soul, yet the bird-conscious soul consistently realizes that it is no other than a bird in the gross world experiencing bird impressions on earth, on water and in air. It realizes itself as a feathered vertebrate capable of flying in air, and with the help of two legs it maintains an erect stand.

Eventually, after ages and cycles of experiences of varied species of bird-form, the bird-conscious soul sheds or drops the most-last species of bird-form as soon as the consciousness of the soul dissociates itself from the most-last species of bird-form; and the consciousness of the soul dissociates itself from the most-last species of bird-form as soon as the consciousness experiences and fully exhausts all the impressions of the most-last but one species of bird-form in the most-last species of bird-form.

Again the conscious soul experiences itself as being without any form for the time being although the consciousness, evolved further and greater, is always there. (Once consciousness is achieved by the soul, this consciousness goes on evolving more and more and can never be lost or devolved). This consciousness of the soul without form now gets centralized in the impressions of the most-last species of bird-form, just dropped. These impressions must necessarily be spent or exhausted by the consciousness of the soul. Therefore consciousness associates itself with a suitable medium and thus tends the conscious soul to identify itself with the most-first species of animal-form. Through this most-first species of animal-form the consciousness of the soul experiences the impressions of the most-last species of bird-form that was dropped or from which it was dissociated. This most-first species of animal-form is nothing other than the consolidated mould of the impressions of the most-last species of bird-form shed.

After innumerable and diverse experiences of the impressions of the most-last species of bird-form through the form of the most-first species of animal-form, the consciousness of the soul completely exhausts the impressions of the most-last species of bird-form and then automatically dissociates itself from identification with the most-first species of animal-form. In this manner the form of that species is shed by the conscious soul, or the form of that species is said to have dropped or died.

Again, the conscious soul, with greater evolved consciousness, finds itself without a form, although the consciousness of the soul is centred in the impressions of the form (just discarded or dropped) of the most-first species of animal-form.

These impressions of the form (just dropped) of the most-first species of animal-form must be experienced or exhausted by the consciousness of the soul, so that the conscious soul should not be aware of any impressions of any form, but be conscious only of the **reality** of its own infinite, eternal state, without forms or impressions, and through knowledge experience the Over-Soul. Throughout the travail of the soul to gain that consciousness for itself which would make it realize the reality of its Self, the conscious soul goes on and on in an apparently unending chain with its consciousness endeavouring ceaselessly to experience and exhaust all impressions that centralize the consciousness of the soul, deviating this consciousness from the reality of the eternal and infinite state of the Self (eternally in the Over-Soul) to the consciousness of duality of illusion of the gross world. Thus the consciousness of the soul, in an effort to gain consciousness of the reality of the Self, is consistently shrouded in an envelope of ignorance.

Therefore, in order that the consciousness of the soul should experience and thus exhaust the impressions of the most-first species of animal-form, the consciousness of the soul now associates automatically with an appropriate medium which will permit and aid it to experience the impressions of the most-first species of animal-form. This association of the consciousness of the soul perforce tends the conscious soul to identify itself with the most-next species of animal-form. This most-next species of animal-form is no other than the consolidated mould of the impressions of the most-first species of animal-form.

As soon as the impressions are experienced and exhausted through the most-next species of animal-form, this species is dropped by the conscious soul. The soul once again experiences that it is not identified with any gross form of the gross world.

When the animal-conscious soul is without any form the consciousness of the soul is centred in the impressions of the most-next species of animal-form just dropped or shed.

These impressions must also be experienced in order that they may be exhausted, and therefore the consciousness of the soul automatically associates itself with another medium and this perforce tends the conscious soul to identify itself with the most-next to the next species of animal-form.

After ages and cycles of varied and innumerable associations with and dissociations from diverse species of animal-form, the consciousness of the soul eventually associates itself with that medium which tends the conscious soul to identify itself as being the most-last of the last species of animal-form.

All throughout the experiences of the animal-conscious soul, the soul identified itself (through its consciousness) with varied species of animals in the gross world in water, on earth and below the surface of the earth, and realized the experiences of an animate creature, usually as a quadrupedal-organized being, endowed with life, sensation and voluntary motion, and which all the while had to struggle for sustenance and survival, sometimes as an herbivorous creature and sometimes as a carnivorous creature. The animal-form has no erect or upright posture and has a tendency to look down with drooping head. Apes, however, are the most evolved types of animals, and they tend to stand erect like human beings. Ultimately, after ages and cycles, when all the impressions of the most-last but one species of animal-form are experienced and exhausted through the medium of the most-last species of animal-form, the consciousness of the soul dissociates itself from the most-last species of animal-form and the conscious soul no longer identifies itself with this most-last species of animal-form. This form is dissociated by the consciousness of the soul and is dropped or shed. However, though the most-last species of animal-form is dropped or shed, the impressions of the most-last species of animal-form are left or retained, and the consciousness of the soul is centralized or focussed on the impressions of the most-last species of animal-form. The conscious soul is once again without form.

These impressions must necessarily be experienced and exhausted, and hence the consciousness of the soul now associates itself with another suitable medium and the soul perforce tends to identify itself through its own consciousness with the most-first human-form. This human-form is no other than the consolidated mould or cast of the impressions of the most-last species of animal-form.

Through the most-first human-form the consciousness of the soul experiences and exhausts the impressions of the most-last species of animal-form.

When all the impressions of the most-last species of the animal-form are experienced and exhausted by the consciousness of the soul, then the consciousness of the soul dissociates itself from the most-first human-form and the conscious soul automatically drops or sheds the body association. This is called the **death** of the most-first human-form. But the consciousness of the soul is now focussed or centralized in the impressions of the most-first human-form and the soul is now temporarily without a form.

In order that the impressions of the most-first human-form may be experienced and exhausted, the consciousness of the soul associates itself with another appropriate medium, and the conscious soul is thereupon inclined to identify itself with the most-next human-form, which form is no other than the consolidated mould or cast of the impressions of the most-first human-form just dropped or shed. This identification of the conscious soul with the next form and those following is called the **birth** of a human being.

As soon as the consciousness of the soul associates with the most-first human-form the EVOLUTION OF CONSCIOUSNESS IS FULL AND COMPLETE.* Because the consciousness [1] of the soul is fully developed in human-form, the evolution of form is also complete, and no new higher forms are now evolved once the conscious soul identifies itself with the most-first human-form. In short, in human-form the consciousness of the soul is full and complete. The process of the evolution of consciousness is brought to a standstill. The human-form is the highest and the most sublime form evolved during the evolution of consciousness. Hence in the human being consciousness is fully developed and the form moulded and cast after ages and cycles is the most perfect form or medium. The consciousness of the soul therefore utilizes this perfect medium to experience and **completely** exhaust all impressions so that the fully conscious soul becomes devoid of any impression whatsoever, and thus is able to realize its own real, eternal and infinite state in the Over-Soul.

---

* [Meher Baba maintains that such subjects should no longer be left indefinite, although he concedes that belief or non-belief in evolution and reincarnation does not in any way hasten or impede man's spiritual progress. He tells us the spiritual significance of evolution and reincarnation in the following words: "It is the evolutionary struggle that enables the soul to develop full consciousness as that in the human form, and the purpose having been achieved, the side-issues or by-products of evolutionary travel (the *nuqush-e-amal* or *sanskaras*) have to be done away with, while retaining the consciousness intact. The process of reincarnation therefore is to enable the soul to eliminate the *sanskaras* by passing through the furnace of pain and pleasure." Ed.]

[1] See also Supplement Note 1 in the Supplement. All numbered references are contained in the Supplement.

Characteristics of the Different Kingdoms

To achieve complete development of consciousness in the human form, the evolutionary process had to take seven major leaps, *viz.*, from stone to metal, from metal to vegetable, from vegetable to worm, from worm to fish, from fish to bird, from bird to animal and finally from animal to the human being, each possessing different characteristics.

Characteristics of the Kingdom of Stones and the Kingdom of Metals

In the stone-forms and metal-forms, the soul has its initial experiences of the gross world. The kingdom of metals, like the kingdom of stones, is inorganic and solid. Both kingdoms include within their range a rich variety of species. In the solid states of stones and metals, life and energy are dormant. Therefore they are regarded as inanimate. The stone-forms and metal-forms cannot move about by themselves, *i.e.*, they have no voluntary motion. For this reason the consciousness, which associates itself with these forms, tends to assert itself through a recumbent, horizontal position(rather than through an erect position or vertical, upright stand) in the gross world.

Characteristics of the Vegetable Kingdom

In the vegetable kingdom, consciousness realizes itself as half animate and half inanimate. The increased consciousness of the vegetable-form asserts its existence in the gross world through an upright or erect stand. The vegetable-forms have to take the help of some other things such as earth or rock for maintaining an erect position. They can neither stand by themselves nor move voluntarily from place to place since they are rooted in one spot.

Characteristics of the Kingdom of Worms

In worm-consciousness the soul gathers experiences of voluntary movement. It experiences itself as animate. In its travail to gain more and further consciousness, the worm-conscious soul experiences itself in the gross world, first as an invertebrate and later as a vertebrate, and goes on creeping in diverse species of worms. Voluntary movements are made by crawling by means of pairs of legs, sometimes by multiple pairs of legs, and sometimes by pairs of legs and pairs of wings. Worms may have surfaces that are hairy, smooth, silky, rough or scaly. The worm goes through a struggle for existence and survival and is endowed with sensation and life. Sometimes it is an amphibian, *i.e.,* it has not only voluntary movement on earth, but has also mobility in water. For the purpose of this explanation, the worm-form includes all worms, insects, reptiles and amphibia, of their species. Even when they have legs and wings, they have a tendency to crawl and they are distinct from birds and from quadruped animals. The worm-form is recumbent, has no upright or erect stand and is prone to lie prostrate.

Characteristics of the Kingdom of Fish

The fish-conscious soul identifies itself with varied species of fish and experiences the gross world as a living creature in water (a vertebrate endowed with life and sensation and voluntary motion), and has fins. It goes through a struggle for sustenance and survival. The fish-conscious soul does not assert its existence in the gross world through an erect stand, but experiences itself as recumbent, never holding its head high and erect.

Characteristics of the Kingdom of Birds

The bird-form enriches (enlightens) consciousness with new experiences since, as a feathered vertebrate, it is capable of flying in the air and, with the help of its two legs, of maintaining an erect stand in the gross world.

Characteristics of the Kingdom of Animals

The animal-form brings to consciousness further expansion, since it can yield new experiences through the greater varieties existing in the kingdom of animals. Endowed with life, sensation and power of voluntary locomotion, quadruped animals have to face a struggle for existence and survival. They are sometimes herbivorous and sometimes carnivorous. Animal consciousness does not assert its existence in the gross world through erect or upright posture, but has a tendency to look downwards with drooping head. Apes, however, are the most evolved type of animals, and they tend to stand erect like human beings.

Characteristics of the Kingdom of Human Beings

In the human-form the evolving consciousness of the soul attains its full development. The process of evolution of consciousness has its terminus in the human form. Here consciousness is full and complete.

When a human being is born, it can only lie prostrate and it continues to experience this state for a fairly long period. But it soon expresses a tendency first to sit erect and then to stand erect. The fully evolved human consciousness of the soul eventually asserts its existence in the gross world through an upright position.*

---

*   THE ASCENDING SOUL

"I died as mineral and became a plant,
I died as plant and rose to animal,
I died as animal and I was man.
Why should I fear? When was I less by dying?
Yet, once more, I shall die as man, to soar
With angels blessed; but even from angelhood
I must pass on; all except God doth perish.
When I have sacrificed my angel soul,
I shall become what no mind e'er conceived.
Oh, Let me not exist! For Non-existence
Proclaims in organ tones, 'To Him we shall return!' "

—Rumi

Reincarnation and the Impressionless Equipoise of Consciousness

DURING the course of evolution of its consciousness, the soul (*atma*), while **consciously** identifying itself with varied, finite gross forms, was also simultaneously, though **unconsciously,** identifying itself with its finite subtle form and its finite mental form, which associated with the soul in compact, homogeneous, unconscious alliance throughout the entire course of evolution of consciousness right from the first urge.

Although the soul frequently and consciously dissociated itself from the finite gross forms which acted as media to experience the impressions gained in the course of evolving greater and higher consciousness, the soul could never dissociate itself, consciously or unconsciously, directly or indirectly, from its finite subtle form and its finite mental form.

On the contrary, while the soul dissociated its identification with any one medium of finite gross form, it was the unconscious association of soul with its finite subtle form that fortified the soul (now without any gross medium) with finite energy (the driving force) to give a tendency to the consciousness of the soul towards identifying itself with the next medium of the next finite gross form, in order to experience the impressions of the last dissociated finite gross form, retained and reflected by the finite mental form of this soul.

It is but natural that, together with the evolution of higher and greater consciousness of soul, the evolution of the finite subtle form of soul also takes place to fortify the soul with greater finite energy to incline the consciousness of the more and more gross-conscious soul to identify itself with higher and higher types of finite gross forms evolved by the impressions of the last lower finite gross form.

Similarly, the evolution of the finite mental form of the soul also takes place simultaneously to accommodate, retain and reflect the increasingly innumerable, varied impressions gained and gathered by the evolution of greater and greater conscious-ness of the soul.

Thus it is that, when the soul tends to identify itself with varied species of vegetable-forms, the evolved finite subtle form and the evolved finite mental form of the soul begin to show greater and visible signs of the soul's association with its much evolved finite subtle form and finite mental form in the shape of varied, rapid cycles of changes taking place in vegetable-forms; and also, in the shape of vegetable-forms showing first signs of peculiar, varied and meaningful tendencies of self-preservation and survival of the fittest.

In the worm-, bird- and fish-forms, this tendency of the finite mental form of the soul is translated gradually and steadily into the shape of instinct, until in the animal-form this instinct is fully manifested as one of the finite aspects of the finite mental form of the soul. Gradually this instinct is further and completely transformed into intellect, this being the highest finite aspect of manifestation of the mental form in the human-form of the gross-conscious human soul experiencing the gross world.

So it is that only in human-form are the subtle body and the mental body fully developed, wherefore the soul, associating itself consciously with human-form is, so to speak, fully equipped with a human body, subtle body and mental body, together with full consciousness of the gross.

Although the soul has gained consciousness in human-form

and thus experiences the gross world, yet the gross-conscious human soul is unconscious of the subtle body and so cannot experience the subtle world. It is also unconscious of the mental body and thus cannot experience the mental world.

Even though the soul has only gross consciousness and is unconscious of the subtle and mental, it does work through the subtle and mental bodies, although indirectly, on the gross plane. Even though the gross-conscious human soul is unconscious of its subtle and mental bodies and their respective subtle and mental worlds, and therefore does not realize the energy of the subtle and the mind of the mental, yet it can **use** energy through various gross aspects of energy such as nuclear energy. And it can **use** mind through various gross aspects of mind such as desires, emotions and thoughts. Of these, **desires** are the predominant aspect of the mind.

So this soul, now fully gross-conscious of the first-most human gross form and still unconscious of the subtle and mental, experiences in the gross world the impressions of the last-most animal gross form dissociated or dropped.

When all the impressions of the last-most animal gross form are exhausted, it is but natural that the first-most human gross form is dissociated from the soul. This experience of the soul is universally termed the death of the human being.

As explained previously, although this soul is dissociated from the first-most human gross form, it is **never** dissociated from its subtle or its mental forms or bodies.

It was also previously explained that though this soul is dissociated from its first-most human gross form, the soul retains and experiences through the subtle and mental bodies the impressions of the dropped or dissociated first-most human-form, and the soul again associates itself with the next-most human-form to experience the impressions of the previous human-form dropped. In fact, the next-most human-form is nothing but the consolidated mould of the past impressions retained of the previous body or form that dissociated from the soul. Thus the association of the soul with the next-most human-form is called universally the birth of a human being.

The apparent gap between the death and the birth of a human being is that period in which the gross-conscious soul, in its association with its fully developed subtle and mental bodies, has experiences of the predominant counterpart of the opposite impressions gathered by the recently dissociated human-form. This state of the soul, in the apparent gap between death and birth, is generally called hell or heaven, and this process of intermittent association and dissociation of consciousness of the conscious soul in human-form, now fully conscious, is termed the "Reincarnation Process."

If the predominant counterpart of the impressions of opposites (such as virtue and vice, good and evil, male and female, etc.), as experienced by the soul now associated only with the subtle and mental, is of virtue or goodness (*i.e.,* the positive aspect of the opposite impressions), then the soul is said to be in heaven. If it is of vice or evil (*i.e.,* the negative aspect of opposite impressions), then the soul is said to be in hell.

The states of heaven and hell are nothing but states of intensive experiences of the consciousness of the soul, experiencing either of the predominant counterparts of the opposite impressions while the soul is dissociated from the gross human body or form. The soul itself does not go to heaven or hell, as is the general belief, because it is eternally infinite and eternally in the Over-Soul. It is the consciousness of the soul which experiences the impressions.

As soon as the predominant counterpart of impressions is experienced and exhausted, and just when equilibrium is about to be maintained between the opposites of impressions of the last human-form that was dropped, at this juncture the soul automatically associates with the next-most human-form, moulded of the consolidated impressions of opposites which were about to be in a state of equilibrium.

Thus the gross consciousness of the soul, after experiencing either hell or heaven, associates with the next human-form (takes another birth) to experience and exhaust the residual opposite impressions of the last birth. As has already been said, this next human-form of the soul is nothing but the consolidated mould of the residual opposite impressions of the last form.

It is in this manner that an apparently unending chain of births and deaths of human-forms or beings continues to form and dwindle. This is the course of reincarnation in human forms of the soul, after it has gained full gross consciousness through the whole series of evolution of the gross consciousness. Right from the unconscious state of the soul (comparable to the deep-sleep state of man), until it has gained full gross consciousness (comparable to the wide-open eyes of man in the awake state) while experiencing the gross world, the soul is One—indivisible, infinite, formless—and is eternally in the Over-Soul.

Throughout the whole process of evolution, reincarnation was an absolutely spontaneous outcome of the first urge, manifested in the unconscious soul, to become conscious of its eternal and infinite Self.

As has been mentioned already, we can now understand that the cycle of evolution of consciousness of **soul** evolved further and greater **consciousness,** together with the evolution of **forms** of higher and higher types, while exhausting the impressions of the dissociated forms of lower types.

Thus the evolution of consciousness of soul apparently causes the soul to identify itself with, and gather varied innumerable impressions of, higher and higher gross species of forms of the gross world.

The clean-cut and major concrete gross forms (after the most-first seven major, most abstract gaseous and fluid forms) with which the consciousness of the soul associated (with every leap of greater and greater consciousness) are separated by the seven leaps from stone to metal, from metal to vegetable, from vegetable to worm, from worm to fish, from fish to bird, from bird to animal and lastly from animal to human being.

The most-finite first impression of the first urge gave to the unconscious soul the most-finite first consciousness. Gradually, varied impressions gained greater finite consciousness for the soul, and eventually the evolution of consciousness was complete when the soul identified itself with the most-first human-form. In human-form the soul achieves full and complete consciousness.

Therefore the soul, having now gained full and complete consciousness in human-form, does not need any more or any other higher forms to evolve consciousness.

This consciousness is full and complete.

Though this soul has gained full and complete consciousness, it is still not at all conscious of its Self as One, indivisible, eternal and infinite, and does not experience infinite knowledge, power and bliss. But it is only fully conscious of its identity with human-form and its varied aspects, and experiences the gross world in full.

The soul with full consciousness is still unconscious of its original infinite state because of the unwanted (though necessary) burden of the gross impressions of the human-form from which the consciousness of the soul dissociates as that form drops dead. These impressions, of the human-form now dead, still cling to the full consciousness gained; and, as usual, the consciousness of the soul centralizes itself in these gross impressions of the human-form just dropped.

In trying to unburden consciousness of these impressions, the gross consciousness of the soul tends the soul to experience and exhaust these impressions through innumerable opposite experiences taken through a series of reincarnations. In this process of reincarnation the consciousness of the soul, while trying to liberate itself from the burden of impressions, gets still further entangled at every stage of reincarnation. When a complete balance of experiences of opposite impressions is just about to be attained, it is just then disturbed by the consciousness of the soul associating itself with the next new human-form. Absence of this association would otherwise have neutralized the effect of the impressions by an equal balance of respective opposite experiences and would thus have liberated the consciousness of the soul from all impressions of opposites.

Here the simile of a "perfect balance" would be appropriate. The consciousness gained by the soul during the process of evolution resembles the indicator at the fulcrum of a perfect balance, and the two pans of the balance are filled with the unequal weights of opposites of impressions such as virtue and vice, etc.

In this way consciousness, acting like the indicator at the fulcrum, tries to gain equilibrium, which is impossible as long as there are in existence unequal impressions of opposites remaining to be experienced. It is therefore that the gross consciousness of the soul constantly seeks to experience the **predominant** opposite impressions in order to gain a total equilibrium of the impressions of opposites.

But the tragedy is this, that as soon as the gross consciousness of the soul tends to reach the zero point of equilbrium by gradually experiencing the predominant opposite impressions, it so happens that the consciousness of the soul invariably gets too engrossed in experiencing the predominant opposite impressions, and experiences them or exhausts them to such a degree that these predominant opposite impressions are now reduced (*i.e.,* through experience) to such a level, that those impressions which were over-balanced by the original predominant opposite impressions, now become predominant; and a great disturbance of balance or equipoise occurs; wherefore consciousness, acting like the indicator at the fulcrum, swings or switches in just the opposite direction of its original experience.

It is at this juncture that the consciousness of the soul turns towards the experience of the **newly** predominant opposite impressions through another human-form. A human being takes form or birth as a medium to satisfy the demanding need of the consciousness of the soul, which now seeks to exhaust or spend or experience the more predominant opposite impressions.

It is but natural that the predominant qualities manifested now by this human soul will be in accordance with the predominant opposite impressions, of which this new human-form is but the mould.

Thus, in the process of reincarnation, the fully gross-conscious human soul, fortified with fully developed subtle and mental bodies, though unconscious of these, must necessarily experience countless varied experiences of impressions of opposites—the impressions which are diametrically opposite—in a chain of unending experiences.

Through its association with the gross body, the soul seeks to exhaust its previously accumulated opposite impressions, but rarely succeeds in doing so. On the contrary, it often accumulates **fresh** impressions of opposites. When the gross form is about to exhaust the impressions which brought it into existence, it is dropped. The residual opposite impressions lead the soul to heaven or hell, in accordance with the predominance of virtue or vice. In discarnate existence also, all opposite impressions seek to be exhausted through the subjective experiencing of vivified impressions. But even here, in the state of heaven or hell, the equipoise of impressionlessness is generally approximated but missed, and the residual predominant opposite impressions goad the consciousness of the soul to associate with a new gross medium. Complete equipoise is lacking in death as well as in birth. It can only be achieved in the gross world. Therefore an endless chain of lives in the gross sphere is sustained by residual impressions, until consciousness succeeds in getting established in impressionless equipoise.

At every stage and in every state of reincarnation, the consciousness of the fully human-conscious soul gets firmly centralized in the more and more concentrated impressions of human-forms with which it has identified and from which it has dissociated. There seems to be no escape * from these concen-

---

* Knowing that Creation is not an accident and that it has a deeper meaning than is apparent to the eye, the seers of all ages have time and again drawn the attention of the world to the fact that, although for a certain period of his life on this planet man may identify himself exclusively with the life of the senses, his transcendental destiny is God-realization.

Maulana Rumi, in his *Masnavi,* has a parable that illustrates this: The cub of a tiger happened to be reared amongst a flock of sheep. As the cub grew up, it developed all the traits of the sheep and grazed and bleated like

trated impressions. These impressions must be experienced and exhausted, and the more the impressions are experienced the more the impressions become concentrated.

The only solution to "thin out" this concentration of impressions is for the consciousness of the fully human-conscious soul to experience increasingly and more rapidly these impressions in such a way, and in so great a frequency that every impression experienced, and the impression that this experience created, should be counter-balanced somehow by an opposite impression.

Throughout the process of reincarnation this play of balancing and counter-balancing the opposites of impressions continues, and on this play is sustained the reincarnation process. On this play depends the eventual emancipation of the human-conscious soul from the chains of ignorance, and the ultimate realization of Self-consciousness.

Thus, in the process of reincarnation, the fully gross-conscious human soul must necessarily experience innumerable and diverse experiences of impressions of opposites—the impressions which are diametrically opposite—in an apparently unending chain of consistent experiences.

Therefore, while the gross-conscious human soul, which is now fully conscious, undergoes the experience of **opposites** in the gross world, the consciousness of the soul has to identify (or reincarnate) itself a number of times as a male, then as a female, and vice versa, in varied castes, creeds, nationalities, colours, and in different places; as rich one time and then as a pauper; sometimes healthy and sometimes sick, and so forth, all the

them, so that it never thought of itself as anything different from the sheep. One day, however, a tiger from the jungle approached the one from the flock and said to him, "Do you know that you are a tiger like me, and not one of the sheep?" Thereafter he coaxed the strayed tiger to look at its image in a rivulet nearby, and succeeded in enlightening it as to its true nature.

The moral of this fable is that man also allows himself to be identified with the world of the senses and seems to have no way of escape. But there is a way of escape, for eventually a Master appears who enlightens him. He is then redeemed, and finds himself in the course of time face to face with his ultimate goal—God-realization.

while reviewing opposite impressions, creating opposite impressions, and simultaneously exhausting them by opposite experiences.

It is only through these diverse opposite impressions and their respective opposite experiences, that the gross-conscious human soul in the gross world could possibly one day, after millions of births and deaths, and through these opposite experiences of births and deaths, be able to balance or thin out the residual or concentrated opposite impressions.*

It is this cycle of deaths and consequent births of human-forms that ultimately results in inciting the fully evolved consciousness of the gross-conscious human soul to **involve** this consciousness to that depth where the fully involved consciousness of this soul realizes the reality of the infinite, eternal state of the Self.

This process of involution of consciousness gradually takes place as the gross impressions of the opposites gradually become fainter and less concentrated.

At this stage the consciousness of the gross-conscious human soul gradually gets dissociated from the gross world, as the involution of consciousness infolds, and gradually dissociates from experiencing the impressions of the gross world.

This involution of gross consciousness is only possible when the opposite impressions gradually, after a very, very long process, thin out through the process of unfailing reincarnation, which leads to the limit of gross impressions of the opposites and gross experiences of the opposites.

---

* *Sarāpā ārzū hone ne bandah kardiyā ham ko*
Vagarnah ham khudā the gar dil-i be mudu'ā hotā.
—Mīr Taqī

"The fact that I am weighed down from head to foot with desires has made a slave of me; I should be God in reality, were my heart and mind desireless."

The Planes

Involution of Liberating Consciousness

When the consciousness of the soul is ripe [2] for disentanglement from the gross world, it enters the spiritual path and turns inwards. Its gross impressions now become less deep. They become fainter or more subtle, with the result that the soul now becomes **subtle-conscious.** This is the first step in the involution of consciousness, which is striving for liberation from the burden of impressions. A number of cycles of births and deaths in the human form have to contribute towards that ripeness of gross experience, which ultimately propels the consciousness of the soul onto the path of liberating involution, on which impressions become fainter and fainter and eventually disappear. Gross impressions become subtle impressions; subtle impressions become mental impressions; and mental impressions are ultimately wiped out, leaving consciousness free to reflect the Truth.

The process of involution is generally gradual. Man's heritage of form as well as impressions is from animals, so the gross impressions are very strong. In extremely rare cases, the gross impressions can suddenly disappear, and the freed consciousness of the soul experiences the Over-Soul. But it is more usual for the gross impressions to become fainter and fainter (thus getting converted into subtle and mental impressions), and then fade away completely. As a general rule the soul, which has started on its homeward journey, does not come back to the gross world in which it had lost itself as if in a wilderness. This does not mean that the subtle-conscious soul does not take a gross form or dwell in the gross world with its gross body. It means that the consciousness of the soul is no longer entangled with the gross form or the gross world, and that it is chiefly engrossed in the subtle world. As a general rule the soul first snaps its link with the gross world, then with the subtle world and lastly with the mental world, and comes to realize itself as beyond all these. While it traverses this path it crosses six planes, of which the first three belong to the subtle world, the fourth is on the border line of the subtle and mental worlds, whereas the fifth and the sixth belong to the mental world. The soul, abiding everlastingly in the Over-Soul, is beyond all planes.

First and Second Planes

As the gross consciousness of the gross-conscious human soul gradually involves, this involving gross consciousness experiences **partially** the first plane [3] of the subtle world through the medium of the fully developed subtle body of the soul.

At this stage the involved gross consciousness of the gross-conscious human soul gets the first glimpses of the first plane of the subtle world and experiences these glimpses or impressions partially through the gross body and partially through the subtle body. Here both the gross and the subtle senses are used simultaneously.

This is the stage when it is said that the human soul stands as it were on the line of demarcation, as shown in the sketch,* which demarks the gross world from the subtle world. The consciousness of this human soul experiences strange things. With his gross eyes he sees glimpses of the subtle plane, with his gross ears he hears celestial music of the subtle plane, and with his gross nose he enjoys subtle scents. In short, the gross-conscious human soul, partially on the first plane of the subtle world,

---

* Facing p. 59.

experiences subtle impressions with gross senses.

Gradually, with further involution of gross consciousness, the gross-conscious human soul experiences completely the first plane of the subtle world. Now the gross-conscious human soul is no longer gross-conscious but he is subtle-conscious. This subtle-conscious human soul gradually becomes conscious of the second plane [4] of the subtle world. This subtle world is the domain of infinite Energy, the infinite power of God, which when translated into the finite, here manifests in the form of the infinite energy of the subtle world.

When in human form the soul has subtle consciousness, it is unconscious of the body (gross) and mind (or the mental body); but it does work through the gross body and through the mind (mental body), not directly, but on the subtle plane.

So even if the subtle-conscious human soul is unconscious of the gross body and mental body and therefore does not realize the gross and mental worlds, he can use the gross body through various aspects of the gross, such as eating, drinking, sleeping, seeing, feeling, hearing, etc.; and he can use the mental body through various aspects of mind (mental body), such as desires, thoughts and emotions.

The subtle-conscious human soul on the second plane, with greater involution of consciousness, is gradually gaining consciousness of the infinite energy of the subtle world and is capable of performing tricks, or minor miracles of lower degree. For instance, with one wish he can make a dry tree green and vice versa; he can stop railway trains and motor cars, fill a dry well with fresh water, and so forth. This subtle-conscious human soul on the second plane experiences the subtle world with the subtle senses of his subtle body. He is now totally unconscious of the gross world, although from all outward appearances he remains and functions as an ordinary man—eating, sleeping and having feelings of pain and pleasure, etc.—yet actually his involving consciousness experiences not the gross but the subtle world and creates fresh subtle impressions only of the sights, scents and sounds of the subtle world.

Third Plane

Further involution of the subtle consciousness of the subtle-conscious human soul makes the soul experience the third plane [5] of the subtle world. Here the subtle consciousness gains greater consciousness of the infinite energy of the subtle world and the soul experiences greater finite power. Here he is capable of performing grand miracles such as giving sight to the blind and restoring limbs to the maimed. Here this subtle-conscious human soul is also capable of experiencing the different planes and worlds of the subtle sphere, just as a gross-conscious human soul is capable of travelling from Asia to Australia or America using the gross vehicles at his disposal.[6]

The second and third planes of the subtle sphere are the two major planes which are solely in the domain of the subtle sphere. The first plane is partially in the domain of the subtle sphere and partially in the gross sphere. Similarly the fourth plane is partially of the subtle sphere and partially of the mental sphere. This fourth plane is known as the threshold of the **mental sphere.**

Fourth Plane

With a gradual and further gain in the involution of the consciousness of the subtle-conscious human soul, the consciousness of the soul inclines the soul to experience the fourth plane. On the fourth plane the soul is fully conscious of **infinite energy.** It is the very same infinite energy which is the shadowy aspect of that infinite power of God. Here the soul is equipped with full power and is even capable of raising the dead and of creating new forms and worlds * breathing with life. On the fourth plane there are no occult powers. They are divine powers.

---

* The *vidnyan*-conscious souls of *Qutub* state or Perfect Masters control such a happening and see that such gross mishaps do not come to pass unless preordained.

As shown in the sketch facing p. 59, the subtle-conscious human soul on the fourth plane, possessing the key to the store of infinite power, is seen on the threshold of the mental world, confronted by the full blast of intense desires and emotions which are the aspects of Mind of the mental world. At this stage, the soul experiences, as it were, a state of the darkest night. He finds himself caught up between the Devil and the deep. The overpowering incitement by intense desires to wield and use this infinite energy at will, proves a treacherous foe at this juncture when the involution of consciousness of this subtle-conscious human soul is unfailingly progressing rapidly towards gaining mastery over all desires.

If these desires at their zenith overpower the soul on the fourth plane, and if the powers are misused, then the experience of liberating this infinite energy invariably proves fatal at this juncture for the soul on the fourth plane. The result is that all of the consciousness gained by the soul is violently disintegrated, and the soul retains only the most finite consciousness and identifies itself once again with the stone-form. This soul then has to pass through the whole process of evolution from the stone-form onward to regain full consciousness.

The soul of the fourth plane has semi-subtle and semi-mental impressions. He is subject to most tantalizing temptations because he has intense and overpowering desires, good or bad. Being in possession of tremendous power, he is impelled to make good or bad use of it. If he misuses his power for the satisfaction of lust or for the sake of craving for name and fame or for some other low purpose, there is a sudden fall of this consciousness of the soul, causing it to revert to the stone stage of consciousness. But if, by overcoming his temptations, he makes good use of his tremendous powers, or does not make any use of his powers, he goes into the fifth plane, where he is safe and has no possibility of downfall. But also if he makes good use of the powers, he is sometimes pulled up into the sixth plane by the *vidnyan*-conscious souls of *Qutub* state or Perfect Masters (but not *Jivanmuktas* nor *Majzoobs*).

Good use of power in the gross world may be directed towards material and spiritual ends. For example, wealth might be spent for the material well-being of others, as for charitable hospitals, relief for the starving and the distressed, etc., or for their spiritual well-being, by providing them with spiritual instruction and spiritual possibilities. But in the fourth plane, good use of powers invariably consists in harnessing them only for the spiritual well-being of others. These powers can never be used to bring about material prosperity for anyone. That definitely is a bad use. We might take the following as an example of good use of the powers of the fourth plane:—Suppose a spiritual pilgrim is going through a desert and is on the point of death due to unquenchable thirst. The soul of the fourth plane can appear to him in the gross body and give him relief by giving him a jug of water and then disappear. Such use can be termed good use.

Powers can be used for individual or collective good. **But even good use binds and arrests the further progress of the soul.** That is why the fourth plane is the most difficult to cross and is fraught with greatest dangers. The person who is stationed on the fourth plane finds it most difficult to abstain from wielding the tremendous powers at his command for the fulfillment of his overpowering desires.

The fourth plane is the threshold of the mental world. On this plane, more than on any other subtle plane, the spiritual pilgrim is particularly susceptible to having a precipitous fall. The crisis which confronts the soul of the fourth plane is grave and hazardous, because he comes into the possession of stupendous divine powers before having brought his mind into complete subjugation. He cannot control his mind completely because, unless and until he rises onto the fifth plane which is of the mental world, he cannot directly experience or use his mind. Like the gross-conscious human soul, the subtle-conscious soul of the fourth plane also uses his mind indirectly. Now on this fourth plane the mind is fully alive. It is functioning in all its fully developed aspects of thoughts, feelings and desires, which are at the zenith of their overwhelming intensity. On the one hand, the soul is trying to gain mastery over its own insurgent mind and bring into subjugation the subversive forces of desires let loose. On the other hand, the limitless energy of the planes is completely at his disposal and is constantly seeking some expression or use.

If the soul yields to the overpowering temptations to put his powers to wrong use, there is an enormous psychic crash of unimaginable magnitude. The explosive forces thereby released bring about a complete disintegration of consciousness, subjecting it to a **cataclysmic downfall from the heights of the subtle consciousness of the fourth plane to the very lowest depths of rudimentary stone consciousness** which the soul experienced in the very beginnings of evolution. This psychic cataclysm of disintegration is comparable to the fusing of an electric bulb due to an irreparable short-circuit. The fallen soul has now no alternative except that of again going through the long and laborious ascent of evolving consciousness, through ages of evolution and reincarnation through numberless forms, and then again gradually and patiently ascending through the planes.

This disintegration of consciousness occurs only in the case of fourth plane consciousness and that, too, rarely—only when the powers of the fourth plane are misused. It is a fact normally that when consciousness is once gained it can never be lost, but the case of fourth plane consciousness is the one exception.

If the soul does not misuse the powers at his command but uses them for good without being overpowered by desires, then, with further involution of consciousness the consciousness of the subtle-conscious human soul sometimes experiences directly the sixth plane of the mental world and skips over the experiences of the fifth plane of the mental world.*

But if this consciousness of soul on the fourth plane of

---

* Entry into the mental world comprising the fifth and sixth planes may be compared to an entry into a room after crossing the threshold—the fourth plane of consciousness.

consciousness neither uses nor misuses the powers of the fourth plane, then gradually, with further involution of consciousness, the subtle-conscious human soul on the fourth plane crosses the threshold of the fourth plane and enters the mental world on the fifth plane.

Fifth and Sixth Planes

With greater involution of consciousness of the subtle-conscious human soul on the fourth plane, the consciousness of the subtle-conscious human soul identifies itself with Mind of the mental planes and experiences the mental world.

This Mind of the mental planes has two sections. In the first section the state of Mind is inquiring or reflecting. In this state Mind functions as thoughts—high thoughts, low thoughts; good thoughts, bad thoughts; material thoughts, spiritual thoughts, and so forth.

In the second section the state of Mind is impressive or sympathetic. In this state Mind functions as feelings—feelings of sufferings, emotions; feelings of desires, longings; feelings of pangs, separation, and so forth.

When Mind of the mental world has distinct dual functions it is necessary that the experiences in the field of Mind (*i.e.,* the mental world) must be distinctively of two kinds also.

Thus the mental world has two domains—the domain of the fifth plane of consciousness of **Thoughts** and the domain of the sixth plane of consciousness of **Feelings.***

Therefore the consciousness of the mental-conscious human soul on the fifth plane [7] identifies with the first section of Mind

---

* The difference between the involving consciousness of the fifth and sixth planes may be compared to the difference between the angles of vision of a man entering a room—the mental world. On entering the room, if the man looks straight ahead of him he spontaneously sees God face to face, thereby gaining directly consciousness of the sixth plane; but if his vision happens to focus on one of the corners of the room, then he first gains only the consciousness of the fifth plane.

only and is conscious of that state of Mind which is inquiring or reflecting Mind. Thus this mental-conscious human soul of the fifth plane is the creator and master of thoughts and is capable of controlling **only the thoughts** of all gross- and subtle-conscious souls. This is often misinterpreted as **controlling the minds** of all gross- and subtle-conscious souls. (He does not control the mind as a whole but controls only that state of Mind which functions as thoughts only.)

The mental-conscious human soul on the fifth plane of consciousness, while identifying himself as inquiring or reflecting Mind, emanates only thoughts, does not identify himself with the second state of Mind and is therefore incapable of establishing mastery over feelings, emotions and desires.

However, with greater involution of consciousness, the mental-conscious human soul on the fifth plane gains consciousness of the second state of Mind of the mental world in the sixth plane and thus tends to identify himself as that Mind in the second state—the impressive or sympathetic Mind. Thus the consciousness of the mental-conscious human soul has involved sixth plane consciousness of the mental world.

The mental-conscious human soul of sixth plane consciousness experiences the mental world through complete consciousness of feelings and thus has no thoughts at all, but actually feels that he is conscious of the feeling of seeing God face to face continuously in everything and everywhere. He "sees" * God continuously but cannot see himself in God as God. Therefore he cannot reconcile his feeling-of-sight of God with his own identity with God; and thus he longs for, feels for, has pangs for union with God Whom he "sees" face to face. This identification with the second state of Mind—feeling—is the predominant aspect of divine love which ultimately leads to union with God.

The fifth plane of the mental world is the state of full consciousness of thought, hence only mastery over the control and

---

* This is not to be confused with our ordinary way of seeing an object with our ordinary eyes. To "see" God face to face is to apprehend God through the one and only sense of the mental plane, and this sense is of "seeing." Here the pilgrim has the intuitive recognition of God.

creation of thoughts is established, whereas no mastery nor control over feelings or emotions and desires is established.

The sixth plane of the mental world is the state of full consciousness of feeling, and thus mastery over the control and creation of feelings is established and no more scope is left for even a single thought to penetrate into the domain of feelings. The sixth plane consciousness is thought-less and governs the feelings of the gross- and subtle-conscious souls. This is often misinterpreted as mastery over the hearts of all gross- and subtle-conscious souls. (A soul with sixth plane consciousness does not govern or regulate the so-called heart but controls and governs that state of Mind in the mental plane which emanates feelings of emotion and desires.)

The loving of God and the longing for His union is really and fully demonstrated in the sixth plane; when even the sixth plane of the mental world is transcended, illusion vanishes and God is realized.

In the human form when the soul is mental-conscious * it is unconscious of the gross body and the subtle body; but it does work through the gross and subtle bodies, not directly, but on the mental plane. So even if the mental-conscious human soul is unconscious of the gross body and the subtle body and therefore does not realize the gross and subtle worlds, he can unconsciously utilize the gross through various **aspects** of the gross and is thus seen eating, drinking, sleeping, seeing, hearing and feeling as an ordinary gross-conscious human being, though he is all the while conscious only of the mental world with his mental sense of "seeing." Similarly, he can unconsciously utilize the subtle through various gross **aspects** of energy in the form of nuclear energies, etc., while all the time being only conscious of "seeing" with his mental sense. The mental-conscious human soul in the mental world has now only one sense and that is of "seeing."

---

* [See also: Meher Baba, "Mental Consciousness," *The Everything and the Nothing* (Beacon Hill, N.S.W., Australia: Meher House Publications, 1963), pp. 63–65. Ed.]

So this mental-conscious human soul on the fifth plane experiences the first state of the mental world with the mental body or the mind and gains consciousness of the first state of Mind. Here this soul is capable of controlling the first state of Mind (*i.e.,* thoughts of the gross-conscious and subtle-conscious human souls) but is now totally incapable of performing any miracles because of his total unconsciousness of the infinite energy of the subtle world and its powers. However, as this mental-conscious human soul controls the first state of Mind of the subtle-conscious human souls, the incitement in the subtle-conscious human soul to perform miracles is checked, controlled or aggravated according to the desire and will of the mind of the mental-conscious human soul, who is capable of creating and controlling thoughts of other minds and is himself stable and can never again slide down to any lower level of consciousness.

Gradually, as the involution of the consciousness of the mental-conscious human soul progresses deeper and deeper, he experiences mastery over the second state of Mind (*i.e.,* feeling) and he now becomes fully conscious of the mind or the mental body, and experiences the whole of the mental body on the sixth plane.[8] This experience is of "seeing" God face to face—seeing God everywhere and in everything.

Right from the first plane up through the sixth plane the involution of consciousness progressed gradually and steadily as the consciousness of the soul had less and less frequent experiences of multifarious and diverse opposite impressions which grew fainter and fainter. Therefore, while the involution of the soul's consciousness was in progress, the diverse opposite impressions became gradually scarcer and fainter until the involved consciousness of the soul on the sixth plane is fully conscious of the mental body and experiences the mental world in full with practically no impressions at all except a faint last trace of residual impressions of opposites. That is, the involved consciousness fully identifies with Mind, and the soul tends to realize that he **is** Mind; and this soul, as Mind, has a last and total impression that he "sees" God face to face in everything but he cannot see himself in God.

This mental-conscious human soul of the sixth plane, almost void of all impressions * and only conscious of mind, now is confronted with God face to face and sees God in everything but does not see himself in God because, being still conscious of mind, he takes himself as Mind. This mental-conscious human soul associates himself with mind, and is conscious of himself as Mind, and experiences himself as still something other than God. This mental-conscious human soul on the sixth plane actually "sees" God face to face more vividly and intensively than the gross- or subtle-conscious human soul sees objects of the gross or subtle worlds.

At this stage the consciousness of the soul, which had experienced diverse, innumerable and opposite impressions, now experiences the last trace of dual impressions of the opposites. This mental-conscious human soul on the sixth plane is still conscious of duality, identifying himself as mind and differentiating himself from God.[9]

Seventh Plane

This experience of duality lingers on and on until the final involution of consciousness of the mental-conscious human soul leads the soul to dissociate itself from the mind (the consciousness of the mind had objectified God), and makes the soul associate itself with its own Self—the Soul or *Atma*.

Thus the consciousness of the soul is now said to experience at last the consciousness of the seventh plane. Here on the seventh plane the Self-conscious human soul is conscious of himself as God and experiences infinite power, infinite knowledge

---

* Like an aching tooth that gradually works loose but does not fall out for a long time, the false ego remains until the last stage of the first spiritual journey, although it becomes increasingly faint as the soul advances on the Path, only to vanish forever in the final *fana* of the seventh plane, to be replaced by the unlimited Real Ego.

and infinite bliss.

For the mental-conscious human soul to cross the sixth plane and experience the seventh plane by his own efforts * is quite impossible.[10] At this stage the **grace** of a Perfect Master is absolutely essential to help the mental-conscious human soul to dissociate himself from the consciousness of mind and to make him realize his unity with the infinite state, to experience infinite bliss consciously and to realize that he (*atma*) was **eternally in bliss.**

So it is that the Self-conscious human soul of the seventh plane is now fully conscious of the Self as infinite and eternal and is now also **conscious of the Source** of energy and mind, which were nothing but the shadowy aspects of his own infinite power and infinite knowledge.

This Self-conscious human soul which is now Self-realized or God-realized, not only experiences infinite power, knowledge and bliss, but simultaneously radiates them. Sometimes, in certain cases, such Self-conscious human souls also make use of this infinite power, knowledge and bliss directly and consciously for the emancipation of other souls from their impressions and their respective associations with the gross, subtle and mental forms and worlds.

In its travail to gain Self-consciousness the individual eternal *atma* (soul), unconscious of its infinite state in *Paramatma,* gathered and experienced innumerable diverse impressions, and all the while associated itself with finite and ephemeral existences, unfurling the gross, subtle and mental worlds while **evolving** gross consciousness of the gross world and while **involving** consciousness of the subtle and mental planes of the subtle and mental worlds.

Involution of consciousness of the *atma* (soul), culminated by the grace of a Perfect Master, led the *atma* to Self-

---

* However, those in the sixth plane of consciousness realize God at the time of dropping their bodies.

realization of its infinite state in *Paramatma*.*

Thus it is that when the consciousness of the *atma* gained Self-consciousness and experienced infinite power, knowledge and bliss, the *atma* realized that it exists—eternally; that all through the travail to gain Self-consciousness, the impressions, experiences and associations of the gross, subtle and mental bodies and worlds were nothing but a vacant dream; and that the identification with gross bodies, creatures and human beings and all the experiences of the three worlds and the six planes, with all of their paraphernalia, had their relative existences sustained and maintained as long as the consciousness of the *atma* was immature. Maturity was only gained in the seventh plane with consciousness fully involved. This led the *atma* to realize the Self, or made the *atma* fully conscious of God-realization. In other words, the *atma's* own infinite state in *Paramatma* was consciously realized.†

It is only after the final annihilation of the mind and the wearing out of the curtain of mental impressions that consciousness can function in full freedom from all impressional bindings. This means crossing the deep abyss which separates the sixth plane from the seventh plane. The seventh plane is the formless abode of the Highest of the High.‡ The Most High or the infinite

---

* *Sav bār tahīrā dāman hā thon mīre āyā*
Jab ānkh khulī dīkhā apnā hī garībān hai.
　　　　　　　　　　　　　　—Asghar

"A hundred times I felt that I held your garment firmly in my hands; When I opened my eyes I was amazed to discover it was my own garment that I was holding."

† The God-realized man is the Almighty, plus knowledge and consciousness. He is in the perfect wakeful state. He is knowledge, knower and the known. He is love, lover and the beloved. He knows that he is in every *jivatma* and that everyone is in him. The God-realized man knows that he is the be-all and the end-all of existence, and that he always was and will remain the same one, infinite Ocean of Truth. But the ordinary man does not **know** whence he came and whither he will go.

‡ [The reader is referred to Fariduddin Attar's *Mantiq-ut-Tayr,* a Sufi allegory generally known as "The Conference of the Birds," for a delightful description of the journey through the planes. Ed.]

God as Truth can be realized only by transcending the entire realm of imagination. Only on this seventh plane does the soul fulfill the initial urge for self-knowledge by experiencing its own Self as identical with the unchanging, eternal, indivisible and formless Over-Soul, with infinite knowledge, infinite reality (Truth), infinite power and infinite bliss.

PLANES AND WORLDS CHART I

GOD (Infinite Power, Knowledge, Bliss)

Consciousness of Self	**7th Plane**	Experiences Consciously (Infinite Power, Knowledge, Bliss)

NO POWER

Fully conscious of second state of
MIND
and Master of minds of all. The
Creator and Controller of
FEELINGS (desires and emotions)

6th Plane

**MENTAL
WORLD**

(DOMAIN OF MIND)

MIND

Conscious of the first state of
MIND i.e. THOUGHTS
and controls only thoughts

5th Plane

4th Plane | **(Threshold)**

POWER

Fully conscious of
ENERGY
(Full Power)
and threatened by
overpowering aspects of
MIND

Gains greater consciousness of
ENERGY

3rd Plane

**SUBTLE
WORLD**

(DOMAIN OF ENERGY)

ENERGY

Gains consciousness of
ENERGY

2nd Plane

With gross nose, eyes, ears,
experiences SUBTLE smell, sights, music,

1st Plane

GROSS WORLD

(INCLUDES UNIVERSES VISIBLE AND INVISIBLE)

(a) Imbibing Energy from Subtle world through gross aspects of Energy
    such as nuclear, solar, etc.

(b) Imbibing the aspects of Mind of the Mental world
    such as desires, thoughts, emotions.

Summary of States of Divine Consciousness

AFTER taking human-form and gaining full consciousness, that full consciousness which the *atma* (soul) craved in order to experience *Paramatma,* the *atma* still does not experience *Paramatma;* because even after attaining full consciousness, as long as this consciousness remains centred in gross impressions, the *atma* perforce is made conscious of the gross body and must therefore experience the gross world.

Without having human-form, it is impossible for the *atma* to gain consciousness of subtle and mental bodies and of Self. Similarly, it is impossible to gather experience of the subtle world, the mental world and of *Paramatma.* For the evolution of consciousness and for the evolution of form and for the experience of the gross world, it is absolutely necessary to have gross *sanskaras* (impressions), and as long as there are gross impressions, the *atma* has no consciousness of the subtle and mental bodies.

In human-form, because of the evolution of full consciousness and because of the evolution of perfect form in the shape of a human being, and because of having taken full experience of the gross world, there is now no more need of gross impressions. Gross impressions can become subtle impressions, subtle impressions can become mental impressions, and mental impressions can disappear. So in human-form the *atma* can have consciousness of the subtle and mental bodies and of *atma* itself, and experience of the subtle world, mental world and of *Paramatma*. But the tragedy is that immediately after gaining full consciousness in human form, the *atma* does not gain consciousness of subtle (*pran*) and mental (*mana*) bodies and Self, and likewise does not experience the subtle and mental worlds and does not have experience of *Paramatma*. This is because gross *sanskaras* do not become subtle *sanskaras* or mental *sanskaras* nor disappear immediately after the *atma* has gained full consciousness in human-form. The reason for this is that the first human-form made out of the last animal-form, when dropped, leaves behind a legacy of impressions of the first human-form, and then each following incarnated human-form is made up of the last human-form *sanskaras*. So the *atma,* in spite of having full consciousness, takes a number of human-forms as long as gross *sanskaras* exist.

Eventually, one of two things happens:—the *atma's* gross *sanskaras* may entirely disappear all of a sudden, and the *atma* lose consciousness of the gross body and gain consciousness of the Self, thus losing the experience of the gross world and gaining experience of *Paramatma*. Or, the second more likely possibility is that eventually the gross *sanskaras* will fade and become subtle *sanskaras,* subtle *sanskaras* fade more and become mental *sanskaras,* and finally mental *sanskaras* fade to such an extent that they disappear. In this case the *atma* first loses consciousness of the gross body and the experiences of the gross world, and gains consciousness of the subtle body and experience of the subtle world. Then the *atma* loses consciousness of the subtle body and gains consciousness of the mental body and loses experience of the subtle world and gains experience of the mental world. Finally, the *atma* loses consciousness of the mental body, thereby gaining consciousness of the *atma* itself and loses the experience of the mental world and gains experience of *Paramatma*.

After the *atma* has gained Self-consciousness and experiences the *Paramatma* the *atma* inherits one of the THREE STATES (not two or four states but three states definitely):

First State A: Soon after this experience of the Highest of the High, the *atma* generally drops all of its shadowy bodies (gross, subtle and mental) and eternally enjoys individualized experience as a whole—the infinite power, knowledge and bliss of God—**without using the attributes thereof.**

First State B: The *atma* may not drop these three bodies until some time afterwards, although it is absolutely unconscious of these bodies. Except that it retains the bodies, its state is actually the same as "A."

Second State: The *atma* retains the three bodies and, simultaneously with Self-consciousness, is also conscious of its three shadows (gross, subtle and mental bodies) and at the same time experiences the infinite power, knowledge and bliss of God. It also experiences the gross world, subtle world and mental world as God's shadows, but it does not use the power, knowledge and bliss of God for the other *atmas* who are mental-conscious, subtle-conscious and gross-conscious and so **it is independent.**

Third State: This is exactly like the second state except that the *atma* **uses** its infinite power, knowledge and bliss in making gross-conscious *atmas* subtle-conscious; and subtle-conscious *atmas* mental-conscious; and mental-conscious *atmas* Self-conscious; **even at one stroke** making gross-conscious *atmas* Self-conscious.

Full Development of Subtle and Mental Bodies in Human Form, and Involution of Consciousness

Only in the human-form are subtle (*pran*) and mental (*mana*) bodies fully developed. Therefore, even when the *atma* has gross consciousness and is unconscious of *pran* and *mana,* it does work through *pran* and *mana,* not directly, but on the gross plane. So even if the gross-conscious human *atma* is unconscious of *pran* and *mana* and therefore does not **realize** Energy and Mind, it can use Energy through various aspects of energy (*e.g.,* nuclear) and it can use Mind through various aspects of mind—such as thoughts, desires and emotions.

In the human-form when the *atma* has subtle consciousness it is unconscious of the gross (*sharir*) and mental (*mana*) bodies, yet it does work through *sharir* and *mana,* not directly, but on the subtle plane. So even if the subtle-conscious human *atma* is unconscious of *sharir* and *mana* and therefore does not realize the gross and mental worlds, it can use the gross, through various aspects of the gross, as eating, drinking, sleeping, seeing, feeling, hearing, etc., and it can use Mind through various aspects of the mind, as thoughts, desires and emotions.

In the human-form when the *atma* has mental consciousness it is unconscious of the gross (*sharir*) and subtle (*pran*) bodies, but it does work through *sharir* and *pran,* not directly, but on the mental plane. So even if the mental-conscious human *atma* is unconscious of *sharir* and *pran* and therefore does not realize the gross and subtle worlds, it can use the gross through various aspects of the gross—such as eating, sleeping, seeing, feeling, hearing, etc., and it can use Energy through various aspects of energy such as nuclear, etc.

To give a simile, let us consider, for instance, a gross-conscious human *atma* as a soul on earth (which we take as a standard for the gross plane) far flung from the sun, which, for instance, for the purpose of our simile only, we take as the source of Energy of the subtle and the source of Mind of the mental. (The simile of sun and earth must never be misconstrued as the sun and earth of the solar system).

This sun, which we have now adopted as our standard, sheds its rays of Energy and Mind continuously and simultaneously on the earth (which we have taken as the standard for the gross); and the gross-conscious human soul on earth—conscious only of the gross—unconsciously imbibes from the sun's rays the Energy of the subtle, by making in the gross world the fullest use of the aspects of this Energy in the form of nuclear energy. Also this gross-conscious human soul on earth unconsciously makes use in the gross world of the aspects of Mind such as thoughts, desires and emotions, which it also imbibes from this sun's rays.

For the purpose of continuing our simile we shall now take the subtle-conscious human soul as a soul in air and hence much nearer this sun than the gross-conscious human *atma* on earth. This subtle-conscious human soul in air is conscious only of the subtle—consciously imbibes the fullest energy from this sun, which is the source of energy, and consciously makes use of this tremendous energy in its nascent form. Thus this subtle-conscious human soul is capable of wielding tremendous power and is quite capable of giving sight to the blind or limbs to the maimed. This is the domain of the first three planes, and the capability of this soul to liberate energy in any intensity is achieved according to the degree of subtle-consciousness gained by it in the second and third planes.

While this subtle-conscious human soul, in its realm of Energy, consciously makes use of energy in its nascent state, it is unconscious of the mental. Therefore, unconsciously, it makes use of the aspects of Mind, such as thoughts, desires and emotions. Thus, though it is capable of wielding tremendous power through its consciousness of Energy, it is susceptible to getting entangled by mind while making use of the aspects of Mind unconsciously. For this reason this subtle-conscious human soul, although mighty powerful, sometimes slides down to the lower level of subtle consciousness while making conscious use of its energy in the form of miraculous powers.

To be more precise, the subtle-conscious human soul is either in the first or second or third plane according to the degree of subtle consciousness gained; or, one may say that the domain of the subtle sphere comprises the first, second and third planes. Now the fourth plane is that state of consciousness which draws a line of demarcation between the domain of the subtle world and the domain of the mental world. In other words, the subtle-conscious human *atma* on the fourth plane is like a human soul standing on the **threshold** (of the mental world), which delimits the subtle world from the mental world.

Therefore the subtle-conscious human soul at the stage of consciousness of the fourth plane is fully conscious of the first, second and third planes and experiences in full the subtle world, and so is completely conscious of the tremendous energy of the subtle world. Thus this human soul on the threshold of the mental world, commanding the energy at its height, is now nearest to the domain of Mind, which is the mental world, and thus is much more susceptible to the overpowering forces of the aspects of the mind, *viz.,* the thoughts, desires and emotions. And although this subtle-conscious human soul on the fourth plane consciously makes use of the subtle world's energy at its zenith, it is still unconscious of Mind. It therefore unconsciously makes use of the aspects of Mind, which are now too overpowering and thus most alluring for this soul which, so to speak, has to face and bear the full blast of the aspects of the mind (thoughts, desires and emotions) at their highest.

This situation for the human soul on the fourth plane is extremely dangerous, since it is extremely treacherous. Here the soul, equipped with highest energy, which can be put to use either for the best or for the worst, has to maintain a sort of equilibrium of two forces at their zenith, *i.e.,* the height of the energy of the subtle world and the overpowering height of aspects of the mind of the mental world. If this human soul on the fourth plane, while unconsciously using the aspects of Mind, is overcome by the overpowering allurements of these aspects (thoughts, desires and emotions), he then cannot resist using energy at its climax for the worst by performing powerful miracles such as raising the dead, curing the blind, the sick and the maimed, etc., just to satisfy his own overpowering desires. He is even capable of creating the whole world of forms with all of its creation, so great is the power obtained from the energy at its height of which this subtle-conscious human soul is conscious.

Thus this misuse of energy at its zenith, through the medium and the overpowering allurements of the aspects of mind, also at their zenith, creates a sort of tremendous, irreparable short-circuit in the two fundamental supernatural forces—of energy at its zenith in the shape of stupendous power, and of mind at its zenith in the shape of irresistible desire—resulting in an unimaginably tremendous clash and explosion in the advanced consciousness of the subtle-conscious human soul of the fourth plane. Absolute disturbance is thus created in the consciousness of this soul resulting in downright disintegration of the advanced consciousness of this human soul. Thereupon this subtle-conscious human soul invariably falls to the lowest level of consciousness, which is the most finite type of consciousness of the crudest form. Therefore this human soul has to take the form of stone and has again to go through the process of evolution.

Example of a Gross-Conscious Scientist

Let us try to explain this situation by an illustration of what sometimes occurs, even on the gross plane, to an ordinary human being who handles tremendous power and who is, more often than not, overcome by an intense desire to demonstrate his powers.

Let us compare then a subtle-conscious human soul on the fourth plane, such as described above, with a great scientist of repute in the gross world. The latter, being fully conscious of the gross plane, by sheer dint of effort and much investigation into the fields of the science of energies, fully realizes the possibility of releasing tremendous energy through certain experiments.

This scientist, we will assume for the purposes of our illustration, gradually becomes fully conscious of the tremendous energy that has come within his reach and which will ultimately come under his complete control. He then desires intensely to make use of it.

Even when this gross-conscious scientist in the gross world is conscious of the highest possible gross aspect of Energy, he is not at all conscious of that Energy in its nascent state, which is only of the domain of the subtle world and which can only be experienced and controlled by the **subtle**-conscious human soul, and which can never, under any circumstances, be experimented with or experienced by any **gross**-conscious human being.

Therefore, when this gross-conscious scientist in the gross world on earth is conscious of the highest possible gross aspects of nuclear energy, he is actually fully conscious of only one of the highest gross aspects of energy of the domain of the subtle world.

And, when this scientist, who is conscious of one of the highest gross aspects of energy, which is now entirely under his control, is overpowered by an intense desire—which is also the highest aspect of Mind of the mental world—to use it, then the scientist's whole career hangs in the balance, and it is thus very often at stake.

It is at this juncture of conflicting thoughts, which on the one hand provoke the scientist to demonstrate his powers, and on the other hand soothe him to become reticent, that the scientist has to be extremely careful to maintain an equilibrium— that is, balancing the tremendous aspects of energy at his disposal. It rests with him either to use it for the welfare of the world, or to misuse it for its devastating effects, or, not to use it at all. He is confronted with the irresistible, overpowering force of the predominant aspect of mind in the shape of intense desires which haunt him with fame, name and power, tickling his ego to the utmost towards selfish ends, irrespective of the potential destruction and devastation which can be wrought.

If the scientist succumbs, therefore, to this overweening desire, which is now at its zenith, and is thereby directed for his selfish ends to misuse the power that he controls in the form of one of the highest aspects of energy, he then consciously leads himself to attempt to explode the most deadly weapon in his control—more powerful than, say, the latest hydrogen bomb.

It is at this stage that the crucial point is reached.

The scientist explodes his weapon, spreading devastating

results; and the equilibrium which was thus far very narrowly maintained between use of power and overpowering desire is absolutely disturbed.

This scientist could not content himself and was incapable of maintaining an equilibrium or balance between the tremendous aspect of energy that lay latent in his weapon, which fortified him with power, and the intense desire to explode the weapon consciously, unmindful of the unimaginable result.

The tragedy of the whole thing was that this scientist, being conscious of and intensely self-interested in the result of the explosion of the bomb, was the first to be directly affected by the blast of the explosion despite all of the necessary precautions taken. The immediate consequence to himself was that at first he was completely overpowered by his own experiment and was aghast; and, he fell flat on the ground, absolutely unconscious. To add to this tragedy, when he regained his consciousness, he regained it at what cost? He had completely forgotten his state as a great and advanced scientist and he was also incapable of remembering his immediate past, his boyhood and his activities as a young man with all of their associations with wife, children and friends. The greatest change that took place in him was that he did not even feel that he had lost anything—*i.e.,* his memory and his consciousness of being a great scientist. The doctors call such an occurrence a case of amnesia. He had consciousness only of the fact that he was a man of the most rudimentary type. He then started his life afresh, never once imagining that he had lived the life of a great man of science, who had had under his control vast and tremendous forces of energy. In a similar fashion occurs the tragedy of the most advanced subtle-conscious human soul on the fourth plane. He, being energy personified, misuses the energy at its zenith in the subtle world, and consequently loses all consciousness except the most finite consciousness which, according to the law of evolution, has to take the most crude form of stone to experience that most finite consciousness.

One of the functions of Perfect Masters is to guard the

soul of the fourth plane from wrecking his spiritual career through the misuse of divine powers.* Very often, if the soul of the fourth plane is about to lose control of his mind, his powers are snatched away by the Perfect Masters, who can control the minds of all subtle-conscious and gross-conscious souls. The cases of actual downfall are accordingly rare and occur as exceptions to the rule. They must ultimately be attributed, not to any failure in the vigilance maintained by the Perfect Masters, but to the original urge within God Himself. So it is literally true that each and every thing, small or great, that happens in the universe, happens only according to the will of the Almighty.

Here it is important to know that though it is an established fact that once full consciousness is gained in the human form, it is virtually never lost; yet, in this case of the subtle-conscious human soul on the fourth plane, there is the possibility of losing the consciousness gained. This occurs if the powers of the fourth plane are misused, and if the equilibrium is not maintained with the highest energy at command, counterbalanced by the overpowering allurement of infinite desires which are the highest aspect of Mind. Though the three fundamental aspects of Mind are thoughts, desires and emotions, the desires form the highest aspect of Mind.

But, if the subtle-conscious human soul on the fourth plane does not misuse the energy commanded by it, and maintains the

---

* Being asked by the editors about Jesus' "temptations," Meher Baba replied:

"The truth is that Jesus was not tempted by Satan, but that Jesus **got Himself tempted,** and He overcame the temptations. There was a great purpose behind this. He had to get Himself tempted; thereby He shouldered the burden of the forces of temptations that predominated in the world. Jesus then overcame all the temptations and in that way created a tremendous force which acted as a great set-back to the forces of universal temptations. The same was true in the case of Buddha, and it is the same every time in *Avataric* periods. Whenever God manifests on earth as *Avatar*, His Godhood gives a universal push and the result is universal, *i.e.*, not only the humanity reaps the benefit but everything in the whole Creation reaps the benefit of the universal push."

equilibrium by discreet use of infinite energy for the best, then this soul on the fourth plane not only crosses this threshold of the fourth plane and enters the domain of the fifth and sixth planes of the mental world but gains consciousness of the sixth plane **directly.** This is because this soul (with subtle consciousness and discreet use of Energy at its zenith) was capable of overcoming and resisting the most alluring and overpowering highest aspects of Mind, the desires, thoughts and emotions, which were most powerfully treacherous at their zenith. Thus this subtle-conscious human soul gains directly the consciousness of the sixth plane by overpowering the desires, thoughts and emotions at their zenith and becomes their master, who now controls them and even has the capacity to create them.

Some subtle-conscious human souls neither use nor misuse the tremendous flood of energy at its height liberated in the subtle world; and when such souls do not fall prey to their desires, which are also at their height, these subtle-conscious human souls cross the threshold of the fourth plane and gain the consciousness of the fifth plane in the domain of the mental world. Here these mental-conscious human souls are no longer the slaves of their minds because they are now conscious of the first state of Mind which controls thoughts.

The mental-conscious human souls on the fifth and sixth planes are now fully conscious of Mind and experience the mental world according to the degree of advancement of consciousness of the fifth and sixth planes. These mental-conscious human souls of the fifth and sixth planes are no longer conscious of the degrees of consciousness of the first, second, third and fourth planes of the subtle world nor do they experience the subtle world any longer. Therefore these mental-conscious human souls are unconscious of the tremendous energy of the subtle world. Hence these mental-conscious human souls, although they are conscious masters of Mind, are now absolutely unconscious of the power of Energy of the subtle world, and it is for this reason that these mental-conscious human souls never can perform any miracles. They can neither raise the dead nor can they give sight to the blind nor limbs to the maimed in spite of their advanced consciousness being greater than the consciousness of the subtle-conscious human soul. However, as these mental-conscious human souls are the conscious masters of Mind, they can create and control the minds of the gross-conscious and subtle-conscious human souls. For them, creating and controlling minds is but child's play, if necessary.

In the case of the mental-conscious human soul, let us suppose that its position is near the sun (which we have taken for our standard as a simile). This soul in human form consciously imbibes and controls the aspects of Mind such as thoughts, desires and emotions, and makes in the mental world the fullest use of Mind which proceeds from the sun (which we, for our purpose of explanation, consider as the source). Thus this mental-conscious human soul, in the realms of the fifth and sixth planes, is not only fully conscious of the mind and its aspects but it is also capable of creating and controlling the thoughts, desires and emotions of all other minds too. The soul is now quite stable and can never fall or slide down to any lower levels of consciousness as could the subtle-conscious human soul on the fourth plane (because the gross-conscious human soul and subtle-conscious human soul are the slaves of their minds, whereas the mental-conscious human soul is the master of his mind).

Finally, the case of the Self-conscious human soul is like a soul in the sun itself. (While trying to understand the explanation, one should bear in mind that the reference to the sun is given only as a form of simile. One must not misunderstand this sun as our earthly sun nor misunderstand our earthly sun as the real standard of the infinite and eternal source of infinite power, knowledge and bliss, nor must we attach any significance whatsoever to our earth's sun, for our earth's sun is nothing but one of the objects of Creation of the soul's own creating.)

This Self-conscious human soul of the seventh plane is conscious of this sun (which we have taken as an example of the source of Energy and Mind), and although he invariably experiences and radiates eternally the infinite power, knowledge and bliss, in some cases such a soul also makes **use** of this infinite power, knowledge and bliss directly and consciously for the emancipation of souls from the *sanskaras* of the gross, subtle and mental worlds.

The Sevenfold Veil

K ABIR was a Perfect Master as well as a poet. *Kabirwani,* his book of poems, is therefore the more unique because of his lucid expositions on God, love for God, the divine path and illusory Creation. Being a Perfect Master, Kabir has said things as much for the man in the street as for the initiate. He does not hesitate to disclose, both allegorically as well as in plain words, some of the spiritual secrets which, though within the grasp of ordinary man, are yet known only to the spiritually illumined ones who alone truly understand the deeper meaning under-lying most of his sayings.

There are yogis (those who practice a systematic course of esoteric knowledge) who can of themselves suspend their physical bodies in mid-air during the time they are in a tem-porary *samadhi* (trance). There are some who can bodily walk on water or fly in the air without the aid of external means, and yet all this is no sign or proof of their having experienced divine love. Weighed on spiritual scales these miracles have no value whatsoever. In fact, miracle mongering by the average yogi is not only poles apart from the spiritual path, but is actually a hindrance to the individual's evolution towards spiritual prog-ress.[11, 12] The following incident in the life of a Hindu Master shows the disregard in which it is held by Perfect Masters, who are Truth personified: The Master was one day by the river's edge waiting for one of the little ferry boats that take passengers across the stream for the diminutive fare of one *anna*. A yogi seeing him thus waiting, came up to him, literally walked across the river and back, and said, "That was much easier, was it not?" The Master smilingly replied, "Yes, and had less value than that of the boat fare—one *anna*."

The ability to exercise constant control over one's low desires is no mean achievement. Success in establishing a lasting sublimation of all desires is indeed a greater one. But the greatest is the burning away of all one's desires once and for all, which divine love alone can do. As there is never any show about divine love, this "burning" in love is always without "smoke," *i.e.*, without show. There are times when an outward expression of God-love may amount to heroism, but to make at any time a mere show of one's love for God, for the sake of show, amounts to an insult to God. That is why Kabir says that in the act of meditation [13, 14] when one assumes an *asan* (posture) to meditate upon God, one should at that time learn to avoid making any display such as the swaying motion of one's body, even if it is only for one's own gratification.

As compared with dreams, the physical life is indeed a reality. Similarly, compared with the reality of the path, the world and all worldly life is vacant dreaming on the part of man. But as the world and all of its experiences are illusory, so is the spiritual path that leads to Reality. The former may be termed false illusion and the latter real illusion. Nevertheless, despite the vast difference between them, they are both illusions, for God alone is the only Reality.

When Knowledge * is gained ignorance is banished, but for ignorance to go, Knowledge must be gained. On the one hand, God, and the capacity of man to see and become one with God, are always there. On the other hand, Truth remains hidden from man until he actually arrives upon the path or realizes God. This apparent anomaly is due to two different factors: man's ignorance of Truth, and the fact that Truth is

---

* [In the sense of "wisdom" rather than of worldly knowledge. Ed.]

beyond the faculty of reason and far, far above the sphere of intellect. The fact remains that man has become God and man can become God for the simple reason that, knowingly or unknowingly, man is God. Only so long as man's ignorance lasts will there seem to be no end to the plural diversity of illusory things. When divine knowledge is gained he realizes that there is no end to the indivisible oneness of God. Under the illusion of cosmic duality the apparent separation between man and God is invariably referred to by masters in terms of the intervenient "veil" and "curtain." Hafiz, who was a Perfect Master as well as a great poet, says:

Miyānah 'āshiq o m'ashūq hīc ḥāyal nīst
Tū khvud hijāb-i khvudī, Ḥāfiẓ, az miyān barkhīz.

"There is no barrier between the lover and Beloved; Hafiz, lift yourself aside, you are yourself the covering over Self."

Kabir, referring to the removal of the seven folds of the veil, says:

Tere ghuṅghaṭa ke paṭa khola tujhe Rāma milegā.

"Open the folds of your veil, and you shall find God."

The *ghunghat* literally means the covering that a woman extends over her head and face in a number of folds; in spiritual parlance it represents the heavy folds of ignorance that keep man hidden from his real identity. The lifting of it, fold by fold, corresponds to the stage-by-stage journey of a pilgrim from the first through the fifth plane of the divine path.

The veil that separates a man-in-ignorance from God Who is All Knowledge, is so subtle that even the highest and finest thought cannot pierce through it. This veil consists of seven folds of seven different, deep colours. Each fold is tied with a separate knot; thus there are seven knots to the seven folds. The seven colours represent the seven root desires, corresponding to the seven fundamental impressions, *i.e.*, lust, greed, anger, etc., connected with the seven openings of sensation in the face, *viz.*, (1) mouth, (2) right nostril, (3) left nostril, (4) right ear, (5) left ear, (6) right eye, (7) left eye.

In Reality and as the only Reality, the soul is **always God** without beginning and without end. False illusion begins with the descent of the soul in seven material stages and real illusion ends with the ascent of the soul to the seventh spiritual plane.

God is a macrocosm, God is a microcosm and God is also **always** beyond both. Knowingly man is body and man is mind, but unknowingly, as in deep sleep, man is also beyond both.

Analogically it is true that man is made in the image of God. The top of his head represents the *vidnyan bhumika, arshe-ala*, the highest spiritual state, or the seat of *Brahman*. The forehead corresponds to the entrance to divinity. The centre of the forehead, just above the two external eyes, is the seat of the inner or third eye. When the veil with all its seven folds is finally removed, man is then able, through the third eye, to see God face to face and sees Him more actually and naturally than what he is ordinarily able to see of his body and the world through the two external eyes. In order to arrive at the divine entrance situated in the forehead, man has to pass through the seven doors as represented by the seven physical openings in the face.

When an initiate succeeds in actually entering the divine path it is for him a single seven-in-one achievement, and it applies to the first of the seven folds of the veil, *viz.*, (1) unfastening of the first knot, (2) disappearance of the first fold, (3) crushing out of the first root desires, (4) wiping out of the relative fundamental impressions, (5) doing away with the first of the seven deep, dark colours, (6) entrance through the first door (as represented by the mouth), and (7) arriving on the first plane in the subtle sphere, the *pran bhuvan* or the *alam-e-malakut.*[15]

In dreams, an ordinary man is able to make **partial** use of his subtle body with subtle consciousness, but only in respect to gross experience and concerning only gross objects. Just as he experiences the gross world with full gross consciousness through his gross body, so the initiate on the first plane begins to experience the subtle world with subtle consciousness through his subtle body.

If the initiate is able to proceed further and manages to maintain progress, he continues in the subtle sphere up to the fourth plane. This progress involves the second and third successive single seven-in-one achievements that parallel the sevenfold results achieved in the first. This passing through the second and third doors (represented by the right and left nostrils) brings a still greater intensification of the real illusion, *i.e.,* higher consciousness of the path. After going through the second door, the initiate realizes even more the wonderful things of the subtle world and at the same time begins to run the risk of being lost in the maze of wonderment. The mystical enchantments of the path beyond the third door are still greater, and so also are the chances of becoming spellbound by them. Just as those with gross consciousness take the gross sphere and its illusory experiences to be real, so the pilgrims in the subtle sphere, while absorbed in the wonder of the plane on which they are, may mistake it for the ultimate Reality. Hence a pilgrim often gets stuck on a plane, deluded by its raptures into accepting it as the Goal, until a Perfect Master or even mental-conscious souls help him by pushing him on to the next plane.

The fourth seven-in-one achievement is a double achievement because at one and the same time (1) the fourth and fifth knots are unfastened, (2) the fourth and fifth folds disappear, (3) the fourth and fifth root desires are crushed, (4) the fourth and fifth deep, dark colours vanish, (5) the fourth and fifth relative fundamental impressions are wiped out, (6) the fourth and fifth doors (as represented by the right and left ears) are passed through, and (7) the pilgrim arrives on the highest plane of the subtle sphere, the fourth plane.

As said before, the fourth plane is the plane of spiritual splendour and of divine powers (*anwar-o-tajalliyat* or *siddhis*). Pilgrims advanced this far can, among many other things, even raise the dead. They run a very grave risk of misusing these powers, thereby inviting disaster, and only a very few can independently cross these dizzy heights safely without the aid of a Perfect Master. It is of them that Hafiz says:

Dar āsitān-i jānān āsmān biyandīsh
Kaz auj-i sar bulandī uftī bikhāk-i pastī.

"On the threshold of the Beloved, beware of the allurements of the heavens, lest you bring about your fall from the heights of progress and greatness to the depths of degradation and ruin."

In such case, a man is not only deprived of the spiritual progress he has made on the path, but is thrown back from the position that he had achieved through physiological evolution to the state of the stone-form.

Just as anything may happen to a man travelling over an unknown path in the pitch blackness of the night, so anything may happen to one who must pass through the fourth plane without the guiding hand of a Perfect Master. That is why, for all its dazzling splendour and power, the period of going through the fourth plane is termed in Christian mysticism, "the dark night of the soul." *

If the advanced pilgrim is at all able to resist the allurements and treacheries of the dark night of the soul, he enters the mental sphere (*mano bhuvan* or the *alam-e-jabrut*) by the fifth and final double seven-in-one achievement which occurs on the same lines as the fourth. All the folds of the veil are re-

---

* For those on the Path the powers of the fourth plane are like the "Devil" who is popularly believed to lead people astray. But for the timely help of the *Sadguru* Dnyaneshwar, the great yogi Chang Deva would have come to grief on this very plane. Similarly, when Baba Farid Ganje-Shakar reached this stage he could not help testing his powers by making birds on the wing fall down dead and trying to raise them to life again. He, too, was saved in time by an aged woman who was a saint of the fifth plane. It was after this incident that Baba Farid came into close contact with his Master, who finally led him to *qutubiyat* or Perfect Masterhood.

moved together with the relative knots, desires, colours and impressions; the sixth and seventh doors (as represented by the right and left eyes) are crossed and the fifth plane of light and love is reached.

Those who have safely arrived on the fifth plane are the *wali Allah* (literally meaning "friends of God"). Their inner sight, or the third eye, is now fully developed, but even though all the seven folds of the veil have disappeared, the **veil itself** is still there. The pilgrim is therefore not yet face to face with God and cannot see the Beloved.

Because of their pure love for God, unadulterated by the false ego, the position of these pilgrims on the fifth plane is secure, and there is no possibility of retrogression. Without any harm to themselves they can and do give, consciously or unconsciously, immense help to others in the subtle and gross spheres.

With rare exceptions further progress on one's own is now impossible. By the help or grace of a Perfect Master one is able to remove the veil entirely and thereby arrive on the sixth plane, the highest plane of the mental sphere, the plane of "divine sight," the entrance to divinity (as represented by the forehead) where one is able actually to see God face to face, everywhere and in everything. This is known as conviction by sight.

Those on the gross sphere who believe in the existence of God have their conviction (*yaqin*) based on their pure and simple faith and belief. This conviction is *ilm-ul-yaqin* (intellectual conviction), and is different from the distinctive convictions that follow:

(1) conviction by intuitive perception (*yaqin-ul-yaqin*);
(2) conviction by sight (*ain-ul-yaqin*);
(3) conviction by actual experience (*Haqq-ul-yaqin*).[16]

Those on the path, up through the fifth plane, **know** there is God, with a definite intuitive certainty (*yaqin-ul-yaqin*); their conviction is based on sure knowledge. Those on the sixth plane see God everywhere; theirs is conviction by actual sight. Those on the seventh plane, having become one with God, have conviction by actual experience.

The highly advanced pilgrim on the sixth plane is still within the domain of duality. Although face to face with God, the "see-er" and the "seen" remain separated by a deep, fathomless valley which can be spanned only by the touch of a Perfect Master. Whereas the first five achievements are possible for man to obtain independently, the actual removal of the veil on the fifth plane is usually accomplished by the grace of a Perfect Master's guidance. The **jump** from illusion of the sixth plane to Reality on the seventh plane is, however, impossible on one's own and **entirely** dependent upon the direct touch of a Perfect One or a Perfect Master (*Sadguru*).

On the seventh plane, the plane of infinite knowledge, power and bliss, the individual merges into God and **becomes** God, a Perfect One for all time and beyond all time. It is then immaterial whether the physical body remains or drops. As a rule, the gross shell falls within a short time after realization, but in some cases the physical body holds on for a long time. These God-realized Ones are known as *Majzoobs* or *Brahmi Bhoots*.

Again, only by the direct and personal help of a Perfect Master does one from among those God-realized Ones return to the level of ordinary man, regaining consciousness of all the spheres (gross, subtle and mental) yet retaining at the same time full God-consciousness. He is then the Man-God, the Perfect Master, *Sadguru* or *Qutub*.

Where there is light, darkness is no more. Where there is Knowledge, ignorance is absent. And, as the folds, the veil and the valley of separation are all in the domain of ignorance, a Perfect Master—who is the "Sun" of all Knowledge—can, in the twinkling of an eye, impart God-realization to anyone he chooses.*

God alone is real, and as we are permanently lodged in the Divine Beloved, we are all one. '

* [See also: Meher Baba, "The Fabric of the Universe," *Beams from Meher Baba on the Spiritual Panorama*, pp. 13–15.

And also see: Meher Baba, "The Ways to the Path and Its States and Stages," *Listen, Humanity*, narr. and ed. by D.E. Stevens (New York: Dodd, Mead and Company, 1957), pp. 160–162. Ed.]

The Beyond the Beyond State of God, the First Urge and the Cycle of Evolution and Involution of Consciousness

The Beyond the Beyond State of God

To begin with the beyond the beginning, there is the original state of the Beyond the Beyond state of God or *Paratpar Parabrahma*. This is the original state of "GOD-IS." In Sufi terms this state is said to be the state of *Wara-ul-Wara*.

In this original state of "God-Is" unbounded absolute vacuum prevails.

In this absolute vacuum there is neither any manifestation of the conscious or unconscious state of God nor is there manifestation of the consciousness or unconsciousness of God. Neither is there the unlimited "I"—the Divine Ego or the Universal Ego—nor is there the limited "I" or the individual ego. Neither is there universal mind nor is there limited mind. Neither is there unbounded energy nor is there limited energy. Neither is there the universal body—the *mahakarana sharir*—nor is there the limited body. Neither are there universes nor are there worlds. There is not even consciousness of either the consciousness—*mahachaitanya*—or of the unconsciousness.

This state is absolutely the **original unbounded absolute vacuum state of God**—neither the *nirguna-nirakar*, nor the *saguna-sakar* states of God—where "God-Is" and "consciousness is-not."

When it is said, "God-Is," it describes the state which prevails beyond the beginning of the beginning of Creation.

This state of God-Is is also called the "original divine sound sleep state of God" in the Beyond the Beyond state.

The God-Is state is the state of infinitude. Infinitude by virtue of being infinite is everything. That is, "EVERYTHING" is the nature of infinitude.

EVERYTHING by virtue of being everything embodies even "NOTHING," or else Everything can never mean everything. This Nothing is **latent** in the Everything. But Nothing, being literally nothing, the very being of being nothing is nothing at all.

As this Nothing is latent in the Everything, the Nothingness of the Nothing is embedded in the Everything as the Latency.

Thus, in the infinitude of the God-Is state all that is latent in the nature of Infinity, which is Everything, is the Nothing. Therefore anything that is latent in Everything is of the Nothing.

In short, except for the infinity of the infinitude, all things are latent in the God-Is state of Everything; and all that is latent is of the Nothing with all its aspects as Nothingness.

In the God-Is state where the Nothing is latent, automatically by the nature of nothingness, consciousness also exists as Nothing. Accordingly consciousness in the Beyond the Beyond state of God is ever and ever latent in God Who is by nature the Everything—infinite and unlimited and unbounded. Thus automatically, by His very nature of being the Everything, God in the God-Is state has in Him ever and ever infinite power, infinite knowledge, infinite bliss and all that is infinitely glorious or beautiful.

Because God is the Everything and the Infinite, the opposite of the Everything, which is the Nothing, must be most finite.

Therefore the Nothing is latent in the God-Is state as the most finite; or, in the infinite state of God which is the Everything there is latent the most finite state of the Nothing.

It is only natural that when this latent and most finite Nothing manifests, it ought to manifest as most finite.

But it is a most paradoxical fact that when this most finite Nothing manifests, its manifestation gradually expands *ad infinitum*.

The thing that gives infinity to this most finite Nothing is God's own latent trio-nature of infinite power, infinite knowledge and infinite bliss which, by virtue of being the nature of God, obviously pervades the infinitude of the God-Is state latently. Naturally, this infinite trio-nature also envelops this most finite Nothing when latent in the infinity of the Everything.

"Om" Point

Therefore, when this most finite Nothing becomes manifested as Nothingness, the manifestation of the most finite Nothing closely linked with, and stretched forth by, the simultaneous projection of the latent all-pervading infinite trio-nature of God, gradually expands *ad infinitum* and gets apparently manifested as infinite Nothingness or the Creation; and hence the universe of Nothingness which is illusory can be called God's **"shadow"** and, God being infinite, His shadow is also infinite.*

When it manifests, the Nothing, which is most finite and latent in the Everything, projects out from a most finite point in the Everything where the Nothing as most finite is embodied.

The most finite point from where the Nothing projects out as Nothingness is called the **Creation Point** or the *Om* **Point.** This creation point is naturally also in the Everything, which means in God in the Beyond the Beyond state.

---

* The whole Creation has come out of the Nothing. Out of the Nothing two things have emerged, evolution and production. Out of the Nothing, seven states of gas came into being. The seventh evolved state is hydrogen. Out of this seventh gaseous state evolution and production came into being.

Creation can be reconciled with evolution because all is in seven stages: seven stages of production, seven stages of evolution, and seven stages of involution. So, it is said that God created the universe in seven days. From the Nothing, most finite shadow and infinite shadow emerged simultaneously.

THE ORIGINAL WHIM

CHART II

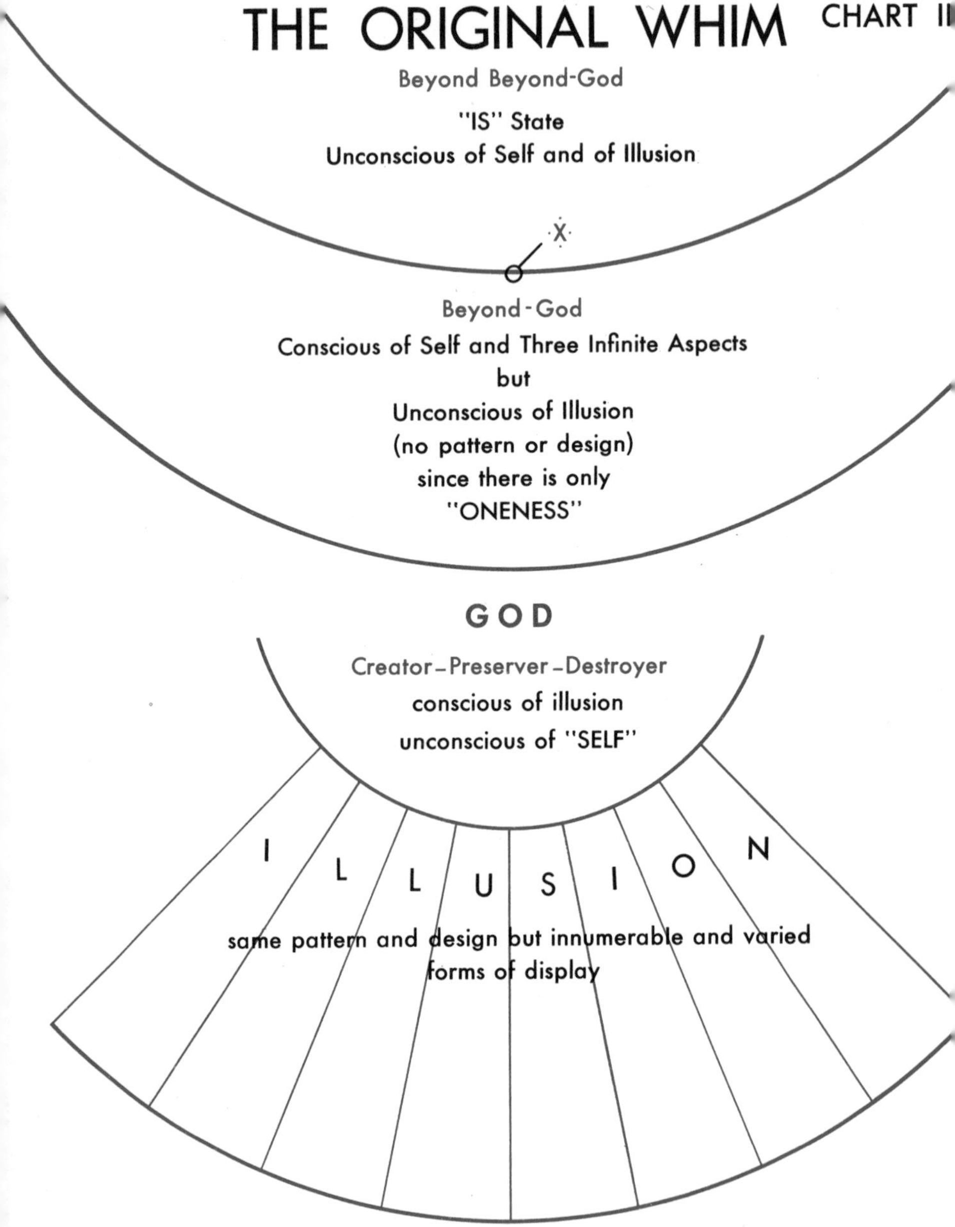

Beyond Beyond-God

"IS" State
Unconscious of Self and of Illusion

Beyond - God
Conscious of Self and Three Infinite Aspects
but
Unconscious of Illusion
(no pattern or design)
since there is only
"ONENESS"

GOD

Creator – Preserver – Destroyer
conscious of illusion
unconscious of "SELF"

I L L U S I O N

same pattern and design but innumerable and varied
forms of display

= Original Whim surged and **GOD** as Creator,

Preserver and Destroyer Manifested with His paraphernalia.

Creator is Himself Created
Preserver is Himself Preserved
Destroyer is Himself Destroyed

So the most finite Nothing projects as the Creation out of the infinite Everything through the most finite "creation point," into the infinity of the infinitude of the God-Is state.

In short, when the most finite Nothing gets projected as Nothingness through the most finite creation point, which is also in the infinity pervaded by the infinite trio-nature of God, the projection of the most finite Nothingness—closely linked with and upheld by the all-pervading infinite trio-nature of God— gradually expands *ad infinitum* and manifests apparently as infinite Nothingness or as infinite Creation.

The Whim or *Lahar*

The cause which led the most finite Nothing, latent in the infinite Everything, to manifest itself as infinite Nothingness, is the **original** cause called the "CAUSE."

This Cause is just nothing but the WHIM or *lahar* of God. This original whim can also be called the first "WORD" uttered by God—"WHO AM I?"

The infinitude of the God-Is state made God absolutely independent, and by virtue of being absolutely independent it is but natural for God to exercise His infinite whim to experience and enjoy His own infinity. To exercise a whim is always the mark of an independent nature, because it is whimsicality that always colours the independent nature.

It is the original infinite whim which is responsible for giving Cause to the latent-all that was of the Nothing to manifest as Nothingness.

But before God exercised His original infinite whim to make manifest the latent-all that was of the Nothing, this whim of God was itself latent as the Nothing in the Everything of the infinitude of absolutely independent God in the God-Is state.

How is it then possible for the latent original infinite whim to surge in God and make manifest itself and all that is latent of the Nothing as Nothingness?

Whim after all is a whim; and, by its very nature, it is such that "why—wherefore—when" can find no place in its nature. A whim may come at any moment; it may come now or after a few months or after years, and it may not come at all.

Similarly, the original infinite whim, after all, is a whim, and too, it is the whim of God in the state of infinitude! This whim may not surge in God at all; and, if it surges, either at any moment or after thousands of years or after a million cycles, it need not be surprising.

Thus it is, that the original infinite whim of God in the state of infinitude **once surged;** and it surged both spontaneously and all of a sudden in absolutely independent God Who is eternally Eternal. Hence this whim, which once surged, once began the Beginning of all things in Creation.

In short, this original infinite latent whim of God in the state of infinitude, once it surged in God Who is absolutely independent, made itself manifest, and simultaneously with its manifestation, it manifested the latent all that was of the Nothing as Nothingness. Thus the whim created the Nothing.

Let us recapitulate how infinite Nothing came out of most finite Everything:

God Beyond is infinite Everything. Infinite Everything may be compared to an infinite, limitless ocean. Therefore this limitless ocean is infinite Everything. Thus every drop in the ocean is most finite Everything. In short, if infinite ocean is infinite Everything then every drop of the ocean is most finite Everything.

Before the whim surges in the limitless ocean and before Creation is manifested, the creation point (*Om* point) through which the Creation is ejected is itself in the limitless ocean as infinite Everything because, prior to the surging of the whim, perfect tranquility prevailed and pervaded the limitless ocean; there was no question of "drops" of the ocean and there was no separateness. There was limitless ocean as infinite Everything.

At the instant when the whim surged in the infinite Everything the creation point or *Om* point manifested as most finite Everything.

Infinite Nothing was latent in the infinite Everything, but when the whim surged the infinite Nothing got manifested through most finite Everything, which is the *Om* point.

Thus, through the **most finite** Everything, the infinite Nothing is ejected gradually, manifesting itself as expanding *ad infinitum*.

Simultaneously with the projection of the latent Nothing and with the manifestation of Nothingness, the consciousness which existed as Nothing, latent in the infinitude of the God-Is state, also got projected and manifested itself gradually as the consciousness of God, and made God experience Himself as God the Creator of all the things that projected out of His state of the Everything as Nothingness.

Whereupon, gradually gaining full consciousness, God in the state of Creator became entangled in the maze of most-finite Nothingness found as infinite, stretched out and upheld through His own infinite trio-nature.

The paradoxical irony is that the infinity itself of God makes it infinitely difficult for God to escape the false apparent infinity of Nothingness which goes on expanding *ad infinitum* through the closely linked infinite trio-nature of God which is infinite power, infinite knowledge and infinite bliss.[17]

But this entanglement is absolutely necessary in order that God in the infinitude of the God-Is state should gain consciousness fully and completely for Himself and of His infinite reality, and in this way experience consciously His unbounded, unlimited, infinite trio-nature of infinite power, infinite knowledge and infinite bliss.

The fundamental fact is that full consciousness once gained can never be lost. It remains eternally, regardless of whether that consciousness fully gained is the consciousness of the false Nothingness experienced as real, or whether that consciousness is the consciousness of Reality Itself.

Eventually consciousness does make God realize His own reality after that same consciousness has attained complete maturity. Consciousness is fully matured to realize Reality only after it is nurtured by the apparent awareness of the false. This awareness of the false as real becomes so intensified during the course of the evolution of consciousness, that the consciousness, steeped in false awareness, makes God aware only of the false, which is experienced by God as the real. That is, God as Creator falsely experiences the manifestation of the Nothing as real and Everything.

In order that the latent consciousness of God in the God-Is state should make it possible for God to realize His own eternal reality, the projection of that latent consciousness in Everything (which, when projected outwards becomes focussed on the false infinity of Nothingness) should be withdrawn inwardly. By such an inward withdrawal, the focus of the same consciousness becomes centred on the infinity of Everything (from which it had projected outwards and given rise to the experience of infinite Nothingness rather than the experience of the infinity of Everything).

As said before, when the projected consciousness withdraws inwards or undergoes full and complete involution, that Nothingness which was once experienced as reality automatically vanishes for the consciousness which is now focussed completely on the eternal Reality of the infinitude of God.

In short, there is no **new** consciousness to be attained to realize Reality—the Eternal. It is the **same** consciousness latent in the Everything which, when it emerges out of the Nothing, first gradually evolves and, associating with the Nothingness, then experiences the Nothingness as real. When the evolution of this consciousness is complete and full, the same consciousness makes God experience the false Nothingness which expands *ad infinitum* as real and infinite. Again, when the same full and complete consciousness reaches full and complete maturity through its own involution, it realizes infinite Reality as the **only reality** and gives God the experience of His own real and eternal infinite state.

God in His original state of infinitude is eternally infinite through His infinite, unbounded and unlimited trio-nature of infinite power, infinite knowledge and infinite bliss. As God eternally **Is,** the only virtual difference between the original state of God and the new states of God that He acquires is that of the consciousness gained progressively through the **impressions** of the projected Nothingness.

God in His original state of God-Is is not conscious of His infinite eternal existence nor of His own infinite nature though He exists infinitely and eternally. Due to His own infinite whim God acquires the consciousness of His reality and realizes His infinite, eternal unlimited Self to experience His unbounded, unlimited and infinite trio-nature.

Thus God, now with His newly acquired state of eternal consciousness, is consciously and eternally aware of His original Beyond the Beyond state of God-Is, which is for ever and ever unconscious of the infinitude of His own God-Is state. Therefore the goal is to realize the eternal and infinite God-state **consciously.**

As already described, the original state of God is that state of unbounded absolute vacuum where God **is** and consciousness **is-not.** This state is the original divine sound sleep state of God beyond the beginning of the Beginning of Creation.

The original infinite whim of God as the "cause" is responsible for breaking the spell of the original divine sound sleep state of God, and the result, which is Creation, is called the "effect."

In order to grasp clearly the divine sound sleep state and understand more clearly all that follows immediately after the original infinite whim surges in God, bestirring Him from the divine sound sleep, let the divine sound sleep state of God be compared with the sound sleep of man.

This sound sleep state of man is literally the same original divine sound sleep state of God. God in the God-Is state is eternally in the original divine sound sleep state, whereas God in the human state daily experiences alternately the sound sleep state and the awake state.

The infinite, impressionless and formless, eternal God experiences Himself as finite, limited, inanimate or animate forms or beings only because of the advent of the first most-finite impression of the Nothing that manifested as Nothingness.

At one stage in the evolution of consciousness the impressions of the Nothing impart to God the experiences of the human state.

These impressions of the Nothing are just the procreation of the original most-finite first impression picked up by the most-finite first ray of consciousness in God made manifest simultaneously when the latent original infinite whim surged in God and projected the latent all of the most-finite Nothing as Nothingness.

The original most-finite impression multiplied and increased simultaneously and concurrently with the evolution of the most-finite original trickle of consciousness.

The multifarious and varied impressions so formed were experienced by the greater evolution of consciousness through multifarious and varied media of finite or gross forms, because the impressions formed must necessarily be experienced by the consciousness; but for consciousness to experience the impressions, suitable media were absolutely necessary.

Thus the evolution of consciousness goes on evolving further and greater consciousness in conformity with the evolution of gross forms of relatively higher and higher types, in order to experience the impressions gathered in conjunction with the preceding relatively lower types of gross media.

In short, the most-finite first impression of the original infinite whim surging in God gave to the unconscious infinite God the most-finite consciousness. Gradually, varied impressions multiplied and increased and gained greater finite consciousness for God, until eventually the evolution of consciousness was complete when the impressions of full consciousness gained identified God with human form. God having now gained full consciousness in human form, the need no longer persists for additional or higher forms to evolve consciousness as this consciousness gained is full and complete.

During the process of the evolution of consciousness, the

consciousness, while identifying God consciously with varied finite gross forms—inanimate and animate—was also simultaneously though unconsciously identifying God with His limited subtle form and His limited mental form. These forms associated with the limited gross form of God in compact and homogeneous unconscious association throughout the process of evolution of consciousness, from the very advent of the first original projection of the latent Nothing in Everything.

It is but natural that, together with the evolution of greater and greater consciousness of God, the evolution of the limited and finite subtle and mental forms simultaneously takes place, till in human gross form the limited subtle and mental forms of God are fully developed.

Though God has gained full consciousness in human form, and though the limited subtle and mental forms are also fully developed in human form, yet the full consciousness so gained is only of the gross which gives experience only of the gross world. Hence, the fully gained consciousness is not yet conscious of the subtle and mental forms nor does it consciously experience the subtle and mental worlds.

In short, though God in the human state has gained full and complete consciousness, He is still not conscious of His limited Energy of the subtle form nor of His limited Mind of the mental form. Much less is He aware or conscious of Himself as the one indivisible, eternal and infinite God with unbounded power and unlimited knowledge. At this stage God is only fully conscious of His identity with human form and its varied gross aspects, and experiences in full only the gross world as an ordinary human being of the world in the form of man or woman.

But the consciousness of man together with his mental form as the mind, his subtle form as energy and his gross form as the body are all the outcome of the manifestation of the most-finite Nothing as infinite Nothingness which was latent in the God-Is state. In other words, the limited mind, the limited energy and the finite body are all of the Nothing, and the consciousness of the limited mind, the limited energy and the finite body is also of the Nothing.

In man, the mind is the seat of desires and thoughts, energy is the seat of force and vigour, and the body, typifying happiness, is the seat of happiness and misery. Hence these desires and thoughts, force and vigour, happiness and misery are respectively the finite aspects of the limited mind, energy and body of man.

Although these aspects of the finite basis of the triple nature of man—the mind, the energy and the body (typifying happiness)—are finite, due to the fact that they are the outcome of manifestation of the most finite Nothing, yet these finite aspects of mind, energy and body demonstrate their capabilities *ad infinitum*.

This is because each of these finite bases of the triple nature of man—the energy, the mind and the body (typifying happiness)—is closely linked with and upheld by each of the three infinite bases of the trio-nature of God (*sat-chit-anand*), infinite power, infinite knowledge and infinite bliss.

The fact is, that when the latent infinite trio-nature of God is gradually manifested out of the gradual projection of the finite Nothing, and when it simultaneously protrudes the projection of the finite Nothing as Nothingness manifested *ad infinitum*, this very same infinite trio-nature of God, at this stage of manifestation, becomes enmeshed in the apparent and false infinity of the Nothingness and thus gets itself expressed as the finite triple nature of man with capabilities demonstrated *ad infinitum*.

How (1) the mind, (2) the energy and (3) the body, as the triple nature of man, demonstrate their capabilities *ad infinitum* in Illusion is clearly experienced through (1) the inventive mind of a scientist, who finds no end to discoveries and inventions; (2) through the release of nuclear energy in Illusion, which has reached a stage where it threatens with its own force of illusion to destroy the very Nothingness out of which it emerged and evolved into such a terrific force; (3) through the body (typifying happiness) which, now keeping pace with the advanced progress of the evolution of the Nothing, is infinitely urged to seek greater and greater happiness to such an extent that happiness actually becomes the very basis of the life of illusion.

The only reason for such infinite demonstration in the field of Nothingness (which is Illusion) is because the basic finite triple nature of man—energy, mind and happiness of Nothingness—is upheld and stretched out *ad infinitum* by the basic infinite trio-nature of God—infinite power, infinite knowledge and infinite bliss of Everything.

Infinite power is unbounded and is never reduced nor exhausted, whereas finite energy, though linked with infinite power, is reduced and exhausted because it is only the outcome of the Nothing manifested as the finite energy of Nothingness.

Infinite knowledge is eternal, uniform and all-pervading and therefore is without a break in its continuity. The limited mind, however, though linked with infinite knowledge, is annihilated and made to vanish ultimately because it is the outcome of the Nothing manifested as the finite mind of Nothingness.

Infinite bliss is bliss eternal and continual and because it is perpetual it is without any opposite aspect. Happiness, on the other hand, although linked with infinite bliss, is not perpetual and therefore it has an opposite aspect of misery. This finite happiness vanishes, even though it is the very basis of the life of the human being, because life itself is transient. As the life of illusion is the outcome of the Nothing manifested as the life of Nothingness, this life must perish.

A stage is reached when man in his travail to realize God ultimately loses his basic finite triple nature, that is body (typifying happiness), energy and mind, and realizes the basic infinite trio-nature of bliss, power and knowledge. In this state man experiences that his nature is not the finite body (typifying happiness) but is infinite bliss; not the finite energy but infinite power; not the finite mind but infinite knowledge. Thus man loses his basic finite triple nature and realizes that his is the basic infinite trio-nature of God. This means that the basic finite triple nature of man, which was upheld by the basic infinite trio-nature of God, is unlinked from the basic infinite trio-nature of God.

Although the man loses his basic finite triple nature, the full consciousness that he gained in his travail is not lost, because full consciousness once gained is never lost, except in gross misuse of the powers of the fourth plane, as previously described.

In this state, with consciousness intact and complete, the limited and finite body (typifying happiness), the limited and finite energy, and the limited and finite mind are all totally unlinked from the unlimited and infinite bliss, power and knowledge respectively.

This is the stage when man is fully conscious and yet no longer experiences the false finite Nothingness as real and infinite. The body (typifying happiness), energy and mind, which were instrumental in giving the experience of the Nothingness, no longer grip the consciousness of man with finite impressions. These are now unlinked and have simply vanished from the focus of the consciousness. They must vanish because they were of the finite Nothing by nature, which literally means absolutely nothing.

But before body, energy and mind ultimately lose their grip over the consciousness of man, there is one predominant experience which he has in his everyday life, that of sleeping and waking each day.

This fundamental experience in a normal man gives rise to three basic states in his everyday life:

The first state is the sound sleep state or the state of complete unconsciousness of the Self in man.

The second state is the dream state or the semi-conscious or semi-awake state.

The third state is the completely awake state or the state of complete consciousness of the Self in man as man.

Now, man's cognizance is **life** in man, and man's life is made cognizant through the **actions** of man. Actions are generated by the impressions of man and vice-versa. These impressions of man are picked up and imprinted on the mind of man by actions. Impressions and actions are thus interdependent because impressions are fed by actions and actions are motivated by impressions.

As said previously, the source of impressions is traced as far back as the latent Nothing in the Everything, which means God in the God-Is state. When the Nothing first became manifested as Nothingness in the shape of Creation, the primal manifestation of the Nothing gave rise to the first trace of consciousness in God and hereupon the first impression of Nothingness manifested. This first impression procreated impressions with the evolution of consciousness.

Accordingly, all impressions are of the Nothing, and as Nothing literally means nothing, these impressions are naturally nothing but mere impressions. But, because it was through these very impressions of Nothing that consciousness evolved fully and completely in man, the consciousness of man is closely linked with these impressions of Nothing and makes man consciously experience this false Nothing as Everything and real.

Impressions as such play a vital role in the life of man until such time as they are completely wiped away, relieving and freeing consciousness from experiencing the false Nothing as Everything and real. Consciousness, when relieved of all impressions, will no longer experience the false Nothing as real but it will experience Reality as the unlimited Self (*i.e.,* God).

As long as impressions persist and continue to impress the consciousness of man, these impressions, activated and generated by the energy of man, are being constantly imprinted on the mind of man and are being retained or stored in his sub-consciousness.

Some of these impressions remain dormant in the sub-consciousness of man for hours, or days, or years, and sometimes for lifetimes. But most of them get projected through the sub-consciousness of man every moment of his life while he experiences semi-conscious and fully conscious states; that is, the dream and awake states, respectively.

When these impressions remain absolutely dormant the man is in his sound sleep state. When these impressions begin to get projected from the sub-consciousness of man, they are hazy in their initial stages, being in varied sub-subtle forms moulded out of the Nothingness, and the man is said to be in a semi-conscious state experiencing dreams through his sub-consciousness. When these hazy impressions grow clearer in their final or ripe stages of projection, the Nothingness in sub-subtle forms is experienced as gross forms and the man is said to be in a fully conscious or awake state, experiencing the gross world through his full consciousness in a completely awake state.

When the man wakes up, the projections of impressions of Nothing manifest the same dream of Nothingness more forcefully and realistically. In other words, the same dream is said to be at its height now in the awake state of man.

Therefore the awake state of man is the experiencing of that same hazy state of dreams, only now they are experienced clearly, being at their height and in their fully ripe and final stages.

The dream of a man is but a drama enacted by the projection of man's own dormant impressions. These impressions, when projected through man's sub-consciousness, create things and creatures of the dream, as sub-subtle forms.

Man in the dream state not only becomes involved in the drama of his dream and plays the roles of both the creator of that dream and of the hero in the drama of that dream, but in this drama man also gets closely associated with the things and the creatures in their sub-subtle forms, which are of his own creation in his dream state. This creation of sub-subtle forms comes entirely as a result of the manifestation of man's own past and present impressions. Thus man in his dream state associates sub-consciously with forms in sub-subtle states.

When recollected by a man in the awake state, these very forms which he has seen and associated with in the dream state, remind him of his conscious associations with the gross forms as things, creatures and beings associated with in his day-to-day life of the present, and link them with his connections and contacts established in his life of the immediate and sometimes distant past.

But more often than not, a man also recollects in his conscious awake state that a particular gross form, whether of a thing, creature or being, with which he closely associates and which he actually seeks, reminds him of having witnessed that same object in his dream at some time in the past, either some days, months or years ago.

Thus it actually happens that a form of the future which he happened to witness in his dream of the past, reappears to the man as a gross form in his life associations of the present.

After a lapse of time the same object, that the man was totally ignorant of ever having seen or contacted before in his lifetime, appears to him (now in the awake state) exactly as he had witnessed it before in his dream state.

Experiences of a similar nature are also recorded in which a man witnesses certain incidents in his dreams years in advance of their actual occurrence.

How is it possible for a man to witness in advance, in the drama of his dream, such forms and incidents of futurity, when this drama of the dream is only the outcome of his past and present everyday life impressions?

Is it really possible in the dream of the present, for one to come across and witness a certain object which is totally of the future, and to establish future associations with it in advance, yet all the while remain ignorant of the object until it is eventually contacted and consciously associated with in an awake state one day in the distant future?

Even if such a thing be really possible, and if the future is being inadvertently probed by man in his dream, then from where does futurity spring into man's present?

How could man living in the present through his own impressions of the past ever come to grips with futurity, even in a dream state, and associate in advance with impressions of future incidents and objects? What is it that endows man with the faculty of prescience?

These very associations with future objects and incidents, though experienced inadvertently and unknowingly by man in the present, are automatically developed and are inevitably there by virtue of man's being the creator of the drama in his dream state.

No sooner does man become the creator of the drama of his dream state through the projection of his dormant impressions, than this very projection of his own dormant impressions reflects his past as if it were really his present, and man, finding himself involved in this drama, gets absorbed in his past while still maintaining his past to be his present.

In this manner, although all the time remaining in the present, the man inadvertently and unknowingly continues to preserve his past, maintaining it to be his present. But when man continues to preserve his past, he (being at the same time the creator) also concurrently becomes the preserver of his own creation through his spontaneous associations with the objects in the drama of his dream state. These very associations, though inadvertently established, maintain the continuity of the drama and endow the creator with the role of the preserver as well.

In every wee-bit act of preservation of all of that which has passed, man in his present, as the preserver of his past, inadvertently and unknowingly, also simultaneously establishes the future in his very present by the very act of preserving his past as his present, which present had remained always as the future of the past.

Take for example a man who finds himself living in the present of today and who looks upon yesterday as all of his past, and tomorrow as all of his future.

Now as soon as this man asserts that he is living in the present of today, he inadvertently and unknowingly has preserved that past of yesterday not only as the present of today but also as the future of tomorrow, just by maintaining himself as alive today in the present.

In every wee-bit act of preserving that past of yesterday while maintaining himself as living in the present of today, that man also inadvertently and unknowingly establishes in his present of today, this today as the future of yesterday.

So it is that although the past and the future have their own stand, yet both of these are consistently and concurrently preserved only in the present. It is only because of the present that both the past and the future find their point of fusion everlastingly in the present.

In the eternity of existence there is no time.* There is no past and no future, only the everlasting present. Therefore, in eternity nothing has ever happened and nothing will ever happen. Everything is happening in the unending NOW, if there is anything happening at all; because all that has apparently happened, all that is apparently happening and all that will ever apparently happen in the illusory cosmic universe is all that which God has already dreamt the moment His own original infinite whim surged as "WHO AM I?" So, really speaking, nothing has happened and nothing will ever happen.

When man in his dream state associates with past, present and even future forms, he simply invents the roles of creating association, then preserving that association and eventually destroying that association, while all the time maintaining that he is the witness to all these in the present of his dream state.

On these very bases of the creation and preservation of all things, creatures and beings created and preserved—whether

* The gross, subtle and mental spheres exist only in imagination, and so time and space exist only in imagination. Time therefore has no absolute value, and in each of the three spheres it has purely relative values that are quite independent of each other. Thus time on the gross sphere is independent of time on the subtle and mental spheres; time on the subtle sphere is independent of time on the gross and mental spheres; and time on the mental sphere is independent of time on the gross and subtle spheres. A dream is nothing more than an experience of gross things by means of the subtle organs, and we have all been told how a long and intricate dream may take place in an impossibly brief moment in that imaginary time which is measured by the movements of the hands on our wrist watch.

in the dream state or in the awake state—there hinges at every step in the present an inevitable destruction as the future of all things created and preserved.

Anything that has its beginning must have its inevitable end; and all things created must inevitably be destroyed however much such things be preserved, anticipating futurity, advertently or inadvertently, as destruction. In the very act of preservation, man in the present automatically becomes the preserver of all things that he created in the past. Man becomes the preserver, being in the know of the future that consistently confronts him in the garb of unfailing destruction that awaits its inevitable turn as futurity. Of course, man himself is really **not aware** that he knows the future, but the very fact that he is the preserver shows that he must be anticipating the destruction; and as destruction belongs to the domain of futurity, the man, though not aware that he knows the future, is knowing it all the time that he is engaged in playing the role of the preserver in the present.

In the very act of becoming the creator, preservation of all things created follows and the creator, perforce, simultaneously has to play the role of the preserver. Concurrently, in the very act of becoming the preserver, destruction of all things preserved is anticipated. Therefore, all things are advertently or inadvertently preserved, and the preserver therefore establishes in the present the future of all things created and preserved, anticipating the inevitable destruction.

God in His original infinite divine dream state eternally plays the three roles of the Creator, the Preserver and the Destroyer simultaneously.

When God is in the process of perserving His own infinite Creation, He is already at the same time in the future, and having preserved what He created, which has passed, the future is definitely established before Him even in His eternal present, which future will destroy what He created in the past and what He preserved in the present. Therefore God, being omniscient and eternally of the present, knows of the past which He eternally preserves as the present; and also, at the same time, He constantly experiences in advance, in His eternal present, all that which is of the future.

Similarly, God in the man state, as man, inadvertently witnesses all the time in his dream state that which is also to be experienced in the future of his awake state. Man thus finds that he sometimes has prescience of things that come to pass after a lapse of time.

To sum up:—In the very act of creation, the acts of preservation and destruction are also present; so, by creating illusion God, as it were, simultaneously preserves and destroys it.

In reality, therefore, nothing is created that remains to be preserved and destroyed, because the created Creation is of the Nothing, and this Nothing in reality means absolutely nothing in all respects.

Though this Nothing is indeed nothing at all, yet when it is said that the Nothing is created by *Brahma,* preserved by *Vishnu* and destroyed by *Mahesh* or *Shiva,* it is spoken of only in terms of the infinite illusion, *i.e.,* in terms of the infinite, divine dream state of God related to the illusory universe—the *brahmand.* *

In the eternity of reality there is absolutely no such thing as creation, preservation or destruction, neither is there space, nor is there any scope for relativity, much less could there ever be the correlated factors of time, such as the past, present and future.

In the eternity of Reality, the one, infinite, eternal, all-pervading existence **is**.

In short, when the consciousness of a man makes him experience the impressions of the Nothing sub-consciously, the man is said to be dreaming a dream. When the consciousness of

---

* Of the three aspects—Creator, Sustainer and Dissolver—Sustainer is the most important because "The Present" which sustains the past and the future is most important. Therefore, *Parvardigar (Vishnu)*—the Sustainer—is the most important aspect of God.

the man causes him to experience more realistically the impressions of the same Nothing full-consciously, the man is said to be dreaming yet another dream into the dream, or he is said to be dreaming into the dream a vacant dream, experiencing the Nothing into Nothing. Hence it is said most appropriately that the world and its affairs are Nothing into Nothing—dream into dream. This means that God in the man state experiences the life of man as a vacant dream into the divine dream, which means Creation. Or, in other words, the life of man is yet but another dream of God in the dreaming of His divine dream or the Creation.

Although God in the man state has gained full consciousness and falsely experiences the multifarious impressions of the false infinity of Nothingness as the reality of the gross world, this full consciousness and these innumerable impressions are all absorbed or gulped in while God in the man state passes away in the sound sleep state, indirectly asserting His original divine state of divine sound sleep. When God in the man state completely wakes up every day from His sound sleep state, the full consciousness which lay dormant during sound sleep and the multitude of impressions which had vanished (*i.e.,* out of sight and out of experience) in the sound sleep, are now all catapulted out to produce once again the false experiences of the finite Nothing manifesting as real and infinite Nothingness.

This unending chain of alternating absorption and ejection of consciousness and impressions in the alternating sound sleep and awake states continues until ultimately all of the impressions are ousted or wiped off clean through the experiencing of the opposite impressions in the processes of reincarnation and involution of consciousness. Thus impressionless consciousness alone remains to give God the conscious experience of His original, eternal, infinite, real God-state.

As God invariably gains full and unimpressioned consciousness through the human-form, the different states of man may be taken as examples with which to compare the different states of God.

The sound sleep state of God in the man state not only resembles the divine sound sleep state of God but is literally the same original divine sound sleep state of God in the Beyond the Beyond state of God-Is where unbounded, absolute vacuum prevails.*

When man passes away in the sound sleep state, absolute vacuum and no consciousness prevails, and though the "self" in man continues to breathe normally, yet in that "self" of man there is no consciousness of its limited "I" or ego, nor is there consciousness of the limited mind, energy, body or the world. The self in man is not even conscious of its own being. In short, in the sound sleep state of man the "self-is" and consciousness "is-not."

When a man wakes up daily from his sound sleep state he normally just wakes up for no reason whatsoever except that his own dormant consciousness of impressions urges or excites his sub-consciousness to eject out the consciousness, and experience the dormant impressions which apparently vanish in sound sleep. Therefore, as soon as the man wakes up, he invariably and simultaneously gains consciousness at first of his surroundings and gradually then of his own "self" with all of its paraphernalia of the limited "I," the mind, energy, the body and the world.

Similarly, no rhyme, no reason and no cause other than

---

* There is a profound and very real relationship between God-realization and sound sleep. The eternal desire of the soul is to become one with God, but because consciousness attaches itself to the gross, the soul seems to become one merely with the gross. In the stone state, for instance, gross consciousness makes the soul identify itself with the stone although, in reality, the soul is all the time one with God. To make this clearer, let us suppose that you take opium or an intoxicating drink. You feel elated or depressed, although there is no radical change in your body, and it is only the consciousness that is affected and gives rise to your feelings. Thus you, as an individual soul, are twenty-four hours within and one-with God, although you feel merely gross-conscious.

Again, let us suppose that you feel tired and fed up and that you go to sleep. What is it that you are trying to do? It is nothing but to try to take refuge in God—your natural and inherent state. The whole Creation therefore has this conscious or unconscious tendency to take shelter in God the Over-Soul by entering the state of sound sleep for a time.

the original, infinite whim of the absolutely independent God was the actual Cause—the original cause—for God in the original divine sound sleep state to wake up out of the unbounded, original vacuum.

Just as a man, who wakes up from his sound sleep state,* has invariably to pass through the state of dreaming first and then wake up completely, gaining full consciousness after the semi-conscious state of the dream (which may last for a very long duration or may last only for a split second), so, too, is it the case with God in the God-Is state. Before completely waking up from His original divine sound sleep state, God necessarily experiences the divine semi-conscious state which is the divine dream state or the creator state.

The original, infinite whim, as the Cause, manifested the first trickle of most-finite consciousness in God. This most-finite consciousness made God, now in a semi-conscious state, experience through sub-consciousness the most-finite impression of the latent Nothing which was also manifested as the Nothingness. This experience of the most-finite first impression of Nothingness began the "divine dream"—the creation of the universe.

Thus the first trickle of consciousness in the God-Is state infused God with the divine sub-consciousness which in turn bestowed the divine semi-conscious state upon God Who was in the divine sound sleep state. In this divine semi-conscious state, God dreams divinely and experiences the divine dream, or the Creation, much before the real, divine awakening state, which state, awakening Him completely, would give Him the experience of God fully conscious of His infinite, unbounded and unlimited divine nature.

This divine sub-consciousness of God also emerged from the Nothing which was latent in the God-Is state of the Everything, and necessarily was projected through the creation point, or *Om* point, in the original absolute vacuum of the Everything.

The very vibrations of the projection of the divine subconsciousness of God, through the creation point in the original

---

* See chart "Real Awakening," facing page 102.

CHART III

REAL AWAKENING

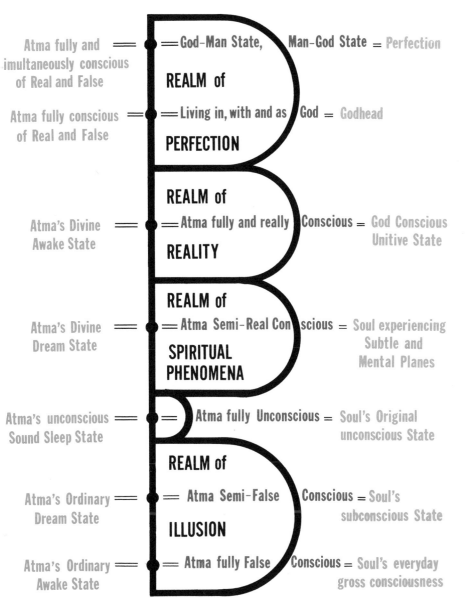

Atma fully and simultaneously conscious of Real and False == ● == God-Man State, **Man-God State** = Perfection

REALM of

Atma fully conscious of Real and False == ● == Living in, with and as God = Godhead

PERFECTION

REALM of

Atma's Divine Awake State == ● == Atma fully and really Conscious = God Conscious Unitive State

REALITY

REALM of

Atma's Divine Dream State == ● == Atma Semi-Real Conscious = Soul experiencing Subtle and Mental Planes

SPIRITUAL PHENOMENA

Atma's unconscious Sound Sleep State == ● == Atma fully Unconscious = Soul's Original unconscious State

REALM of

Atma's Ordinary Dream State == ● == Atma Semi-False Conscious = Soul's subconscious State

ILLUSION

Atma's Ordinary Awake State == ● == Atma fully False Conscious = Soul's everyday gross consciousness

The so many deaths during the one whole life, from the beginning of evolution of consciousness to the end of involution of consciousness, are like so many sleeps during one lifetime.

*   *   *

One who lives for himself is truly dead and one who dies for God is truly alive.

— Meher Baba —

absolute vacuum, bestirred the divine sound sleep state of God and made manifest the original breath of God, or the original Word—the divine *nad*—together with space, time and the cosmic universe, with all of its paraphernalia of the limited and finite ego, mind, energy and the individual and multiple forms.

As the projection of the infinite divine sub-consciousness of God in the divine dream state gathers momentum, the divine dream, or the Creation, begins to evolve, and God in the divine semi-conscious state not only begins to experience the divine dream but simultaneously gets involved in His divine dream by identifying and associating Himself with all the things which He experiences in the field of cosmic evolution.

When the infinite divine sub-consciousness of God has projected infinitely through the creation point in the absolute vacuum, the whole Creation projects forth gradually and evolves in size, shape, form, colour, and so forth, in accordance with the intensity of the projection of the divine sub-consciousness.

At this stage God, in the Beyond the Beyond state of divine sound sleep, is just aroused from the divine sound sleep—not completely but semi-consciously—even after the complete emergence of the divine infinite sub-consciousness that was latent in God.

God, being now in the more evolved divine semi-conscious state, experiences more forcefully the divine dream and also identifies and associates Himself more intensely with His very Creation.

Gradually, though now more forcefully, God experiences Himself as everything in the cosmic evolution and identifies Himself with the universes, the airs, the inanimate and animate beings—such as stones, metals, vegetation, birds, worms, fishes, animals and human beings. God in this way receives apparently real, but really false, answers to His **First Word** "Who am I?", such as—"I am stone," "I am metal," and so forth, and finally obtains the answers "I am man," "I am woman."

When God identifies Himself with human beings, He is no longer semi-conscious; because at this stage in the divine dream state, as soon as God identifies Himself with a human form He gains full consciousness.

Full consciousness now having been gained, this consciousness ought to dispel all dreams and cause God to experience the real awake state, giving Him the realization that He is God. At this stage, although God identifies Himself with human beings and although God is now fully conscious, with a feeling of greatest awareness,* yet God has not realized His real, divine awake state because the full consciousness thus far gained is of the Nothingness of the Nothing which was latent and which is now manifested apparently as Everything through the projection of His own divine infinite sub-consciousness. This leads God to identify Himself with His projected creation rather than to become conscious of Himself as the real Everything and of His own identity as God.

In short, this is the stage at which God, while identifying Himself with human beings in full consciousness, still remains quite oblivious of His own real and original state of God-Is.

Even in this state of full consciousness God still continues to experience the world of His own creation, and with greatest awareness simultaneously continues to identify Himself with human beings, thus finding Himself sometimes as man and sometimes as woman according to the predominance of impressions which are opposite in nature. In other words, God in the man state, although fully conscious and completely aware, experiences Himself not as God in the God-Is state but as man in the human state, not as infinite but as finite.

The paradoxical irony is that God the Real now finds false creation as real, having lost His own reality in illusion and having made His own reality an obstacle to experiencing Reality.

In order that God-in-man should experience Himself as God-in-Reality, the projection of the full consciousness of God, which is now fixed on man, should be so drawn inward that the

---

* Before attaining human form there is consciousness but not awareness. In sound sleep there is neither consciousness nor awareness. Till the sixth plane there is awareness. In the seventh plane there is only consciousness.

same full consciousness, which when projected outward identified God as man, should now identify Him as Himself. This is realization of the God state and this realization is the divine goal which alone brings about the end of the divine dream.

Attainment of the divine goal would mean that at this stage God-in-man, through the gradual process of involution of consciousness, should eventually experience the passing-away-in that original divine sound sleep state of absolute vacuum while retaining the legacy of the full consciousness which has been gained. Thus God would be able to realize His eternal "I am God" state consciously. Whereupon, attaining His original state consciously, God would experience His own divine eternal existence and His own divine nature which is the Everything—infinite and real; and so at last get the real answer to His First Word or question of "Who am I?", as "I am God."

To make it clearer, to attain the divine goal with full consciousness evolved, the human-conscious God strives, through further experiences by the process of reincarnation, to withdraw inwards towards Himself the already projected full consciousness, which He gained as soon as He identified Himself with the first human-form in His divine dream (Creation).

As this stage of the beginning of the end of the divine dream approaches, the full consciousness of God which experiences the false awake state in the human form strives to the utmost through the process of involution to withdraw inwards, unto Himself, this fully evolved consciousness which is projecting outwards onto all things in the cosmic universe rather than unto Himself.

In order to describe the various stages by which the complete unconsciousness of God in His original sound sleep state gradually projected full consciousness through the process of evolution of consciousness, and how the projected consciousness was eventually withdrawn inwards through the process of involution of consciousness, after numerous reincarnations, before actually experiencing the real divine awake state of "I am God," let the different stages be visualized step by step, comparing each stage of gradual gain in consciousness of God with the relative states of a normally conscious man who is at first in sound sleep and who subsequently gains consciousness enough to realize eventually his ordinary awake state every day.

FIRST STAGE

Visualize a man with eyes completely shut and in sound sleep. This man is completely unconscious and is oblivious of all that surrounds him. Now picture at the same time the original divine sound sleep state of God as He is in the original absolute vacuum of the God-Is state. In both cases, that is, both in God's formless state and God's state of human-form as man or woman, there is complete absence of consciousness, and in both cases absolute vacuum prevails. Simultaneously, also picture the total absence of consciousness in both cases as comparable to the completely shut eyes of a man in sound sleep.

SECOND STAGE

Visualize the next state of the man as being still asleep but beginning to open his eyes very, very slightly, because he is just bestirred from his sound sleep state and the spell of absolute vacuum is shattered by the emergence of the dormant impressions now commencing to project through the sub-consciousness of the man which also lay latent in him in his sound sleep state. Because of the projection of the varied impressions through the sub-consciousness of this man, he now begins to experience dreams while still asleep, although no longer in the sound sleep state, because the absolute vacuum no longer prevails. For the man to commence experiencing dreams means that in his initial stage of the semi-conscious state he begins to experience through his sub-consciousness the dormant impressions of the Nothingness in sub-subtle forms. The man now is not only in the initial stage of the semi-conscious state and is not only beginning to experience dreams, but he is also starting to get involved in the dreams by beginning to associate with the creatures in sub-subtle forms of his own creation. Thus the projection of impressions, which lay dormant in the sub-consciousness of man, makes man play the role of the hero or the creator in the drama of his dreams. Because this man in this dream state has only just stirred from his sound sleep and has just attained the semi-conscious state, picture this man experiencing the dreams as one who is starting now to open his eyes very, very slightly. The beginning of the opening of the eyes resembles the advent of the first trace of consciousness as sub-consciousness manifested in man.

While visualizing this state of man, as a parallel, picture likewise that state of God in which He has just stirred from His original divine sound sleep state. God now only begins to experience the divine dream state, or the Creator state, as soon as the first most-finite impression of the Nothingness is projected through the divine sub-consciousness of God. Both of these— *i.e.,* the Nothingness and the divine sub-consciousness of God— were latent as of Nothing in the original state of God as the Everything. God, now in the initial stage of the divine semi-conscious state, just begins to identify Himself with the creatures of His own Creation (*i.e.,* His own divine dream) through the infinite divine sub-consciousness which just begins to project the Creation, that is, the impressions of the Nothingness.

THIRD STAGE

Visualize the third state of the man as still asleep, but with half-open eyes, because a man in this state now completely experiences the semi-conscious state. In order to picture this complete semi-conscious state of the still-sleeping man, continue to visualize him with eyes very, very slightly open, representing the beginning of the semi-conscious state. In this state, as said above, he starts to experience dreams due to the false, illusory impressions of the Nothingness which were collected sub-consciously and are now ejected out through the projection of the sub-consciousness, giving rise to the beginning of the dream state of man. But, as the dreams continue, and as they gather momentum due to the intensity of the projection of multi-farious and varied dormant impressions through the sub-consciousness of the man, he gets more and more involved sub-consciously. As a result he now firmly associates himself with the creatures of his own creation in the dreams and he is completely in the semi-conscious state. This semi-conscious state of the man represents that state which is neither the complete sound sleep state without consciousness nor the complete awake state with full consciousness. This state, so to speak, is the semi-awake state. Now visualize this third state of the man as the state of semi-consciousness represented by half-opened eyes experiencing the dreams more forcefully and much more intently.

While visualizing this state of the man, picture as a parallel that state of God in the divine dream state where God is experiencing a semi-conscious state. At this stage, God as the creator of Creation experiences the creator state through the infinite, divine semi-conscious state. Here the infinite divine sub-consciousness, intensively projecting Creation into being, continually affirms God's identification with the creatures of His own creation. This gives rise to infinite experiences of a more forceful nature in the divine dream of God, when God actually finds Himself as the creatures of His Creation.

FOURTH STAGE

Visualize the fourth state of the man as that in which he is still asleep but trying gradually to open wider his already half-opened eyes in accordance with the greater and greater intensity of the projection of more and more impressions through the sub-consciousness of the man still in his dream state. Here the man is not only in a semi-conscious state but is verging on being fully conscious, and is about to realize his awake state.

Now paralleling this, picture also that state of God in the fourth stage of His divine dream state. Compare the fourth state of the man in the semi-conscious state with a very critical stage in the divine dream state of God. Here the projection of infinite impressions, through the infinite divine sub-consciousness of God, is so intensified in the course of the cosmic evolution of the consciousness of God, that this projection is about to be so completely fixed, or so perfectly focussed, onto the infinity of Nothingness as to identify God with His own most perfect image in His divine dream of Creation. Thus at this stage in the divine dream state, God the Creator is about to identify Himself with a human form after innumerable identifications with all and everything that is in His Creation including inanimate and animate objects. God, in the divine infinite semi-conscious state, is now nearing the verge of gaining full consciousness concurrently with His identification with human form.

FIFTH STAGE

Visualize the fifth state of the man as being still asleep but with eyes now **almost** open. The man in this state is **still** in the semi-conscious or semi-awake state, experiencing the dreams at their height in their final stage, in which the impressions are projected through his sub-consciousness with the greatest intensity. The zenith is reached both by the intensified projection of the impressions in much less hazy forms, or in greater degree of realism, and by relevant dreams which are dreamt in a greater degree of clarity or in their ripe stage. This is the stage in dreams when the sub-subtle forms of Nothingness have reached their zenith and appear more clearly. The dreams at their height now must stop, because the zenith reached by the projections of impressions through the sub-consciousness of the man is at this point sufficient to excite and urge the emergence or manifestation of full consciousness at any moment. This state of the man **almost** fully conscious may therefore be pictured as a man with his eyes almost wide open, though still asleep. This is the stage reached a split second before the man has roused from his dream state to become wide awake. This is the completely matured semi-conscious state of sub-consciousness.

While visualizing the fifth state of the man, side by side with it picture that state of God in His divine dream state where God is experiencing the completely matured state of the divine, infinite semi-conscious state and is almost about to gain full consciousness. At its zenith the intensity of the projection of infinite impressions through the divine, infinite sub-consciousness of God has almost ceased to identify God semi-consciously with the last of the creatures in the cosmic evolution of Creation and forms. With divine, infinite sub-consciousness, God is in His divine, infinite semi-conscious state, which when **almost matured** identified God with infinite impressions of animal forms. But now in the fifth stage of the divine dream state where God is in the **completely matured** divine, infinite semi-conscious state, God can no longer be made to identify with impressions of animal forms even though they are intensively and infinitely projected through His divine, infinite sub-consciousness. At this point a stage is reached in the divine dream state wherein, with the projection to infinity of impressions projected infinitely through the divine, infinite sub-consciousness of God at its zenith, this infinite projection has almost identified God with a human form and God is almost fully conscious.

SIXTH STAGE

Visualize the sixth state of the man as having completely awakened from his sleep and as having his eyes completely wide open. In this state the man is no longer in the semi-conscious state, dreaming the dreams which were nothing but the hazy and faint projection of the dormant impressions of Nothingness which were stored in the sub-consciousness of the man, and realized through his sub-consciousness in sub-subtle forms of Nothingness. This is the stage in the state of the man where he has just awakened completely, but albeit he is fully conscious, he is not conscious of his "Self" as yet. The man is no longer in his sound sleep and semi-conscious states and, with full consciousness gained, is pictured now with wide-open eyes. This means the end of the dream, or the end of the false state of man where he experienced the latent or dormant Nothing manifested in its raw state as Nothingness in the shape of hazy and faint sub-subtle forms. The man now in the awake state no longer experiences or sees the Nothingness as something hazy or faint as he used to see it in his dream state. With his eyes just opened wide and fully, he is dazed and stares vacantly at things that now confront his sight more realistically. The man now observes things that confront his sight as if he were seeing the ripe, the clear and the fully developed forms of the same Nothingness that he saw in his dream as raw, hazy and faint. In this state the man sees, as it were, yet another dream, but he sees it much more realistically than the dream from which he awakened a split second before.

This is the sixth stage in the state of man where the man, dazed, simply experiences the sight of things much more realistically but still as if it were just a vacant dream. That is, the man sees more forcefully and realistically but still vacantly the dream of his dream state, giving him the sense of yet another dream within the dream of his dream state.

This state corresponds to the few seconds immediately after a man has awakened and cannot help but see at first the objects that come within range of his vision rather than his own self. This is because, as soon as his eyes open after the sleep state, the spontaneous opening of the long-shut eyes creates in him a sort of dazed state and, although the man has awakened and is fully conscious, he is still unaware of his Self or of its position in relation to the objects surrounding his very self. He simply stares at the objects upon which his gaze falls.

While visualizing the sixth state of the man, make a parallel of it by picturing in the same way that state of God as of that instant when God has **just** identified Himself with a human form and has **just** gained full consciousness. At that moment God is no longer in the divine, infinite semi-conscious state, dreaming the original divine dream which was the projection of the latent Nothing released by the divine, infinite sub-consciousness as the Creation, or as completely evolved Nothingness.

In this sixth state, God is now out of His original, divine sound sleep and His divine, infinite semi-conscious states because He is now fully conscious. Here God is conscious not of His unlimited Self nor of His infinite, unbounded and unlimited trio-nature of infinite power, knowledge and bliss, but is **just** fully conscious. God is fully conscious now in the sense that God is consciously absorbed in the Nothingness which now manifests through His full consciousness as clear and well defined, realistic gross states apparently demonstrating their infinite aspects *ad infinitum.*

SEVENTH STAGE

Visualize the seventh state of the man where he has his eyes wide open and is completely and fully awake in the sense that he now asserts his limited self or ego, and is conscious of his human form or the gross body, of his surroundings and of the gross world. Though this man is fully conscious and completely aware of the gross, and experiences the gross world in full, yet he is still unconscious of the limited energy and mind of which he indirectly makes unconscious use, being aware of their aspects through the limitations of his gross body alone. In this state the man is fully conscious, but gross-consciously, and is fully aware of his self as a man in the world of his surroundings.

The man is not only completely aware of the gross world, and of all things in the world which confront his view, but he also actually experiences them by involving his fully conscious and fully aware state of limited self in them. He now recognizes the objects of the gross world through his five predominant gross senses and differentiates them one from another, using them discriminately or indiscriminately, automatically and indirectly utilizing energy and mind which are now fully developed, in attaching to them their relative values as and when his limited self asserts in his awake state before he passes away once again in sound sleep.*

---

* In the awake state, it is the mind that sees through the gross eyes, hears through the gross ears, smells with the gross nose, eats through the gross mouth and acts through the gross limbs.

In the dream state (sub-conscious state) it is the mind that sees through the sub-subtle eyes, hears through the sub-subtle ears, and so on.

In the sound sleep state, it is the mind that is at peace and at rest.

While visualizing the seventh state of the man, picture likewise that state of God where God identifies Himself completely with the human form and gains full and complete consciousness. God now no longer dreams divinely the original divine dream but, with full consciousness now completely gained, He experiences falsely the complete awareness. This awareness makes God falsely aware of that original Nothing which was latent in His own state of infinitude, and which, with the present gain of full consciousness, makes God experience that Nothing realistically as the Everything, infinite and real. In other words, God, when He was in the divine, infinite semi-conscious state, was experiencing the latent Nothing manifested as the Nothingness as His divine dream. Now, when God is in a fully conscious state, He apparently experiences that Nothing, not as the divine dream of Nothingness, but He now actually experiences the awareness of this Nothing as the Everything.

In this stage with the advent of awareness, although God in the state of creator has stopped dreaming divinely the original divine dream, yet, because of His having gained full consciousness and complete awareness, God now becomes completely aware of the original divine dream not as a dream but as something realistic, not as illusion but as reality, not as the Nothing but as the Everything, preserving the Nothing that He created. Thus it is that, although God gained full consciousness and experienced complete awareness in the state of creator, this very awareness of God the Creator proves a deception and makes God now experience His own divine dream (or the Creation) of the Nothing as Reality while He identifies Himself with the human being.

In short, God the Creator as the God-in-man, though now fully conscious and completely aware and out of His original divine dream state, yet finds Himself not as God but as man with complete gross consciousness, experiencing the creation of His own original divine dream state as Reality. Here it is to be said that the God-in-man continues to experience in the awake state with the awareness of false reality the vacant divine dream as yet another dream of God within that original divine dream. This is the most alluring stage in the state of God when, with full consciousness gained, God is led astray, by the false awareness attained, to identify Himself not with His unlimited and infinite Self, but with His most perfect image in the shape of the human being, while God continues to experience the vacant divine dream.

Although it appears as the most fantastic imagination, yet it is a fact that the very life of man is the veil that shrouds the reality of the eternal existence of God.

It is the irony of divine fate that God gets lost in man to find Himself, and the instant that man gets lost in God, God realizes His Reality as Existence, eternal and infinite.

In other words, infinite God becomes infinitely absorbed in His own infinitely perfect image intently seeking His infinity; and although God does gain full consciousness through it, He does not realize the reality of His own eternal, infinite existence in it. But, the instant the full consciousness thus gained ceases to identify God with the infinite reflection of His infinitely perfect image, this image vanishes from the consciousness of God, and God spontaneously and automatically and consciously realizes His own identity as God, the infinite Existence, and finds that He alone ever was, always is and eternally will remain the **Only Reality.**

Thus God in the man state, at first realizing Himself as man, asserted His limited aspects through the limited self or the limited ego, the limited mind, the limited energy and the finite gross body. Then eventually and ultimately realizing Himself as God, He manifests His unlimited, unbounded, infinite trio-nature of infinite knowledge, infinite power and infinite bliss through His divine unlimited Self.

While depicting, through the seven different primary stages, the process of unfoldment of the latent consciousness of God in His original, unconscious, divine sound sleep state, as compared with the seven different primary states of man gaining consciousness right from his unconscious sound sleep state to the state wherein he gains full consciousness and wakes up completely with wide-open eyes, it is found that this is the process of the evolution of consciousness of God which eventually identifies the fully conscious God with the fully conscious man, after identifying God with all and everything inanimate and animate in the drama of the divine dream of Creation.[18]

Right from the unconscious state (compared to the divine sound sleep state) until full and complete consciousness is gained in the man state (compared to the wide-open eyes of man experiencing the gross world), God remains One, indivisible, infinite, formless and eternally all-pervading. But it is the all-pervading, infinite nature of God that expresses consciously and unconsciously His eternal divine existence, directly and indirectly, in one and all states and forms, through their expressions of their very being.

The whole process of evolution was an absolutely spontaneous outcome of the original, infinite whim surging in the unconscious God to become conscious of His eternal and infinite existence. And, paradoxical as it may seem, in the process of evolution the **unconsciousness** of God urged the gradual unfoldment of the latent **consciousness** of God, which consciousness grew greater and greater through a gradual, systematic and progressive process of gathering and experiencing varied and innumerable impressions through identifying God with varied and innumerable gross forms.

So it is that the evolving consciousness of God gives rise to the identification of God with forms and states of forms of higher and higher types. This identification of God in turn gives rise to an apparently unending chain of associations and dissociations, or the so-called births and deaths, of forms and beings which continue to form and assert and then dwindle away in the Nothingness, leaving behind the legacy of impressions which in turn again lead the evolving consciousness of God to identify Himself with yet another form moulded of the very impressions left behind by the form that dwindled away.

Through the process of evolution, the unconscious God

did eventually gain full consciousness when the evolved consciousness of God eventually identified God with the human form. But this full consciousness gained was impressioned consciousness and therefore did not make God realize the original infinite state of God. On the contrary, God realized that He is man. Thus God, after having the original whim of His first Word ("Who am I?"), at this stage finds Himself to be man and experiences the gross world, apparently living in it as man and quite oblivious of His infinite and eternal existence until He finds the real answer to His first Word of "Who am I?" to be "I am God."

So it is that the original whim **created** the Nothing; and the impressions or the *sanskaras* **preserved** that Nothing as the Nothingness, *i.e.,* the Creation and the creatures of Creation; and eventually the opposite impressions will ultimately uproot these impressions and destroy that Nothingness to give realization of Reality.

It was the original whim of God that effected in the absolutely independent God the infinite triune attributes of God the Creator—God the Preserver—God the Destroyer (*i.e., Brahma—Vishnu—Mahesh*). It is God's original whim itself that is responsible for bestowing upon God infinite attributes such as the Creator—the Preserver—the Destroyer.

These infinite triune attributes of God consistently force assertion through consistent formation, conservation and dissolution of all things and beings in existence. Even in the everyday life of man and of all creatures in Creation, this infinite triune aspect of God consistently appears to assert through consistent births, procreations (maintaining the preservation) and deaths.

The original first word, through the original whim of God, created out of the latent Nothing the latent original first impression of "Who am I?", and this original first impression procreated the latent Nothingness as the original Creation. In turn, the procreation of the Nothingness procreates the impressions which continue to preserve the Nothingness consistently as the original Creation, until eventually this Nothingness is destroyed by opposite impressions through the processes of reincarnation and involution of consciousness, and the final answer of "I am God" is obtained to the first word "Who am I?"

It is in accordance with the procreated impressions of the varied individualized conscious assertions of inanimate and animate forms and beings that illusion consistently maintains its apparently infinite and varied stand. It is because of this unfailing and apparently unending chain of varied individualized procreated impressions that the original Creation, originating out of the original whim of God, is consistently preserved, while being concurrently evolved so that every individualized form and being in existence may consciously experience the answers to the first word "Who am I?" as "I am an inanimate thing," "I am an animate creature," "I am a rational being," "I am a man" and "I am a woman."

For example, when God in the man state, as man, is in sound sleep, and when time and space as the day and the universe of the man have all been apparently destroyed for him, then what is it that every day unfailingly creates his daily morning for him? And again, when man wakes up every day, then what is it that unfailingly creates for him his universe and all the things that are of it and in it? It is the man's own dormant impressions gathered during the course of the evolution of consciousness, and during the process of reincarnation, that incite his own dormant consciousness during sound sleep to wake him up inadvertently every day, so that the man's own dormant impressions may have the necessary scope to become exhausted through conscious experiences during his awake state. In this manner the man's own impressions in the dormant state **create** for the man his own morning and his own universe every day. Although both the daily morning and the universe of the man were simultaneously created for him by his own dormant impressions, yet both were already handily **preserved** for him by his own impressions of his life in the everyday awake state, and also through the procreation in his own everyday life of deeper and deeper impressions or *sanskaras* of the already existing Illusion, or of the original Creation, which sprang from the original whim of God. Eventually, both the morning (or the day) and the universe of that man are **destroyed** by the man's own opposite impressions experienced in his sleep state, which are diametrically opposite to the impressions of his awake state.

Hence, in regular unfailing succession, God in the man state as man, consistently asserts Himself as the Creator of His own Creation through the dormant impressions of man; as the Preserver of His own Creation through man's leading the everyday life in the awake state, procreating the impressions of creation; and as the Destroyer of His own Creation through the opposite impressions of man when he falls asleep and ultimately passes away in the sound sleep state. Every day, finally destroying the very creation as individualized by his consciousness, man once again creates, preserves and destroys the whole creation through the play of impressions. Even through the very being of every thing and of every creature, God consistently asserts His infinite triune attributes as the Creator, the Preserver and the Destroyer.

As in the nature of the man state, so also in the nature of every state of God, God consistently asserts directly and indirectly, apparently and really, His infinite triune attributes of Creator, Preserver and Destroyer at one and the same time. Even in the very pulsation of the heart and in the functioning of the lungs, the three aspects of the infinite triune attributes never fail to assert. With every pulsation of the heart, the heart expands, relaxes (in the refractory period) and contracts, simultaneously heralding the advent of the birth of a being on the one hand, and sustaining the life of the being on the other hand, and finally, with the eventual and final contraction, leading to the physical death of the being.

Thus it is that the triune attributes of God, as God the Creator, God the Preserver and God the Destroyer (*Brahma, Vishnu,* and *Mahesh* or *Shiva*), assert independently as well as simultaneously in all things and in every creature and in all beings, in every state of God at every stage in the evolution of consciousness, and on every plane in the involution of consciousness, until eventually the original cosmic Creation, having sustained the ages, cycles and periods, and being preserved by the play of cosmic impressions, is finally destroyed by the play of cosmic opposite impressions of God. This final destruction is generally known as *mahapralaya,* meaning the "Greatest of the great event of absorption," when the whole cosmic Creation as Nothingness is absorbed infinitely by the Everything.

In the process of evolution, unconscious God did obtain full consciousness, not of His original infinite state but of the gross and finite. After all the struggle during the course of evolution, which achieved full consciousness for God, no doubt—at what price was it gained? The cost was the burden of the legacy of impressions accumulated in the gross form—the last medium of association of the evolving consciousness of God—through which full consciousness was completely evolved in the instant that God identified Himself with the human form. Therefore God in the man state is still unaware of His original state despite having gained full consciousness. This unawareness is due to the unwanted (through necessary) burden of the gross impressions still clinging to the full consciousness gained.

The process through which God in the man state struggles to unburden these finite impressions is one which takes place through opposite impressions, and is called the process of reincarnation.[19]

In trying to unburden consciousness from the finite impressions the gross consciousness of God necessarily has to experience these impressions and then exhaust them by innumerable opposite experiences through a series of reincarnations. Experiences opposite by nature are absolutely essential to exhaust the impressions, because opposite experiences alone can shake up the roots of thickly set or firmly established varied impressions.

In the process of reincarnation the fully gross-conscious God in man, fortified with fully developed subtle and mental bodies, which are consistently though unconsciously used, must necessarily experience a series of unending chains of varied and innumerable experiences, opposite by nature, in order that the impressions of opposites might be exhausted. These impressions are constantly being imprinted upon, or picked up by, the mental body or the mind of man, and are retained or released by the sub-consciousness in man. When these impressions are released through the sub-consciousness and full consciousness of God in man, as man, he has varied experiences according to the variety and the intensity of the impressions released. Whereas the subtle body of man, which is the seat of energy, energizes these impressions to activate man into committing actions in his everyday life of either the dream or awake state (as the case may be). These actions are also opposite in nature to the varied related opposite impressions.

Thus in the man state on the gross plane, although energy and the mind are fully developed and are continually and consistently used, yet they are employed indirectly and unconsciously. When on the planes of Energy (*i.e.,* on the subtle planes), this Energy is divinely and consciously made use of; but on the subtle planes the Mind is made use of indirectly and unconsciously. On the mental planes, when this Mind is made use of divinely and consciously, Energy is only made use of indirectly and unconsciously.*

It necessarily follows that while this gross-conscious God in the man state experiences the opposites in the gross world, He reincarnates a number of times, sometimes as a male, sometimes as a female, in the varied castes, creeds, nationalities and colours and in varied different places and continents, always reviewing opposite impressions and exhausting them by experiences of opposites.

It is always through these diverse oppositional impressions and their respective opposed experiences that gross-conscious

---

* [See also: Meher Baba, "Control of Mind over Energy and Matter," *Life at its Best,* ed. by Ivy O. Duce (San Francisco: Sufism Reoriented, Inc., 1957), p. 38. Ed.]

God in the man state on earth can possibly one day, after millions of rebirths, thin out the thick-set impressions. It is the process of this cycle of so-called deaths and births of human-forms that ultimately urges the consciousness of the gross-conscious God in the man state to involve. This process of involution of consciousness gradually takes shape when the gross impressions gradually grow fainter and scarcer.

Involution of the consciousness of God in the man state is only possible when the opposite impressions, after a very, very long process, gradually thin out through the process of unfailing reincarnations which leads to the limit of gross impressions.

When the limit of gross impressions is reached, then the stage is attained where gross-conscious God in the man state gradually becomes dissociated from the gross world as the involution of consciousness begins to **infold** the consciousness. Simultaneously with the beginning of the involution of consciousness, God in the man state gradually dissociates from experiencing the impressions of the opposites of the gross world.

It was seen that God attained full consciousness through the process of evolution of consciousness; but the full consciousness gained was a consciousness that was impressioned. In order to wipe the impressions off of the full consciousness gained, the process of reincarnation and the process of involution of consciousness must be followed through.

The process of the evolution of consciousness of God was compared to the gradual opening of the eyes of man. When man opened his eyes completely it was compared with the end of the evolution of consciousness, because God then had gained full consciousness.

The process of the reincarnation of God in the man state may be compared with the man completely awake with full consciousness and with eyes wide open, gaining diverse experiences opposite to the impressions he gathered during the years of his life, and which he now actively experiences during the course of his days, forgetting his own self amid the execution of his multifarious activities.

Now the urge for the involution of the consciousness of God in the man state may be compared with a man who, having been engrossed in his activities of the day, at last finds time, when the day's work is practically over, to pay attention to his own self rather than to his activities. Thus urged, man's attention shifts automatically from external activities towards paying proper attention to his own self.

Just as full consciousness was evolved in seven different stages, so too, evolved full consciousness is completely involved through the process of involution in seven different stages. These seven stages of involution of consciousness are named "the seven planes of consciousness." The seventh plane is the seventh and last stage in the process of involution of consciousness where consciousness is completely involved and God consciously realizes His eternal infinite existence. That is, God, Who was originally unconscious, now becomes oblivious of oblivion itself.

These seven stages of gradual involution of the consciousness of God in the man state may be compared with the wide-open eyes of a man, at first gazing straight ahead of him and away from him. Then, in an attempt to behold his own self, he lowers his eyes gradually, shifting them in seven stages, until eventually his range of vision includes his own self.

Through unfailing, numerous reincarnations wherein a limit to gross experiences is reached, and when the gross impressions become faint and almost defunct, the gross consciousness of gross-conscious God in the man state gradually begins to involve, and God in the state of man is initiated into the process of involution of consciousness.

At this stage the involving gross consciousness experiences **partially** the first stage or plane of the subtle world through the medium of the already fully developed subtle body of God in the man state. This is the initial stage before the first plane where the involved gross consciousness of gross-conscious God in the man state obtains the first glimpses of the first plane of

CHART IV

EVOLUTION AND INVOLUTION

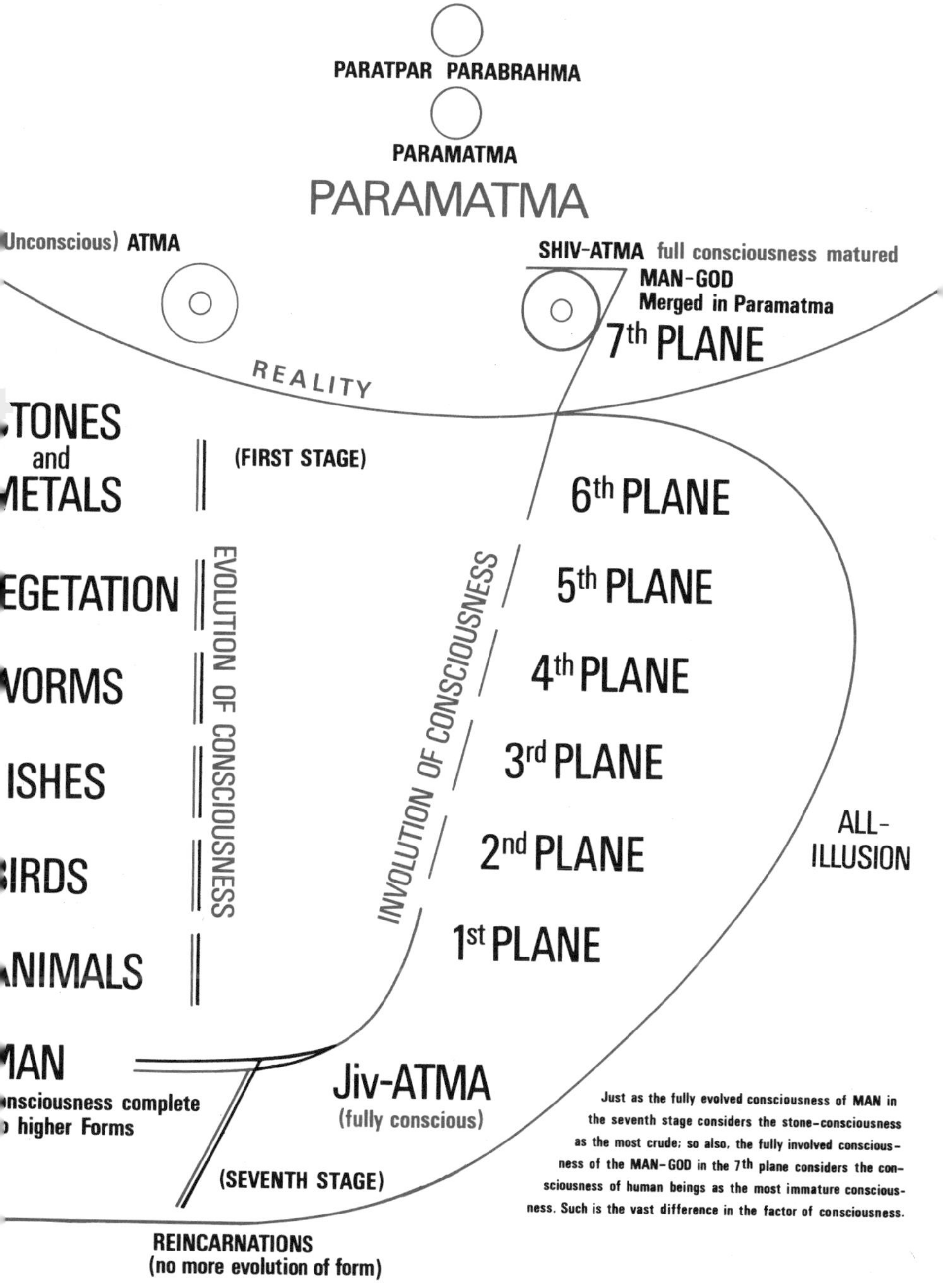

PARATPAR PARABRAHMA

PARAMATMA

PARAMATMA

(Unconscious) ATMA

SHIV-ATMA full consciousness matured

MAN-GOD
Merged in Paramatma
7th PLANE

REALITY

STONES
and
METALS

(FIRST STAGE)

6th PLANE

VEGETATION

EVOLUTION OF CONSCIOUSNESS

5th PLANE

WORMS

4th PLANE

INVOLUTION OF CONSCIOUSNESS

FISHES

3rd PLANE

BIRDS

2nd PLANE

ALL-
ILLUSION

ANIMALS

1st PLANE

MAN

consciousness complete
no higher Forms

Jiv-ATMA
(fully conscious)

(SEVENTH STAGE)

Just as the fully evolved consciousness of MAN in
the seventh stage considers the stone-consciousness
as the most crude; so also, the fully involved consciousness of the MAN–GOD in the 7th plane considers the consciousness of human beings as the most immature consciousness. Such is the vast difference in the factor of consciousness.

REINCARNATIONS
(no more evolution of form)

the subtle world, and experiences their impressions partially through the gross body and partially through the subtle body. Here both the gross and the subtle senses are simultaneously used.

This is the stage where God in the man state stands, as it were, on the line of demarcation which delimits the gross world from the subtle world and where the consciousness of God in the man state experiences strange things. With His gross eyes He obtains glimpses of the subtle plane, with His gross ears He hears celestial music of the subtle plane, with His gross nose He enjoys subtle scents. In short, gross-conscious God in the man state, partially on the first plane of the subtle world, experiences subtle impressions with the gross senses.

With further involution of gross consciousness, gross-conscious God gradually experiences completely the first plane of the subtle world. Now the gross consciousness of God in the man state is no longer **gross** consciousness, but is **subtle** consciousness.

Subtle-conscious God in the man state gradually becomes conscious of the second plane of the subtle world as the involution progresses on and on to infold consciousness further and further.

This subtle world is the domain of infinite energy. The infinite and unlimited power, which is an aspect of the infinite trio-nature of God, when radiated from unbounded infinity into the finite worlds of illusion, is translated into the finite and manifested in the domain of the subtle world in the form of infinite energy of the subtle world.

Thus, in the second plane, God in human-form is subtle-conscious, and therefore He is not conscious of the gross body and the mental body—the mind. But God in human-form does work through the gross body and through the mind (the mental body), not directly but on and from the subtle plane.

Therefore even if subtle-conscious God in the man state is unconscious of the gross body and of the mental body, and does not experience directly the gross and mental worlds, still, God in the man state does make use of the gross body (though not directly but from the subtle plane) through various aspects of the gross, and is therefore observed from all outward appearances as an ordinary gross-conscious human-form which eats, drinks, sleeps, sees, feels, hears, and so forth. Similarly, God in the man state, when conscious of the second plane of the subtle world, does use His mental body (*i.e.*, the mind), not directly but through various aspects which give it the outward appearance of being an ordinary gross-conscious human-form having thoughts, desires and emotions.

At this stage, with greater involution of consciousness, subtle-conscious God in the man state on the second plane, gains greater awareness of the infinite energy of the subtle sphere and is now capable of performing tricks or minor miracles of lower degree through the release of this infinite energy, and can demonstrate such powers as converting a dry tree into a green one and vice versa, stopping railway trains and motor cars, filling a dry well with water, and so forth.

This subtle-conscious God in the man state on the second plane experiences the subtle world with the subtle senses of His subtle body. He is now totally **not-conscious** of the gross world, though from all outward appearances He remains and functions as an ordinary man, eating, sleeping, having feelings of pain and pleasure, and so forth, yet actually His involved consciousness experiences not the gross but the subtle sphere and creates fresh subtle impressions through His subtle senses, which are three in number, with faculties only of seeing, smelling and hearing.

Further involution of consciousness makes it possible for God in the man state to experience the third plane of the subtle world. Here subtle consciousness gains greater awareness of the infinite energy of the subtle sphere, and God in the man state experiences greater finite power. In this stage He is capable of performing grand miracles such as giving sight to the blind, restoring limbs to the maimed and sometimes even raising the dead * into life. In this state subtle-conscious God in the man state is also capable of experiencing the different planes and worlds of the subtle sphere, just as a gross-conscious human-form is capable of travelling from one continent to another, using the gross vehicles at his disposal.

The second and third planes of the subtle world are the two major planes which are solely in the domain of the subtle world. The first plane is partially in the domain of the subtle world and partially of the gross world. Similarly the fourth plane is partially of the subtle world and partially of the mental world. For this reason the fourth plane is said to be the threshold of the mental world.

Now, with gradual though progressive gain in the involution of the consciousness of subtle-conscious God in the man state, the consciousness of God experiences the fourth plane of the subtle-*cum*-mental.

In the fourth plane God in the man state is fully conscious of the subtle body and completely experiences the subtle sphere, and therefore He is completely aware of the subtle nature of the subtle sphere which is infinite energy. This is the very same infinite energy which is the finite aspect in the Nothingness of that infinite and unbounded power of God which was latent in God's state of the Everything.

In the fourth plane God in the man state is fully equipped with infinite energy and thus He is now capable of raising the dead and of even creating new forms, in new worlds, breathing with life. Subtle-conscious God in the man state in the fourth plane is in reality infinite energy personified.

This infinite energy of the fourth plane of the subtle-*cum*-mental worlds is not the ordinary so-called energy of the gross world. It is that infinite energy which is called the "breath of all life," or *"pran,"* and which can cause all things to become alive. It is this energy which when infinite can create living things out of dust.

---

* Those on the third plane of consciousness can only raise the dead of the sub-human species.

Although this energy be infinite, it is yet by no means equivalent to the reality of that infinite power of God. This infinite power of God, when translated into Illusion, becomes the finite aspect of the infinite energy of the fourth plane of the subtle-*cum*-mental worlds.

Subtle-conscious God in the man state, possessing the key to the store of the infinite energy of the fourth plane, is now firmly established on the threshold of the mental world, and is confronted by the full blast of the intense desires, emotions and thoughts which are the aspects of Mind of the mental world.

Though the fourth plane is the exalted stage of consciousness where God in the man state consciously experiences Himself as infinite energy personified, yet it is the state of experiences of the so-called "darkest night," because here the consciousness of God in the man state undergoes the experience of being caught, as it were, between "the Devil and the deep." Fired by intense desires and emotions, the overpowering incitement or temptation to wield and use the infinite energy which is at His command, proves a treacherous foe at this juncture when the involution of consciousness of subtle-conscious God in the man state is unfailingly and rapidly progressing towards the mental sphere where it will gain mastery over all desires, emotions and thoughts.

If desires at their zenith emanated by the mental plane, confronting the consciousness of God in the man state in the fourth plane, overpower God (in the man state on the fourth plane), and if the forces generated by the infinite energy at His command are released by Him, then the experience of the liberation of infinite energy at this juncture often proves fatal, especially when He grossly misuses the forces liberated by infinite energy to satisfy selfish ends indiscriminately.

At this juncture on the fourth plane if the power of the infinite energy of the subtle world is indiscriminately liberated, the resultant effect of the complete liberation of that energy is almost unimaginable by gross consciousness. However, an idea could be gathered of that result from the fantastic experiences of the liberation of nuclear energy, which is merely one of the gross aspects of the infinite energy of the subtle world.

Thus, if the involved consciousness of God in the man state succumbs to the temptation of experiencing the complete liberation of infinite energy in the fourth plane of consciousness, the inevitable experience is so severe that the full consciousness gained, and the subtle consciousness experienced, totally disintegrate into the most-finite consciousness, identifying God once again with the most-finite gross form of stone. Consequently, the consciousness of stone-conscious God must once again go through the whole process of the evolution of consciousness, identifying Himself with gross forms until He identifies with man and again wins full consciousness.

It is a fact that when consciousness is once gained it can never be lost, but the disintegration of consciousness from the fourth plane is the one exception to this rule. This disintegration of consciousness occurs only in the case of fourth plane consciousness and that, too, only very, very rarely, when He succumbs to the temptation of misusing the powers of that plane.

If God in the man state in the fourth plane does not misuse the powers of infinite energy but uses them discriminately, without being overpowered by desires,* then with further involution of consciousness the subtle-conscious God in the man state experiences directly the sixth plane of the mental world, skipping over the experiences of the fifth plane of the mental world.

But if God in the man state in the fourth plane neither uses nor abuses the powers of infinite energy, then gradually, with further involution of consciousness, subtle-conscious God in the

---

* [Desires must be **consciously** wiped out because they can create new impressions and in turn further desires which may lead to further binding actions. Consciousness is preoccupied with such impressions and their physical expression rather than with the real Self. If these impressions are wiped away consciously, the soul (*atma*) will then begin to perceive the Truth, and will begin to emancipate itself from the tyranny of worldly desires. The individual (*jivatma*) minus life (of desires) becomes soul (*atma*), and is always the unconscious Almighty. It is while we are living that life must be given up. To renounce worldly desires while retaining consciousness of unconsciousness is the goal of life. Ed.]

man state in the fourth plane of consciousness crosses the threshold of the mental world and begins to experience the fifth plane of consciousness.

The fifth and sixth planes of consciousness are fundamentally the planes of the mental sphere of the Mind. In the mental world mental-conscious God in the man state is master of His mind, whereas in the gross and subtle worlds when gross- and subtle-conscious, He was the slave of His mind.

With the progress of the involution of consciousness of subtle-conscious God in the man state, the experiences of the fifth plane of the mental world are realized by the mental sense which is only that of **seeing.**

In the man state, when God is mental-conscious He is not conscious of the gross or subtle bodies but He does work through the gross body and sutble body, not directly but on and from the mental plane. So even if mental-conscious God in the man state is not conscious of the gross and subtle bodies, and therefore does not realize the experiences of the gross and subtle worlds, He still can unconsciously utilize the gross body through various aspects of the gross. He is thus observed eating, drinking, sleeping, seeing, hearing and feeling as in an ordinary gross-conscious human-form, although He is all the while conscious only of the mental body with His mental sense of only "seeing." Similarly He can unconsciously utilize His subtle body through various aspects of infinite energy and is thus observed moving about actively and performing acts while all the time He is only conscious of the mental body—the mind—and only consciously experiences the mental world with His mental sense. Mental-conscious God in the man state in the mental sphere has now only one sense, and that is of "seeing." The mind persists through the fifth plane of consciousness. In the sixth plane of consciousness, the mind itself becomes the Inner Eye and sees God. In the seventh plane of consciousness, the mind is annihilated.

Hence it is that mental-conscious God in the man state on the fifth plane experiences the impressions generated through

His mental sense of "seeing" and consequently experiences the mental world with the mental body (mind). He is now conscious only of mind. In this stage, God in the man state is capable of controlling the minds of gross-conscious and subtle-conscious states of God in subtle-conscious and gross-conscious human-forms.

But in the fifth plane, mental-conscious God in the man state is totally incapable of performing any miracles because He is now in the mental sphere and no longer in the subtle sphere of infinite energy which, when released, resulted in miraculous powers. Yet, because He is mental-conscious and is about to become "Mind" personified, He controls the minds of the subtle-conscious state of God and becomes the source which incites those in the state of subtle consciousness to perform miracles. He is the One Who, in the mental-conscious state, according to the desire and will of His mind, is capable of checking, controlling or guiding the minds of those in the subtle-conscious planes either to perform the miracles or not, though He Himself in His mental-conscious state cannot perform any miracle.

God in the man state of mental consciousness is capable of creating and controlling the thoughts, desires and emotions of all minds in gross- and subtle-conscious states. He is Himself stable as soon as He experiences the state of the fifth plane, from which state the consciousness involved thus far can never devolve nor disintegrate.

As the involution of consciousness of mental-conscious God in the man state gradually progresses deeper and deeper, He experiences His mastery over the mind, and the conscious-ness of mental-conscious God is said to be Mind personified. Thus God in the man state now becomes fully conscious of the mind or the mental body and experiences the whole of the men-tal sphere or the mental world in the sixth plane of mental con-sciousness. This experience is of "seeing" God in His original state face to face. This "seeing" is the seeing of the mental con-sciousness with the mental sense of "seeing." In other words, God in the man state sees God everywhere and in everything.

Right from the first plane up through the sixth plane the involution of consciousness progressed gradually and consistently as the consciousness of God underwent fewer and scarcer experiences of multifarious and diverse opposite impressions, which grew fainter and fainter. Therefore, during the progress of the involution of consciousness of God, the diverse opposite impressions gradually lessened and became fainter until the involved consciousness of God in the sixth plane was fully conscious of the mental body and experienced the mental world in full with practically no impressions at all except for a last faint trace of residual impressions of opposites. In other words, the involved consciousness fully identifies with the mind and God tends to realize that He is Mind. Now God in the man state as Mind has the last finite impression that He as Mind sees God face to face in all things except in His Self. This is the state of God in the man state in the sixth plane of consciousness.

This mental-conscious God in the man state of the sixth plane, practically void of all impressions at this point and only conscious of Mind, is now confronted by God Himself and sees Him face to face, and also sees Him in all things, but He does not see His Self in God because He is still impressed with the consciousness of Mind and takes Himself as Mind.

This mental-conscious God in the man state, associating Himself with Mind, is conscious of Himself as Mind and experiences Himself as still something other than God, because He actually sees God face to face with His mental consciousness. Then, too, He sees God much more vividly and intensively than, in the gross or subtle states of God, He can see the gross and subtle objects in the gross and subtle worlds.

In this stage the consciousness of God, which had experienced diverse and innumerable opposite impressions, now experiences the last trace of dual impressions of opposites. Therefore, mental-conscious God in the man state on the sixth plane is yet conscious of duality, that is, identifies Himself as Mind and differentiates Himself from God.

In order to understand the involution of consciousness in

the mental sphere more clearly it is necessary to understand that the mental sphere of the fifth and sixth planes of consciousness is the domain of the Mind. This Mind of the mental planes has two sections.

In the first section the state of Mind is inquiring or reflecting. In this state Mind functions as Thoughts—high thoughts, low thoughts, good thoughts, bad thoughts, material thoughts, spiritual thoughts and thoughts of every kind, type and state.

In the second section the state of Mind is impressive or sympathetic. In this state Mind functions as Feelings—feelings of sufferings and emotions, feelings of desires and longings, feelings of pangs of separation and feelings of every kind and type and state.

Since Mind of the mental sphere has distinct dual functions, it is inevitable that the experiences in the field of Mind (*i.e.*, the mental sphere) must be distinctively of two kinds also.

Thus the mental sphere has two domains. Therefore the domain of the fifth plane of consciousness is of thoughts, and the domain of the sixth plane of consciousness is of feelings.

Consequently, the consciousness of mental-conscious God in the man state in the fifth plane identifies with the first section of Mind, which is inquiring or reflecting Mind. Therefore, this mental-conscious God in the man state of the fifth plane is the creator and master of thoughts, as He is "Thoughts" personified, and is accordingly capable of controlling only the thought section of all minds of all gross- and subtle-conscious states of God. This is often misinterpreted as controlling the **minds** of all gross- and subtle-conscious states of God, but the fact is that God in the fifth plane of consciousness does not control the mind as a whole, but controls only that state of Mind which functions as **thoughts.**

Mental-conscious God in the man state in the fifth plane of consciousness, while identifying Himself as inquiring or reflecting Mind emanating only thoughts, does not identify Himself with the second section of Mind and is therefore still incapable of establishing mastery over feelings (*i.e.*, emotions and desires).

With greater involution of consciousness, mental-conscious God in the man state of the fifth plane progresses into the sixth plane of consciousness wherein he gains consciousness of the second section of Mind of the mental sphere and thus tends to identify Himself with that second section of Mind (*i.e.,* impressive or sympathetic Mind).

Mental-conscious God in the man state in the sixth plane of consciousness experiences the mental world, with the mental sense of seeing, through complete identification with feelings, and thus God in the man state is not Thoughts but is Feelings personified. Wherefore He experiences consciously the feelings of seeing God face to face continuously in all things and everywhere. He feels seeing God everywhere continuously but He cannot feel seeing Himself in God as God. For this reason He cannot reconcile feelings of sight of God with His own identity as God, because He still identifies Himself with feelings. He feels for, longs for and pangs for **union with God** Whom He at this stage feels seeing face to face.

This identification with the second section of Mind (feelings) is the state of God in the man state where the predominant aspect of divine love, which eventually leads to union with God (*i.e.,* realization of the God state consciously), is manifested most forcefully.

Hence it should be clear that the fifth plane of the mental sphere is the state of full consciousness of thoughts only. The mastery over control and creation of thoughts alone is established, and there is no mastery or control over feelings of desires and emotions. But the sixth plane of the mental sphere is the state of full consciousness of feelings, and thus the mastery over control and creation of feelings is established and no more scope is now left for even a single thought to penetrate into the domain of feelings.

The sixth plane consciousness is **thought-less** and governs the **feelings** of all of the gross- and subtle-conscious states of God. This is often misinterpreted as mastery over the **hearts** of all those in the gross- and subtle-conscious states of God. He does not govern or regulate the so-called hearts but controls and governs that second section of Mind in the mental sphere which emanates feelings of emotions and desires.

The loving of God and the longing for His union is really and fully demonstrated in the sixth plane of consciousness. Only when the sixth plane of the mental sphere is transcended, does Illusion vanish with the vanishing of the last trace of impressions, and Reality is realized.

Mental-conscious God in the man state on the sixth plane is still experiencing duality, because God in this state of consciousness finds Himself as Mind and not as God.

This experience of duality lingers on and on until the final involution of consciousness attains the seventh plane of consciousness. This is the final and seventh stage in the process of involution of consciousness when the full consciousness of God in the man state is now fully withdrawn inwards, so completely that it is now fixed and focussed onto Himself rather than onto the objects of His own creation.

Now that full consciousness has been fully involved, the objects of Nothingness, which apparently appeared to exist, vanish completely together with their impressions.

With complete annihilation of impressions of the associations of the Nothing, the impressioned consciousness of God in the man state is spontaneously transformed into the unimpressioned or impressionless consciousness of God which makes God in the man state experience the "passing-away-in" His original state of absolute vacuum. It is but natural that the full consciousness, fully involved, and now free from even the slightest trace of any impression, should give no other experience but that of the original, absolute vacuum state of God which once prevailed and which is now experienced **consciously.**

This full consciousness, fully involved, is the super-consciousness or the *mahachaitanya*. The unconscious God in the original, absolute vacuum state is now fully conscious, or super-conscious, of His original state of God in the Beyond the Beyond state.

This "passing-away-in" the absolute vacuum of the original state of God is called attaining the *fana* of the seventh plane of consciousness.

In Sufi terms *fana* means "passing-away-in." *Fana* has two stages: the first stage of *fana* is the conscious experience of the absolute vacuum state, and the second stage of *fana* or *fana-fillah* is the conscious experience of the "I am God" state.

Fana-fillah, the second stage, is the Goal of God in the man state where God in human form, that is, as man, ultimately realizes the "I am God" state with full consciousness. This is the state of final *majzoobiyat* as it is termed by the Sufis.

Much before the first stage of *fana* is attained, God in the man state, as man, had full consciousness of the limited ego or "I," mind, energy, body and the world in an ordinary awake state, because the full consciousness of God in the man state, as man, was directly focussed on them through their finite impressions. And as soon as the consciousness of God in the man state, as man, began to involve, the involved consciousness experienced gradually the six planes of sub-super-consciousness through impressions gathered and spent in each of the six planes. When the sub-super-consciousness completely involved, that is, was withdrawn inwards towards Himself, then God in the man state, as man, gained the seventh plane of super-consciousness devoid of all impressions. This was the final stage in attaining the Goal.

Simultaneously with the complete involution of consciousness, and on gaining super-consciousness, the mind is finally completely annihilated and vanishes once and for all time together with all impressions. The false experiences of the limited ego or "I," mind, energy, body and the world all disappear forever, vanishing completely, because all these experiences were but the outcome of the impressions generated out of the Nothing, which literally meant nothing and were nothing.

Consequently, with the vanishing of the limited ego or "I," mind, energy, body (typifying happiness) and worlds with all of their corresponding paraphernalia, a state of absolute vacuum is spontaneously experienced by the consciousness, which remains eternally when once it is gained. At this stage God, in the man state as man, with full consciousness as super-consciousness, is now only conscious of absolute vacuum—the consciousness is now fixed and focussed on "Absolute Vacuum" itself.

This vacuum is absolute in its entirety; vacuum alone prevails and there is an entire absence of the Nothing as well as of the Everything. This is therefore called the "Divine, Absolute Vacuum," and it is not born of Illusion, but it is born of Reality.

This state of divine vacuum prevails just at the instant when the Nothing disappears or vanishes and just immediately before the Everything fills in that vacuum to give conscious experience of the reality of the "I am God" state.

This is the first stage of *fana* where all that is of the Nothing vanishes completely and where the super-consciousness is focussed only on absolute vacuum, which now prevails as it prevails eternally in the original God-Is state of God in original, divine sound sleep.

Therefore, in the first stage of *fana* the consciousness of God, in the man state as man, is not of the limited self or ego or "I," mind, energy, body and worlds, nor is the consciousness even of God or of the unlimited Self or Ego or "I," universal mind, unbounded energy, universal body and universes; because, in this first stage of *fana* only the consciousness of absolute vacuum prevails. This vacuum is also divine; it is not of Illusion but it is of Reality. In this first stage of *fana* the super-consciousness of God, in the man state as man, experiences the "passing-away-in" the absolute vacuum state of the original God-Is state, and is thus conscious now only of absolute vacuum.

As has already been said, this same absolute vacuum state is also established in the everyday sound sleep state of a normal man where the limited ego or "I," mind, energy, body and the worlds also vanish and the consciousness gained remains dormant.

The only difference, which truly makes a world of difference, between the absolute vacuum state of the everyday sound sleep state of man and the experience of the absolute vacuum in the first stage of *fana* is, that although the same absolute vacuum is established also in *fana,* yet in *fana* the consciousness no longer remains dormant. In this stage it is fully and completely matured consciousness, now actually experiencing the very same absolute vacuum state as the original state of God.

The experience of the first stage of *fana* is of the *nirvana* state.

Nirvana is that state where apparently "God Is Not." This is the only state where "God Is Not" and "Consciousness Is." This experience of the first stage of *fana* is what Buddha emphasized, but later on it was misinterpreted as Buddha having emphasized that there was no God. The reality, however, is that God Is; but in the absolute vacuum state of the first stage of *fana* only consciousness remains, experiencing absolute vacuum.

As it can never happen for God not to exist, in the state of *nirvana* God plays the part of consciousness itself, which consciousness is sometimes termed super-consciousness or *mahachaitanya.*

The second stage of *fana* follows this *nirvana* state and the "I am God" state is experienced consciously.

However, it is only in some cases that the first stage of *fana* is immediately followed by the second stage of *fana* called *"fana-fillah"* where the annihilated false and limited ego or "I" is replaced by the real and infinite, unlimited "I" on which the super-consciousness now becomes automatically focussed. Simultaneously the absolute vacuum is automatically filled by the experience of the Infinite.

The super-consciousness of God in the man state, as man, now fixed and focussed on the unlimited "I," spontaneously identifies man with God the Infinite. Simultaneously with the identification, the super-consciousness of God the Infinite experiences the "I am God" state. This is the Goal.

Attainment of the Goal is to attain the *nirvikalpa samadhi.**

---

* The soul has necessarily to pass through the state of *nirvana* to attain Liberation (*mukti*). Escape from the round of birth and death is attained

Just as man goes to sleep every night and must wake up every day in the state of man, so also when one goes into divine sleep one must wake up in the Divine. Similarly the first stage of *fana* is the sound sleep state with full consciousness, and the second stage of *fana* which is *fana-fillah* is the state of awakening in God as God.

When the first stage of *fana* is immediately followed by the second stage of *fana-fillah,*[20] in some cases the consciousness of the limited "I," "self," mind, energy, body and the worlds does not come back; but the consciousness, now as super-consciousness, of the unlimited "I" only exists as identified with the universal Self, God. The super-consciousness now experiences the "I am God," *"Aham Brahmasmi"* or *"Anal Haqq"* state. This is the experience of *nirvikalpa samadhi,* meaning thereby "Undoubtedly I am God." This is experienced because in *fana-fillah* the *atma* consciously merges completely in *Paramatma,* or in *fana-fillah* the soul achieves complete union with the Over-Soul.

This experience is the Goal and it was attained only after the evolution of the consciousness, latent in the Nothing, took place when the latent finite Nothing manifested as infinite Nothingness. The evolved consciousness, while infinitely entangling itself in the field of the Nothingness, experienced this false and finite Nothingness as real and infinite. Ultimately, when this consciousness involved, it could gradually experience the infinite falsity of the infinitely false Nothingness, and eventually realize the infinite reality of the God-the-Infinite as the Everything beyond doubt and beyond limitations and as eternal existence in the "I am God" state of *fana-fillah.*

This *fana-fillah* is the goal where the "I am God" state is experienced, for example, by those persons who are called *"Majzoobs"* (one being overpowered by God, or one whom God controls). These persons are also known as *"Brahmi*

---

both in *nirvana* and *nirvikalpa.* It is because of this that *nirvana* is supposed to be the Goal, but the fact is that the real Goal for one in human form is to attain *nirvikalpa.* And, there is a world of difference between *nirvana* as Goal and *nirvikalpa* the Goal.

Bhoots." In this state one constantly, continually and consciously experiences the "I am God" state together with the continued and conscious experience of the infinite trio-nature of God, *sat-chit-anand* (*i.e.,* infinite power, infinite knowledge and infinite bliss), as one's own infinite nature.

So it is that self-conscious God, in the man state as man in the seventh plane, is now fully conscious of Self as infinite and eternal. He is now also conscious of the source of energy and mind which were nothing but the finite aspects of His own infinite power and infinite knowledge, which He experiences now, while being continually in infinite bliss.

In His travail to gain Self-consciousness, the indivisible, eternal God, unconscious of His infinite state, gathered and experienced innumerable diverse impressions, and all the while associated Himself with finite and ephemeral existences, unfurling the gross, subtle and mental worlds, while **evolving** gross consciousness of the gross world and while **involving** consciousness of the subtle and mental planes of the subtle and mental worlds. The final involution of the consciousness of God culminated in conscious realization of His Self in His infinite state.

Consequently when the consciousness of God gained consciousness of Self and experienced infinite power, knowledge and bliss, God realized that He exists eternally in infinite bliss and that all through the travail of gaining Self-consciousness, the impressions, experiences and associations and dissociations of the gross, subtle and mental bodies and worlds were of the Nothing and were but vacant dreams. He realized, too, that identification with gross bodies, creatures and human beings, and all experiences of the three worlds and the six planes with all of their paraphernalia, had their relative existences sustained and maintained as long as His consciousness was immature. Maturity was only attained in the seventh plane with consciousness fully involved. This led God to realize His Self, or made God fully conscious of God-realization. In other words, God's own infinite state was consciously realized by God Him-

self when He attained the "I am God" state.*

In other words, God first goes through the becoming process in the gross; that is, in the gross, God becomes the **body** of *anna bhuvan* (gross sphere). Then in the subtle He becomes the **energy** of *pran bhuvan* (subtle sphere). Then in the mental He becomes the **mind** of *mano bhuvan* (mental sphere). Beyond this in *vidnyan,* God becomes God—that which He was and is and always will be. Therefore God, Who was originally unconscious, now becomes oblivious of oblivion itself and gets the real and final answer to His original first word, "Who am I?", as "I am God." Thus in the gross, subtle and mental spheres God becomes actually what He really **is not;** and in *vidnyan* He becomes actually what He really **is.** Originally God was God; now God has become God.

Just because God, after "passing-away-in" His original state of absolute vacuum in the first stage of *fana,* realizes His own infinite state of "I am God" in the second stage of *fana,* this *fana* (*i.e., fana-fillah*) becomes and is the goal.

Attainment of this goal means the end of the First Divine Journey, which began with gnosis and which ended, after traversing all planes of consciousness, in deification.

The second stage of *fana* is deification which means man has become God. Man now is God and experiences God's knowledge, God's powers, and God's bliss; but this is not "Perfection" as yet, although it is the goal. At the second stage of *fana* or the *fana-fillah,* which is the end of the first divine journey, man has **entered** God and thus has become God, but has not yet entered God's life. Man at the end of the first divine journey simply realizes that he is God and simply experiences the "I am God" state together with the experiences of infinite

---

* The happiness of God-realization is the Goal of all Creation. The real happiness which comes through realizing God is worth all physical and mental sufferings in the universe. Then all suffering is as if it were not. The happiness of God-realization is self-sustained, eternally fresh and unfailing, boundless and indescribable; and it is for this happiness that the world has sprung into existence.

power, knowledge and bliss, and enjoys the state of infinite bliss.

After the Goal is attained at the end of the first divine journey, but very rarely however, God as man, now in the God state, can leave infinite bliss and come down to normal consciousness from the super-conscious "I am God" state and begin to experience the state of *baqa*, thus entering the Second Divine Journey.

The Sufi term *"baqa"* means "abiding-in." [21]

To come down to normal consciousness from the super-conscious "I am God" state and to experience the "abiding-in" God state would mean getting established in the very life of God. Thus in *baqa* the life of God in a human being is established. This means that in *baqa* man establishes himself as God consciously. This consciousness is called *"sulukiyat"* or the normal consciousness of being "established in the life of God." Distinct from this is the *majzoobiyat* or "being drowned or absorbed by infinite bliss" in the state of "I am God." Accordingly, God as man, experiencing the state of *baqa,* is called the **real** *"Salik"* in Sufi terminology. This *baqa* of Reality and Divinity is called *"baqa-billah."* In Vedanta it is known as *"atmapratisthapana."*

The *Salik* not only experiences infinite power and infinite knowledge while in infinite bliss, as in *majzoobiyat,* but, now being the *Salik,* He consciously accumulates all the infinite power, infinite knowledge and infinite bliss while being established in the life of God with the normal consciousness of His *sulukiyat.*

But before finally and really "passing-away-in" the reality of the ultimate *fana-fillah* state with full consciousness completely matured, and before getting established in the final *baqabillah* of Divinity, generally speaking in terms of Illusion, there are as many individualized experiences of *fana-baqa* as there are varied and innumerable species and states of life in Creation.

Nevertheless, three fundamental types of *fana-baqa* include all the individualized experiences of *fana-baqa.*

The first of the three fundamental types is the rudimentary. This type is the *fana-baqa* of the phenomenal, false life in

Illusion experienced by all who, daily "passing-away-in" *fana* gain *baqa* to "abide-in" Illusion every day. This rudimentary *fana-baqa* of the ordinary phenomenal, false life is composed of the ordinary sound sleep state and the ordinary awake state.

As stated before, even when one with all of the impressions of Illusion "passes-away-in" sound sleep, the same original divine absolute vacuum of the God-Is state is established, where never anything existed and where nothing ever exists except the one infinite and only Reality as the Everything, which is called the Infinitude of God in His God-Is state. When the impressions of Illusion, with which one goes to sleep, wake one up, one abides in Illusion itself in the awake state and establishes everyday life in Illusion.

Accordingly, in everyday life, when one goes into sound sleep, *fana* is established as one daily "passes-away-in" the original God state without consciousness. And when one wakes up daily, *baqa* is gained to "abide-in" the everyday life of Illusion, as long as sound sleep does not overpower and drag one, once again, into the state of the daily *fana* which is the One's original, divine state of absolute vacuum.

The second type of *fana-baqa* is of the planes on the Path towards attainment of the goal and differs from the rudimentary type of the ordinary phenomenal, false life in Illusion, although this second type of *fana-baqa* of the planes is also illusion.

In every plane, from the first through the sixth plane on the path, the full consciousness evolved is being gradually withdrawn inwards or involved. Hence the *fana-baqa* of the planes is in accordance with the impressions impregnating the involving consciousness and differs from the first type of rudimentary *fana-baqa* of the impressioned consciousness that is fully evolved or is still in the process of evolution.

Every plane on the path towards the goal of *fana-fillah* has its *fana-baqa* while the fully evolved consciousness is being gradually involved in conjunction with progressive advancement in the planes.

But the generalized meaning of the Sufi term *"fana"* is the "passing-away-in" the absolute vacuum of the original God-Is state. Therefore, whether the *fana* is of the rudimentary type of the ordinary, phenomenal false life or of the second type of the planes on the path, it does not make any difference at all. In both types the *fana* ("passing-away-in") is fundamentally the same, for daily in the sound sleep state the impressioned consciousness, in both cases, "passes-away-in" the same state of absolute vacuum, regardless of all the differences in the types of impressions of Illusion.

Although the *fana* is always the same in both the **evolving** consciousness and the **involving** consciousness, yet it is the type of impressions of Illusion with which the consciousness is impregnated, while abiding in Illusion during the awake state, that really matters, and that does create the differentiation when "passing-away-in" the sound sleep state or in the state of *fana*.

For example, the *fana* of an animal or a creature in the sound sleep state "passing-away-in" the absolute vacuum, with its own particular impressions of Illusion, differs completely from the *fana* of a human being in the sound sleep state "passing-away-in" the absolute vacuum with his own particular impressions of Illusion. Similarly, the impressions of Illusion of an ordinary human being will be quite different from the impressions of Illusion of a human being in the planes of the path.

In all cases, though the different types of *fana* remain always as *fana,* yet the different impressions impregnating individual consciousness in the *baqa* of the awake state give rise to the individualized *fana* of each and all species and states of life in Creation.

In contrast with that, when the *baqa* of the individualized life is gained in the awake state after the sound sleep state of *fana,* the *baqa,* which in Sufi terms means "abiding-in," establishes in Illusion the everyday individualized life of Illusion in accordance with the predominant impressions with which the individualized life had "passed away" from the variety of impressions of Illusion in the state of its individualized *fana,* in the sound sleep state. As such, every individualized *baqa* completely differs from every other *baqa*, because when this individualized *baqa* is gained in the awake state, the impressions of the impressioned consciousness of every individualized life are solely responsible for establishing in Illusion the individualized life of Illusion.

Hence it is that in regular, unfailing succession the *fana* of Illusion in the sound sleep state is invariably followed by the *baqa* of Illusion in the awake state, which in turn gets lost in the inevitable *fana* only to alternate and re-establish again and again—day after day, year after year, and life after life—irrespective of whether this *fana* or *baqa* is of the ordinary, phenomenal false life or is of the planes on the Path. It is never stable as long as it is of the Illusion.

As long as individualized life does not really and finally "pass-away-in" the *fana-fillah* of Reality and become established in the abiding *baqa-billah* of Divinity, it is obvious that there are bound to be innumerable and diverse types and groups of *fana-baqa* of Illusion in accordance with the persisting impressions that consistently impress the evolving and the involving consciousness of individualized life in *baqa*.

In every plane also, from the first through the sixth plane of involving consciousness, there is bound to be a particular type of *baqa* for each of the six planes, in accordance with the particular impressions of the Illusion of each plane.

When a man is said to be on the first plane his fully evolved consciousness is beginning to involve, and his full consciousness remains focussed on the first plane of the subtle sphere, because the impressions of the first plane consistently impregnating his involving consciousness make him abide in the first plane and lead him to experience the illusion of this plane. Even though the gross body of the man on the first plane is exactly like the gross body of a man **not** on the first plane, and though the man on the first plane also sleeps and wakes up exactly like an ordinary man of the everyday phenomenal, false life, yet, because his involving consciousness is directly focussed on the first plane, he "passes-away-in" the sound sleep state of the first plane *fana* with the impressions of the illusion of the first plane, and wakes up daily to get established in the first plane *baqa* to "abide-in" the first plane, and to experience the impressions of that plane.

The difference between the *fana-baqa* of the man who enters the planes of the path and of the man who is not on the planes of the path is that the former can be likened to a man who, after living for many years in a certain place, severs all of his past connections and sets out on a world tour, travelling from one place to another, crossing continents one after the other. Although this man would be daily going to sleep, and awakening the next day, as he was accustomed to sleeping and awakening every day in his first habitat, yet now in the course of his world tour he would be "passing-away-in" sound sleep and would be daily waking up evidently with the predominant impressions of his completely changed environments and novel experiences.[22]

In short, he who enters the first plane of involving consciousness eventually experiences the first plane fully. This man, who is getting established in the first plane, establishes his living in this "world of his own" and therefore he sleeps in this plane and wakes up every day in this plane as well. In exactly the same way, all individualized consciousness in all other planes "passes-away-in" the *fana* of those particular planes to wake up in such planes and establish the everyday life *baqa* in these particular planes.

Nevertheless, the *fana-baqa* of every plane of the path is fundamentally of the same type, because it pertains only to consciousness that is **involving** gradually and not to that of the evolving nor of the evolved consciousness. Whatever difference there is to differentiate the *fana-baqa* of one plane from another plane would only be such as would exist between two men living on two different continents of the same earth and having their own individual impressions of that particular part of the earth on which each lives. The man in America has his own impressions and relative experiences of his individualized life; the same is true of the man in Asia who has his own impressions and experiences related to his continent which is quite different from America.

But the fundamental fact remains that both men live on the same earth. Despite the vast difference between the impressions and the consequent experiences of these two men, yet when both sleep, they both "pass-away-in" sound sleep. And, whether one sleeps on a bed of velvet and the other on a bed of hay, it is quite immaterial when both can equally enjoy the same sound sleep state. In like manner, when both wake up they both can live their individual lives in illusion on the same earth, irrespective of the difference in their impressions and their consequent relative experiences due to living on different continents. Thus the *fana-baqas* of all the planes on the path are not in any way different fundamentally, although each and every plane on the path has its own *fana* and *baqa* when individualized life on the planes is under consideration.

Just as the rudimentary first type of *fana* and *baqa* includes all the individualized *fanas* and *baqas* of dogs, horses, camels, elephants, of all creatures and human beings that live the phenomenal, false life of illusion in the gross world, so also the second type of *fana* and *baqa* of the planes on the path includes all the individualized *fana-baqas* of each and all on every plane from the first through the sixth planes of the illusory subtle and mental worlds.

When a man in a particular plane, with his consciousness gradually involving, becomes completely dazed by the enchanting experiences of the plane, the man is said to be a *majzoob* of this particular plane.* Such a *majzoob* is completely absorbed and overpowered by the impressions of Illusion of the plane which consistently impregnate his consciousness. Even in the awake state this *majzoob* of the plane behaves as if he were completely intoxicated by and drowned in the enchantment of

---

* The *majzoob* and *salik* of the planes should not be confused with the **real** *Majzoob* of the seventh plane known as *"Majzoob-e-Kamil"* (perfect *Majzoob*), nor the **real** *Salik* of the seventh plane.

the plane. Such a man is commonly known as a *"mast,"* meaning thereby that the man is "God-intoxicated."

On the other hand, if a man in a particular plane does not get absorbed in and overpowered by the fascinating experiences of the plane, but continues to maintain his poise throughout while his involving consciousness is persistently impressed by the impressions of Illusion of that plane, he is then said to be a *"salik"* of the particular plane.* Such a *salik,* to all external appearances, behaves like a very normal man of the world even though his consciousness is progressively involving and is completely dissociated from the gross world as far as his consciousness, fully focussed on the particular plane, is concerned. The *sulukiyat* and *masti* of each plane are different.

There are, however, certain cases when a man in a particular plane is sometimes completely drowned in and absorbed by the fascination of the experiences of the plane and behaves like a *majzoob,* and at other times he regains his poise and behaves like an ordinary, normal *salik* of the plane. Such a man on the plane is said to be a *majzoob-salik* of the plane if the predominant behavior is that of a *majzoob,* and a *salik-majzoob* of the plane if the predominant behaviour is that of a *salik.* Such a state in Illusion may be compared with the *turiya avastha* at the Divine Junction in Reality.

The third type of *fana-baqa* is of the seventh plane of the final involution of consciousness and is the real *fana-fillah* of the Reality and the real *baqa-billah* of the Divinity. When the impressioned consciousness of individualized life is totally and finally relieved of all impressions of the Illusion, and when this unburdened or impressionless individualized Self consciously "passes-away-in" the original, divine absolute vacuum to gain the *fana-fillah* or the "I am God" state, the goal is finally attained. This is the state of **real** *majzoobiyat.*[23]

The only but infinite difference between the *fanas* of all the different individualized species and states of illusory life and

---

* [See footnote page 145. Ed.]

the final and real *fana* of the divine life is that in the former the consciousness is **nil** while in the latter full consciousness prevails.

After the state of *fana-fillah,* the state of *baqa-billah* is established by some individualized selves to live the life of God as "Man-God" on the earth. Such a "Man-God" lives at one and the same time in all states of life and in all planes, the life of man in Illusion—knowing Illusion as Illusion—and of God in Reality. This is the state of **real** *sulukiyat.*

After attaining the state of *fana-fillah* and before establishing the state of *baqa-billah,* there is also a state of *turiya avastha* at the Divine Junction between *fana-fillah* and *baqa-billah.* In this state there is sometimes the experience of real *majzoobiyat* of the *fana-fillah* and sometimes the experience of real *sulukiyat* of the *baqa-billah.* This is the state of the **real** *Majzoob-Salik* or *Salik-Majzoob* as the case may be.

The consciousness of the false limited "I," which was there before *fana,* matured through the process of involution, and the limited false "I" was replaced by the real unlimited "I" in *fana-fillah.* In *baqa-billah* this matured consciousness is now focussed once again and is fixed on the "I" as the real unlimited "I," on the mind as Universal Mind, on energy as Unbounded Energy and on the body as the Universal Body called the *"mahakarana sharir."* An important fact must be noted here:—that in the state of *baqa-billah* **simultaneously** the same consciousness is also focussed and fixed on the limited "I," mind, energy and body, wherefore the *Salik* consciously experiences the false as falsity with the false, and the Real as Reality with the Real.

Consequently, in God's state of *baqa-billah,* the same consciousness **simultaneously** experiences the dual experiences of "I am God" and "I am human." Along with this dual experience the same consciousness spontaneously also experiences, without break, the infinite knowledge, power and bliss of God along with the experiences of the weaknesses and sufferings of humanity.

It follows that in God's state of *baqa-billah,* God, in the form of an ordinary human being, establishes Himself in His divine life or, man "abides-in" the life of God.

In short, *baqa-billah* is that state of God where "abiding-in" or getting established in God is experienced by those who are defined as "*Saliks*" or "*Jivanmuktas.*" [24, 25] The *Salik* continually and consciously experiences simultaneously the dual experience of the "I am God" state and "I am human" state, and accumulates infinite knowledge, power and bliss, simultaneously experiencing human weaknesses and sufferings, knowing their falsity to be based on the manifestation of the finite Nothing that manifests out of His own state of being Everything and Infinite.

In *baqa-billah,* the life of God-in-human being established, man as God experiences the *sahaj samadhi.* This means that man as God simultaneously, without the least effort, has continually and automatically the dual experience of God and of man. This is the state of Perfection.

Perfection generally carries with it the sense of the highest pitch of, or the extreme type of, accomplishment, and Perfection as such cannot become more perfect. But when the term "Perfection" is used in terms of Divinity, there are three types of Perfection in the state of *sulukiyat* of *baqa-billah:*—

The first type is known as "*Kamil*"—The Perfect One.

The second type is known as "*Akmal*"—The Most Perfect One.

The third type is known as "*Mukammil*"—The Supremely Perfect One.

There is absolutely no difference whatsoever in their continual and conscious experience of the eternal Reality, but the degrees of comparison that are attached to the perfection are due to the difference in the function of the **offices** of "Perfection." Hence, due to differences in function, different attributes are attached to each type of Perfection.

The *Kamil* can spontaneously give conscious experience of the realization of God to only **one** man and make only that man

THE FOUR JOURNEYS

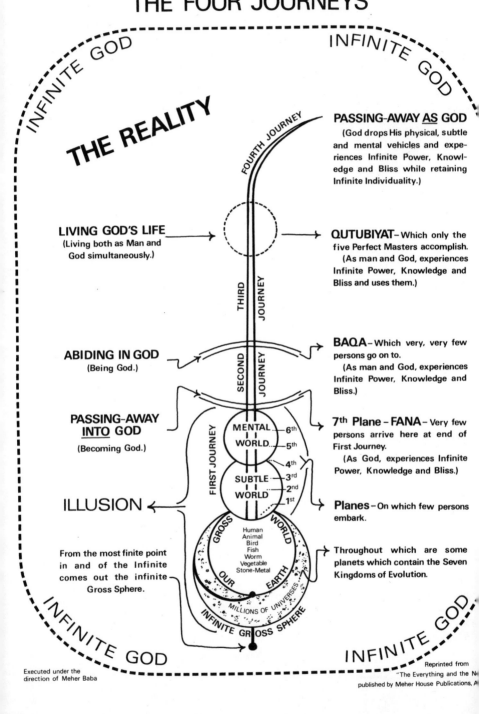

THE REALITY

FOURTH JOURNEY

PASSING-AWAY AS GOD
(God drops His physical, subtle and mental vehicles and experiences Infinite Power, Knowledge and Bliss while retaining Infinite Individuality.)

LIVING GOD'S LIFE
(Living both as Man and God simultaneously.)

THIRD JOURNEY

QUTUBIYAT—Which only the five Perfect Masters accomplish.
(As man and God, experiences Infinite Power, Knowledge and Bliss and uses them.)

ABIDING IN GOD
(Being God.)

SECOND JOURNEY

BAQA—Which very, very few persons go on to.
(As man and God, experiences Infinite Power, Knowledge and Bliss.)

PASSING-AWAY INTO GOD
(Becoming God.)

FIRST JOURNEY

MENTAL WORLD — 6th
— 5th
— 4th
SUBTLE — 3rd
WORLD — 2nd
— 1st

GROSS WORLD

7th Plane – FANA – Very few persons arrive here at end of First Journey.
(As God, experiences Infinite Power, Knowledge and Bliss.)

ILLUSION

Human
Animal
Bird
Fish
Worm
Vegetable
Stone-Metal

OUR EARTH

MILLIONS OF UNIVERSES

INFINITE GROSS SPHERE

Planes—On which few persons embark.

From the most finite point in and of the Infinite comes out the infinite Gross Sphere.

Throughout which are some planets which contain the Seven Kingdoms of Evolution.

INFINITE GOD   INFINITE GOD

INFINITE GOD   INFINITE GOD

Executed under the direction of Meher Baba

Reprinted from "The Everything and the No published by Meher House Publications, A like unto him in the eternal experience of the Reality. The *Akmal* can make **many** like unto him in experience; whereas the *Mukammil* can make not only **any number,** even all in the Creation,* like unto him in the experience of the eternal Reality, but he can also spontaneously bestow on **any number** the transfiguration of their physical bodies and even make their physique **appear and live and experience** like unto his own physical body in the gross world, together with giving the eternal conscious experience of the Reality.

Baqa-billah is the end of the second divine journey. In between the states of *fana-fillah* and *baqa-billah,* at the Divine Junction (*muqam-e-furutat*), there is the state of *turiya avastha* (*fana-ma-al-baqa*).

Turiya avastha is that state where **sometimes** the superconsciousness gives the experience of the "I am God" state and where **sometimes** super-consciousness gives the experience of the "I am human" state of normal consciousness.

This state is experienced by those who are termed *"Majzoob-Salik"* or *"Paramhansa"* and who in this state of *turiya avastha* **sometimes** experience consciously as "I am my own God" and **sometimes** experience consciously as "I am my own creature."

At the Divine Junction, between the end of the first and the beginning of the second divine journey, the fluctuating divine experiences of "divine" and "human" are experienced alternately until the "I am God" state of *fana-fillah* gradually becomes established in the state of *baqa-billah* where the "abiding-in" God state is established and where man as God simultaneously, without the least effort, automatically undergoes the dual experience

---

* A *Mukammil* can make **all** Creation God-realized if he wishes. All Creation means all human beings and everything that is in Creation from a particle of dust to an elephant. But a *Mukammil* will never wish to do so because the carrying out of such a wish would mean the end of cosmic Illusion (the whole Creation). To put an end to cosmic Illusion would amount to putting an end to the divine play. And to end the divine play would go against the very nature or characteristics of God in His original State II (described on page 172) when He remains infinitely conscious and simultaneously infinitely unconscious.

of God and man at one and the same time.

As soon as the Divine Junction is crossed the *majzoobiyat* of *fana-fillah* becomes established as *sulukiyat* in *baqa-billah*. The *Majzoob* of *majzoobiyat* could only consciously experience infinite knowledge and power while being drowned * in infinite bliss. The *Salik* of *sulukiyat,* however, not only consciously experiences but also consciously accumulates infinite knowledge, power and bliss, although He does not use these infinite aspects for others as *Qutubs* of the *qutubiyat* do.

The end of the second divine journey leads to the third divine journey which is the state of *qutubiyat* where **living** the life of God is actually experienced by those who are termed "*Qutubs*" or "*Sadgurus*" or "Perfect Masters."

The state of *qutubiyat,* which follows the *sulukiyat* of *baqa-billah,* is where man as God, established in the life of God in *baqa-billah,* now begins to **live** the life of God in the state of *qutubiyat* as a *Qutub* or a *Sadguru.* He now not only consciously experiences as in the state of *fana-fillah* and consciously accumulates, as in the state of *baqa-billah,* infinite knowledge, power and bliss, but uses these infinite aspects in this state of *qutubiyat* for those who are still in Illusion. Such a Man-God of the state of *qutubiyat* is called a Perfect Master,[26] who as man has not only become God and established himself in God but **lives** the life of God as God's individual representative in Illusion.

The dual role of "I am God" and "I am human" which was established in *baqa-billah* is now not only simultaneously experienced but is also lived through in the state of *qutubiyat;* and the Man-God (*Qutub, Sadguru* or Perfect Master) now simultaneously lives the life of God and the life of man with all

---

* [Meher Baba was asked, "If *Majzoobs* are utterly unconscious of all the spheres (gross, subtle and mental), of everything except the 'I am God' state, then how is it they react to the physical side of life (eating, drinking, showing preference to certain things, antipathy to others)?"

Meher Baba replied, "The *Majzoob* may apparently like or dislike, ask or reject, seem happy or angry; it is an automatic reflex action of which he is unconscious, like the sound of snoring is to the fast-asleep man emitting it. Like the sleep walker who is unconscious of his actions, however normal or varied they may be, the *Majzoob* is oblivious to his body and surroundings, **and is conscious only of his divine state of 'I am God.'** " Ed.]

of the strength of the infinite knowledge, power and bliss of the God state together with all of the weaknesses and sufferings of the man state.

At the end of the third divine journey the Perfect Master not only lives a dual role and displays strength and weakness simultaneously, but also simultaneously utilizes this display of infinite strength through infinite knowledge, power and bliss, and infinite weakness through infinite suffering for those who are in ignorance and who still conceive the false, finite Illusion to be infinite and real. In contrast to this state, in the state of *baqa-billah* God experiences His Godhood constantly, simultaneously with the continual and constant experience of His manhood; and yet He cannot use the infinite knowledge, power and bliss and also cannot utilize the infinite weakness and suffering for those in ignorance because God does not **live** the life of God in this state as in the state of *qutubiyat*.

It is very, very rare and it is for only very, very few to begin and to end their third divine journey in the *Qutub* or *Sadguru* state. In this state man as God now **lives** the life of God. He now **uses** the infinite knowledge, power and bliss that He experiences. He is that "God and man" or Man-God who has brought down the One indivisible existence into the Many. He is that Man-God who brought down Independent Reality into Illusion and controls Illusion from the divine office of His Beyond state *vidnyan bhumika* or *muqam-e-Muhammadi*.[27]

The very life of this Man-God or Perfect Master is the *sahaj samadhi*. Such a Perfect Master is at one and the same time, simultaneously, in all the universes and in all the worlds, on all the levels and on all the planes, living the life of the "One and the All." His life is that of living also on particular levels and on particular planes, as every creature, and as an individual of that certain level, and of that particular plane. At the same time, together with living the life of God, he lives the life of man on this earth.*

---

* [In the words of Meher Baba, "Perfection does not belong to God as God, nor does it belong to man as man. . . . The finite being, who is conscious of his being finite, is obviously short of Perfection; but when he is

In this state of *qutubiyat* it may be said that God overlaps Godhood, which means that the consciousness of God **after pervading everything** still **remains** infinite, unlimited and unbounded in this Beyond state of God, while remaining eternally conscious of the Beyond the Beyond state of God.

The fourth divine journey pertains to the dropping of the *Qutub's* body (*sharir*).

Even after dropping his body, the *Qutub* eternally remains consciously and individually as God the Infinite; and the individual and indivisible state of "I am God," of the state of *fana-fillah*, which is the goal, is everlastingly experienced. That is, even after the body or the human-form is dropped in the fourth divine journey, the experience of conscious, infinite, indivisible individuality is retained eternally as "I am God," Everything, infinite and unbounded, "One without a second."

Similarly, God in the state of *baqa-billah*, where the apparently dual role of consciousness of "I am God" and "I am human" is manifested, is naturally enacted until the cloak of Illusion, knowingly and consciously donned, is dropped. That is, when the human form or the body is dropped the experience of conscious, infinite, indivisible individuality is retained eternally as "I am God," Everything, infinite and unbounded, "One without a second."

God is Existence eternal, infinite and all-pervading. Since God is eternally infinite existence, it follows that there are an infinite number of states of God, infinitely and eternally existing. But fundamentally there are only two states of God: the original state and the final state.

The original state is the Beyond the Beyond state of God where eternally God "Is" and consciousness "Is Not." The final state is the Beyond state of God where consciousness "Is"

conscious of his being one with the Infinite, he is Perfect. . . . Thus we have Perfection when the finite transcends its limits and realizes its Infinity, or when the Infinite gives up its supposed aloofness and becomes man; in both cases the finite and the Infinite do not stand outside each other. When there is a happy and conscious blending of the finite and the Infinite we have Perfection." Ed.]

eternally of the "God-Is" state of the Beyond the Beyond state of God.

The same Existence, as God, prevails eternally, whether it is as the Beyond the Beyond state of God or as the Beyond state of God. The only difference is one of consciousness. In the Beyond state of God, the Existence **consciously** realizes Itself as existing eternally as the Beyond the Beyond state of God-Is.

Therefore the divine goal is to realize the "I am God" state where Existence consciously realizes Itself as existing eternally as the Beyond the Beyond state of God-Is. This is the Reality, and the conscious realization of this Reality once gained is retained eternally. Invariably It manifests Itself in no other forms but in human forms of the earth in **different divine states** of God through different divine statuses of *majzoobiyat,* of *turiya avastha* or *fana-ma-al-baqa,* of *sulukiyat* and of *qutubiyat.*

All other intermediary states of God are **illusory states** where the same eternal, infinite, all-pervading, one, indivisible, formless Existence, as God, though not realized as the eternal Reality, asserts through its very being, in assuming forms of infinitely innumerable inanimate and animate things and creatures, as lifeless and living states of God, while in the process of gaining full consciousness of the eternal reality of infinite existence.

All these intermediary illusory states of God thrive in the illusion of cosmic Creation through multifarious and diverse gross, subtle and mental impressions of illusion; and though the entire cosmic Creation is illusion, yet it serves the purpose of a divine incubator, where consciousness of the Divine incubates, and where such incubation produces the maturity to realize the eternal Reality after the consciousness is nurtured and progressively developed through multifarious, diverse and finite impressions and experiences of the opposites of the gross, subtle and mental forms and worlds of the cosmic Creation.

In the illusory states of God, the eternal, formless, infinite God, while being impressed by His own cosmic creations, gains consciousness first of the gross forms and experiences the gross worlds, then of the subtle forms and experiences the subtle worlds, then of the mental forms and experiences the mental worlds and, eventually attaining consciousness of His unlimited Self, experiences His eternal state.

Consequently, when God is conscious of His gross forms He identifies Himself with the gross bodies and finds Himself as a particular gross body according to the special impressions of that gross body. This means that the infinite, eternal, formless God finds Himself as finite, mortal and having gross form. The cause of this ignorance is but the impressions—*sanskaras*.

So God, Who is eternally in the Beyond the Beyond state of *Paratpar Parabrahma* or in the infinitude state of God-Is, in the beginning acquires ignorance through being impressed by the impressions rather than by acquiring knowledge of His reality.

Hence when God acquires a particular form, body or *sharir* according to particular impressions, He feels and experiences Himself as that particular form, body or *sharir*. God in His stone-form experiences Himself as stone. Accordingly, in consonance with impressions and their consciousness, God feels and experiences that He is metal, vegetation, worm, fish, bird, animal or human being. Whatever be the type of the gross form and whatever be the shape of the form, the evolving consciousness of God tends God spontaneously to associate Himself with that form, figure and shape which tends Him to experience Himself through impressions that He is that form, figure and shape.

Similarly, when God is conscious of the subtle body (*i.e.,* the *pran*) then God experiences the subtle world and regards Himself as the subtle body or *pran*. Likewise, God becomes conscious of the mental body (*i.e.,* the *mana* or the mind), experiences the mental world and regards Himself as the mental body or the *mana* (*i.e.,* the mind).

It is only because of impressions that the infinite God, the Over-Soul, without form and infinite, experiences that He is veritably but a finite gross body in the gross sphere (*i.e.,* the *jiv-atma* in *anna bhuvan*), or a subtle body in the subtle sphere (*i.e.,* the *jiv-atma* in *pran bhuvan*), or a mental body in the mental sphere (*i.e.,* the *jiv-atma* in the *mano bhuvan*). God, while experiencing the gross world through gross forms, associates with and dissociates from innumerable gross forms. The association with and dissociation from gross forms are called "birth" and "death," respectively.

It is because of impressions that the eternal, immortal, formless God, or the Over-Soul, without births and deaths, has to experience births and deaths a number of times. While God has to experience these innumerable births and deaths because of impressions, He has not only to experience the gross world which is finite and therefore false, but together with it He has also to experience its happiness and misery, its virtue and vice.

All forms, figures and shapes, all worlds and planes, all births and deaths, all virtue and vice, all happiness and misery, experienced by God, Who is eternal, formless and infinite, are the outcome of impressioned consciousness. Since all impressions are but the outcome of the Nothing that manifested as the Nothingness, it means that whatever God experiences through His evolved consciousness in the gross, subtle and mental worlds is the experience of the Nothing; and as this Nothing by nature is nothing, therefore all the experiences in the intermediary illusory states of God are nothing but literally illusion and, as such, false and finite.

Only when the impressioned consciousness is freed from all impressions is liberation or *mukti* in human form attained as *nirvana* or *fana,* where only consciousness "Is" and where all else of the Nothing, which was as Nothingness, vanishes forever. Only in the case of the one who retains the body * for three to four days † after *nirvana* does the liberated (or the unimpressioned or impressionless) consciousness invariably realize eternal

---

* [Meher Baba explained: "Those who do not retain their bodies for three to four days but drop their bodies immediately after *nirvana* attain Liberation (*mukti*)." Ed.]

† [Time does not exist for anyone who is in *nirvana* or for the one who has attained Liberation. The period mentioned (three to four days) holds meaning only for the understanding of those who are gross-conscious and are bound by time. Ed.]

Godhood in the second stage of *fana* (*i.e.,* in *fana-fillah*) and assert itself as "I am God" **without doubt.** This is the *nirvikalpa* state of "Undoubtedly I am God" when, literally, the impressionless or unimpressioned consciousness, linked with human-form, realizes "I am God, I was God and forevermore will remain God" as Existence, eternal and conscious. In this way man becomes God; and it is said that man is God-realized, or that the *jiv-atma* in *Paramatma* has become the *Shiv-Atma* in *Paramatma,* or the Over-Soul.

The eternal reality is that *Paramatma,* or the Over-Soul, is *atma* or the soul; and this reality is realized only when the impressioned consciousness as *jiv-atma* becomes the impressionless or unimpressioned consciousness as *Shiv-Atma,* merging in *Paramatma* to assert and realize the identity of *Paramatma.*

If in reality *atma* is *Paramatma,* how then could any situation arise for *atma* to merge in *Paramatma?*

In order to clarify this situation and understand that *Paramatma* is *atma* in reality, we compare *Paramatma* with an infinite, limitless and shoreless ocean. Therefore *atma,* which is *Paramatma,* can never be out of bounds of the limitless and shoreless ocean (*i.e., Paramatma*). *Atma* can never be out of *Paramatma* because *Paramatma,* which we have compared to the limitless and shoreless ocean, is infinite and unlimited. How could *atma* come out of or have a place beyond the expanse of the limitless when *atma* is *Paramatma?*

Hence, *atma* is in *Paramatma,* too.

Now, in order to understand that the *atma* which is **in** *Paramatma* is in reality *Paramatma* Itself, let us imagine that it is possible to separate or take one iota of the ocean out of the limitless expanse of the unlimited and shoreless ocean. It follows then that this iota of ocean, when in the limitless ocean, is ocean itself before separation, and was in the unlimited ocean not as an iota of the ocean but as the ocean itself (because every iota of ocean when not limited by the limitations of being an iota is unlimited ocean itself).

It is only when the iota of the ocean is separated from the

unlimited ocean, or is taken out of the unlimited ocean, as a drop, that this separated iota of the ocean is looked upon as the limited drop of the unlimited ocean.

In other words, the infinite, unlimited and shoreless ocean now is made to look upon itself through the drop as merely the limited drop of that infinite, unlimited and shoreless ocean; and in comparison to the infinite, unlimited and shoreless ocean, this drop of ocean is most finite, most limited, and has now infinite limitations.

Similarly, *atma,* as compared to the drop of the infinite ocean, can never be out of any limitations of the limitless and infinite *Paramatma* as compared to the infinite, unlimited and shoreless ocean.

But just as the iota of ocean acquires its limitations as a drop through a bubble on the surface of the ocean, and just as this bubble bestows upon the iota of the ocean an apparent separative and limited existence apart from the infinite ocean, likewise *atma,* which is not only in *Paramatma* but which is *Paramatma* Itself, apparently experiences and asserts separative existence from the infinite, unlimited *Paramatma* through the limitations of the bubble of impressions, which bestow conscious ignorance, and with which *atma* shrouds itself and experiences itself as limited and separate from *Paramatma.*

Through these limitations, formed by the bubble of impressions, self-created by *atma, atma* apparently inherits a separative and limited existence from *Paramatma,* and because of this self-created separativeness from infinite *Paramatma, atma,* which is Itself infinite, unlimited and unbounded, bestows upon Itself the aspects of being most finite and most limited, with infinite limitations acquired through impressions.

As soon as the bubble of impressions bursts on completion of total involution of consciousness, and conscious ignorance, as impressioned consciousness, is transformed into conscious knowledge, as unimpressioned consciousness, the limited and the most finite experiences of the *atma* vanish. *Atma,* liberated from apparent separative finite existence, automatically merges in, or finds itself as one with and in *Paramatma*—eternally infinite, unlimited and unbounded in the Beyond state of God; and this is called *atma's* union with *Paramatma* or *Allah*. In this state of consciousness, *atma* is now completely conscious of the Beyond the Beyond unconscious *Paratpar Parabrahma* state of God, which is the original state of God when it is said "God-Is." In Sufi terms, God in the Beyond state is termed *"Allah,"* and God in the Beyond the Beyond state is termed *"Wara-ul-Wara"* or *"Ghaib-ul-Ghaib."*

In human form the highest and the most exalted divine status of God is that of *qutubiyat* where the *Qutub,* or the *Sadguru* or Perfect Master, not only consciously experiences infinite knowledge, infinite power and infinite bliss and all-goodness and all that is infinite beauty, meaning glory, but He consciously uses these infinite aspects for those *jiv-atmas* still undergoing the illusory states of God in Illusion.

In this exalted divine status of *qutubiyat* not only man becomes God but man **lives** the life of God, too. To worship this Man-God is to worship God with infinite attributes.

This highest divine status of living the life of God consciously in human-form is attained very, very rarely by very, very few *Shiv-Atmas*, after the unconscious *atmas* pass through the process of evolution, reincarnation and involution of consciousness as *jiv-atmas*, and attain *nirvana* which in some cases is immediately followed by *nirvikalpa samadhi* of super-consciousness asserting as *Shiv-Atmas*.

At all times and in all ages, and at one and the same time, there are always on this earth fifty-six *Shiv-Atmas* or God-realized *Atmas*. Of these fifty-six *Shiv-Atmas* some remain in the state of *majzoobiyat;* some remain in the state of the Divine Junction— in *turiya avastha*—known in Sufi terms as *"fana-ma-al-baqa";* a very few of them, crossing the Divine Junction, remain in the state of *sulukiyat;* and only five of them are always there in the state of *qutubiyat,* as long as **all** these retain human-forms.

Thus, at all times and in all ages, there are always five

Qutubs (*Sadgurus* or Perfect Masters) living on the earth amongst humanity, wielding infinite aspects of *ahadiyat* of the *arsh-e-ala* or *vidnyan* of the *vidnyan bhumika* of the Beyond state of God in the form of infinite knowledge, power and bliss for the progressive emancipation of all in the field of Illusion.

According to the divine law, these five *Qutubs* or *Sadgurus* or Perfect Masters, at the end of every cycle, precipitate the advent of the direct descent of God on earth in human male form. Hence, at the end of every cycle, when God manifests on earth in the form of man and reveals His divinity to mankind, He is recognized as the *Avatar*—the Messiah—the Prophet. The **direct descent** of God on earth as *Avatar* is that **independent status** of God when God **directly becomes man** * **without undergoing or passing through the processes of evolution, reincarnation and involution of consciousness.** Consequently, God directly becomes **God-Man,** and lives the life of man amongst mankind, realizing His divine status of the Highest of the High, or the Ancient One, through these *Qutubs* or *Sadgurus* or Perfect Masters of the time.[28]

Fundamentally there is absolutely no difference in the experience of Reality, whether the *Shiv-Atmas* are in the divine status of *majzoobiyat, turiya avastha, sulukiyat* or *qutubiyat.* Once the goal is attained, all *Shiv-Atmas* in all divine statuses undoubtedly and consciously begin to enjoy for ever and ever that divine heritage of infinite bliss while spontaneously and continuously experiencing their own triune nature of infinite knowledge, infinite power and infinite bliss.[29]

However, the difference in their divine status is due not to their experience of their infinite triune nature but to a difference in the scope of wielding infinite power after establishing themselves in the *vidnyan bhumika* of infinite knowledge or *sulukiyat,*

---

* *Fana-ul-fana* = the state of God becoming man (the direct descent of God on earth as *Avatar*).

  Baqa-ul-baqa = the state of God becoming God-Man (God's knowing Himself as *Avatar*).

State of ordinary man is the state of God as man.

and then living the life of Man-God, as *Qutub*, exercising their infinite knowledge to wield infinite power while enjoying infinite bliss.

The difference between the divine status of a *Qutub* or *Sadguru* and the *Avatar* of the Age is that a *Qutub*, after having gone through the whole process of cosmic evolution, enters and lives the life of God as Man-God, while the *Avatar* does not have to go through the process of evolution at all because the *Avatar* is that highest status of God where God directly becomes man and lives on earth as God-Man.

In living the life of God, both the *Sadguru* (or *Qutub*) and the *Avatar* (or the *Saheb-e-Zaman*) are equal in having the same experiences. Both are leading God's life and also both are on every level and plane of life in Illusion. Both are simultaneously on the level of the lowest to the highest. In spite of this, the most important and the only difference is that the *Qutub* **acts** on that level and the *Avatar* **becomes** [30] that on that level.

To make the point of "acting" and "becoming" clear, many and innumerable examples can be quoted, but for ordinary human understanding let illness serve as an example.

For instance, a *Qutub* or *Sadguru* cannot and will not **fall ill,** and when he appears to have fallen ill, it is just his "acting" of illness. When people actually see him ill they do not **see him ill** but in reality they **see his illness** perfectly enacted because he is the Perfect Master and perfection personified; he acts as if he were ill. On the other hand, when people see the *Avatar* ill, He has **actually fallen ill** and He has **literally become ill.** But though the *Avatar* has actually become ill, He has at His back simultaneously infinite power, infinite knowledge and infinite bliss.

On every level, in every state and in all planes simultaneously a *Sadguru* **behaves** as the creature or the thing of that level and state and as a man of that plane; whereas the *Avatar* **becomes** as the creature or the thing of that level and state and as a man of that plane all at once. And, at one and the same time becoming and being one and all on all levels, states and in all planes and beyond all levels, states and all planes, the *Avatar* is the **only one** infinitely capable of giving a universal **push** to all things, all creatures and to all mankind, at one and the same time, accelerating the maturity of consciousness.

In Reality God is Everything and is in every one. The *Avatar* of God is not only Everything and in every one but he actually becomes Everything and every one.

Hence the fundamental and only difference between an *Avatar* and a *Sadguru* is that on every level and on all planes a *Sadguru* acts whereas an *Avatar* does not act but actually "becomes" that.[31]

In short, there are always, at all times and in all ages, fifty-six God-realized souls or *Shiv-Atmas* in human form on the earth.[32]

It must be noted that all of the fifty-six God-realized ones may be called Perfect Ones; but all of these fifty-six Perfect Ones are not all Perfect Masters; although all fifty-six experience the same experience of the eternal Reality, without the least difference of experience whatsoever, and although all the fifty-six are one in consciousness of the ultimate goal—Reality, perfect in all respects and God-realized, yet there is a difference in their function. Therefore the term for the fifty-six God-realized ones may be "Perfect Ones" but **not** Perfect Masters or *Sadgurus* or *Qutubs*.

Out of the fifty-six Perfect Ones or *Shiv-Atmas* in human-form, there are always at all times in all ages, five Perfect Masters or *Sadgurus* or *Qutubs;* and these five control the affairs of the whole universe.

When the age is **not** of the *Avataric* period, these five Perfect Masters conjointly look to the affairs of the universe, and the one from amongst the five Perfect Masters who is responsible for the control of all of the affairs of the whole universe is called by the Sufis *"Qutub-e-Irshad."*

But, when the age is of the *Avataric* period at the end of

every cycle,* the *Avatar* (Ancient One, the Highest of the High), the Independent Reality (Infinite Consciousness of the Beyond state of God), is made to manifest in Illusion directly on the earth through a male human being. This manifestation of Infinite Consciousness of the Beyond state of God, through a male human-form on earth, is commonly called "the direct descent of God on earth" in human form. This descent of God on earth is generally known as the *"Avatar."*

Hence it is obvious that when the age is of the *Avataric* period and when the *Avatar* (or the Reality, or the God-consciousness of the Beyond State of God) is made to manifest into Illusion on the earth, by giving this Reality a human form to be made presentable to the humanity of the world, this *Avatar,* or this God-Man, must necessarily be other than the fifty-six God-realized ones.

The then existing and functioning five Perfect Masters, at the appropriate time of the *Avataric* period, individually and conjointly bring about the advent of the *Avatar;* [33] and exercising their infinite mercy and love for all in Ignorance living the illusory life in Creation, use their infinite power and grace to precipitate this advent and make manifest the infinite Reality of the eternal, infinite God-consciousness in the Beyond state, onto this earth into Illusion; and they bestow, through their infinite power, knowledge and bliss, onto the Reality a most suitable "cloak" of Illusion in the shape of a human male form, so that the divinity of the Reality may be made most presentable, in the world of Illusion.

Thus, when Infinite Reality (*i.e.,* God) manifests on earth in the form of a man and reveals His divinity to mankind, He is recognized as the *Avatar,* the Messiah, the Prophet. God thus becomes man.

In this manner, infinite God, age after age, throughout all cycles, wills through His infinite mercy to effect His presence

---

* All cycles of time in Illusion end and begin after 700 to 1400 years, and there have been and will be millions and billions of such cycles in a Cycle of cycles; thus there is no end to Illusion which always remains illusion.

amidst mankind by stooping down to human levels in human-form, but His physical presence amidst mankind not being apprehended, He is looked upon as an ordinary man of the world. When, however, He asserts His divinity on earth by proclaiming Himself the *Avatar* of the Age, He is worshipped by some who accept Him as God; and glorified by a few who know Him as God on earth. But it invariably falls to the lot of the rest of humanity to condemn Him while He is physically in their midst.

Thus it is that God as man, proclaiming Himself as the *Avatar,* suffers Himself to be persecuted and tortured, to be humiliated and condemned by humanity for whose sake His infinite love has made Him stoop so low, in order that humanity, by the very act of condemning God's manifestation in the form of the *Avatar* should, however indirectly, assert the existence of God in His infinite, eternal state of Reality.

The *Avatar* is always One and the same because God is always One and the same,* the eternal, indivisible, infinite One who manifests Himself in the form of man as the *Avatar,* as the Messiah, as the Prophet, as the Buddha, as the Ancient One,—the Highest of the High. This eternally One and the same *Avatar* is made to repeat His manifestation from time to time, in different cycles, adopting different names and different human-forms, in different places, to reveal Truth in different garbs and different languages, in order to raise humanity from the pit of ignorance and help free it from the bondage of delusions.

During the *Avataric* period, the one, from amongst the then living five Perfect Masters, who used to function as *Qutub-e-Irshad,* ceases to hold this divine office with the advent of the *Avatar* and delivers his **duty** and **charge** of the sole responsibility for the affairs of the universe into the hands of the God-Man as soon as He is able to assume His office as the Christ—the *Avatar* of the Age—and remains himself, as long as he is in a gross body, holding the same office of *Qutub* as the other

---

* [Meher Baba was asked whether a Perfect Master, after leaving the body, ever comes back to earth, *i.e.,* does he ever take birth again. Baba replied, "No, never. Only the *Avatar* takes birth again and again." Ed.]

four hold.

In spite of the advent of the *Avatar,* there must be fifty-six God-realized ones in human body, and from amongst these fifty-six there must be the five Perfect Masters living on earth. When one from amongst these five Perfect Masters drops his physical body, the office is never left vacant; it is invariably filled by another living God-realized one who has realized the eternal Reality at the time. Hence, even when the *Avatar* is on earth, there are fifty-six God-realized ones, including the five Perfect Masters in human-form, but the *Avatar* becomes the sole **Authority.**

CHART VII

GOD IS REALITY AND ALL ELSE IS ILLUSION

EVERYTHING

THROUGH Gross Body = Small Gross Shadow ⬤ OF ⬤ Gross Sphere = Big Gross Shadow = Gross Nothing = Nothing into nothing –into nothing

THROUGH Subtle Body = Small Subtle Shadow ⬤ OF ⬤ Subtle Sphere = Big Subtle Shadow = Subtle Nothing = Nothing into nothing

THROUGH Mental Body = Small Mental Shadow ⬤ OF ⬤ Mental Sphere = Big Mental Shadow = Mental Nothing = Nothing

EVERYTHING

MAN
IS GROSS CONSCIOUS
MAN
IS SUBTLE CONSCIOUS
MAN
IS SUBTLE CONSCIOUS FUNCTIONING
MAN
IS MENTAL CONSCIOUS
MAN
IS MENTAL CONSCIOUS FUNCTIONING

ILLUSION

GOD'S MOST ORIGINAL UNCONSCIOUS STATE OF BEYOND THE BEYOND

REALITY

God is conscious of everything except nothing

MEN GOD ~ARE~ GOD MAN

simultaneously conscious of everything including all nothing

EVERYTHING   **EVERYTHING**

GOD IS EVERYTHING AND ALL ELSE IS NOTHING

With the energy from the subtle and the illumination from the mental spheres, for trillions upon trillions of years in the past and in the future, the gross universe has been and will be forming and disintegrating into countless stars, suns, planets, worlds, moons and meteors. Yet, in fact, there are no such things as time and space. Once the soul is freed of illusion, Illusion does not merely cease to exist, but is then found never to have existed at all.

After a gradual evolution through the mineral, vegetable and animal kingdoms of the gross universe for a definite yet immeasurable period of millions, billions and trillions of years, consciousness reaches perfection in man. Man then rightly ought to be God-conscious, but does not become so because of the *sanskaric* bindings born of impressions of the illusory experiences gathered during the evolution of consciousness. Thus man remains fully conscious only of the gross.

Before man's perfect but gross consciousness can involve into the Reality of God-consciousness, it has first to involve into subtle consciousness, and from the subtle into full mental consciousness. For that, the gross impressions have to turn into the subtle and from the subtle into the mental impressions regaining, in degree, the faintness and fineness of earlier impressions as gathered in the vegetable and mineral forms—the fundamental difference being in consciousness.

Unlike the definite course followed in the process of evolution, man as man can make use of his consciousness fully and freely. Therefore the fully gross-conscious man, according to the resultant tightening or loosening of his *sanskaric* bindings, can become fully subtle-conscious, and thereafter fully mental-conscious, sometimes after a few or sometimes after numerous human reincarnations between each of the two involutions of his consciousness. And if one happens to be blessed with divine love from a "Lover of God," or if one has the guiding hand of a Perfect Master, the emancipation from all bindings, however great and complicated they may be, is achieved much more easily and quickly. In exceptional cases, an instantaneous emancipation is also possible without involving a single reincarnation.

However, in order to loosen the bindings through the opposite experiences of the duality of Illusion, *i.e.,* pain and pleasure, good and bad, man and woman, strong and weak, etc., on his own, man has to remain conscious of multifarious experiences for eighty-four *lakhs* of times through something like fifty *crores* of sleeps of death; yet invariably, on account of the all-pervading grace of God, man becomes subtle- and mental-conscious, and is thus able to cut short more or less the stalemate of recurring physical births and deaths.

Finally, by the grace of the God-Man or the Man-God, in far, far less than an instant's flash of time, man becomes fully conscious God and finds that time and space are born of His own eternity and infinitude in which time and space have no existence at all.*

---

* [Asked for further clarification, Eruch B. Jessawala wrote in reply:

"The reference to fifty *crores* of sleeps of death is approximately what one soul has to undergo during the processes of evolution of consciousness of forms and of reincarnation with the help of changes in the media, *i.e.,* association with and dissociation from different forms of different species.

"Eighty-four *lakhs* of shakings or reincarnations are in *human form,* but 'fifty *crores* of sleeps of death' include pre-human forms' associations with and dissociations from media and the experiences of their impressions.

"Man need not die more times than he can be born! Man is born once with the birth of mind, and man dies once with the annihilation of mind. As such, there is indeed no reincarnation; it is just a process of *crores* of sleeps of death for the mind that is born once and that dies once! Birth of mind involves the processes of evolution, reincarnation and involution. Death of mind is realization of the Self." Ed.]

The Ten States of God

BY ERUCH B. JESSAWALA

"The Ten States of God" which follows was written by Eruch B. Jessawala under the direct supervision of Meher Baba, describing and interpreting an original diagram, "The Ten States of God," devised by Meher Baba.

—*The Editors*

The Ten Principal States of God

DEPICTED BY MEHER BABA *

STATE I	GOD	IN	BEYOND-BEYOND
STATE II	GOD	IN	BEYOND Sub-States A, B, C.
STATE III	GOD	AS	EMANATOR, SUS- TAINER AND DIS- SOLVER
STATE IV	GOD	AS	EMBODIED SOUL
STATE V	GOD	AS	SOUL IN THE STATE OF EVOLUTION
STATE VI	GOD	AS	HUMAN SOUL IN THE STATE OF REINCAR- NATION
STATE VII	GOD	IN	THE STATE OF SPIRIT- UALLY ADVANCED SOULS
STATE VIII	GOD	AS	THE DIVINELY AB- SORBED
STATE IX	GOD	AS	LIBERATED INCAR- NATE SOUL
STATE X	GOD	AS	MAN-GOD and GOD- MAN

---

* See chart.

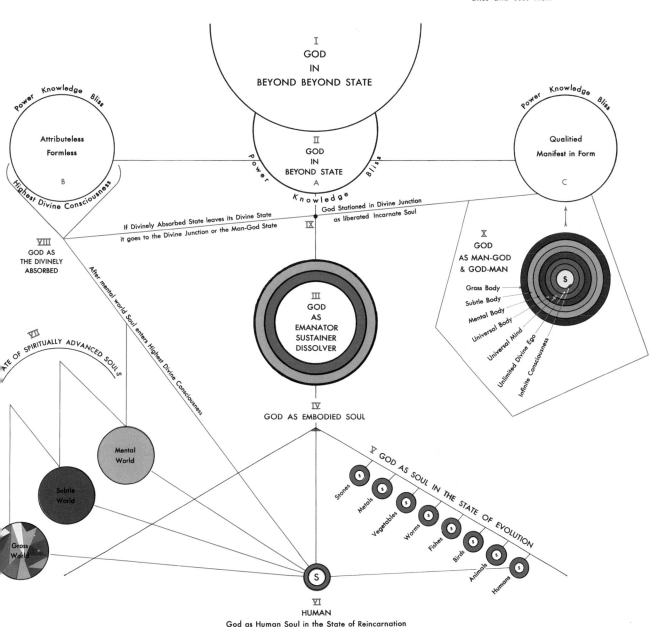

THE TEN STATES OF GOD

A God neither consciously experiences Power, Knowledge, Bliss nor uses them

B God consciously experiences Power, Knowledge, Bliss but does not use them

C God consciously experiences Power, Knowledge, Bliss and uses them

CHART VIII

VEDANTIC *	MYSTIC	SUFI
Paratpar Parabrahma	God's Beyond–Beyond State	Ghaib-ul-Ghaib Wara-ul-Wara
Paramatma	God in Beyond State	Allah
Anant	Infinite	La Mahdood
Nirguna	Attributeless	La Sifat
Nirakar	Formless	La Surat
Sat-Chit-Anand	Power, Knowledge, Bliss	Qudrat, Marefat, Musarrat
Vidnyan Bhumika	Realm of Mastery	Alam-e-Hahut Arsh-e-Ala
Atmapratisthapana Sahaj Samadhi	Established in the Life of God	Baqa-Billah
Vidnyan	Highest Divine Consciousness	Ahadiyat Alam-e-Lahut
Saguna	Qualitied	Ba Sifat
Sakar	Manifest in Form	Ba Surat
Brahma	Emanator	Afridgar
Vishnu	Sustainer	Parvardigar
Mahesh	Dissolver	Fanakar
Mano Bhuvan	Mental Sphere	Alam-e-Jabrut
Pran Bhuvan	Subtle Sphere	Alam-e-Malakut
Anna Bhuvan	Gross Sphere	Alam-e-Nasut
Utkranti	Evolution	Irteqa
Punar Janma	Reincarnation	Rij'at, or Awagawan
Bhumika	Plane	Asman
Atma	Soul	Jan, or Ruh
Jiv-Atma	Embodied Soul	Jan-e-Jismi
Manava	Human	Insan
Yogi (Sadhak)	Aspirant	Rahrav
Sadhu	Advanced Soul	Mutawassit
Mahatma	Great Soul	Akhyar
Mahapurush (Sant)	Saint	Abrar = Wali
Satpurush	Adept Pilgrim (Saint)	Afrad = Pir
Manonash (Nirvana)	Annihilation of Mind (self)	The final Fana
Nirvikalpa	Oneness with God	Fana-Fillah
Brahmi Bhoot	The Divinely Absorbed	Majzoob-e-Kamil
Turiya Avastha	Divine Junction	Fana-ma-al-Baqa at Muqam-e-Furutat
Paramhansa	Divine Super-Man	Majzoob-Salik or Salik-Majzoob
Jivanmukta	Liberated Incarnate	Azad-e-Mutlaq
Sadguru	Man-God	Qutub
Avatar	God-Man	Saheb-e-Zaman

*Vedantic and near-Vedantic terms

The Ten States of God

THE pages of this chapter are built around the diagram depicting THE TEN STATES OF GOD. This diagram has been given by Meher Baba himself; it is a gem from the fathomless treasure of his supreme gnosis. The spiritual terms of this diagram have been linked up with the most generally accepted Sufi, Vedantic and Christian mystical equivalents.

If we were to take a bird's-eye view of this diagram we should find that it depicts what is really the downward journey of the Over-Soul to the lowest point of devolution as man (*insan, jiv-atma*), and its upward journey again through the unfolding planes of consciousness, back to the original source, first as the divinely absorbed *Majzoob-e-Kamil* and culminating finally in the Perfect Man (*Insan-e-Kamil, Shiv-Atma*). The ten different states of God are principal stages on this journey, a journey in which unconscious God becomes conscious man, in order to become conscious God.

Although these states of God are depicted as apparently distinct from one another, they are in effect ten **aspects** of the One God Who is, and will always remain, One. The descent and ascent of the Over-Soul is in imagination only, and with the

169

cessation of imagination comes the realization with full consciousness for the individual soul that God alone exists and that anything and everything else which appears to exist is but His shadow.

Meher Baba's gnosis upholds without equivocation both the theory of Identityism (*wahdat-ul-wujud*) [34] and the theory of Advaitism. In the chart "The Ten States of God by Meher Baba," it is made clear that it is God alone who plays the different roles, real and imaginary. The beginning is God and the end is God; the intermediary stages cannot but be God. The spiritual dictum of Islamic theology is *"Huwal awwal, Huwal akher, Huwal zaher, Huwal batin"* (He is the first, He is the last, He is the external, He is the internal).

Maulana Shabistari, in *Gulshan-e-Raz,* says:

Gar andar āmad avval ham bidar shud
Agar cih dar ma'ād az dar bidar shud.

"He returns to the door from which he first came out, although in his journey he went from door to door."

We shall now try to describe concisely each one of these ten states of God as explained by Meher Baba.

State I
God in the Beyond-Beyond State

This state of God is so transcendent that nothing can really be conceived of it. It is utterly pure and immaculate and has no tinge of "otherness." It is the hidden of all hidden knowledge and the internal of all internal realities. It is beyond all words and so it cannot be adequately described. It is neither finite nor infinite, neither attributeless nor with attributes. In this domain the wings of thought, inference, discrimination and understanding are limp and useless.

Bikhiyāl dar nagunjad, tū khiyāl-i khvud maranjān
Zi jahat buvad mubarrā maṭalab bihīc sūyash.

—Hafiz

"He cannot be grasped by the mind, therefore do not exert yourself to understand Him; He is free of all directions, therefore do not try to seek Him anywhere."

Meher Baba says that when one who has **realized** this state of God tries to describe it to others, this act results in a description not of the first, but of the second, state of God—God in the Beyond state.

It is the Eternity of all eternities (*Azl-ul-Azal*) because no eternity can be conceived of to precede or to follow it. Here all indications are blotted out (*Munqata-ul-Izharat*), since no other thing exists that can be pointed out or referred to. This pure essence (*Zat-al-Baht*) is not aware of anything, even of itself.

This state has been referred to by the Sufis as *Wara-ul-Wara*—The Beyond-Beyond State of God. Vedanta calls it *Paratpar Parabrahma*.

This is the state in which God is neither *nirguna* (attribute-less) nor *saguna* (with attributes), neither *nirakar* (formless) nor *sakar* (with forms).

Of all the principal ten states of God, the first and the most-original state is the Beyond-Beyond state of God.

When there were no other states of God in the beyond the beginning of the Beginning, only the most-original infinite state of God (that is, "God-Is" state) prevailed as the Beyond-Beyond state of God.

In the infinitude of this Beyond-Beyond state of God only the infinity of Infinitude is manifest as the unbounded, absolute, infinite Divine Vacuum; and all other states, attributes and aspects of God, including infinite consciousness and infinite un-consciousness, are all latent as the Nothing in that Infinitude of the unbounded, absolute, infinite Divine Vacuum as the Everything (Everything also includes the Nothing).

Thus, the most-original Beyond-Beyond state of God is that state where one can only say: God-Is eternally; and that in this most-original state, God is neither infinitely nor finitely conscious, nor unconscious, of Self or of His own state of Infinitude. In this state, God is also neither conscious nor unconscious of Illusion or Reality.

State II
God in the Beyond State

We have already stated that the Beyond-Beyond state of God can never be adequately described. God-realized beings, when they try to describe the Beyond-Beyond state, succeed only in describing the Beyond state of God, which is the *Allah* of Sufis, the *Ahuramazda* of Zoroastrians, the *Paramatma* of Vedantists, God the Father of Christians, and the Over-Soul of some philosophers. God in the Beyond state is absolute, unlimited and infinite—the One without a second.

Meher Baba, while explaining this second state of God, stressed that fundamentally State II is in no way different from State I of God; the sub-states A, B and C of State II of God are what create the difference.

How, when and where the difference came into being is described as follows from the explanations of Meher Baba:

At the instant when the latent original infinite whim of the infinite God to know Himself ("Who am I?") is about to surge in the unbounded uniformity of the unbounded, absolute, infinite Divine Vacuum of the **most-original** Beyond-Beyond state of God, the very prospect of this infinite urge-to-know, prompting the eternally tranquil poise of God in the unbounded, absolute, infinite Divine Vacuum, becomes inconceivable.

But the **fact** of the insurge of the infinite whim and its very inconceivability, spontaneously brings into being another aspect of God's state other than the most-original Beyond-Beyond state of unbounded, absolute, infinite Divine Vacuum, where there is neither prospect of aspect nor attribute; neither the infinite or finite consciousness nor the infinite or finite unconsciousness; and where, except for the infinity of God which is eternally manifest, every other thing is latent including the infinite whim and the consequent infinite urge-to-know.

Thus it is that the very inconceivability of the prospect of the infinite whim surging in the Beyond-Beyond state automatically unfolds the prospectiveness, which is also latent in the infinite state; and this manifestation (of prospectiveness) bestows upon the most-original Beyond-Beyond state of God the prospect of an infinite aspect different from that of the most-original and eternal state.

The second state of God accordingly comes into being only as another infinite aspect of the most-original first state. This second state of the ten principal states of God is called the Original Beyond State of God.

It is to be heeded well that this original second state of God, denoted in the chart as II and termed "God In Beyond State," is in no way to be taken as a state of God altogether other than the most-original first state of God, denoted in the chart as I and termed "God In Beyond-Beyond State."

The only difference between State I and State II of God is that State I is of unbounded, absolute, infinite Divine Vacuum, where even the remotest prospect of the insurge of the infinite whim is inconceivable. Therefore, only at the instant when the original infinite whim insurges in the infinitude of the God-Is state, could infinite God conceive the infinite original urge-to-know, as "Who am I?"—that is, only when the aspectless State I of God In Beyond-Beyond gets the aspect of State II of God In Beyond. *Paratpar Parabrahma* thus gets the infinite aspect of *Paramatma*.

It is also to be noted very carefully that the Beyond State marked in the chart as II is fundamentally the same as the Beyond-Beyond State of God marked in the chart as I. But in the chart these two states, State I and State II, are depicted separately, because even though State II of God In Beyond State is the same **original** state of God, yet it is not the **most-original** state of God which is the Beyond-Beyond State. This necessarily follows because God could conceive the infinite insurge of the infinite original whim and could get the infinite original impulse of the infinite original urge-to-know, as "Who am I?", **only** in State II, when God eternally in State I assumes the infinite original aspect of State II within His own eternal State I which is the most-original Beyond-Beyond State.

To be more explicit, in both these states of God (States I and II), except for the eternally manifest infinity of the eternal infinitude of God (as the unbounded, absolute, infinite Divine Vacuum), all attributes, all aspects, all states, infinite and most-finite consciousness and unconsciousness of God, including God's own infinite trio-nature of power, knowledge and bliss and all other things, are all latent in the unbounded, absolute, infinite Divine Vacuum.

All this that is latent in the Infinitude could only have the scope of manifestation in State II of God, which may be said to differ from State I only in this respect, of having this infinite scope of manifestation of all that is infinitely, and most finitely, latent as the Nothing in the infinitude of God as the Everything.

Consequently, the infinite original whim of God, when it once surged, had the feasibility of surging only in State II of God; and when it surged, it did so uniformly in the infinitude of God. But when the whim surged, the insurge of this whim could never be **experienced** by God in His infinitely most independent Beyond-Beyond State I; it was experienced by God, eternally in the most-original Beyond-Beyond state, only through the infinite aspect of His State II as "God In The Beyond State."

Hence, the infinite insurge of the infinite original whim and its consequent infinite repercussions are in reality effected in the State II of God In The Beyond State.

At the instant when the infinite original whim surged and God had the infinite original urge-to-know, as "Who am I?", the infinite uniformity of the infinite insurge of the whim spontaneously made manifest both the latent infinite consciousness and the latent infinite unconsciousness of God simultaneously in the original Beyond state of God, Who is nevertheless eternally in the most-original Beyond-Beyond state.

This spontaneous manifestation of the latent infinite consciousness and infinite unconsciousness **simultaneously,** is beyond the grasp of human intellect to understand and digest. It is indeed a paradox of the realm of Reality, and it defeats all human understanding. How could God gain spontaneously His own infinite consciousness and His infinite unconsciousness simultaneously? Meher Baba, while explaining this, declared that this is a fact, and it is of the realm of Reality, but it can never be understood or grasped by the mind; it is only to be realized on realizing the Reality. At the same time, in order that we may get at least some concept of this fact effected in Reality, and that we may not take it as a mere paradoxical mystery, Meher Baba made us understand this apparent paradox through the example of a child in a mother's womb.

When the mother conceives, the child is under development in the mother's womb; and as soon as the development reaches a stage when, along with other developments, the eyes of the child are fully moulded, the child gains the faculties of "seeing" and "not-seeing" simultaneously. Irrespective of whether the child, after birth, sees or does not see, the very fact that the eyes have been moulded in the womb of his mother, gives to the child the dual aspect of his own eyes. In the eyes, as soon as they are developed, the faculties of seeing and not-seeing are simultaneously contained. When the child opens his eyes he will see and when he closes his eyes he will not-see; but the fact still holds good that no sooner were the eyes developed than there was contained in them the dual faculty of seeing and not-seeing simultaneously.

Similarly, with the insurge of the original infinite whim in God, both the infinite consciousness and unconsciousness, latent in God, were manifested simultaneously, which to the limited mind appears paradoxical.

Thus God in His most-original State I of the Beyond-Beyond gained spontaneously, through His original State II of the Beyond, His own infinitely unconscious state and His own infinitely conscious state simultaneously, depicted in the chart as states "A" and "B," respectively.

Consequently, on the one hand, with the spontaneous manifestation of infinite unconsciousness, God in His infinite, **unconscious** Beyond state, shown as "A" in the chart, eternally remains not only infinitely unconscious of His own eternal, infinite existence, as in the most-original Beyond-Beyond state of Infinitude-Absolute, but He also eternally remains infinitely unconscious of His own begotten infinite original Beyond state, shown in the chart as II.

On the other hand, simultaneously with the spontaneous manifestation of infinite consciousness, God in His infinite, **conscious** Beyond state, marked in the chart as "B," eternally becomes not only infinitely conscious of His own eternal infinite existence, as in the most-original Beyond-Beyond state of Infinitude-Absolute, but He also becomes, most obviously, infinitely conscious of His own begotten infinite original Beyond state, shown in the chart as II.

In other words, only in the Beyond state of God, marked in the chart as State II, God spontaneously, with the insurge of the infinite original whim, simultaneously begets His eternal, infinite unconscious state, marked as sub-state "A," and His eternal, infinite conscious state, marked as sub-state "B."

Sub-state A is of God In Beyond State, marked as State II. This sub-state A is of divine infinite unconsciousness of God's own infinite power, infinite knowledge and infinite bliss. God in this sub-state A neither consciously experiences His own trio-nature of infinite power, knowledge and bliss, nor uses them.

Sub-state B is also of God In Beyond State, marked as State II. This sub-state B is attributeless and formless, but is of highest divine consciousness of God's own infinite trio-nature of infinite power, knowledge and bliss. God in this sub-state B consciously experiences His own infinite power, infinite knowledge and infinite bliss but He does not use them. He is conscious of His Reality but is unconscious of Illusion.

In Vedantic terminology, it is thus that the State I of *Paratpar Parabrahma* begets the State II of *Paramatma;* and in this State II, God as *Paramatma* is eternally unconscious and simultaneously eternally conscious of His own most-original state of *Paratpar Parabrahma*. This infinite dual aspect of the *Paramatma* state is pointed out in the chart as state A and state B respectively.

It naturally follows, therefore, that the eternal unconscious state of *Paramatma,* marked A, in the eternal original Beyond state, marked II, eternally aspires to attain the eternal conscious state of *Paramatma,* marked B, which is the second of the dual infinite aspects of the original Beyond God state (*Paramatma*) marked II.

Consequently, the divine goal is that the unconscious state of God in A should attain the conscious Reality of the conscious state of God in B.

In short, when state A consciously realizes state B, the divine goal is attained.

For state A to realize consciously state B, there is no other alternative but that state A must gradually experience transmutation into state B and eventually become state B in all respects consciously.

This gradual transmutation of the unconscious, infinite state of God into the conscious, infinite state is depicted through States III, IV, V, VI and VII as different states of God in the chart of the ten states of God. In State VIII, state A of God becomes fully conscious of state B.

In this State VIII, the unconscious infinite state A of God not only gains the highest divine consciousness of state B, but God becomes divinely absorbed in the Reality of His own infinite conscious state and so realizes His eternal identity with the infinite conscious state B of God.

If God, divinely absorbed, as in State VIII, recovers and maintains normal consciousness of the mental, subtle and gross spheres through His mental, subtle and gross aspects as an embodiment of a perfect human being, then State IX, at the Divine

Junction between States VIII and X, is attained. After this ninth state, the tenth state of God is depicted in the chart and connected with the God state "C."

This tenth state of God is the state of God qualitied and manifest in the human form of a Perfect Master. In State X God consciously experiences His own trio-nature of infinite power, infinite knowledge and infinite bliss, and also uses them through the Divine Office of God-state X marked in the chart as "C."

It is also to be well noted that God in the infinite, unconscious state A is neither *nirguna* (attributeless)-*nirakar* (formless), nor *saguna* (with attributes)-*sakar* (with form). But state B is of *nirguna-nirakar* (attributeless and formless), and state C (which is also of the original Beyond God state) is of *saguna-sakar* (with attributes and form). It is that highest state of Man-God where God is infinitely conscious of both Reality and Illusion.

State III
God as Emanator, Sustainer and Dissolver

In this state God brings into play His three principal attributes (*sifat*) of emanating, sustaining and dissolving. This three-in-one state corresponds to the trinity of Vedanta: *Brahma* (Creator), *Vishnu* (Preserver), and *Mahesh* (Destroyer)—the Sufi synonyms of which are the terms *Afridgar, Parvardigar,* and *Fanakar.*

The three attributes of God are expressed through the three Archangels, *Israfeel* (the angel who creates life), *Mikaeel* (the angel who sustains life) and *Izraeel* (the angel who destroys life).

The triple attributes of State III of God were latent in the most-original State I of God; these, simultaneously, unfolded themselves spontaneously at that instant when the original infinite whim surged in God and when He conceived in His State II the infinite urge-to-know Himself, as "Who am I?" At that instant of the insurge of the infinite whim, God in His State II gained simultaneously the infinite, dual aspects of being infinitely unconscious as in His state A and at the same time, of being infinitely conscious as in His state B.

Nevertheless the infinite original urge-to-know Himself obviously persists still in God state A which is yet infinitely unconscious of Himself. The infinite urge-to-know Himself persisting in this infinitely unconscious state A of God made possible the **manifestations of all the qualities and aspects of God latent as the Nothing in the infinitude of the most-original State I of God as the Everything.** But all that is latent as the Nothing in the Everything could be possibly conceived as latent in the Beyond State II of God only.

Wherefore, all that is latent in the Beyond state of God is gradually unfolded, propelled by the infinite urge, and is spontaneously made to manifest as all that is of the Nothing. Hence the Nothingness of the Nothing that is manifested is the Creation; and this Creation springs forth out of the infinite urge-to-know in the infinite, unconscious state A of God. Consequently, it is only natural that the infinite, unconscious state A of God gains the first attribute as Emanator, of the three infinite attributes: God the Creator, God the Preserver and God the Dissolver or Destroyer.

For God to have gained the attribute of Emanator, He obviously becomes the Creator of Creation, as in His State III.

It then follows most naturally that when God creates, He must spontaneously also sustain what He creates. He then obviously becomes also the Preserver of Creation, as in His State III.

And in the very act of preserving what is created, God also simultaneously establishes the inevitable dissolution or destruction of Creation. Preservation would be meaningless if dissolution or destruction were not anticipated. Accordingly God obviously becomes also the Dissolver or Destroyer of Creation, as in His State III.

State III of God is that state in which God becomes the Creator and simultaneously remains the Sustainer or Preserver, and Dissolver or Destroyer of His own Creation. At one and the same time, God thus becomes the Creator, Preserver and Destroyer in State III.

The infinite original whim that surged in God and the consequent infinite urge-to-know Himself made manifest in God the infinite triple attributes of Creator, Preserver and Dissolver, with all the paraphernalia of the Nothingness of the latent Nothing. This Nothingness literally is nothing, although it appears to exist through Illusion (sometimes called *Maya* [35]) as the Creation.

Meher Baba has told us that there is no Creation in the literal sense of the word. What we call Creation is a manifestation of countless forms of the Nothing. This Nothing is really "no-thing"—but it exists in its own field of Illusion. It cannot be denied, but it is not beyond the Everything, that is, God. Although the Everything includes this Nothing, the Nothing never does and never can include or mean the Everything. The Almighty alone is the Everything, including the Nothing; and before Creation manifested itself, there was literally and absolutely "no-thing" but the Almighty as the Everything.

> *Ẕāt thī Allāh kī aur jalve sab rūposh the*
> *Īk saut-i sarmadī thā naghme sab khāmosh the*
> *Thā faqaṯ maīkhānah sāqī thā nah vāṇ maīnosh the*
> *Kā-yi nāte dahar kyā rūḥ ul-amīn bihosh the*
> *Zindagī jab muskurā'ī hai qaẕā ke sāmne.*
>
> —Munsiff–Asghar

"The existence of *Allah* alone was and all manifestations were latent therein;

One Eternal Sound prevailed, and all musical notes were dormant therein;

Only the tavern was there—no cup-bearers and wine-drinkers;

The gross universe was out of the question—even the angelic world was not in existence,

When, with the divine command 'Be,' life smilingly sprang up."

The Almighty alone existed, but He was only latently conscious, and hence He did not know Himself, and in the same way that consciousness was latent in Him, so also Creation was latent in Him.

The difference between the latent and the manifest Creation may be compared to that between a seed and a tree. But, whether seed or tree, latent or manifest, Creation is always "no-thing," because it is the latent Nothing that is manifested as the Nothingness.

All that is latent as the Nothing in the Beyond State II of the infinitude of God as the Everything is expressed and manifested through a most finite point in the infinitude of God. This point is called the "creation point" or the "Om point." * Through this point Creation has been precipitated. This creation point was also latent in the most original State I of God, in the Beyond-Beyond state.

The process of emanating, sustaining and dissolving, which is constantly and uniformly going on, may be illustrated by an analogy. Let us imagine that a human body is God. The human body sleeping with eyes shut may then be compared to the Beyond State of God, as State II-A. The very first moment of opening the eyes may be compared to the state of God as Creator. The subsequent condition of remaining awake may be compared to the state of God as Sustainer, and going back to sleep again with eyes shut may be compared to the state of God as Dissolver. Thus God is the Creator, Sustainer and Dissolver, all three in One, at one and the same time.

State IV
God as Embodied Soul

> Dīd apnī thī ūse khvāhish
> Āp ko har tarah banā dekhā.
> —Niyāz

---

* [See also: Francis Brabazon, *Stay with God* (Woombye, Queensland, Australia: Edwards and Shaw for Garuda Books, 1959), pp. 65–66. Ed.]

"He desired to see Himself; hence He assumed to Himself varied aspects involving names and forms."

In order to understand how the infinitely unconscious state A of God becomes gradually transmuted into the infinitely conscious state B of God and attains full and infinite consciousness, Meher Baba gave the following analogy:—

Imagine the infinitely unconscious God state A, before the Creation came into being, as motionless infinite ocean. A puff of wind then stirred the tranquil uniformity of this ocean, and immense waves, countless drops of water, and innumerable bubbles appeared from out of the uniformity of the limitless, infinite ocean. The puff of wind that set the ocean into commotion may be compared to the impulse of the infinite, original urge-to-know originating with the infinite, original whim of God, surging in God to know Himself through His infinite God State II.

The stir on the surface of the ocean, caused by the infinite urge, surcharged every drop of that infinite ocean with the infinite original urge-to-know itself.

Thus *Paramatma* in His infinitely unconscious state A, being urged to know Himself, simultaneously bestirs the tranquil poise of every *atma* in *Paramatma* with an urge to know itself. This could only be understood when *Paramatma* is compared to an infinite ocean and the *atmas* to the drops of that infinite ocean. But it must also be well noted that every drop of the ocean, when in the ocean, is ocean itself, until the drops inherit individuality through bubble formations over the surface of the ocean. Every bubble thus formed would then bestow a separate and a particular individuality upon every drop. And this created separateness would exist within the uniform indivisibility of the drops of the infinite ocean as long as these bubbles creating separateness exist. As soon as the bubbles burst, the drops, which are and were already in the ocean itself, come to realize that they are and were one with the infinite ocean; and they gain this consciousness of their **eternal infinity in the infinite ocean** only after **they** first experience separateness and then dispel the bubbles of ignorance that were instrumental in bestowing upon them the experience of their apparent separateness from their inherent indivisibility.

As long as the infinitely innumerable drops of the ocean do not experience apparent separateness, they fail to realize their own homogeneous and indivisible eternal, infinite existence as ocean itself. It is only through the experience of apparent separateness that *atmas* can consciously realize their indivisible Oneness as *Paramatma.*

In order to describe the God State IV of "God As Embodied Soul," let us think of one infinitely unconscious soul (*atma*) of *Paramatma* in state A.

In the beginning, in state A, the soul (*atma*) has no consciousness and has no impressions (*sanskaras*).

Therefore, at that stage and in that state the soul (*atma*) has no gross form, gross body, subtle body nor mental body, **because the existence of gross, subtle and mental impressions** (*sanskaras*) **only can give existence to gross, subtle and mental bodies;** and only the existence of these bodies can make possible the existence of gross, subtle and mental worlds.

Hence in the beginning the soul in God state A, being infinitely unconscious and being impressionless, had no consciousness of gross, subtle and mental bodies, and was also unconscious of its infinite Self. The soul naturally then had no experience of the gross, subtle and mental worlds, and also had no experience of the Over-Soul (*Paramatma*).

Now this infinite, impressionless, unconscious, tranquil state of the soul reverberated with the first impulse, which we called The First Urge (the first urge to know Itself).

Simultaneously with reverberations of the first urge to know Itself, a **most-gross** first impression emerged, objectifying the soul as the absolutely opposite and most-finite counterpart of the absolutely infinite Over-Soul.

The soul, being eternally in the Over-Soul and one with the Over-Soul, has also the infinite potentialities of the Over-Soul, though latent in its unconscious state. Thus the soul is also the possessor of infinite power, knowledge and bliss.

Therefore, when the impressionless, infinite soul receives the very first impression, this impression could be nothing other than the most-gross impression, because the soul itself, which is the possessor of infinite knowledge, tries to gain knowledge of its own "Self." This very conception on the part of the possessor of infinite knowledge is infinitely crude or gross, and this infinitely crude or gross conception of the infinite soul imparted to the impressionless soul the most-gross first impression. Simultaneously with the most-gross first impression, the infinitely unconscious soul also gained the **most-finite** first consciousness. With the increasing gross impressions, the consciousness evolved and the evolution of gross forms gained momentum.

Consequently, the evolution of consciousness, the evolution of gross forms and the evolution of the experiences of the gross world were all effected as the result of the first urge of God to know Himself.

Because of this most-gross first impression of the first urge, the infinite, unconscious soul gained the aspects of **experience** for the first time. This first experience of the infinite soul was that it (soul, *atma*) experienced a contrariety (absolutely opposite by nature) in its identity with the infinite, impressionless, unconscious state A of *Paramatma*.

This experience of contrariety effected changeableness in the eternal, indivisible stability of the infinite soul; and spontaneously there occurred a sort of eruption, disrupting the indivisible poise and unconscious tranquility of the infinite soul with a recoil or tremendous shock, which impregnated the infinite unconsciousness of the infinitely unconscious soul (*atma*) with first consciousness of its apparent separateness from the indivisible state of *Paramatma*. But the soul being infinite, the first consciousness that it derived from the recoil or shock of the **absolutely opposite** and most-gross first impression of its separateness, was naturally and necessarily most-finite first consciousness.

The first consciousness gained by the soul was obviously

most-finite in proportion to the experience of absolute opposites of its own original, infinite state as in "A."

Consequently, it then means that in the beginning when the impressionless, infinite soul was first impressioned, such first impression was an absolutely most-finite gross impression. The first consciousness it (soul, *atma*) derived was most finite. Naturally, at that instant, the unconsciousness of the infinite soul actually experienced a most-finite first consciousness of the most-gross first impression.

Now if the soul is conscious of impressions (*sanskaras*), then the soul **must necessarily experience these impressions.** And in order to experience the impressions, the consciousness of the soul must experience them through proper and suitable media. As the impressions are, so are the experiences of the impressions, and likewise so are the proper media to experience the impressions. That is to say, the impressions give rise to experiences, and to experience the impressions, the use of appropriate media is essential.

Therefore, as the infinite, eternal and formless soul has now gotten the most-finite first consciousness of the most-gross first impression, most obviously and necessarily this first consciousness of the soul must utilize the most-finite and the most-gross first medium to experience the most-gross first impression.

This first medium adopted by God in His State IV (God as embodied soul) is a first form which, although it is gross, yet it is so inconceivably, infinitely finite that it cannot even be considered as gross. It is so very infinitely shapeless and sub-stanceless, matterless and formless that it cannot lead one even to imagine that it is gross. Yet this form is the very first gross form that emerges simultaneously as if in three prongs, as the first three of the foremost seven **"gas-like"** forms. If a description of these first three gas-like forms could ever be attempted, they could only be described from the standpoint of density,—the first having infinitely negligible density, then in the next stage negligible density, and in the third stage as having the first traces of density. These first three forms have no evolution. The next three forms may come within the scope of our imagination and may be described as "semi-gaseous and semi-material" forms. Evolution begins with the fourth gas-like form. And finally, there is the seventh gas-like form, of the series of seven foremost gas-like forms, which is hydrogen, and which may be said to include the electron.

It should be noted well that the first six gas-like gross forms bear no resemblance to the various gases such as hydrogen, nitrogen, and so forth. They are much, much finer (not subtler) * than those with which the scientists of the age are well conversant.

State V
God as Soul in the State of Evolution

God as embodied soul now **begins** to become conscious and **begins** to "know" the Creation (the Nothingness), although His "knowing" of the Creation at this stage is infinitely negligible. Even this most finite consciousness and this minutest "knowing," however, creates more impressions (*sanskaras*) that cause the "drop" (soul, *atma,* self) to leave or dissociate from the original first bubble (form). Leaving the bubble is equivalent to a dropping off of, or dissociating from, the first form.

Even after the form is dropped, the impressions gathered by the evolving consciousness of the soul do not vanish. These impressions remain associated with the evolved consciousness and cause the evolving consciousness of the soul to associate with another appropriate and superior bubble (form). The soul is thus able to know or experience more of the Creation through the second form. The "angle of vision" widens and the consciousness of "knowing" increases in proportion to the simultaneous evolution of form. With the evolution or growth in gross consciousness the impressions (*sanskaras*) also increase and cause the soul to assume or associate with a still more complex gross form in accordance with the impressions retained by the consciousness

---

* This is in no way to be connected with any form or object of the subtle world, because these forms are solely of the gross world.

when the second gross form is abandoned.

In this way the evolution of consciousness progresses for ages, concurrently with the evolution of forms which help to experience, and concurrently exhaust, the impressions gathered, until after countless changes of forms, through more concrete and successive stages of stones, metals, plants, worms, fishes, birds and animals, the soul takes on the human form.

In other words, the cycle of evolution of consciousness of soul continues evolving further and greater consciousness with the evolution of forms of higher and higher types, while experiencing and exhausting the impressions of the dissociated forms of the next lower type.

Consequently the evolution of consciousness of souls apparently tends the souls to identify themselves with, and gather varied innumerable impressions of, higher and higher gross species of forms, unlimited in number, in the gross world. The clean-cut major forms with which the souls associate, with every leap of greater and greater consciousness, are in accordance with the leaps from stone to metal, from metal to plant, from plant to worm, from worm to fish, from fish to bird, from bird to animal, and ultimately the last and seventh leap is from animal to human form.

It is very important to understand that the process of evolution of consciousness concerns the evolution of bubbles or forms only, and not the "drops" or the souls. The souls remain as indivisible and infinite as the unlimited ocean (*Paramatma*) from the beginning until the end of evolution of consciousness, which terminates with the completion of evolution of form.

Only through this evolution of form does the consciousness of ignorance, or the "knowing" of Creation, increase step by step due to varied impressions; and only in the human form can the individualized soul (*atma*) eventually realize the Over-Soul or *Paramatma*. As the soul is infinite, the consciousness of the soul must also become infinite; and because consciousness can become infinite only in human form, the human form is therefore the final stage of evolution of form.

The soul has to pass through eight million, four hundred thousand (eighty-four *lakhs*) human forms after it has once commenced to reincarnate in the human form until it has attained God-realization. The prehuman forms through which it has to pass before it can incarnate in the human form are innumerable.

Strictly speaking there is only one form—the human form—which is latent in all of the previous forms. The mineral, the plant and the animal forms actually contain the human form in its latent state, and this is gradually and increasingly manifested until it is at last completely expressed as a human being in a human body.

Before the human form becomes completely manifested in a human body, such as a man or a woman, the latent human form makes a series of partial turns. In the crystalline rock state (such as granite) the latent human form is completely upside down, and is almost so in the plant state as well. As the forms progress or evolve, the axis of the body rotates slowly, so that it becomes more and more horizontal; and when we reach the higher vertebrates, we find the head rising up more and more, as the axis of the body approaches the vertical. In men and women we find the human form completely expressed and completely vertical.

The details of this evolution of form are extremely complex. There are, for example, certain species of stone, metal, plant and animal that have what Meher Baba described as a special "seat" in evolution. These key species of forms are mostly those that are milestones on the evolutionary road, and they mark the first and the last of a certain general class of species of forms. For example, the first species of bird-form to follow the last species of fish-form and the first species of the animal-form to follow the last species of the bird-form have a special "seat" significance in evolution.

Meher Baba tells us that this whole theme has been explained down to the last detail in his own book * that is still

---

* [The book referred to should not be confused with this publication. Meher Baba has authored an additional work, which might be published later. Ed.]

to be handed over to the world.

Just as there is evolution of consciousness and evolution of forms, so also there is evolution of the worlds.

The evolved consciousness of the soul, identifying the soul with evolved forms, gets more and more impressioned; and in order to exhaust these impressions, it consistently finds its field of expression; and it experiences these impressions on the earth, which is also evolving concurrently with other worlds in accordance with the progressive evolution of the entire cosmic Creation.

During the course of evolution of consciousness of the soul, the soul, while **consciously** identifying itself with varied, finite gross forms, was also simultaneously, though **unconsciously**, identifying itself with its finite subtle form and its finite mental form, which associated with the soul (*atma*) in compact, homogeneous, unconscious association throughout the course of evolution of consciousness, right from the first urge.

During the whole course of the evolution of consciousness while the soul frequently and **consciously** dissociates itself from the finite gross forms, which act as media to experience and exhaust the impressions while evolving greater and greater consciousness, the soul never dissociates itself, consciously or unconsciously, from its finite subtle form and its finite mental form.

On the contrary, when the soul dissociates its identification with any one medium of finite gross form, it is the unconscious association of the soul with its subtle form that fortifies the soul, then without any gross medium, with finite energy—the driving force—to tend the consciousness of the soul towards identifying itself with yet another form, *i.e.*, the next medium of the next finite gross form, to experience the impressions of the last dissociated finite gross form, retained and reflected by the finite mental form of the soul, which is also in unconscious association with the soul.

It is only natural that together with the evolution of greater and greater consciousness of the soul, the evolution of the finite subtle form of the soul also takes place to fortify the soul with greater finite energy to tend the consciousness of the more and more gross-conscious soul to identify itself with higher and higher types of finite gross forms evolved by the impressions of the last lower and finite gross form.

Similarly, the evolution of the finite mental form of the soul also takes place simultaneously to accommodate, retain and reflect the increasingly innumerable, varied impressions gained and gathered by the evolution of greater and greater consciousness of the soul.

Thus it is that only in a human form are the subtle body and the mental body fully developed. Hence the soul, associating itself consciously with human form is, so to speak, fully equipped with gross body, subtle body and mental body in human form, together with the full consciousness of the gross gained in the human form.

Nevertheless, although the soul has gained full consciousness in human form and so experiences the gross world, yet the gross-conscious human soul is unconscious of the subtle body and therefore cannot experience the subtle world; the gross-conscious human soul is also unconscious of the mental body and therefore cannot experience the mental world.

State VI
God as Human Soul in the State of
Reincarnation *

The most-finite first impression of the first urge gave to the infinite unconsciousness of the unconscious soul the most-finite first consciousness. Gradually, varied and innumerable impressions, experienced through varied and innumerable gross media, gained greater and greater consciousness of the finite gross world for the soul, and eventually the evolution of consciousness was complete when the consciousness of the soul identified itself with the most-first human form. Therefore the

---

* [See also: Meher Baba, "Reincarnation and Karma," *Discourses*, 3: 51–98. Ed.]

soul, having now gained full consciousness in human form, does not need any more or any other higher forms to evolve consciousness. The consciousness gradually gained in the process of evolution is full and complete in human form.

Though the soul in this state has gained full and complete consciousness, it is still not conscious of its subtle and mental bodies nor of its unlimited Self as One—indivisible, eternal and infinite; it is only fully conscious of its identity with human form and its varied aspects and experiences of the gross world.

Consequently the soul at this stage, only fully gross-conscious of the most-first human gross form, and still unconscious of the subtle and mental, experiences in the gross world all of the impressions of the most-last animal gross form dissociated or dropped by the consciousness of the soul in the latest stage of evolution of consciousness.

When all of the impressions of the most-last animal gross form are exhausted through incessant experiences by the most-first human gross form, then it is but natural that this most-first human form is dropped or dissociated from the consciousness of the soul. This experience by the fully conscious soul is universally accepted as the death of the human being. As explained previously, although the consciousness of the soul gets dissociated from the most-first human form, yet it can never get dissociated from the unconscious associations of its subtle and mental bodies.

The consciousness of the soul retains and experiences the impressions of the dropped or dissociated most-first human form through its subtle and mental bodies. In order to exhaust these impressions the consciousness of the soul must necessarily associate with a gross form; and therefore, it associates itself with the next human form to exhaust and experience the residual impressions of the previous human form dropped. In fact this next human form is nothing but the consolidated mould of the past impressions retained of the previous body or human form that dissociated from the conscious soul. The association of consciousness of the soul with the next human form is universally accepted as the birth of a human being.

In short, in State VI of God as human soul in the state of reincarnation, the soul has developed full consciousness in human form, and therefore there is no need for any further evolution of the gross form. The evolution of gross consciousness thus comes to an end with the attainment of the human form; and to experience the impressions (*sanskaras*) cultivated in the human and the sub-human forms, the soul has to incarnate again and again into the human form.

The kind of human forms with which the consciousness of the soul has to associate is determined by the nature of previous impressions (*sanskaras*) of virtue or vice, happiness or misery, and so forth. While experiencing the gross world, the soul identifies itself with the gross body, which is destructible, although the soul itself is eternal.

In the sub-human stage the evolutionary process of form and consciousness is involuntary, yet sustained and continuous, with no possibility of slipping down to the lower forms of evolution. In the human stage, which marks the end of the evolution of form and the attainment of full consciousness, the spiritual progress of man, through the reincarnation and realization processes, is voluntary, and is also absolutely free from any danger whatsoever of slipping down to a sub-human state except in flagrant misuse of the powers of the fourth plane. Once full consciousness is gained, it is gained forever and is never lost; and the evolution of consciousness is completed only when the consciousness of the soul associates itself with human form. Therefore retrograde incarnation is an impossibility once the consciousness of the soul identifies itself with a human form.

With the development of full consciousness of the gross world in the human gross body, the soul simultaneously is associated with the fully developed subtle and mental bodies. But as long as consciousness is confined to the gross world, the consciousness of the soul cannot make use of its subtle and mental bodies directly. The soul becomes conscious of these bodies and experiences the corresponding impressions of these bodies through the corresponding spheres of the subtle and mental worlds only when full consciousness, which is conscious only of the gross at this stage, turns inwards toward itself and the process of the involution of consciousness begins. This becomes possible only when the consciousness of the individualized soul becomes satiated with the incessant experiences of the varied and innumerable impressions of the material or gross life, and only when it has suffered oscillations between the opposites of pain and pleasure, for what may seem interminable ages, through the unfailing chain of births and deaths in the process of reincarnation. In the stage of evolution of consciousness the "winding process" of impressions (*sanskaras*) is at work with a view to evolving consciousness, developing higher and higher types of gross forms. In the human stage the fully evolved consciousness remains, but the grip of impressions (*sanskaras*) begins to loosen and thin out as a result of continuous jolts experienced by the consciousness of the soul through the seemingly unending chain of births and deaths in the reincarnation process.

State VII
God in the State of Spiritually
Advanced Souls

After a long drawn out struggle with the life of the gross senses in the gross world, the consciousness of the soul **begins** to get drawn towards the Self of the soul rather than to remain focussed on the gross body and its gross environment. After a number of births and deaths the gross-conscious human soul is at last inevitably drawn to embark upon the process which will lead the man ultimately to the goal of God-realization in human form.

The consciousness of the soul therefore begins to withdraw itself from the world of gross senses and is now ready to undergo the process of involution. The soul is thus said to advance spiritually through the subtle and mental spheres.

The subtle sphere, or the subtle world, is the domain of the first three planes of the involving consciousness of the soul; the fourth plane lies between the subtle sphere and the mental sphere; and the mental sphere contains the fifth and sixth planes.

This seventh state of God comprises the advance by the pilgrims on the spiritual path through the subtle and mental spheres. The greater the advance, the greater the involution of consciousness.

When the soul becomes conscious of the subtle sphere through the subtle body, it identifies itself with the subtle body; and when it is conscious of the mental sphere through the mental body, it identifies itself with the mental body, just as it identified itself with the gross body when it was conscious of the gross sphere through the gross body.

The spiritual progress of the soul through these spheres is entirely in imagination. The pilgrim's progress in the involution of his consciousness consists in replacing one realm of imagination for a better and higher level of imagination, right from the first through the sixth plane of involving consciousness. In the seventh plane the involving process is complete, imagination comes to an end and Reality is realized and is no longer a concept.

Those who enter the spiritual path and tread upon it without the help of a Master to guide them very often get lost in the labyrinths of sights and illuminations, and have little or no chance of redeeming themselves from that position. They are like children who, on their way to school, get distracted by the sights and attractions of the market place.

The enchantment on the spiritual path is so great and the enticement so intense that even in the earlier stages of the journey the pilgrim has a pseudo-sense of God-realization from which he cannot emerge unless helped by Perfect Masters. Many an advanced pilgrim in the subtle sphere thinks that he has gained complete freedom from births and deaths—although this is not so. The delusion remains up to the sixth plane of involving consciousness, but it is most conspicuous between the third and fourth planes. The fourth plane of consciousness is the most treacherous stage in the pilgrim's progress, because this is the stage when all the powers of the infinite Energy of the subtle sphere are under his direct command. The misuse of these powers means the downfall and disintegration of the consciousness of the soul. Though it is a fundamental fact that once consciousness is gained it can never be lost, yet an exception to this rule can occur, but only **at the fourth plane** where there is a good possibility of the consciousness gained by the soul being disintegrated. While it is never lost completely, it disintegrates as far back as the consciousness of the stone form. The whole process of evolution of consciousness then has to be repeated to regain the full consciousness and the human form.

Thus it is that from the fourth plane the pilgrim on the spiritual path may either fall back due to the abuse or wrong use of *tajalliyat* (*siddhis*), or progress by further involution of his consciousness to fifth plane consciousness, and capture the experience of the mental sphere or the mental world. Crossing the fourth plane and stepping into the fifth would mean gaining approach to the Divine Gate!

In the sixth plane the pilgrim "sees" God face to face. This seeing is through the mental eye when the consciousness of the soul identifies the soul with the mental body. Even when the pilgrim sees God face to face in the sixth plane of his involving consciousness, the grip of duality is not overcome, because the seer and the seen are still differentiated through the seeing.

Imagination on the planes ceases as soon as the pilgrim crosses the field of Illusion and enters the realm of Reality in the seventh plane of completely involved consciousness, where he is absolutely free of all traces of impressions. The seventh plane consciousness is full, as well as mature, and is the impressionless consciousness which identifies the soul with its "Self." The soul then feels and experiences consciously its eternal existence as God. The "drop" (soul), devoid of any bubble (form of ignorance in Illusion), realizes its eternal existence in the infinite ocean, as the ocean itself (the *Paramatma* or the Over-Soul).

State VIII
God as the Divinely Absorbed

This state of God signifies for the soul the end of the long evolutionary struggle, the end of the reincarnation process and the end of the realization process through the planes. For the individual soul there is no higher stage toward which to aspire, because it has reached the goal by becoming one with God. The God-realized pilgrim of this stage is known to the Sufi world as a *Majzoob* and the Vedantist calls him a *Brahmi Bhoot*. The *Majzoob* has no body-consciousness and no consciousness of the three spheres, the gross, the subtle and the mental. This means that in this State VIII, God as *Majzoob* **consciously experiences** His own infinite trio-nature of infinite power, knowledge and bliss, but does not make **use** of these infinite aspects of His nature.

In this State VIII, the unconscious, infinite state A of God (the unconscious *Paramatma*) not only gains the highest divine consciousness of state B of God (the conscious *Paramatma*) but in this state God becomes divinely absorbed in the reality of His own infinite, conscious state, and thus realizes His eternal identity with the infinite, conscious state B of God.

This State VIII of God is of the highest divine consciousness, which is the *ahadiyat* (*halat-e-Muhammadi*) or the *vidnyan*. All God-realized beings—the *Majzoob-e-Kamil* (*Brahmi Bhoot*), *Majzoob-Salik* (*Paramhansa*), *Azad-e-Mutlaq* (*Jivanmukta*), *Qutub* (*Sadguru*), and *Rasool* (*Avatar*)—retire to this state B of God in the Beyond after disembodiment. Meher Baba explained that such a disembodied state of the Perfect Master is referred to by the Sufis as *halat-e-Muhammadi* (State of Muhammad), as distinguished from *muqam-e-Muhammadi* (Office of Muhammad), when in a physical body. *Haqiqat-e-*

Muhammadi is the tenth state of God in a physical body, and the *muqam-e-Muhammadi* (Office of Muhammad) is the *Vidnyan Bhumika* (the office of *vidnyan*) depicted in the chart as C.

State IX
God as Liberated Incarnate Soul

If God, divinely absorbed as in State VIII, recovers and maintains normal consciousness of the mental, subtle and gross spheres through His mental, subtle and gross aspects as an embodiment of a perfect human being known as *Majzoob* (divinely absorbed), He then experiences State IX at the Divine Junction between God States VIII and X.

If the soul recovers the normal consciousness of the mental, subtle and gross bodies and spheres, it comes out of the *Majzoob* State VIII, crossing the *fana-fillah,* to get the experience of the *baqa-billah* state. But, before becoming established in *baqa-billah*, it may enter the state known to Sufis as *"fana-ma-al-baqa"* of the *"muqam-e-furutat,"* which the Vedantists call *"turiya avastha."* This is State IX at the Divine Junction between the *fana-fillah* and *baqa-billah* of Divinity.

The God-realized souls in a human body at this state are either the *Paramhansa* (*Majzoob-Salik* or *Salik-Majzoob*) or the *Jivanmukta* (*Azad-e-Mutlaq*). They both enjoy infinite knowledge, power, and bliss, and are conscious of the "I am God" state. They differ from the *Majzoob-e-Kamil,* however, in that they can and do become conscious of the three bodies and the three spheres (mental, subtle and gross). While the *Majzoob* state is a continual state of being divinely absorbed, the state of the *Paramhansa* is one of **sometimes** being divinely absorbed and **sometimes** recovering normal consciousness of one who experiences the *suluk* of *sulukiyat*. His conscious experience is sometimes that of "I am my own God" and sometimes "I am my own creature." The state of the *Jivanmukta* is of one who normally experiences the *suluk* of *sulukiyat* (*i.e.,* of one permanently established in the state of *baqa-billah*). Both the *Paramhansa* and *Jivanmukta* differ from the *Qutub* in not being able to use the infinite knowledge, power and bliss that they experience continuously.

No direct * spiritual benefit accrues to the world from a *Paramhansa* or *Jivanmukta*. However, a *Jivanmukta*, towards the end of his life, does make one single soul perfect like himself; although he has no duty in the three spheres, he enjoys the *baqa-billah* state.

State X
God as "Man-God"

This is the state of God in a human body such as a Perfect Master (*Qutub*, *Sadguru*). In this state the Perfect Master or the Man-God is divinely, unattachedly and unlimitedly above the law of Illusion that governs the cosmic Creation in an infinitely systematical order; and yet He permits Himself to be bound by the limitations of time, space and causation while continually experiencing consciously His "I am God" state and His infinite power, knowledge and bliss. He not only experiences these infinite attributes, but He also uses these for the emancipation of other souls in the grip of ignorance who are still unconscious of their own eternal reality.

This is the state of absolute perfection; here God is with attributes and with form (*saguna* and *sakar*).

According to the Sufis, the *Qutub* connotes the highest point on the upward journey; he is the *summum bonum* of Creation and the fairest flower of humanity. In the *Majzoob* state, the soul enjoyed the infinite bliss of the "I am God" state; but the Perfect Master (*Qutub*, *Sadguru*) enjoys the infinite bliss of the "I am God" state and also the highest divine consciousness of "Everything is I" and "Everything is from Me."

This tenth state of God in the human body is the state of

---

* [Nevertheless, indirectly, anyone coming in contact with him automatically benefits. Ed.]

haqiqat-e-Muhammadi. The Perfect Masters (*Qutubs* or *Sadgurus*) and the *Avatar* (*Rasool*) are all of this state. Whether God is in the state of Man-God, as Perfect Master, or in the state of God-Man, as *Avatar,* He is in this tenth state and functions as a Man-God and as a God-Man from the divine office *muqam-e-Muhammadi* or *vidnyan bhumika,* depicted in the chart as "C". The first manifestation of God, with His infinite consciousness, assumed this divine office, and this office will ever continue to function eternally to radiate infinite power, knowledge and bliss which the Perfect Masters and the *Avatar,* not only eternally experience, but also use for the emancipation of all souls who are still in the grip of ignorance, trying to gain consciousness of their eternal state of oneness with the Over-Soul.

In other words, God in a human body will everlastingly manifest Himself in all of His perfection only through this divine office marked "C" in the chart "The Ten States of God."

It was only through this divine office that God, as God-Man, in the form of Zoroaster, Rama, Krishna, Jesus, Buddha, Muhammad and others, manifested Himself and proclaimed in every cycle, age after age, that He is the Saviour, the Prophet, the Messiah, the Son-of-God, the *Avatar,* the *Rasool,* the *Buddha* and so forth. And it is only through this divine office that the five Perfect Masters or the *Qutubs* or the *Sadgurus* function as the *summum bonum* of the whole cosmic Creation.

The Sufis call this divine office *"muqam-e-Muhammadi,"* after the name of the Prophet Muhammad, the *Rasool* of God, in His *haqiqat-e-Muhammadi.* Similarly, Jesus of Nazareth, the Son of God, is—like Muhammad, Zoroaster, Krishna, Rama, Buddha—the God-Man; whilst "Christ," like *haqiqat-e-Muhammadi,* is the divine state of Jesus.

When we try to put together all the different stages of God in a nutshell, five distinct stages, in the travail of the unconscious *Paramatma* to gain complete consciousness, become conspicuous.

THE FIRST STAGE

(A) To begin with, *atma* (soul) and *Paramatma* (Over-Soul) are both one in the infinite, indivisible "Oneness of Reality."

(B) Before the beginning of the Beginning, *Paramatma* and all *atmas* were unconscious and unimpressioned.

(C) In the beginning, *atma* had no consciousness of the gross body, subtle body or mental body, and therefore had no experience of the gross world, the subtle world or the mental world. *Atma* was even unconscious of its own Self and therefore had no experience of its own *Paramatma* state.

This is the stage depicted as state A in the chart of the Ten States of God.

THE SECOND STAGE

Atma gains consciousness and has impressions. At this stage *atma* is conscious either of the gross body or the subtle body or the mental body and experiences either the gross world or the subtle world or the mental world; but *atma* is still unconscious of its own Self and therefore does not experience the *Paramatma* state yet.

This is the stage as in States III, IV, V, VI and VII according to the chart.

THE THIRD STAGE

Atma becomes impressionless but retains full and complete consciousness. This complete consciousness is now no longer of the gross body, the subtle body or the mental body, and therefore *atma* no longer experiences the gross world, the subtle world or the mental world.

This consciousness that is retained is of *atma's* own infinite Self, and therefore *atma* now experiences the *Paramatma* state consciously and experiences the infinite power, knowledge and bliss of the "I am God" state.

This is the stage noted as State VIII in the chart.

THE FOURTH STAGE

Atma recovers the so-called normal consciousness of the gross body, the subtle body and the mental body and therefore once again experiences, at one and the same time, the gross world, the subtle world and the mental world. At this stage, *atma* is simultaneously also conscious of its own infinite Self and experiences the infinite power, infinite knowledge and infinite bliss of its own *Paramatma* state, but *atma* **cannot use** these infinite attributes even though, at this stage, it is conscious of its gross, subtle and mental bodies and experiences simultaneously the three worlds.

This is the stage of State IX in the chart.

THE FIFTH STAGE

Atma is fully and completely conscious of the gross body, the subtle body and the mental body, and experiences the gross world, the subtle world and the mental world simultaneously with having the highest divine consciousness of its infinite Self, and also experiences and **uses** the infinite power, infinite knowledge and infinite bliss of its own *Paramatma* state.

This is the stage of State X as shown in the chart of the Ten States of God.*

---

* [A summary by Meher Baba of different terms for status, state, stage or aspect and gnosis in the eternal sphere of Reality appears on pages 296–7. The gnosis of "I am God" is common to each one of the four types of perfection and does not end on physical death. Ed.]

Conclusion

G OD cannot be explained, He cannot be argued about, He cannot be theorized, nor can He be discussed and understood. God can only be lived.[36a, b, c.]

Nevertheless, all that is said here and explained about God to appease the intellectual convulsions of the mind of man, still lacks many more words and further explanations because the TRUTH is that the Reality must be realized and the divinity of God must be attained and lived.

To **understand** the infinite, eternal Reality is **not** the GOAL of individualized beings in the Illusion of Creation, because the Reality can never be understood; it is to be **realized** by conscious experience.

Therefore, the GOAL is to realize the Reality and attain the "I am God" state in human form.

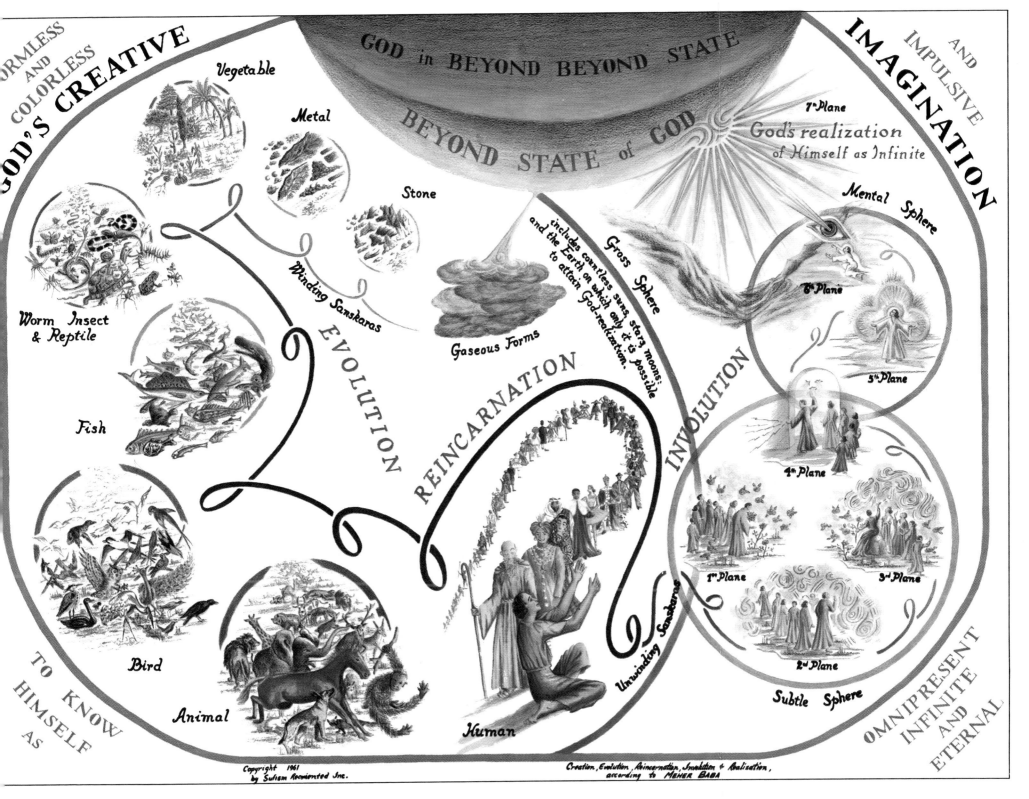

GOD in BEYOND BEYOND STATE

BEYOND STATE of GOD

FORMLESS AND COLORLESS

GOD'S CREATIVE

AND IMPULSIVE

IMAGINATION

Vegetable

Metal

Stone

Worm Insect & Reptile

Winding Sanskaras

EVOLUTION

Fish

Bird

Animal

Gaseous Forms

Gross Sphere

includes countless suns, stars, moons; and the Earth on which only it is possible to attain God-realization.

REINCARNATION

Human

Unwinding Sanskaras

INVOLUTION

7ᵗʰ Plane
God's realization
of Himself as Infinite

Mental Sphere

6ᵗʰ Plane

5ᵗʰ Plane

4ᵗʰ Plane

1ˢᵗ Plane

3ʳᵈ Plane

2ⁿᵈ Plane

Subtle Sphere

TO KNOW HIMSELF AS

OMNIPRESENT INFINITE AND ETERNAL

Copyright 1961
by Sufism Reoriented Inc.

Creation, Evolution, Reincarnation, Involution & Realization,
according to MEHER BABA

CHART 8A: *Creation, Evolution, Reincarnation, Involution & Realization, according to Meher Baba.*

This chart, painted by Rano Gayley under the supervision of Meher Baba, is a pictorial version of the book *God Speaks*.

God in the Beyond Beyond State represents God as pure Essence, infinite, original and eternal, unaware of anything, even of Himself. God Is.

God in the Beyond State represents the Oversoul (Paramatma), essentially the same as God in the Beyond Beyond State except that here surged the whim to know Himself and He became conscious of infinite power, knowledge and bliss, and simultaneously conscious of Illusion which manifested as the Creation. By completing His journey through the worlds of forms He sheds the illusion of their apparent reality.

Reading counter-clockwise, the first forms taken by souls emanating from the Creation point are gaseous. As consciousness evolves, souls take the innumerable forms indicated, experiencing increasing impressions (sanskaras). Arriving at the state of man, the soul has achieved complete consciousness and reincarnates innumerable times until it is ready to experience involution, all of which takes place while embodied in the gross world.

While getting free of sanskaras, the ascending soul gradually becomes aware of the seven planes and higher spheres until it is liberated from all bindings and becomes one with God (God-realized).

The first three planes depict subtle awareness; the fourth portrays the vast powers and energies encountered there; the fifth is the plane of sainthood and is in the mental sphere; the sixth is the plane of illumination and the seventh is the plane of God-realization, i.e. unity with God.

Contents of Supplement

Supplement

1 Impressioned Consciousness (29) *

At the request of the editors, Meher Baba added the following information:

Consciousness is definitely complete as soon as the first human form is taken, but it does not start involving at that point. When consciousness first begins to involve it means that the human being is only beginning to take the first step on the spiritual path.

Between the time of the first human incarnation and the time of going on the path, the complete consciousness of a human being, which is still an impressioned consciousness, has necessarily to indulge in a process that eventually must dislodge these impressions from retaining their hold on it (the consciousness which is complete).

It is to be noted that during that period, which covers thousands of reincarnations, the impressions which were hard-set or dense get shaken up so thoroughly by the reincarnation process that their tight grip on consciousness becomes loose. These hard-set (dense or gross) impressions thin out or become

_____
* Numbers refer to the page number of this book.

feeble through innumerable and varied experiences of opposites. The limit to these experiences is reached by persistent reincarnations which give experiences of opposites.

It is also to be noted that it is only when these dense, hard-set or gross impressions become less dense or become feeble, that the limit to the experiences of the gross world through gross impressions is reached by the gross medium, the human body. When the dense, hard-set impressions become less dense, they no longer give rise to gross experiences because these less dense (feeble) impressions are refined or fine and no longer crude or gross. The aggregate of such refined or fine impressions is called subtle impressions. These subtle impressions give rise to experiences of the subtle type (*i.e.*, pertaining to the subtle world) and the subtle body experiences these subtle impressions and tries to exhaust them.

When these subtle impressions become even less dense and still more refined, the aggregate of such impressions is called mental impressions. These mental impressions give rise to experiences pertaining to the mental world, and the mental body experiences these mental impressions and tries to exhaust them.

When the last traces of mental impressions are exhausted through experiences by the mental body, the complete consciousness of the soul (which was all along in the grip of impressions from the instant it identified itself with the most-first human-form up to the last human-form—which is the mental-conscious human being), is unburdened of impressions. Only such impressionless complete consciousness can realize the final experience of the "I am God" state of the soul.

When the gross or hard-set impressions get thinned out by the reincarnation process, they become subtle impressions. These subtle impressions can no longer give rise to experiences of the gross world. At this stage the consciousness of the gross-conscious human being automatically begins to indulge in experiences of the subtle world. This marks the advent of the process of involution of consciousness and the aspirant begins to tread the Path. It is obvious that the subtle impressions must give rise to the subtle experiences of the subtle world. These subtle impressions get exhausted by the subtle body through experiences of the subtle world and the process of involution of consciousness continues.

2 Practical Mysticism (44)

APPROACH TO TRUTH IS INDIVIDUAL

There is no general rule or method applicable to all who aspire to realize God. Every man must work out his own salvation, and must choose his own method, although his choice is mostly determined by the total effect of the mind impressions (*sanskaras*) acquired in previous lives. He should be guided by the creed of his conscience, and follow the method that best suits his spiritual tendency, his physical aptitude and his external circumstances. Truth is One, but the approach to it is essentially individual. The Sufis say, "There are as many ways to God as there are souls of men" (*Aṭ-ṭuruqu īlāllahi kanufūsi banī ādam*).

> *Jamāl-i fiṭrat ke lākh partao*
> *Qubūl partao kī lākh shākhīṇ*
> *Ṭarīq-i 'irfāṇ maīṇ kiyā batāūṇ*
> *Yah rāh kiskī wāh rāh kiskī.*
> —Akbar

"Nature's beauty has thousands of facets for which there are thousands of ways and means of acceptance (understanding); in the Path of Gnosis, who can determine which particular mode or mood is earmarked for a given individual?"

RENUNCIATION

When a pilgrim, and by pilgrim we mean here aspirant or disciple, feels drawn to renunciation, it means that the spirit of renunciation was already latent in him. This readiness results from the swinging of the terrible pendulum from pain to pleasure and pleasure to pain, in the countless forms of evolution and in the countless entrances and exits through the doors of birth and death experienced during reincarnation. Because this spirit of renunciation is latent, it needs only some exciting cause to bring it to the surface, and it is only when it comes to the surface that we are able to see the power and nature of the latent spirit.

If the latent spirit is simply a spiritual indigestion from a temporary surfeit of pain, combined with a mild desire for something more pleasant, the overt renunciation will be only of a fleeting and feeble kind, a mere temporary escape from unpleasantness. At its best however, this latent spirit is a secret pact of aggression between an incurable disgust for the world and an ardent and burning thirst for God. When it comes to the surface it shows itself as an invincible determination to marshal the entire being to the attainment of victory over the lower self, and to reject everything that is irrelevant to this great and terrible struggle. Note this word "reject"; it means that such a pilgrim casts aside irrelevancies. We might call renunciation the fruit of the flower of spiritual longing, fertilized by the pollen of disgust for the futility of endless births and deaths. Once renunciation expresses itself there are many ways of looking at it, of which the simplest is to divide it into two main types, internal and external.

External renunciation means giving up completely all worldly delights and physical attachments to material things. In the early stages, this renunciation is helpful to the extent to which it leads to internal renunciation and preoccupation with God. Tens of thousands of so-called *sanyasis* (renunciators) are to be found in India, of whom far too many have adopted this external renunciation only as a profession that enables them to indulge in an unproductive life of idleness. External renunciation, however, can be and often is real. When this is so it will inevitably lead on to internal renunciation, and this is the renunciation that matters. Internal renunciation means the control of desires at their very source so that the mind does not fall a prey to the demands of lust, greed and anger. This does not mean that one shall cease at once to **have** such thoughts. This is impossible, as such thoughts will continue to be troublesome as long as the *sanskaras* from which they arise are part of one's being. The fight is necessarily hard and long.

For the West in particular, external renunciation is inadvisable and impracticable. It should be internal and of the mind from the start. One should live in the world, perform all legitimate duties and yet feel mentally detached from everything. One should be in the world but not of it. The Sufis say, *"Dil bā yār, dast bikār"* (The heart with God; the hands for work).

Hazrat Nizamuddin Awliya, the Perfect Master of Delhi, was once asked by a visitor how one should live in the world. At that moment it so happened that a few women were passing by with pitchers of water balanced on their heads, and, as they walked, they gossiped and gesticulated. Pointing to them Nizamuddin said, "Look at those women—that's how you should live in the world." Asked to explain this cryptic remark, the Master continued, "These women returning from the well with pitchers balanced on their heads seem to be thinking of nothing else but exchanging tid-bits of gossip with each other; and yet they are all the time concentrating on something far more important, on balancing the pitchers on their heads. Thus, whatever your body, your senses or the purely surface part of your mind may be occupied with, see that the root of your mind is constantly focussed on God."

Vaitag AND *Vairagya*

If we look upon renunciation as being a state of mind, we can understand how this state of mind may be either temporary or permanent. The former is known as *vaitag* and the latter as *vairagya*.

Vaitag (temporary renunciation) is simply a temporary disgust for the world and its affairs resulting from some shock, disappointment or loss, combined with a vague desire for God; or it may come from a sudden impulse. In *vaitag* the mind turns away from the world and takes to godly ways; but this attitude is not lasting, and the mind returns to its old ways as soon as circumstances alter, or as soon as the impulse dies down.

Vairagya (irrevocable renunciation) however is an attitude of mind involving such a longing for God and such a deep indifference to things worldly that, once roused, it knows no retreat and is proof against all temptations to give it up. The famous example of Gautama Buddha is illustrative of *vairagya.*

We have already explained that renunciation is the overt expression of a latent desire for union with God combined with a latent spirit of disgust for the world, and we used an analogy of flower, pollen and fruit. As far as fertilization is concerned the flower and the pollen by themselves are helpless, for the two can only be brought together by some outside agency, such as the wind, the bee or the insect. Whether or not fertilization takes place in nature may depend upon so many thousands of unknown factors that modern science gives up trying to predict it, and labels it chance. That, however, is beside the point at the moment, and in our analogy we shall think of this fertilization as a gift.

To return to *vairagya,* let us remember that the longing for union with God is latent in **every** living being. However, it only pushes its way into consciousness when the soul approaches the beginning of what Meher Baba, in the "Divine Theme," calls "the realization process." The disgust for the world is also something that develops naturally in all of us and which grows more and more powerful as we draw nearer to the beginning of this realization process. When the flower is in full bloom and the pollen ripe, the wind or the bee gives the gift of fertilization that produces the fruit. In the same way also, when this moment of inner readiness comes, a divine gift descends upon the soul which fertilizes the longing for God and the disgust or indifference for the world, and so brings about the priceless fruit of *vairagya.* This divine gift may be a touch of inner grace from the indwelling God, or it may be the result of contact with a saint or a Perfect Master. But it is always a gift.

Vairagya, when it first becomes manifest, will almost certainly express itself for a time as an external renunciation. But *vairagya,* being permanent, will always lead sooner or later to the real renunciation which is internal.

When an aspirant has such an intense longing for Truth he is qualified to enter the Path. There is a story of a Master who was pestered by a disciple as to when he would realize God. Once when they went to bathe in a river the Master held the aspirant under water for a few moments. When the disciple was on the verge of suffocation the Master pulled him out and asked what he had thought of and longed for most while under the water. The aspirant replied, "Air." The Master explained that when the disciple had just as intense a longing for God then Realization would come. Maulana Rumi says:

Āb kamjū, tishnigī āvar bidast.

"Call out for water less, but create thirst for it more."

In the words of Meher Baba, "The Path begins with a conscious longing for a deeper reality. As the fish which is taken out of water longs to go back to the water, so the aspirant who has sensed the Goal longs to be united with God.

"In fact, the longing to go back to the Source is present in each being from the very time that it gets separated from the Source by the veil of ignorance, but it is unconscious till the aspirant enters the Path." *

The Sufis call this attitude of mind *"tauba"* meaning repentance and implying the turning away from or renouncing of the life of the senses for the life of the spirit. One who has taken this great step does not look back again at that which he has left behind.

Meher Baba says that there may be a thousand seekers enjoying as many spiritual experiences, but there is only one Path of Gnosis. It is an internal but an actual pathway. Though not an ordinary path it is distinctly perceptible as such to the internal eye of the true pilgrim who travels along it. But even those mystics who have truly "experienced" can only explain

---

* [See also: Meher Baba, "The Stages of the Path," *Discourses,* 2: 18–26. Ed.]

the sections of the Path that they themselves have traversed. Those who have reached the critical point on the third plane can know nothing about the fourth plane, nor can they lead any one up to their own level. Their knowledge and experience are limited to themselves. Only those on the fifth and sixth planes can bring others up to their own level and anyone upon whom their grace descends will be greatly benefited.

The individual souls of the world are within the limits of the gross sphere which includes all the gross suns, moons, worlds and all space. A savage, ignorant of the most elementary scientific laws and of the code of right and wrong, and a great philosopher or scientist are both within the bounds of the gross sphere. The philosopher may be quite familiar in theory with the subtle sphere; and the scientist may be an authority on the extreme frontiers of modern physics; but, from the standpoint of the subtle, they and the savage belong to the gross sphere. Until the subtle sphere is experienced, gnosis remains a subject for intellectual quibbling for all those belonging to the gross sphere because by "subtle" we do not mean merely the finest form of the gross. In the ordinary sense of the word it may be correct to call very fine substances such as ether, the atom, vibration, light and space, "subtle"; but they are unquestionably gross, though in a very fine form.

Spiritually speaking, subtle means something completely different from the physical, however attenuated physical things may be. Although the gross sphere is the outcome of the subtle sphere and is dependent on it, the subtle sphere is completely independent of the gross sphere. As an example, we may take the act of eating. The gross act is the outcome of the thought, and depends upon it; but the thought is independent of the physical act.

FORGETFULNESS

The whole philosophy of approaching and realizing the Truth hinges on the question of what we may call forgetfulness. The word "forgetfulness" used here must not be associated with its commonly accepted meaning of forgetting to post a letter, or of a state of mind that is simply dull and blank. Forgetfulness in this special sense is an attitude of mind that develops gradually into spiritual experience. External renunciation is not forgetfulness, because it is mostly physical and partly mental; but internal renunciation, when it becomes purely mental, does assume the quality and dignity of forgetfulness. Thus one may renounce the world, but it is not so easy to forget it.

Forgetfulness in this special sense thus explains the secret that lies behind all happiness, spiritual or otherwise, that human beings experience. The Sufi term for this forgetfulness is *bikhudi,* and it should not be mixed up—though it often is—with *bihoshi* (unconsciousness).

The difference between forgetfulness and unconsciousness is important, and a few examples of types of unconsciousness will help to make it clear. To begin with, one must remember that forgetfulness is the partial or total **detachment** of the mind from the physical world, and unconsciousness the partial or total **deadening** of the mind to the physical world. The former gives rise to various degrees of spiritual ecstasy and the latter to various degrees of cessation of pleasure and pain.

Let us then look at one or two examples of unconsciousness. In perfect health one does not bother about the functioning of a vital organ like the heart. This means that one forgets that this organ is beating ceaselessly and perfectly in the human body for the maintenance of life and health. If, however, there is a disturbance in the cardiac rhythm there is immediate discomfort, and if there is a cardiac infarct there is immediate precordial pain. In either case one is reminded that one has a heart. The sensation of discomfort or pain, though it arises from the heart, is felt only because of the functioning of the mind. The more the mind is directed to the heart, the more the discomfort or pain is felt. When pain reaches its climax, unconsciousness may supervene—a break in the threads of consciousness that enables one to forget the pain. But this is unconsciousness and not forgetfulness in its spiritual sense. A surgeon by performing a pre-

frontal leucotomy can interfere with some of the nervous path-
ways that serve this focussing of the mind on the intractable pain
of some incurable disease like cancer. After this operation the
pain is still there, but the patient ceases to direct his mind towards it, and so ceases to bother about it. This again is a partial
unconsciousness brought about by purely physical means, and
not true forgetfulness in its spiritual sense. Sleep is a state of
unconsciousness that affords a temporary respite from the wear
and tear of life; but sleep is not true forgetfulness in its spiritual
sense.

The whole philosophy of happiness and unhappiness therefore hinges on the question of forgetfulness of some kind or another, and of remembrance of some kind or another. Remembrance is an attachment of the mind to a particular idea, person,
thing or place, and forgetfulness is its opposite. Once it is understood that remembrance causes pain, it follows that the only
cure is some kind of forgetfulness, and this forgetfulness may
be either positive or negative. The positive forgetfulness is one in
which the mind remains aware of external stimuli, but refuses
to react to them. The negative forgetfulness is either mere unconsciousness—a stopping of the mind as in sound sleep—or
an acceleration of it as in madness, which has been defined as a
way of avoiding the memory of suffering. Either sleep or madness may be artificially induced in various degrees by the use
of intoxicants or drugs; but this also is a negative way of overcoming remembrance.

Positive forgetfulness, then, is the cure, and its steady
cultivation develops in man that balance of mind which enables
him to express such noble traits as charity, forgiveness, tolerance,
selflessness, and service to others. One who is not equipped with
this positive forgetfulness becomes a barometer of his surroundings. His poise is disturbed by the slightest whisper of praise or
flattery, and by the faintest suggestion of slander or criticism;
his mind is like a slender reed swayed by the lightest breeze of
emotion. Such a man is perpetually at war with himself and
knows no peace.

In the exercise of this positive forgetfulness, not only is non-reaction to adverse circumstances essential, but also non-reaction to favourable and pleasurable circumstances. Of these two the latter is the harder and is less often described, although it matters just as much.

Positive forgetfulness, although it lies at the very root of happiness, is by no means easy to acquire. Once a man attains this state of mind, however, he rises above pain and pleasure; he is master of himself. This forgetfulness, to be fully effective for the spiritual life, must become permanent, and such permanence is only acquired through constant practice during many lives. Some people, as a result of efforts towards forgetfulness in past lives, get spontaneous and temporary flashes of it in a later life, and it is such people who give to the world the best in poetry, art and philosophy, and who make the greatest discoveries in science.

In such moments of true forgetfulness there is a mental detachment from all material surroundings in which the poet allows his imagination to soar. An artist, when he gives form to an ideal in which he completely forgets himself and all irrelevant surroundings, creates a masterpiece. The best of philosophy is uttered when a man surveys the problem of life without reference to the ups and downs of his purely personal circumstances; and some of the greatest scientific discoveries have been made in this same frame of mind. Such manifestations of genuine spontaneity of forgetfulness are very rare indeed, and although it is said that poets, artists and philosophers are born and not made, these fleeting phases of real forgetfulness are the result of efforts made in past lives.

In an attempt to make life bearable some people develop a feeble kind of stoicism—a sort of "who cares, anyway" outlook —and others plunge recklessly into epicurism. The former is the apathetic acceptance of defeat, and the latter the effort to forget defeat in the arms of pleasure. Neither is true forgetfulness. But when a man acquires the true forgetfulness, he enters the spiritual kingdom and passes through different degrees of forgetfulness until the Goal is reached. Meher Baba tells us, "Forgetfulness of the world makes one a pilgrim (*rahrav*, *sadhak*); forgetfulness of the next world makes one a saint; forgetfulness of self means Realization; and forgetfulness of forgetfulness is Perfection."

3 The First Plane (45)

Hafiz evidently refers to the first plane when he says:

*Kas nadānist kih manzilgah-i maqṣūd kujāst
In qadar hast kih bāng-i jarasī mīāyad.*

"It is not known where the real abode of the Divine Beloved is; only this much is clear, that I hear the sound of bells (from the travelling caravans)."

On this subject of sound and the planes Meher Baba says: *
"However, know this, that sound exists throughout all the seven planes, differing in its expression of feeling, ecstasy and bliss.

"The sound, sight or smell of the higher planes can with no stretch of the imagination be likened to what we are used to on the physical plane. . . . Our physical organs of hearing, seeing, and smelling are useless for experiencing and enjoying the higher planes. Therein it is a different eye that sees, a different ear that hears and a different nose that smells. You know already that there are inner senses, counterparts of the external senses in man, and it is with the former that one experiences the higher planes.

"Avoid the mistake of likening the sound of the higher planes to something different in intensity and frequency of vibrations to the sound of the physical plane; know it for a certainty that there is actually what may be called 'sound' in the first three planes. The form, beauty, music and bliss of this

* "Questions Baba Answers," *Meher Baba Journal*, vol. 1, no. 3, (January, 1939), pp. 83–84.

sound are beyond description. The *nad* or celestial music is peculiar to the first plane, which Hafiz refers to as *bāng-i jarasī* (the ringing of bells).

"As stated above, although there is sound in all the seven planes, it is smell that is peculiar to the second and third planes, while sight belongs to the fifth and sixth planes . . .

"The seventh plane stands unique. Here the sound, sight and smell are divine in essence and have no comparison to those emanating from the lower planes. In this plane one does not hear, smell or see but one **becomes** sound, smell and sight simultaneously, and is divinely conscious of it."

4 The Second Plane (46)

Hafiz evidently refers to the second plane when he says:

Cigūyamat kih bimaykhānih dūsh mast o kharāb
Surūsh-i 'ālam-i ghaybam cih muzhdihā dādast?

"How should I reveal to you that last night in the tavern, intoxicated and unsteady as I was, great good tidings were brought to me by the angel of the hidden world?"

5 The Third Plane (47)

Hafiz refers to the third plane in the following words:

Cih rāh mīzanad īn mutrib-i muqām shinās
Kih dar miyān-i ghazal qūl-i āshinā āvard.

"What perturbation and distress this musician with knowledge of (spiritual) states and stages is causing the listeners (lovers), by interpolating in the midst of his performance the words of the Divine Beloved."

6 The Stage Between the Third and Fourth Planes (47)

The journey between the third and fourth planes is at once difficult and dangerous because between these two planes there is the point of enchantment (*muqam-e-hairat*). It is very difficult to pass out of this state of enchantment if the pilgrim once stops there, although most pilgrims pass directly from the third to the fourth plane. Unless the pilgrim gets out of this state quickly and proceeds onwards to the fourth plane, his progress will be held up indefinitely. Once a pilgrim becomes thus enchanted he remains so for days, months or years together. He can neither make further progress nor can he retrogress. He is neither gross-conscious nor subtle-conscious. Neither can he be called **unconscious** because he is fully conscious of the enchantment, and it is because of this consciousness of the enchantment that he lives this living death.

The physical condition of the deeply enchanted pilgrim is no less strange, for if he seats himself in a particular position, he remains in that position for months or years together. Similarly, if he becomes enchanted while standing, he will continue standing until the enchantment ends. In short, he remains stationary in the position in which he first becomes enchanted, and, although he may appear to be a lifeless statue, he is in fact more alive than the ordinary man of the world.

It is well known to the Sufi world how Ali Ahmed Sabir of Piran Kalyar, who afterwards became a Perfect Master, once remained standing for years near a certain tree. During this period Sabir's mind was absorbed in the enchantment of this *muqam-e-hairat* and he was delivered from it by a *Qutub*. Only natural death or divine help from a living Master can help such a dazed pilgrim out of his spiritual stalemate. A Master would help such a pilgrim either by bringing him back to the third plane or by pushing him onwards.

Hafiz no doubt thinks of this stage of the pilgrim when he says:

Mastam kun ān cunān kih nadānam zi bīkhvudī
Dar 'arṣih khiyāl kih āmad kudām raft.

"Make me so dazed and intoxicated that, on account of this state of forgetfulness, I should be oblivious of what came into my mind and of what passed out of it."

Meher Baba explains that a pilgrim runs the risk of entering *muqam-e-hairat* (state of enchantment) when he passes from the third to the fourth plane. There are, he says, states of enchantment on other parts of the Path also, but the most important is that between the third and the fourth planes. This *hairat* (enchantment) may be strong or feeble. If there is no hitch or disturbing factor present at the moment that a pilgrim becomes enchanted, then the *hairat* is deep, or strong. If there is a disturbing factor present at that moment then the *hairat* is feeble. If a pilgrim experiences either strong or feeble *hairat* between the third and fourth planes and is then pushed forward by accident to a higher plane, he invariably goes to a position between the fifth and sixth planes, again with the same strong or feeble *hairat*. However, such instances are very rare. Ali Ahmed Sabir of Kalyar and Baba Abdur Rahman of Bombay both were precipitated from a very strong *hairat* between the third and fourth planes into a very strong *hairat* between the fifth and sixth planes, the former by a gift of grace from a *Qutub* and the latter through God's gift in the shape of an accident.

A complete fixity of posture that lasts until death, or until a Perfect Master is contacted, is seen only in those pilgrims who have a very strong *hairat*. A *mast* (God-intoxicated) who has been with Meher Baba for many years was in this *muqam-e-hairat* between the third and fourth planes when he was brought to Meher Baba in Rahuri in 1936; but his *hairat* was feeble, and although he would stand for many hours at a stretch in one position, this position would not be maintained permanently. The enchantment of Ali Ahmed Sabir, however, was a strong one, and he remained in one posture until he was finally delivered from the enchantment by a *Qutub*.

This state of enchantment should on no account be confused with the catatonic stupor of a schizophrenic, although it may appear similar. Both are states of enchantment, but they are poles apart.

7 Pilgrim of the Mental Sphere (51)

Meher Baba says that if a pilgrim of the mental sphere is in India and conceives the idea of seeing America, simultaneous with the wish on his part, either mentally or physically as he wishes, he will be there. One may ask how he travels as fast as thought itself. The answer is that the mind is everywhere, and therefore the pilgrim of the mental sphere does not have to travel. He can be anywhere he likes without using his gross or subtle organs. He can know anything and everything about the gross, subtle and mental spheres as far as the sixth plane, simply by willing to know. More important still, he can help less advanced souls and also ordinary human beings to come up to his own level of progress. When he wants to help anyone directly, the pilgrim of the fifth plane can lead an aspirant "by the hand" along the Path. When he does so, the aspirant himself also perceives internally the continual presence of the master of the mental plane (known to Sufis as a *"wali"*), and also feels himself being actually led by him along the path to perfection. Hafiz, in the following couplet, evidently visualizes the particular sensation of one who is being led in this way:

Tū dastgū shū āy khizr-i pay khujastih, kih man
Piyādih mīravam o hamrahān savārānand.

"O august master, lead me by the hand because I am traversing the Path on foot (helplessly) as compared with other companions who are riding along it."

Generally, however, a *wali* (*mahapurush*) helps an aspirant by gazing into his eyes, thereby tearing away the inner veil from the real eye within. This spiritual influence of the *wali* through sight is known to Sufis as *tawajjoh*. The term *tawajjoh* does not apply to Perfect Masters. In their case the term "will" is correct for they can also render this help without the physical contact that is necessary in the case of masters of the planes.

Meher Baba explains that on the fifth plane the pilgrim sometimes desires to have the divine presence, and sometimes attends to worldly duties. In fact so far as divine presence on the fifth plane is concerned, God is always present, but the pilgrim may not always desire this presence when he turns his attention to worldly duties. On the sixth plane the pilgrim persists in desiring the presence of God one hundred percent. Hafiz evidently refers to his experience of the fifth plane when he says:

Ḥuẕūrī gar hamī khvālū
Āzū ghāyib mashū Ḥāfiẕ.

"O Hafiz, if you desire the divine presence, then do not allow yourself to be absent."

8 The Sixth Plane (54)

The traveller who succeeds in reaching this plane is entitled to be called a *pir* or *satpurush*. There is no adequate translation of these words in English. The word "saint" would perhaps do, but it suffers from the handicap of very loose usage.

Hafiz remembers this sixth plane in the following words:

Mā dar piyālih 'aks-i rukh-i yār dīdih īm
Ay bīkhabar zi laẕẕat-i shurb-i mudām-i mā.

"We have seen the face of the Beloved reflected in the cup (of our mind or heart). O ignorant one, no notion have you of the bliss that we imbibe therefrom."

9 Gnosis of the Sixth Plane (55)

Concerning the gnosis of the sixth plane Meher Baba tells us: "Only God exists, and if anything exists due to ignorance, its reality is illusory. It then exists as God's shadow, which means that God is both in the stage of Knowledge and ignorance. The following four angles of the one experience, written in the language of Sufi gnosis, are different aspects of gnosis of souls in the sixth plane when they are face to face with God, but still in the domain of duality. All of these aspects are experienced together at the same time.

(1) *Hama ust*	—This means, 'Everything is He'; and for one who experiences this gnosis, only God exists.
(2) *Hama az ust*	—This means, 'Everything is from Him'; and for one who experiences this gnosis, all phenomena, diversities and manyness exist as illusion when ignorance prevails.
(3) *Hama ba ust*	—This means, 'Everything is with Him'; and for one who experiences this gnosis, God is both attributeless and with attributes. His attributes are unlimited when Knowledge prevails, and limited when ignorance prevails. Body, mind and the three worlds do not exist; but if they seem to exist, they exist as shadows.
(4) *Hama dar ust*	—This means, 'Everything is in Him'; and for one experiencing this gnosis, even ignorance has no reality in itself. Its existence, when expressed, comes out of God's unconscious and infinite Knowledge; and so whatever exists in duality due to ignorance has come out of God where it everlastingly existed."

10 The Seventh Plane (56)

It should be understood that at the moment of being merged into the seventh plane, all links with the gross, subtle and mental bodies and with the universe are necessarily snapped. In ordinary gross existence there is no parallel to this snapping of these long-enduring vital connections that bind the individual to his three bodies and to the universe. Physical death is, by comparison, an insignificant thing, about as significant as the snapping of a piece of string. Ordinarily at the instant of death the subtle body and vital force are separated completely from the gross body. But the mind maintains the connection with the gross body for the first four days after death and, to a slighter degree, for seven days more after that. In the final annihilation (*fana*), however, the separation is not between body and mind; it is the actual annihilation of mind and of all *nuqush-e-amal* (*sanskaras*).

11 Different Types of Miracles (72)

Meher Baba has given us an explanation of the difference between the miracles of:—

(1) A Saviour (*Avatar*)
(2) A Perfect Master (*Sadguru*)
(3) A *pir* and a *wali* (*i.e.,* one on the 6th or 5th plane, respectively)
(4) Those on the lower planes (*i.e.,* 1st, 2nd, 3rd and 4th)

In connection with these four types Meher Baba tells us:

1. The miracles of a Saviour are of a universal character and are performed when universally necessary. When a Saviour intends working a miracle, he stations himself for the time being on the 6th, 5th or 4th plane, as demanded by circumstances. When, however, it is desired that the miracles be very forceful, he stations himself for the time being on the 4th plane.

2. The miracles of a Perfect Master are on a very large scale, but they do not cover the whole universe. Like the Saviour's miracles, however, they are wrought solely for the spiritual awakening of others. Like the Saviour also, the Perfect Master who intends working a miracle stations himself on the 6th, 5th or 4th plane for the time being; and for a very forceful miracle, he stations himself for the time being on

the 4th plane. No miracles are ever wrought by the *Majzoob-e-Kamil* of the 7th plane for the simple reason that the three spheres, the mental, subtle and gross, do not exist for such a soul.

3. The miracles of a *pir* or *wali* are on a limited scale. In fact they perform no miracles directly. However, such miracles as can be attributed to them are wrought from their mental influence over the thoughts and feelings of others, yielding both spiritual and material benefits. They do not come down to the 4th plane—the plane of almighty spiritual powers.

4. Pilgrims of the 1st, 2nd and 3rd planes can use or demonstrate powers from their own plane, such as reading the minds of others, producing things from nowhere, reciting words or passages from a book without seeing it, stopping trains, allowing themselves to be buried alive for hours together, levitation, etc., etc. These are actual powers acquired by the pilgrim on the different planes and, as such, cannot be called mere jugglery. Perfect Masters and the *Avatar* can snatch away a pilgrim's ability to use the powers from the lower planes *viz.* 1st, 2nd and 3rd, and can even snatch away the almighty powers of one on the 4th plane. Such a snatching away of powers of those on the lower planes is known to the Sufis as *salb-e-wilayat*.

On the fourth plane are stored all the almighty powers * which, if misused by the pilgrim, result in his utter ruin. But such miracles do not affect the world adversely, because the *Qutub-e-Irshad*—the head of the spiritual hierarchy of the age—takes care to make these actions ineffective.

Meher Baba further explains that the indiscriminate display of powers by a pilgrim of the first three planes is fraught with serious dangers, but that one who misuses the powers of the fourth plane invariably falls back to the lowest phase of evolution—the stone state.

Kabir has referred to these dangers when he says:

---

* One on the fourth plane is known as a *mahayogi* (a great *yogi*).

Sāheba kā ghara dūra hai jaisī lambī khajūra
Caṛhe so cākhe prema-rasa gire cakanācūr.

"The Lord's house is high, like the top of the tallest date palm. If he climbs it, he tastes the nectar of love; if he falls, he breaks his neck."

CONSCIOUS AND UNCONSCIOUS OCCURRENCE OF MIRACLES

The miracles wrought by Saviours and Perfect Masters have a divine motive behind them and may be either voluntary or involuntary. The voluntary miracles of a Saviour or Perfect Master are those that he deliberately performs by the expression and force of his **will,** and the involuntary ones are those that occur independently of the will of the Saviour or Perfect Master and are wrought by means of the ever-active force that surrounds these great beings. In the latter type of miracle the Saviour or Perfect Master is unaware of the incidents of the miracle of which he himself is the source and prime cause. Both voluntary and involuntary miracles of these Perfect Ones are nevertheless always directed towards the spiritual awakening of the world.

WHY DO SAVIOURS AND PERFECT MASTERS PERFORM MIRACLES?

Very worldly people are spiritually obtuse, and they sometimes need miracles to save themselves or other quite innocent people from the results of this insensitivity. The following analogy shows what is meant thereby.

Let us suppose that a child is holding a sparrow in his hand and in so careless a way that he is on the point of strangling it. In order to save the sparrow's life it would be inadvisable to try to snatch the bird from the child's hand, for the child would probably tighten his grip on the sparrow and so kill it. But if the child is offered a coin, he will almost certainly relax his hold on the sparrow and so release it. The child is thus prevented from killing the bird out of sheer ignorance of what he is doing. The miracles of a Perfect Master accomplish the same sort of thing; they prevent people from doing themselves and others harm out of sheer ignorance of spiritual values.

If gold is defined to represent miracles, a yogi of the lower planes dazzles worldly people by dangling this gold in front of their eyes so that they are astounded by his prowess. Should they surrender themselves to such a yogi they will ultimately suffer a cruel disillusionment. But when the Saviour or a Perfect Master dangles this gold in front of the eyes of worldly people, he uses one form of *Maya* to drag them away from other and more binding forms of *Maya,* and so draws them towards the Path that leads to their true destiny, Self-realization.

Let us take another illustration and imagine a man with monochromatic vision to whom the world appears blue for example. His eyes thus act like blue spectacles so that when he looks through them everything seems to be blue. Spiritually speaking the world is illusion and so has no colour at all. It is colourless. A yogi demonstrating his miraculous powers merely replaces this man's blue "spectacles" by green or red ones so that he sees everything as green or red. To his ignorant eyes, accustomed to seeing the world blue, this sudden change to green or red is astounding, and reflects great apparent credit on the yogi.

A Perfect Master, knowing that neither blue nor red nor green is the true colour, but that everything is colourless (*i.e.,* nothing), wastes no time in changing "spectacles," thereby enabling the man to see the world as it really is: colourless, or nothing. The yogi and those lesser masters who are not perfect merely replace one illusion by another. But a Perfect Master permanently tears away the veil of all illusion and reveals the truth that Creation is imaginary and that God alone is real. This working of the Perfect Master is a slow and painful process that lacks the colourfulness of the yogi's spectacular and misleading method, and it is for this reason that the working of the Perfect Masters is unfathomable.

WHO OWNS THE POWERS BY WHICH MIRACLES ARE WROUGHT?

The miraculous powers of a Perfect Master appear the same as those of a yogi of the fourth plane, but there is this important difference, that the powers of a Perfect Master are his own, because he is Power itself. He has simply to will a thing and it is done. "Be and it was" (*Kun faya kūn*) refers, according to the Sufis, to the divine manifestation of power.

The yogis' powers, however, are not their own and they have to depend on extraneous sources of power for working miracles. The inherent powers of Perfect Masters are continually over-flowing, and yogis and pilgrims of the lower planes borrow these overflowing powers and work miracles with them. This is quite in consonance with the Sufi belief that *walis* are the Prophet Muhammad's witnesses, and that all their miracles, like drops oozing from a skin filled with honey, are derived from him. Endorsed by orthodox Muslims, this belief is limited in scope however, because it is applied only to the personality of the Prophet Muhammad. Its universal applicability is at once suggested though by the Sufi belief that from the beginning there has been only **one** *Rasool* who appears from time to time in different countries under different names.

Illuminating this point still further, Meher Baba has explained, "In *fana-fillah* (the *Majzoob* state) there are no miracles, direct or indirect. In Divine Junction (*turiya avastha* or *muqam-e-furutat*) the *Jivanmukta* (*Azad-e-Mutlaq*) has no duty and performs no miracles. But there is always a possibility of miracles happening through the *Jivanmukta* without his being aware of it. The agents or pilgrims of the lower planes very often borrow his powers and work miracles with them, but the powers of the *Jivanmukta* are not in any way lessened thereby."

MIRACLES OF THE SAVIOUR (*Rasool* OR *Avatar*)
AND PERFECT MASTERS (*Sadgurus*)

When God becomes man, He becomes a Saviour (*Rasool* or *Avatar*) and when man becomes God, he becomes a *Majzoob*, and, if he has duty to perform to humanity, he traverses the second and third divine journeys and becomes a Perfect Master (*Sadguru*). Both the Saviour and the Perfect Master are spirit-ually perfect, because both are one with God, and although both have a duty towards humanity, that of the Saviour is of a special kind.

The Sufis say that the "relationship" (*qurbat*) with God differs in the Saviour and the Perfect Master, and they refer to them as *qurb-e-farayiz* (involuntary necessary nearness) and *qurb-e-nawafil* (voluntary nearness) respectively. *Qurb-e-farayiz* thus belongs to the Saviours and *qurb-e-nawafil* to the Perfect Masters.

The Sufis explain that in the working of miracles by the *Rasool* (the *Avatar*), God is the actor and man the instrument; while in a Perfect Master it is the other way round—man is the actor and God the instrument. The famous incident of the Prophet Muhammad throwing a handful of dust at the enemy in the battle of Badr and thereby routing them, is an example of a Saviour working a miracle. Although to all appearances it was Muhammad as a man who threw the dust, in reality it was God as Muhammad who threw the dust, and Muhammad as a man who routed the enemy. A miracle such as this is therefore an illustration of *qurb-e-farayiz*.

The miracles performed by Perfect Masters are, however, illustrations of *qurb-e-nawafil,* of which the miracle of Shamsi Tabriz—that of raising the dead to life—is a good example. When Shams uttered the words *"Qum bi iznillah"* (arise in the name of God) the prince did not come to life; but when he said *"Qum bi iznī"* (arise in my name) the prince at once came to life. Here Shamsi Tabriz as man gave the order, and God as Shamsi Tabriz clothed himself with the attribute of Himself—in this case with the attribute of life—and so restored the prince to life. In *qurb-e-nawafil* man is the actor and God the instrument.

Let us for a moment discuss the difference in the attitude of East and West towards miracles. The East, which possesses a long record of familiarity with Perfect Masters and advanced souls, has come to accept that God, because He is infinite, cannot be comprehended by the finite mind. The East knows that human intellect, which is limited in scope, has its use only up to a certain stage in tackling metaphysical problems. As sung by the philosopher Dr. Iqbal,

> *'Aql go āstān se dūr nahīn*
> *Ūskī taqdīr maīn ḥuẓūr nahīn*
>
> "Intellect, though not far away from the threshold (of the Beloved) is not destined to enjoy the Divine Presence."

The East thus knows that at the point where intellect gives up its efforts in grappling with that which is transcendental, love must take up the link. The West sets great store by the intellectual approach, and that which refuses to come within the orbit of intellect is apt to be either denied or scoffed at. As a by-product of this occidental attitude we may cite the utter misuse of the word "mystic" in current American idiom. The ardent religious enthusiasm of medieval Europe has been almost replaced by great enthusiasm for culture and science.

The doctrines of science are, however, fluid to a certain extent, and the genuine scientist does look facts in the face, but Meher Baba has often declared that in spite of its great progress science is yet far from the core of material things, and further from the outermost fringe of spiritual things. The heart must cooperate with the head.

It may be that some of the purely physical feats of yogis, which pass for miracles with the multitude, can be explained away by medical science. But real miracles, particularly the miracles of Perfect Masters, do not admit of scientific explanation. Many of the miracles wrought by Saviours, Perfect Masters and saints, are recorded in the spiritual legends and classics of all peoples and all religions, and the ever-functioning spiritual hierarchy is daily adding to these miracles. The facts are there; Jesus and other Perfect Ones have raised the dead to life, and have healed diseases. But even if one were to see a miracle take place before one's very eyes, and even if one were convinced that it was a miracle and not trickery, one would never be able to formulate a rational explanation of it, for miracles are utterly beyond the reach of intellectual explanation. They are a mystery as deep as life itself.

Perhaps, however, the fault is not entirely without reason, for the world at large seldom gets an insight into the workings of Perfect Masters, and, in truth, most of these workings lie treasured in the breasts of a few intimate associates and deserving initiates, and are safely hidden from curiosity. In the words of the famous Sufi Abdul Hasan Kharqani, "If a few drops of that which is under the skin of a Perfect Master should come forth between his lips, all the creatures of heaven and earth would fall into panic."

In spite of the mass appeal of miracles and of the claims of spiritual masters, the East, like the West, is also very circumspect in its attitude towards them. It may be said to its credit, however, that the East has learned by long experience not to **deny** the actions of the spiritual hierarchy, even if it cannot see its way to accept or believe in them. One of the earliest Sufis has declared, "Miracles are only one of the thousand stages on the way to God"; and the *Avatar* of this cycle, Meher Baba, affirms that the greatest miracle a Perfect Master can perform is to make another man spiritually perfect like himself.

12   Kinds of Powers (72)

Spirituality and spiritualism are two different things. Spirituality has nothing to do with any kind of power in any form. Spirituality is the path of love for God and obedience and surrender to the Perfect Master.

As one travels the Path, one comes across powers on the planes of consciousness. Those on the planes from first to fourth are sometimes tempted to demonstrate these powers.

There are three kinds of powers:

(1) The divine powers of the fourth plane.
(2) The occult powers of the first three planes of consciousness. These are called the mystic powers.
(3) Other occult powers.

(1) The divine powers of the fourth plane are the almighty powers of God. They are the source of all powers, whether mystic or other occult powers.

The mystic and other occult powers are infinitely insignificant in comparison with the divine powers.

The divine powers remain always the same because God is always One and the same. The occult powers, whether they are of the planes or not, are different in kind and vary in expression.

The miracles performed through the manifestation of the divine powers by the *Avatar* and the *Qutub* are called *mojezat.* These are performed for the good of all—on a limited scale by the *Qutub* and on a universal scale by the *Avatar.* However, these can be performed for any individual in close association with the *Avatar* or the *Qutub.*

The miracles performed indirectly by those on the fifth and sixth planes with the help of the divine powers are called *karamaat.*

The display of the mystic powers by those on the first up through the third plane cannot in fact be termed miracles. Such a display is nothing but a show of powers that they come across while traversing the planes; such a display of powers is called *shobada.*

When the one on the fourth plane makes good use of the divine powers and performs a miracle, it can be termed as *karamat-e-mojeza;* when he makes a bad use of them, *i.e.*, misuses the divine powers of the fourth plane, it is termed *mojeza-e-shobada.*

The fourth plane is regarded as the "threshold" of the mental sphere, and so the misuse of the divine powers on the fourth plane results in a "fall" as far back as the stone-state and results in disintegration of consciousness.

(2) The occult powers of the first three planes, called the mystic powers, **cannot** be misused by the aspirant on these planes, though they sometimes are tempted to display them. These mystic powers are different and vary in expression, such as: reading the minds of others; reciting words or passages from a book

without seeing it; allowing themselves to be buried alive for hours together, etc.

The powers of the planes are not induced. These powers are ever accessible to those on the planes, within their own limited environment, and as such need no concentrated effort to display them. This display of powers should not be confused with the demonstrations of mind readers and of others who put on stage performances.

The one on the third plane of consciousness can raise dead sub-human creatures but can never make a dead human being alive. This he can do because of the nearness to and "warmth" of the divine powers of the fourth plane.

But one on the fourth plane can raise the dead including human beings by the use of the divine powers of the fourth plane.

The one on the third plane can change his physical form at will, and one who does this is known as *abdal*. This act is also a display of the mystic powers, but not the misuse of powers. However, this act should not be confused with the dematerialization or materialization of the human forms by the *tantriks*.

(3) Other occult powers have nothing to do with spirituality or with the mystic powers of the planes.

These occult powers are of two types:

(a) Superior occult powers.

(b) Inferior occult powers.

The one who has these occult powers can make good or bad use of the same. Good use of occult powers helps one to put himself on the planes of the Path and may even make one a *mahayogi*. Bad use of these occult powers makes one suffer intensely in the next human form. Good use of superior occult powers puts one on the fifth plane of consciousness after four lives (reincarnations).

(a) Superior types of occult powers are derived from *tantrik* exercises such as *chilla-nashini* or repetition of certain *mantras*, etc.

The one who holds these powers can perform the so-called

miracles such as levitation, flying and floating in the air, de-materialization and materialization, etc.

(b) Inferior types of occult powers need no *tantrik* or any special exercises. They are had through *sanskaras* of past lives. For example: if someone has done certain good deeds many times in the past, his next incarnation may give him the faculty of inferior occult powers without undergoing any strenuous exercises. His *sanskaras* give him the faculty of inferior occult powers such as clairvoyance, clairaudience, healing, producing sweets or money seemingly out of nothing, etc.

All such capabilities form part of the lower or inferior type of occult powers.

If one makes good use of the inferior type of occult powers, he derives superior type of occult powers in his next life without undergoing any *tantrik* exercises. Likewise, the one who puts to good use his faculty of hypnotism gains the superior type of occult powers in his next life.

13   Meditation (73)

A SCHEME FOR BEGINNERS BASED ON A STUDY OF THE DIVINE THEME BY MEHER BABA

Meditation has often been misunderstood as being a mechanical process of forcing the mind upon some idea or object. It is therefore only natural that most people should find great difficulty in their attempts to coerce the mind in a particular direction or to pin it down to one particular thing. Any purely mechanical handling of the mind is not only irksome but is ultimately bound to be unsuccessful.

The first principle which the aspirant should therefore remember is that the mind can be controlled and directed in meditation only according to the laws inherent in the make-up of the mind itself, and not by the application of any feats of simple will power.

Many people who do not technically "meditate" are often found to be deeply and intensely engrossed in systematic and clear thinking about some practical problem or theoretical subject. In a sense, their mental process is very much like meditation, inasmuch as the mind is engrossed in intense thinking about a particular subject matter to the exclusion of all irrelevant things. The reason meditation is often easy and spontaneous in such a mental process is that the mind is dwelling upon a subject in which it is interested and which it increasingly understands. But the spiritual tragedy about ordinary trains of thought is that they are not directed towards things that really matter. The subject matter of meditation must therefore always be carefully chosen and it must be spiritually important. In order to attain success in meditation we must not only get the mind interested in the divine subjects or truths, but we must also begin by trying to understand and appreciate them. Intelligent meditation is a natural process of the mind, which avoids the monotonous rigidity and regularity of mechanical meditation. It therefore becomes not only spontaneous and inspiring, but easy and successful.

Since intelligent meditation consists in thorough thinking about a particular subject, it follows that the best way to meditate would be to make a brief and clear exposition of an appropriate subject. For this purpose there could be nothing better than the Divine Theme with its charts which is reproduced in the following section.

The process of meditation which Meher Baba recommends has three stages:

1. In the first stage the aspirant will read through the Divine Theme daily, studying the charts also, and thinking about it thoroughly as he does so.
2. In the second stage when the aspirant has the entire subject at his fingertips, actual reading becomes unnecessary, but the subject matter of the exposition will be mentally reviewed with the help of the charts when necessary.
3. In the third stage, which will develop naturally out of the second, it will be quite unnecessary for the mind to review

the words or the thoughts in the exposition separately and consecutively or even to refer to the facts, and all discursive thinking about the subject matter will come to an end. At this stage of meditation the mind will no longer be occupied with any trains of thought, but will have a clear understanding of the sublime truths expressed in the exposition.

14 The Divine Theme (73)
By Meher Baba

EVOLUTION, REINCARNATION AND THE PATH TO REALIZATION
(Introduction to the Charts)

A soul becomes perfect * after passing through evolution, reincarnation and the process of realization. To gain full consciousness, it gets increasing *sanskaras* in the process of evolution, till in the human form, it gets full consciousness as well as all the gross *sanskaras*.

In the process of reincarnation, this soul retains its full consciousness and exchanges (*i.e.,* alternatingly experiences) the diverse *sanskaras* in itself; and in the process of realization, this soul retains its full consciousness, but its *sanskaras* become fainter and fainter till they all disappear and only consciousness remains. While becoming faint, gross *sanskaras* become subtle *sanskaras*, subtle *sanskaras* become mental *sanskaras;* and finally they all disappear.

Up to the human form, the winding process of *sanskaras* becomes stronger and stronger in the process of evolution. In the human form, in the process of reincarnation, the winding retains its full strength; but in the process of realization, the *sanskaras* gradually unwind themselves, till in the God-state, they are completely unwound.

God, the Over-Soul, alone is real. Nothing exists but God. The different souls are in the Over-Soul and one with it. The processes of evolution, reincarnation and realization are all necessary in order to enable the soul to gain self-consciousness.

---

* See chart IX. "A" soul becomes "Z" soul.

In the process of winding, *sanskaras* become instrumental for the evolution of consciousness though they also give *sanskaric* bindings; and in the process of unwinding, *sanskaric* attachments are annihilated, though the consciousness which has been gained is fully retained.

In the process of the winding of *sanskaras,* the soul goes through seven stages of **descent;** and in the process of unwinding, the soul goes through seven stages of **ascent.** But the phenomena of descent as well as ascent are both illusory. The soul is everywhere and indivisibly infinite; and it does not move or descend or ascend.

The souls of all men and women, of all nationalities, castes and creeds, are really one; and their experiences of good and evil, of fighting and helping, of waging wars and living in peace are all a part of illusion and delusion, because all these experiences are gained through bodies and minds, which in themselves are nothing.

Before the world of forms and duality came into existence, there was nothing but God, *i.e.,* an indivisible and boundless ocean of Power, Knowledge and Bliss. But this ocean was unconscious of itself. Picture to yourself this ocean as absolutely still and calm, unconscious of its Power, Knowledge and Bliss and unconscious that it is the ocean. The billions of drops which are in the ocean do not have any consciousness; they do not know that they are drops nor that they are in the ocean nor that they are a part of the ocean. This represents the original state of Reality.

This original state of Reality comes to be disturbed by an urge to know itself. This urge was always latent in the ocean; and when it begins to express itself, it endows the drops with individuality. When this urge makes the still water move, there immediately spring up numerous bubbles or forms around the drops; and it is these bubbles which give individuality to the drops. The bubbles do not and cannot actually divide the indivisible ocean; they cannot separate the drop from the ocean; they merely give to these drops a feeling of separateness or limited individuality.

Now let us study the life of one drop-soul through its different stages. Owing to the arising of the bubble, the drop-soul which was completely unconscious is invested with individuality (or a feeling of separateness) as well as with very slight consciousness. This consciousness, which has sprung up in the drop-soul, is not of itself nor of the ocean; but it is of the bubble or the form, which in itself is nothing. This imperfect bubble at this stage is represented by the **form** of a stone. After some time, this bubble or form bursts and there springs up in its place another bubble or form. Now, when a bubble bursts, two things happen: (1) there is an increase in consciousness and (2) there is a twist or consolidation of impressions or *sanskaras* accumulated during the life of the previous bubble. The consciousness of the drop-soul has now slightly increased; but the drop-soul is still conscious only of this new bubble or form and not of itself nor of the ocean. This new bubble is represented by the form of the metal. This new bubble or form also bursts in due course of time; and simultaneously there is a further increase in consciousness and a fresh twist or consolidation of *sanskaras,* which gives rise to the emergence of another type of bubble or form.

This process continues right through the course of evolution, which covers the stages of stones, metals, vegetables, worms, fishes, birds and animals. Every time that the previous bubble or form bursts, it gains more consciousness and adds one twist to the already accumulated *sanskaras,* until it reaches the human bubble or form, in which the ever-increasing consciousness becomes full and complete. The process of the winding up of *sanskaras* consists of these regular twists; and it is these twists which keep the consciousness, gained by the drop-soul, directed and fixed towards the bubble or the form instead of towards its real Self, even when consciousness is fully developed in the human form.

On gaining the human form, the second process begins; this process is that of reincarnation. At this point, the process of the winding up of *sanskaras* comes to an end. The drop-soul takes numerous human forms one by one; and these forms are exactly eighty-four *lakhs* in number. These human forms are sometimes those of man and sometimes those of woman; and they change nationalities, appearance, colour and creed. The drop-soul through human incarnations experiences itself sometimes as a beggar and sometimes as a king, and thus gathers experiences of the opposites of happiness or misery according to its good or bad *sanskaras*. In reincarnation (*i.e.,* in its successive and several human forms) the drop-soul retains its full consciousness but continues to have alternating experiences of opposite *sanskaras,* till the process of realization begins. And during this process of realization the *sanskaras* get unwound. In reincarnations, there is a spending up of *sanskaras;* but this spending up is quite different from the unwinding of the *sanskaras,* which takes place during the process of realization. The spending up of *sanskaras* itself creates new *sanskaras,* which bind the soul; but the unwinding of *sanskaras* does not itself create fresh *sanskaras;* and it is intended to undo the very strong grip of *sanskaras,* in which the drop-soul is caught.

Up to the human form, the winding up of *sanskaras* becomes stronger and stronger during the process of evolution. In the human forms of reincarnation, the winding continues to operate as a limiting factor; but with every change of the human bubble or form, the tight twists, gained during the process of winding, get loosened through eighty-four *lakhs* of shakings,* before they are ready to unwind in the process of realization.

---

* [Many readers do not discern that Meher Baba customarily described the life cycle as: evolution, reincarnation, involution and the **process of** realization.

Fearing the statement in the text above might seem contradictory to that in paragraph 1, page 188, we asked Eruch B. Jessawala for clarification.

He replied: "Once one is on the planes of consciousness, the reincarnation process may be said to have come to its fag end. On the Path leading to Beloved God, the impatience to 'see' Him and to be One with Him is intense. Such reincarnations as are necessary, due to impressions burdening the consciousness, seem almost nil when compared to eighty-four *lakhs* of shakings." Ed.]

Now begins the third process of realization, which is a process of ascent. Here, the drop-soul undergoes the gradual unwinding of the *sanskaras*. During this process of unwinding, the *sanskaras* become fainter and fainter; and at the same time, the consciousness of the drop-soul gets directed more and more towards itself; and thus, the drop-soul passes through the subtle and mental planes till all the *sanskaras* disappear completely, enabling it to become conscious of itself as the ocean.

In the infinite ocean of the Over-Soul, you are the drop or the soul. You are the soul in the ordinary state; and you use your consciousness in seeing and experiencing the bubble or the form. Through the gross layer of the bubble, you experience that part of the huge gross bubble which is the earth. You are eternally lodged and indivisibly one with the Over-Soul; but you do not experience it. In the advanced stage, up through the third plane, you use your consciousness in seeing and experiencing the huge subtle bubble called the subtle world, through the subtle bubble or form called the subtle body; but you do not see and experience the Over-Soul which you are in, since your consciousness is not now directed towards the Over-Soul. In the advanced stage from the fourth through the sixth plane, you use your consciousness in seeing and experiencing the huge mental bubble, which is called the mental world, through the mental bubble or form which is called the mental body, but even now you do not experience the Over-Soul. But in the God-realized state, you continually use your consciousness for seeing and experiencing the Over-Soul; and then all the forms are known as being nothing but bubbles.

So, now, picture yourself as the soul-drop, lodged in the Over-Soul, behind five layers after the gross body. You, the soul-drop, are now looking at the gross body and through it at the gross world. When you look at the second layer and through it, the first layer will appear to you as nothing but a layer only, and thus, looking behind each layer, you will find all these layers as only your shadow covers; and finally, when you (*i.e.,* the soul-drop) look at and get merged in the Over-Soul, you

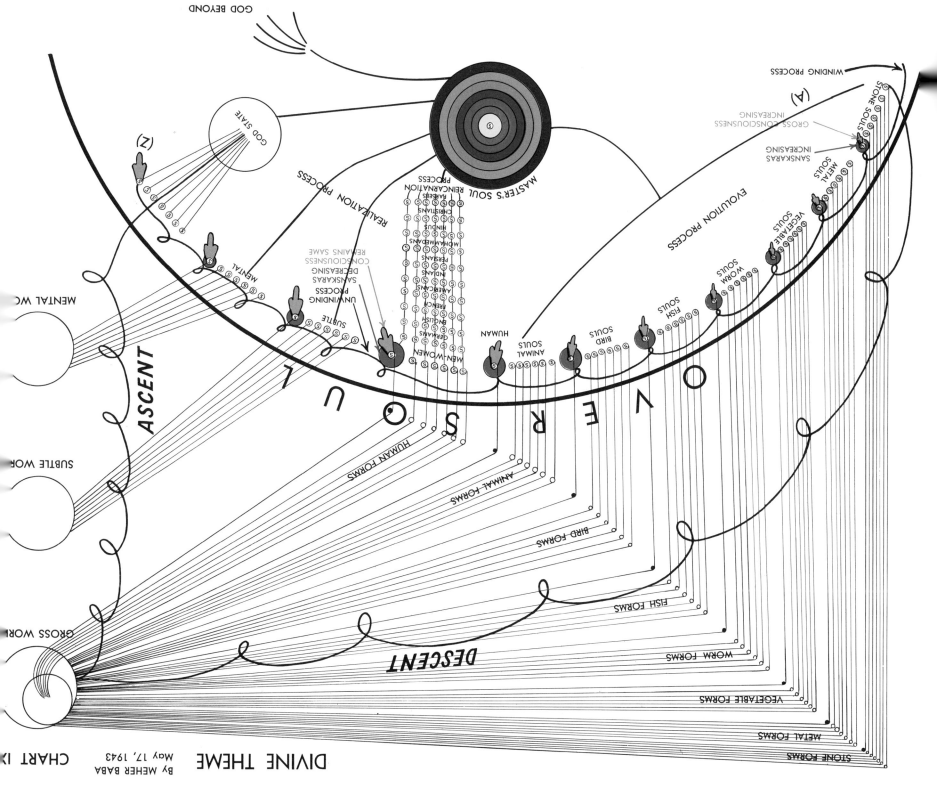

GOD BEYOND

GOD STATE

(Z)

MENTAL

SUBTLE

MEN-WOMEN

HUMAN

ANIMAL SOULS

BIRD SOULS

FISH SOULS

WORM SOULS

VEGETABLE SOULS

METAL SOULS

STONE SOULS

(A)

WINDING PROCESS

GROSS CONSCIOUSNESS INCREASING

SANSKARAS INCREASING

EVOLUTION PROCESS

MASTER'S SOUL REINCARNATION PROCESS

PARSEES
CHRISTIANS
HINDUS
MOHAMMEDANS
PERSIANS
INDIANS
AMERICAN
FRENCH
ENGLISH
GERMANS

REALIZATION PROCESS

UNWINDING PROCESS

SANSKARAS DECREASING

CONSCIOUSNESS REMAINS SAME

ASCENT

OVER SOUL

MENTAL WORLD

SUBTLE WORLD

GROSS WORLD

DESCENT

HUMAN FORMS

ANIMAL FORMS

BIRD FORMS

FISH FORMS

WORM FORMS

VEGETABLE FORMS

METAL FORMS

STONE FORMS

DIVINE THEME

By MEHER BABA
May 17, 1943

CHART IX

realize that only you were real and all that you were seeing and experiencing till now was your own shadow and nothing else.

(Explanation of the Charts No. IX and No. X)

CHART IX

The big semi-circle in Chart IX represents the Over-Soul, which contains everything in the universe. The life of a single individual soul is depicted in the three main stages of evolution, reincarnation and the process of realization. "S" stands for the individual soul. Before attaining the human form, it goes through seven stages of each of the following kinds of existence, *viz.,* stone, metal, vegetable, worm, fish, bird and animal. At the seventh stage, *i.e.,* just before entering a new kind of existence, you will note a pictorial representation of a twist or a knot, which stands for a consolidation of previously acquired *sanskaras.* The outer red circle round the individual soul "S," represents the *sanskaras* accumulated during the process of evolution; and the blue appendage to "S" represents the consciousness, which comes to be developed simultaneously. "A" soul becomes "Z" soul after going through evolution, reincarnation and the process of realization. It is only in the God-state that consciousness is free from *sanskaras.*

The gross, subtle and mental worlds (*i.e., anna bhumi, pran bhumi* and *mano bhumi*) are each represented by a big circle on the right-hand side. Since consciousness of the gross world is not fully developed in the pre-human stages of evolution, the lines which connect the stone, metal, vegetable, worm, fish, bird and animal souls, through their respective stone, metal, vegetable, worm, fish, bird and animal forms, are shown merely as touching the gross world only partially; while, since consciousness is fully developed in the human form, it is shown (through corresponding lines) as being capable of understanding the entire gross world in all its different aspects.

In the process of reincarnations, the soul may take a male or a female form; and it may belong to any nationality, creed or religion. From the point of view of self-knowledge, the process up to the attainment of the human forms represents an actual descent, though it looks like an ascent; and the process of realization represents an actual ascent, though it looks like a descent; and these two processes are respectively represented by a line (representing descent) of winding knots of *sanskaras,* which goes **up** from the stone-stage to the gross world, and by a line (representing ascent) of unwinding knots of *sanskaras,* which comes **down** from the gross world to the God-state. The process of ordinary reincarnations begins after the winding is complete; and it continues till the unwinding has begun.

In the process of realization, advanced souls from the first through the third planes are conscious only of the subtle world, through their subtle bodies. They are aware of ordinary souls who are gross-conscious and can act upon them in the subtle world; but all this is done by them through the subtle body and in the subtle world; and they have no connection with the gross world through the gross body. In the same way, advanced souls from the fourth through the sixth planes are aware of gross-conscious as well as subtle-conscious souls; but they act upon them in the mental world through the mental body; and they have no connection with the gross world through the gross body, nor with the subtle world through the subtle body. Therefore, the lines in the chart connect the subtle-conscious souls only with the subtle world; and the corresponding lines connect the mental-conscious souls only with the mental world.

In the God-state, in which all the *sanskaras* are unwound, consciousness is turned only to God; this is the state of *Majzoobs-e-Kamil,* who have no connection with the gross nor the subtle nor the mental worlds. But a few who enjoy the God-state also come down and regain the consciousness of the entire Creation. These are the souls of the Masters. The soul of the Master is represented by seven concentric coloured rings.* The following points (which have been brought out by connecting lines) should be carefully noted:—(i) The Master's soul is connected

---

* For their significance see Chart X.

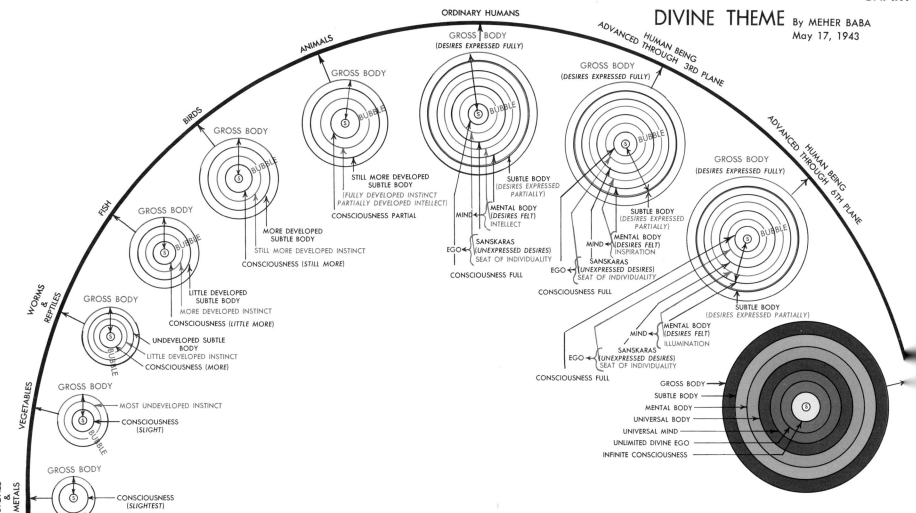

CHART

DIVINE THEME By MEHER BABA
May 17, 1943

ORDINARY HUMANS

GROSS BODY
(DESIRES EXPRESSED FULLY)

ADVANCED HUMAN BEING
THROUGH 3RD PLANE

ANIMALS

GROSS BODY

GROSS BODY
(DESIRES EXPRESSED FULLY)

ADVANCED HUMAN BEING
THROUGH 6TH PLANE

BIRDS

GROSS BODY

BUBBLE

BUBBLE

GROSS BODY
(DESIRES EXPRESSED FULLY)

STILL MORE DEVELOPED
SUBTLE BODY

SUBTLE BODY
(DESIRES EXPRESSED
PARTIALLY)

FISH

GROSS BODY

(FULLY DEVELOPED INSTINCT
PARTIALLY DEVELOPED INTELLECT)

CONSCIOUSNESS PARTIAL

MENTAL BODY
(DESIRES FELT)
INTELLECT

SUBTLE BODY
(DESIRES EXPRESSED
PARTIALLY)

BUBBLE

BUBBLE

MORE DEVELOPED
SUBTLE BODY

MIND

MENTAL BODY
(DESIRES FELT)
INSPIRATION

STILL MORE DEVELOPED INSTINCT

EGO

SANSKARAS
(UNEXPRESSED DESIRES)
SEAT OF INDIVIDUALITY

MIND

CONSCIOUSNESS (STILL MORE)

SANSKARAS
(UNEXPRESSED DESIRES)
SEAT OF INDIVIDUALITY

WORMS & REPTILES

GROSS BODY

LITTLE DEVELOPED
SUBTLE BODY

CONSCIOUSNESS FULL

EGO

GROSS BODY
(DESIRES EXPRESSED FULLY)

BUBBLE

MORE DEVELOPED INSTINCT

CONSCIOUSNESS FULL

CONSCIOUSNESS (LITTLE MORE)

BUBBLE

UNDEVELOPED SUBTLE
BODY

LITTLE DEVELOPED INSTINCT

SUBTLE BODY
(DESIRES EXPRESSED PARTIALLY)

CONSCIOUSNESS (MORE)

MENTAL BODY
(DESIRES FELT)
ILLUMINATION

VEGETABLES

GROSS BODY

MIND

MOST UNDEVELOPED INSTINCT

EGO

SANSKARAS
(UNEXPRESSED DESIRES)
SEAT OF INDIVIDUALITY

CONSCIOUSNESS
(SLIGHT)

BUBBLE

STONES & METALS

GROSS BODY

CONSCIOUSNESS FULL

GROSS BODY

SUBTLE BODY

MENTAL BODY

CONSCIOUSNESS
(SLIGHTEST)

UNIVERSAL BODY

UNIVERSAL MIND

UNLIMITED DIVINE EGO

INFINITE CONSCIOUSNESS

BUBBLE

with God-Beyond, which is the *vidnyan* or the resting place of the Masters, (ii) it is connected with the God-state and (iii) it is not only connected with all the three worlds, but all the souls, whether they are mental-conscious, subtle-conscious or reincarnating human beings (who are gross-conscious), or souls who are in the pre-human evolutionary stage.

CHART X

Chart X brings out the details pertaining to the process of evolution up to the human form and the process of realization up to the state of a God-realized being. The innermost small circle which is referred to by "S" represents the individual soul. The soul is shown as having an increasing number of circles around itself up to the human stage; and it is shown as retaining all these circles later on. The second circle, which is next to the soul, represents consciousness, which goes on increasing up to the human form; but afterwards it remains constant. In evolution, vegetables acquire the most undeveloped instinct, but not the subtle body,* which emerges in an undeveloped form in worms and reptiles. This subtle body goes on developing until it is fully developed in the human form. Side by side with the development of the subtle body, there is a simultaneous development of instinct. Intellect, in its partial development, makes its first appearance at the stage of animals; but the mental body appears only at the last stage represented by the human form.

In the human form, the first innermost circle represents the individual **soul**; the next outer circle represents **full consciousness**; and then the other outer circles (in the order in which they are drawn) respectively represent (i) the seat of individuality, (ii) *sanskaras* or unexpressed desires, (iii) intellect, (iv) felt desires of the mental body, (v) subtle body (in which there is a partial expression of desires) and (vi) the gross body (in which the desires come to be fully expressed). All the circles

---

* Nevertheless, in the gaseous or stone or metal or vegetable form the soul also identifies itself, **though unconsciously,** with its most-finite subtle form and its most-finite mental form. [See page 34 of text. Ed.]

round the innermost circle of the soul, with the exception of the first circle of consciousness, are **layers** of consciousness. Of these layers, the outermost circle and the circle next to it respectively represent the gross and the subtle bodies, while the other four layers around consciousness represent four functions of one mental body. Of these four functions of the mental body, two (*i.e.,* felt desires and intellect) are usually included under mind; and the other two (*i.e., sanskaras* or unexpressed desires and the seat of individuality) are included under the ego. Thus, at the human stage, the soul, with its consciousness, has **three bodies,** but **six layers** (including the gross layer known as the gross body).

When (after reincarnations) the human soul launches upon the process of realization, intellect is replaced by inspiration, which finds its expression from the first to the third plane; and from the fourth to the sixth plane, this inspiration is transformed into illumination.

The coloured rings or concentric circles represent the soul of a God-realized person, with all the vehicles at its disposal. In respect to this diagram, the following points should be carefully noted: (i) The three outer rings respectively represent the gross, subtle and the mental bodies. We find all these bodies also in ordinary human beings. (ii) In the God-realized person, there has emerged a new spiritual body, known as the universal body or *mahakarana sharir,* which is the seat of the universal mind. Just as water is contained in a cup, the universal mind may be said to be contained in the universal body. Therefore, though the universal body and the universal mind are represented by two different circles, they are inseparable from each other. (The universal mind of the Master, which works through his universal body, is in direct contact with the mental bodies of all the individual souls in Creation; and it can, through these mental bodies, bring about any changes in the mental, subtle or gross worlds. Though the Master has a mental body like ordinary humans, he always works only through his universal mind.) (iii) In the Master's soul, the limited ego of the human stage is transmuted into the unlimited Ego, *i.e.*, the feeling of separateness and narrow individuality is replaced by the realization of unlimited indivisible and all-comprehensive existence. (iv) The soul of the Master is endowed with infinite consciousness. The full consciousness at the human stage does not reveal or express the infinity of the soul, owing to the limitations of *sanskaras;* but in the God-realized person, this full consciousness is not limited by any *sanskaras* and, therefore, it reveals or expresses the infinity of the soul.

15   The Five Spheres Described by Meher Baba (75)

Meher Baba says there are five spheres:—(1) gross, (2) subtle, (3) mental, (4) composite and (5) Real. The first four concern relative existences and the fifth one is composed of the one and only Real Existence.

The question of details is all the more important when a subject is beyond ordinary human experience. On the one hand, more details confuse one more, and less details explain things less. This gives rise to a variety of terms and expressions for use from different viewpoints and in different contexts. In the absence of underlying experience, descriptions of the same one thing often sound contradictory. But in the light of relative experiences or the final realization of Truth, the very contradictions prove to be complementary expressions about the same one Truth. The facts and the fact of facts underlying the five spheres will bear this out.

The first, the gross sphere, although entirely depending for its existence on the subtle, is distinctly different in very many respects from the subtle. The gross sphere consists of numberless worlds, suns, moons, stars, and in fact everything material from the crudest to the finest. Some of the worlds in the gross sphere contain minerals and vegetation only; some others contain countless embodied beings also, and in some there are included human beings. The point of prime importance in the gross sphere is our world (Earth). Here, amongst all other beings who are conscious in greater or lesser degree of the gross, man with his full consciousness is superior to all other beings of all gross worlds.* But until man **here** awakens to the subtle, his full consciousness remains fully occupied with the gross, even when he reads and thinks of spiritual subjects such as the one discussed here.

The second, the subtle sphere, is the sphere of energy, and although it is divided into seven divisions, it is one world by itself. Its subsistence depends upon the mental sphere but it exists entirely independent of the gross sphere. In the parlance of time and space, the domain of the gross sphere, with its infinite space comprising universes of innumerable suns, planets and worlds, including our Earth, is but a speck as compared with the subtle sphere.

The path of Self-realization, the *rah-e-tariqat* of the Sufis and the *adhyatmic marga* of the Vedantists, consisting of seven planes (*muqams* or *sthans*), is the one and only bridge between the first sphere of the gross and the fifth, the Real sphere. The path has its first three planes in the subtle, the second sphere.

The subtle sphere through its energy, its angels, and above all through man's partial and full subtle-consciousness (human consciousness partly or fully freed **from** the gross, **in** the gross), while penetrating the gross sphere itself, also penetrates infinite space with its suns, stars, planets and, in fact, every thing and every being in all the worlds within the gross sphere.

The unlimited diversity and intensity of subtle sights, sounds, feelings and powers have no parallel in the gross sphere,

---

* This means also superior spiritually amongst all human beings of the gross sphere. Meher Baba tells us that of the three worlds in the gross sphere which are inhabited by human beings, ours (the Earth) is the one where man is the highest spiritually. He explains that, whereas man on this Earth possesses in his personality equal degrees of head and heart (50% head and 50% heart), man on the other two worlds possesses 100% head, and 75% head and 25% heart, respectively. Man, in the course of his reincarnations, is born on any one of the three worlds, but must finally take form and reincarnate on this Earth to fulfill his divine destiny which is God-realization. In the gross sphere, the Earth is the last and nearest stepping stone to the Path. The two other worlds are most close to the Earth in the pattern of habitation. Altogether there are 18,000 worlds with life, but these two worlds and the Earth are akin to one another in the pattern of human life.

save energy which becomes limited within the bounds of the gross, and human consciousness which is surrounded by gross limitations.

The third, the mental sphere, is the sphere of the spheres. It is absolutely independent of both the subtle and gross spheres and is independently sustained by Divinity. The mental sphere is the very abode of Mind, individual, collective and universal. The Mind pervades its own sphere as much as it does throughout the subtle and gross spheres.

This sphere of the Mind includes everything relating to intellect, intuition, insight and illumination. Herein are also contained the loftier planes of the Path, the fifth and the sixth. The fourth plane is but a junction between the third plane in the subtle sphere and the fifth plane in the mental sphere.

Nevertheless, the mental sphere does not and cannot touch the Real Sphere, as nothing can touch it save its own Reality, conscious of itself in the eternal "I am God" state of God.

The fourth, the composite sphere, is the most named and the least understood one. It is composed of twenty-one sub-spheres and as such it is both a sphere and not a sphere by itself.

The twenty-one connecting links are made up of seven sub-gross and sub-subtle spheres between the gross and the subtle spheres; seven sub-subtle and sub-mental spheres between the subtle and the mental spheres; and seven sub-mental and sub-supramental spheres between the mental sphere and the Real Sphere.

The peculiar nature and position of the composite sphere could be grasped more easily through either of the following tables:

TABLE I

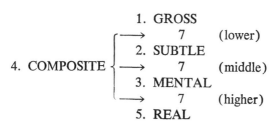

TABLE II

(1) The Gross Sphere (First Sphere)
Seven **lower** sub-spheres
of
(4) The Composite Sphere (Fourth Sphere).

(2) The Subtle Sphere (Second Sphere)
Seven **middle** sub-spheres
of
(4) The Composite Sphere (Fourth Sphere).

(3) The Mental Sphere (Third Sphere)
Seven **higher** sub-spheres
of
(4) The Composite Sphere (Fourth Sphere).

(5) The Real Sphere (Fifth Sphere).

The seven lower sub-spheres are spiritually superior to the gross sphere and they do touch the gross, whereas the seven higher sub-spheres are neither spiritually superior to the mental sphere nor can they ever touch the Real Sphere as will be clear from further details which follow.

On the one hand, the all-important Path, the one and only bridge between man and God, runs through the two spheres of the subtle and the mental, and on the other hand, there are innumerable things and beings in these two spheres as well as in between the seven lower and seven higher sub-spheres, and each one of the things and beings is directly or indirectly vital to the Path.

From the seven lower to the seven middle sub-spheres, inclusive of the subtle sphere, amongst other things there are the abodes of the disembodied souls (spirits) and the un-embodied souls (angels). From the seven middle to the seven higher sub-spheres, inclusive of the mental sphere, amongst other things there is the abode of the archangels.

The spirits (disembodied souls), both good and bad, have to remain in the "state of waiting," both before and after experiencing the states of pleasure and pain—states commonly known as heaven and hell.[37]

The angels (unembodied souls) are mere automatons for the will of God and they do nothing which is not desired or prompted by God. These wishes happen to be mere expressions of divine power and activity which are all-pervading. In short, angels are pure and not contaminated with physical embodiment. In this they are superior to the man whose consciousness has not extended beyond the limitations of the gross (meaning a man not yet on the Path). Paradoxically, man, the inferior, who has succeeded in being contaminated with physical embodiment, is actually the superior in the strength of the potentialities latent within him. Experiencing his imperfections, limitations and weaknesses, he is potentially ripe to realize his real strength and purity which are far above those of, and beyond the reach of, even the archangels.

The archangels are the mediums for the expression of God's principal divine attributes of creating, preserving and destroying limited life on an unlimited scale, and of communicating unlimited Knowledge on a limited scale. The archangels are entities who always enjoy and never suffer.

The abode of the archangels, the sub-supramental spheres of the fourth, the composite sphere which is discussed here, comes after the third—the mental sphere—and is nearest the fifth, the Real Sphere. This is true, yet not the whole truth; for in spite of its proximity it cannot touch the Real Sphere. An archangel, from the highest sub-supramental sphere, can never see God, whereas man in the sixth plane of the third, the mental sphere, can and does see God face to face everywhere and in everything. The last point of the last of the sub-supramental spheres is what the Sufis call the *sadrat-ul-muntaha* (the last limit), beyond which, as is popularly and rightly believed by the Muslims, even the archangel Gabriel cannot go.

Man has and man shall (because man alone can) jump over the last seven links of the really non-existent relative existences of all the four spheres into his really own—the fifth, the Real Sphere. In short, angels must necessarily cease to be angels and become man before they can reach the Reality attainable to man. And when man ceases to be man and enters the "I am God" state, he realizes that angels and archangels are in fact his own attributes in one sense or another.

Finally the dissolution of the higher seven sub-spheres of the fourth—the composite—sphere, is the phenomenon called *qiamat* or *mahapralaya,* and when this takes place the whole of the non-existent existence of Creation, with all its spheres and sub-spheres, like a manifested tree, recedes into the unmanifested seed form of non-existent non-existence, only to be manifested anew once more in the very next moment of eternity.

The fourth, the composite sphere, is commonly included in the first three spheres as follows:

1) The gross sphere plus part of the fourth, the composite sphere, is the *alam-e-nasut* of the Sufis and the *anna bhuvan* of the Vedantists.
2) The subtle sphere plus part of the fourth, the composite sphere, is the *alam-e-malakut* of the Sufis and the *pran bhuvan* of the Vedantists.
3) The mental sphere plus part of the fourth, the composite sphere, is the *alam-e-jabrut* of the Sufis and the *mano bhuvan* of the Vedantists.

The latter also call the three (including the fourth) spheres collectively the *tribhuvan* (triple sphere), and the Sufis call them collectively *do alam* (two spheres) meaning the gross on the one hand, and the subtle and the mental (including the composite sphere) on the other hand.

The fifth, the Real Sphere, is also the seventh plane of the Path, the plane of full superconsciousness which, in simple words, means the full human consciousness fully freed from any vestige or tinge of duality inherent in varying degrees in all of the four spheres of relative existence. It would not be wrong to say that the fifth sphere or the seventh plane is neither any sphere nor plane but the Reality of God's very Selfhood—referred to by humanity as *Allah, Paramatma,* Almighty God, *Yezdan,* and so on. According to the different states of the same one God from is to "I am God," and from "I am God" to "I am everything," there are different terms for the different stages or aspects of the Real Sphere—such as *alam-e-hahut* and *alam-e-lahut* of the Sufis or *vidnyan bhumika* and *vidnyan*.

16   The Types of Conviction and of Knowledge (78)

According to the Sufis, the spiritual life consists of four stages, and man's life on earth in all its aspects is but a preparation, conscious or unconscious, for the ever-unfolding realms of knowledge and illumination that lead to God-realization. These four stages are *shariat* (*dharma shastra*), *tariqat* (*adhyatma marga*), *haqiqat* (God-realization or *aikya*) and *marefat-e-haqiqat* (Gnosis or *satyanubhuti*).

Imam Muhammad Ghazali has compared these four stages to a walnut, which has four constituents: the outer skin or husk, the inner skin or lining, the kernel, and the oil within. To make the analogy more explicit, we may say that *shariat* is the outer husk, *tariqat* the inner lining, *haqiqat* the kernel, and *marefat-e-haqiqat* the oil.

As the aspirant advances through these four stages, he acquires an ever-increasing measure of certainty concerning Truth. These enduring certainties are known to the Sufis as:

(1)   *Ilm-ul-yaqin*
(2a)   *Yaqin-ul-yaqin*
(2b)   *Ain-ul-yaqin*
(3)   *Haqq-ul-yaqin*
(4)   *Urf-ul-yaqin*

(1)   *Ilm-ul-yaqin*, or intellectual certainty (conviction), is derived through rock-like faith.

(2a)   *Yaqin-ul-yaqin*, or perceptual certainty through awareness of God, is derived from inner feelings, visions or spiritual experiences on the Path. It is conviction of the soul on the first up through the fifth plane.

(2b) *Ain-ul-yaqin*, or visual certainty (*i.e.*, conviction by sight), is the experience of actually seeing God everywhere and continually; this is *antar drishti*.

(3) *Haqq-ul-yaqin*, or certainty of Realization (*i.e.*, conviction by actual experience), is attained by the soul on the seventh plane of the spiritual journey, which is *haqiqat*. Here the soul realizes itself through itself. This state is *aikya* (union with God).

(4) *Urf-ul-yaqin;* or certainty of gnosis, concerns the perfection of divinity in man by which man living the life of God knows all the mysteries of the Self and of the universe. The faculty brought into play here is the universal mind (*sarvabhaumic manas* or *aql-e-kull*), which is the seat of all divine discrimination.

To illustrate these types of conviction still further, let us suppose that a man comes to know that there is milk in a certain vessel. To have implicit faith in this knowledge through intellect and intuitive perception is *ilm-ul-yaqin* and *yaqin-ul-yaqin*. If he is not satisfied with this intellectual and intuitive conviction and actually takes the trouble to go over to the vessel and see the milk with his own eyes, and thus feel convinced that the actuality tallies with his intellectual and intuitive knowledge, he experiences the certainty known as *ain-ul-yaqin*. To drink the milk, and to become to all intents and purposes one with it, gives him the experience of *Haqq-ul-yaqin;* and to find within himself the knowledge of all that expresses and represents milk, such as sugar, water, fat, vitamins, etc., and to be able to describe these and the various uses of milk to others in detail, is the certainty of knowledge or gnosis, *i.e.*, *urf-ul-yaqin* which is the stage of *marefat-e-haqiqat*.

FIVE TYPES OF KNOWLEDGE

According to the Sufis, there are five types of knowledge affecting human beings:

The first is the knowledge of the world, which is confined to the attainment of material well-being.

The second is the knowledge of *shariat*, which is mostly

used by those who have acquired it to overthrow their opponents with the wordy warfare of logic and argument. This knowledge is that of the exoteric divines.

The third type of knowledge is that of the spiritual Path; and it is found with those who have seriously taken to some inner discipline and have shunned the society of exoterics. In this knowledge the ego still persists, and the consciousness of good and evil still clings to the soul. The knowledge of philosophers and thinkers is on the borderline between the second and third types of knowledge.

The fourth type of knowledge is that of God—the Self (*haqiqat*). One who arrives at this knowledge has no tinge of false ego left and all vestige of duality disappears.

The fifth type of knowledge is the real gnosis—the *marefat* of *haqiqat,* which, Meher Baba explains, is a complete knowledge of God and a complete knowledge of the universe. This is the knowledge of Perfection possessed by the *Rasool* (*Avatar*) and the *Qutub* (*Sadguru*).

Unless a soul goes through all the different stages of knowledge, the highest stage of *tasawwuf* (Wisdom) which is *suluk* (return to normal consciousness) can never be attained. Arriving at this stage of gnosis entitles one to be called a perfect Sufi (Perfect Master). There are, however, instances where persons have reached the fourth stage of knowledge without going through the intermediary stages, but they are quite exceptional, and occur only when such persons are led by a Perfect Master.

Meher Baba divides all spiritually advanced souls into five basic types: God-merged (Perfect One), God-intoxicated, God-absorbed, God-communed and God-mad. The reader is referred to Chapter I, pages 21–37 of Dr. William Donkin's book *The Wayfarers* which delineates Baba's treatment of this subject.

17 *Paramatma* Is Infinite and Everything (85)

Paramatma is Infinite and Everything.
All *atmas* are in *Paramatma*.
Some *atmas* experience the gross world, some experience

the subtle world and some the mental world, and some experience *Paramatma.*

As all *atmas* are in *Paramatma* they also have these different experiences in *Paramatma.* Those who experience (the experiencers) and the very experiences are all in *Paramatma.* Although the experiencers and the experiences are in *Paramatma* they are not of *Paramatma!* They are of the Nothing.

Paramatma is the Everything, and the Nothing is in the Everything.

Hence, the *atmas* that are conscious of only *sharir, pran* or *manas* are not conscious of Self. In other words, such *atmas* are conscious of the Nothing and not of the Everything. Such *atmas* experience the gross, subtle or mental world and do not experience *Paramatma.* That is, they experience the Nothing and do not experience the Everything. Therefore it can be said that the *atmas* that are in *Paramatma* are not conscious of the Self, and are not experiencing *Paramatma,* but they are conscious of the Nothing and are of the Nothing, and they experience the Nothing.

These *atmas* identify themselves with the Nothing so realistically that they apparently become Nothing.

Every being is Nothing personified.

All beings and things are personifications of the Nothing—that is in the Everything.

18   Five Spiritual Facts (115)

(1) ORDINARY HUMAN BEING:—	Man, as man, sees himself in everyone and everything.
(2) *PIR* IN SIXTH PLANE:—	Man, as man, sees God in everyone and everything.
(3) *MAJZOOB* IN SEVENTH PLANE:—	God, as God, sees Himself in everyone and everything.
(4) *QUTUB:—*	God, as man, sees Himself simultaneously in everyone and everything.
(5) SAVIOUR:—	God, as God and man, sees Himself simultaneously in everyone and everything.

—Meher Baba

19   Real Birth and Real Death (119)

There is one real birth and one real death. You are born once and you really die only once.

What is the real birth?

It is the birth of a drop in the ocean of Reality. What is meant by the birth of a drop in the ocean of Reality? It is the advent of individuality, born of indivisibility through a glimmer of the first most-finite consciousness, which transfixed cognizance of limitation into the Unlimited.

What is meant by the real death?

It is consciousness getting free from all limitations. Freedom from all limitations is real death. It is really the death of all limitations. It is liberation. In between the real birth and the real death, there is no such reality as the so-called births and deaths.

What really happens in the intermediate stage known as births and deaths is that the limitations of consciousness gradually wear off until the consciousness is free from all limitations. Ultimately consciousness, totally free from all limitations, experiences the unlimited Reality eternally. Real dying is equal to real living. Therefore I stress: Die for God and you will live as God.

You are first a child. Then you grow old and drop the body, but you never die and never were born. In the East, Vedantists believe in reincarnation, and in a number of births and deaths until one attains Godhood. The Muslims believe in one birth only and one death only. The Christians and the Zoroastrians hold the same belief. All are right. But Jesus, Buddha, Muhammad, Zoroaster, all meant what I mean by real birth and real death. I say you are born once and die once.

All the so-called births and deaths are only sleeps and wakings. The difference between sleep and death is that after you sleep you awake and find yourself in the same body; but after death you awake in a different body. You never die. Only the blessed ones die and become one with God.

20   *Fana* and *Fana-Fillah* (137)

Fana is the state of unconscious Consciousness.

In *fana-fillah* soul is unconscious of everything except Self being God.

Before the soul loses its human state and gains the divine state of *nirvikalpa*, it has to experience the vacuum state of *nirvana*.

Nirvana is the infinite vacuum, a state in which the soul is fully conscious of real Nothing, and if in the state of *nirvana* the human body is dropped, one passes into a state of the infinite bliss of God.

In some cases *nirvana* is immediately and inevitably followed by *nirvikalpa* or *fana-fillah,* where the soul is fully conscious of real Everything. *Nirvana* and *nirvikalpa* are so closely linked that each can be said to be the divine goal;

false nothing = false everything

real Nothing = neither everything nor nothing

real Everything = God the Infinite

False nothing leads to false everything; and real Nothing leads to real Everything. False nothing is linked to false everything; and real Nothing is linked to real Everything. Eventually false nothing ends in false everything, and real Nothing ends in real Everything. In duality false nothing is false everything. In unity real Nothing and real Everything are one.

Meher Baba has also made the following points:

1. The real goal is to realize God in human form; but those who drop their bodies before attaining God-realization (*i.e.,* those who drop their bodies in the state of *nirvana* before attaining the state of *nirvikalpa*), their goal is liberation

(*mukti*) from the cycle of rebirth. They experience infinite bliss only.

2. The individuality of the one who attains *nirvikalpa* state is retained as infinite and unlimited even after dropping the human body and there is a continuous experience of "I am God." But the one who attains *mukti* (liberation), experiences "I am *anand*" (I am infinite bliss); and this limits his experience of unlimited individuality of "I am infinite Power-Knowledge-Bliss" simultaneously.

3. Infinite knowledge is the most important aspect of the trio-nature of God, when an individual realizes God in human form. Infinite bliss remains the important aspect of one's experience when one has dropped one's body in the state of *nirvana* and attains *mukti, i.e.,* liberation as the goal.

4. *Majzoob-e-Kamil* experiences infinite Knowledge-Power-Bliss simultaneously and when he comes down to normal consciousness, *i.e.,* when he is also duality-conscious and is no more in the state of *Majzoob-e-Kamil,* he not only experiences Knowledge-Power-Bliss but also uses them while having his human body.

21 The Sufi Conception of *Fana* and *Baqa* (140)

This is a short study of the terms *fana* and *baqa* as understood by the Sufis. Every plane has a *fana* and *baqa* of its own. It must be remembered that the *fana* of the planes is not the *fana* of the seventh plane, and that the *baqa* of the planes is not the *baqa* of the *Qutub* state—the state of perfection.

The following are some of the chief points of comparison in Sufi gnosis, and it will be seen that their exposition is mostly in relation to the seventh plane and that their terms have, of course, a transcendental application.

Fana literally means effacement or annihilation. It is a state that is not permanent.

Baqa literally means permanence and is a state that abides forever.

Fana signifies the end of travelling **towards** God.

Baqa signifies the beginning of travelling **in** God.

Fana is not to be considered as an attribute; it is not like the dissolution of sugar in water. According to Hujwiri, it does not signify the disappearance of essence.

Baqa represents that which was not non-existent before, and will not be non-existent afterwards, like the essence of God.

Fana is the disappearance of the cognition of *ghair* (the other, *i.e.,* duality).

Baqa is the knowledge of God that one gains after the disappearance of *ghair.*

Fana according to Mahmud Shabistari in *Gulshan-e-Raz,* is death of passion, of self-will and of the ego, resulting in the spirtual awakening to eternal life (*baqa*). It also means the forgetfulness of the false ego (*khudi*) which has so long been concealing man's reality (God) from himself. If it occurs to the aspirant that he is effaced from self, it is a defect. The highest state is to be effaced from effacement.

Fana is of two kinds, outward and inward:

Outward *fana.* This is the *fana* of deeds and the glory of divine deeds. The possessor of this *fana* becomes so immersed in divine deeds that he is oblivious of himself and of everything except of the desire and the will of God. Some holy aspirants have attained this *muqam* wherein they are so indifferent to physical needs that God appoints someone to look after them.

Inward *fana.* This is the *fana* of qualities in *zat* (Reality). The possessor of *hal* (experience) in the revelation of the attributes of God is immersed sometimes in the *fana* of his own qualities, and sometimes in the manifestation of the influence (*asar*) and the glory (*tajalli*) of God.

Outward *fana* is a portion of the lords of the heart and of the companions of *hal.*

Inward *fana* is peculiar to the noble ones who have outgrown the sway of *hal* and have pierced the veil of the heart; and from the society of the men of the heart they have joined the society of the converter of hearts (God).

Baqa that is in relation to outward *fana* is this: After *fana* of desire and of will God makes the slave into a master of desire and will and gives him absolute control of the reins of guidance.

Baqa in relation to inward *fana* is this: The soul becomes neither God as the veil of Creation nor Creation, the veil of God. In *fana* God is the veil of Creation, and to those who have not reached the state of *fana,* Creation is the veil of God.

22 Involution of Consciousness (144)

Meher Baba comments further:—

"Full consciousness, which is complete as soon as the first human form is taken, gradually withdraws, plane after plane. This involution of consciousness (which consciousness is already complete) begins for the first time when the hard-set gross impressions become thinned out. Consciousness thus experiences the first plane. As the impressions get thinned out still more the consciousness withdraws (involves) more and experiences the second plane, and so forth until the seventh plane is attained.

"Withdrawal of consciousness means that at first the consciousness which was complete was focussed on gross impressions and far from being focussed on Self. Later on, in the process of involution, as the impressions thin out more and more gradually, with the help of diverse experiences of opposites, the consciousness also concurrently shifts its focus gradually towards Self. In the seventh plane the consciousness is no longer impressioned consciousness, and this naturally results in the consciousness focussing upon its Self. This means that the consciousness identifies itself with Self as all impressions have vanished."

23   Five Algebraic Definitions (146)

(1) GOD = Infinite Existence + Infinite Knowledge + Infinite
         Bliss — Unconsciousness
       = *sat* + *chit* + *anand* — unconsciousness
       = *satchitanand* **minus** unconsciousness

(2) Perfect Master = *Qutub* = *Sadguru*
       = Infinite Existence + Infinite Knowledge + Infinite
         Bliss + Consciousness
       = Conscious of being infinite and conscious of finite
         simultaneously.

(3) Saviour = Perfect Man = *Insan-e-Kamil* = *Puratan Pur-
         ush* = Buddha
       = *Saheb-e-Zaman* = *Rasool* = *Avatar* = Living
         Christ
       = Infinite Existence + Infinite Knowledge + Infinite
         Bliss + Consciousness
       = Conscious of being infinite and conscious of being
         finite simultaneously.

(4) Man
     or
     jiv-atma ⎬ = Body + Energy + Mind + Consciousness
     or   + Soul
     insan

(5) *Majzoob-e-Kamil* = Divine "I"
                        = Divine Consciousness — finite con-
                          sciousness

24   The Four Types of *Mukti* or Liberation (148)

Certain well-known terms to describe various types of perfection are stated here briefly so that the seeker may fit them
into the framework of the subject of God-realization. In describing these types of perfection, the key word *mukti*, which

literally means "liberation," is used here to define four types of liberation.

In the following table all the four types of liberation (*mukti*) of the soul belong to the seventh plane.

1) Ordinary *mukti* (Ordinary *moksha*)
2) *Videh mukti*
3) *Jivanmukti*
4) *Param mukti*

1) Ordinary *mukti* (*moksha*)

Ordinary *mukti* (*najat*) is achieved only after death by some exceptionally God-fearing, Truth-loving, good souls; and this *mukti* usually comes three to five days after the soul has left the body. Since this *mukti* is attained without the body, the individual soul enjoys only bliss (*anand*); and although power and knowledge are there, such a *Mukta* cannot experience them. Such a liberated soul is conscious only of the bliss of Union, and for him Creation no longer exists, thereby bringing to an end the constant round of births and deaths.

Nirvikalpa samadhi must not be confused with this ordinary *mukti* or *moksha* state. Should a soul reach the *mukti* state, it does so **after** the death of the physical body. Such a soul reaches God, but this occurs only after death. Thus there is an important distinction between ordinary *mukti* on the one hand and *nirvikalpa samadhi* on the other, because the latter is experienced while the soul retains the body and thus becomes *Videh Mukta*.

2) *Videh mukti*

Some God-realized souls known as *Videh Muktas* retain the body for three or four days after becoming realized. Their consciousness is merged completely in their own Real Self (God), and they are not, therefore, conscious of their bodies or of Creation. They experience constantly the infinite bliss, power and knowledge of God, their own Self now, but they cannot consciously use them in Creation, nor help others to attain liberation. Nevertheless, their presence on earth, for the few days they remain there, is a centre for the radiation of the infinite power, knowledge and bliss of God; and those who approach them, serve them and worship them, are immensely benefited. Others retain the body for years according to the momentum of their *"prarabdha."* The *Videh Mukta* is the *Brahmi Bhoot,* or the *Majzoob-e-Kamil* of the Sufis, and he experiences the trio-nature of God—*sat-chit-anand*—automatically.

3) *Jivanmukti*

The *Jivanmukta* (*Azad-e-Mutlaq*) in *turiya avastha* (*fana-ma-al-baqa*) enjoys All-Bliss, All-Knowledge and All-Power, and his consciousness is of the "I am God" state, and also of the three spheres—the gross, subtle and mental; but, being without duty, he does not use the bliss, knowledge and power for others.

4) *Param mukti*

The *Param Mukta,* who is known as the Perfect Master, *Qutub* or *Sadguru,* comes back to normal consciousness after God-realization, and is simultaneously conscious of the "I am God" state and the three relative existences and their corresponding spheres. He not only enjoys All-Power, All-Knowledge, All-Bliss, but uses them in all the planes of existence through the universal mind and the universal body.

Such *Param Muktas* are conscious of themselves as God, both in His unmanifest and manifest aspects. They know themselves both as the unchangeable divine essence (*zat*) and as the infinitely varied manifestations (*sifat*). They experience themselves as God apart from Creation; as God the Creator, Preserver and Destroyer; and as God Who has accepted and transcended the limitations of Creation. This means that such a one is conscious of every one of the ten states of God shown on the chart facing page 168.

The *Param Mukta* constantly experiences and uses the absolute peace and perfection of the trio-nature of God—*sat-chit-anand*. He fully enjoys and suffers the divine sport of Creation.

He knows himself as God in everything and is therefore able to help everyone spiritually, and can make other souls realize God as any of the four types of *Mukta*. He is indeed the helper of humanity in particular and of Creation in general.

25 A Summary of the Four Types of *Mukti* (148)

Meher Baba summarizes these four types of *mukti* in the following way:

Type of *Mukti*	Consciousness	Duty in Duality
Ordinary *Mukti*	*Anand* (bliss) only; no consciousness of "I am God" or of duality.	No
Videh Mukti	"I am God" (*sat-chit-anand* or Knowledge, Power and Bliss) without consciousness of duality.	No
Jivanmukti	"I am God" (*sat-chit-anand*) with consciousness of duality.	No
Param Mukti	Simultaneously "I am God" (*sat-chit-anand*) with duality and divinity in action.	Yes

[See also Summary, pp. 296–7. Ed.]

26 Signs of Perfection (150)

In answer to a question by a disciple requesting some infallible method of recognizing a Perfect Master, Meher Baba explained: "An ordinary man may not be able to discriminate satisfactorily between the different stages of spiritual attainment up to the sixth plane. He may be able to know that such souls are advanced, but not the extent of their advancement. But when a sincere and patient seeker of Truth comes into contact with one who is spiritually perfect, he will observe certain outer signs that are inseparably associated with inner spiritual perfection.

"The most important of these signs are three: firstly, Perfection is not only 'Oneness with God,' but the continual and uninterrupted experience of 'Oneness in everything.' A Perfect Master continually, without break, experiences and realizes his own Self as the Self in all. This inner experience objectively manifests itself in the spontaneity of love that such a one feels or expresses towards all Creation. To him nothing is attractive or repulsive. Good and bad, saint and sinner, beauty and ugliness, wisdom and idiocy, health and disease—all are modes of his own manifestation. When embodied Perfection loves, fondles, or feeds any living creature, it feels and enjoys as if it were loving, fondling and feeding its own Self. In this stage no vestige of 'otherness' is left.

"The second sign is the atmosphere of bliss that Perfection radiates in its immediate vicinity, an atmosphere that a stranger in search of it cannot help feeling. A Perfect Master not only enjoys infinite bliss but also experiences universal suffering. The acuteness of suffering however is nullified or subdued by the overwhelming feeling of bliss. Hence Perfection can outwardly appear blissfully calm in the face of every kind of suffering and persecution.

"The third sign of Perfection is its power to adapt itself to any level of humanity. It can be as nonchalant on a throne as in a gutter. It can very naturally be thrifty with the poor, extravagant with the rich, regal with kings, wise with the learned and simple with the illiterate and the ignorant. Just as a Master of Letters teaches English in different ways to beginners and graduate students, so also a Perfect Master adapts himself to the level of those whom he wants to uplift spiritually."

Once Ghaus Ali Shah Qalander, while discoursing on spiritual perfection (*faqiri*), said, "Giving perfection to a disciple is a matter of a fraction of a second. A word in the ear is enough to lift a man at once from finiteness to infinity, and such a transformation is not dependent on prayers or fasts."

Maulana Rumi has said:

*Dād-i ūrā qābilīyat-i shart nīst
Balkih shart-i qābilīyat dād-i ūst.*

"Divine Grace is not limited by conditions of ability. Ability, in fact, is conditioned by Divine Grace."

Hearing this, one of the disciples remarked, "Sire, if realization be so easy of attainment, then why is it that disciples are invariably made to undergo a long period of trials and austerities?" In reply, Ghaus Ali Shah related the following anecdote:

"A certain man having two vessels encrusted with the rust and dirt of many years, decided to have them cleansed. He gave one vessel to a professional who promised to cleanse it in forty days, and the other to a man who undertook to do the job in a single day. The professional began to work at his vessel scientifically. He subjected it to many different processes over a period of forty days, and he made the vessel not only spick and span but also a thing fit for use.

"The second man, who had promised to finish the job in one day, adopted the very drastic procedure of burning the vessel in a huge fire. This cleansed the vessel quickly and completely, but made it brittle and worthless. It can be seen, therefore, that although both the vessels were made clean, only that which underwent the lengthy process was of any use."

The Master went on to say that it was for this reason that a Perfect Master seldom gave realization to an aspirant instantaneously, but led him to it slowly so that he might become a robust, useful vessel for God's work.

In this connection, Meher Baba once remarked to his disciples, "Realization can be imparted to anyone in a second. It will then be for one's own self only with no benefit to others. The period of austerity, self-denial and hardship which one undergoes with a Master, engenders power and gives authority to use Realization, when achieved, for the spiritual awakening of others." *

27   *Hal* and *Muqam* (151)

Here is a gist of *hal* (experience) and *muqam* (stage) in the light of Sufi gnosis. Some Sufis believe there is no appreciable difference between *hal* and *muqam;* they maintain that every *muqam* is *hal* at the beginning and develops into *muqam* at the end. This applies to all the planes included in the subtle and mental spheres. Many however distinguish *hal* from *muqam.*

According to Abdullah Haris Muhasibi of Basra:

Hal is the gift of God; it is as fleeting as lightning, and is secured by practice (*mujahida*).

Muqam is the result of repentance, and is secured by the constant overshadowing of *hal.*

The author of *Awarif-ul-Maarif* has it thus:

Hal signifies a hidden event that descends from the upper world upon the heart of the pilgrim, and keeps going and coming until the divine attraction draws him from the lowest to the highest level.

Muqam is the station on the Path at which the pilgrim arrives. It becomes the place of his stay until he advances further.

Hal is not under the control of the pilgrim; the pilgrim is controlled by it.

Muqam is in the traveller's sway.

Hal is a gift (*maohib*).

Muqam is an acquisition (*kasb*).

Hal can never be without being related to *muqam.*

Muqam can never be without being related to *hal.*

---

* [See also: Meher Baba, "Perfection," *Discourses,* 1: 115–120, for the understanding of the difference between spiritual perfection and the relative perfection pertaining to the domain of duality. Ed.]

Sheikh Mohammed Ibrahim, also known as Ghazur-e-Ilahi, in his *Irshadat* says:

When *hal* continues, it becomes *muqam*. Whoever gets *hal* once is a beginner, and whosoever continues in it becomes an adept.

Meher Baba explains that:

In the general sense of the word, *hal* is the inner experience (which includes ecstasy, both controlled and uncontrolled) of relative existences on the first through the sixth planes (stages) of the Path. In the particular sense, *hal* is the state of divine ecstasy and is always experienced in degrees of potency according to its relative *muqam*. *Hal* in Vedanta is called *bhav* and *muqam* is called *sthan*.

Muqam is the staying of the pilgrim on a given plane, in that particular *hal*.

Hal and *muqam* go together up to and onto the sixth plane. *Hal* always dominates *muqam*.

Hal and *muqam* do not exist on the seventh plane.

Where there is *hal* there is duality. When one from the seventh plane comes down to normal consciousness and establishes himself on any plane for the sake of duty, then that particular plane becomes his *muqam*. Thus for the *Qutub* (*Sadguru*) there is no *hal*, there is only *muqam*. Ordinary men, who are by nature emotional, can enjoy ordinary *hal* while listening to music, but this is a pseudo-*hal* and is not to be compared with the spiritual *hal* of a pilgrim on the Path.

28 Advent of the *Avatar* (159)

Being questioned as to whether or not the *Avatar* is the first individual soul to have become God-realized, Meher Baba replied:—

"It was God Who first became infinitely conscious (see explanation in God State II-B). All this means that God realized Himself first. Simultaneously, God in His State II-A is infinitely unconscious (see explanation in God State II-A). The other states of God and all divine statuses are the outcome of God's State II-A eternally aspiring to gain infinite consciousness.

"As a result of all this, we find that man becomes God.

"The *Sadguru* is Man-God (*i.e.*, man becoming God) and had to pass through the process of evolution and involution, whereas the *Avatar* is God-Man; that is, God directly becomes man without passing through the process of evolution and involution.

"The five *Sadgurus* (*Qutubs*, Perfect Masters) effect the advent of the *Avatar* (*Rasool*, Christ, Buddha) on earth and therefore the advent of the first *Avatar* on earth was not possible without there first being the five *Sadgurus* to effect that coming. Consequently in the beginning the five Perfect Masters became realized first and then there took place the first advent of the *Avatar* on earth.

"Whether there have been twenty-six *Avatars* since Adam, or one *lakh* and twenty-four thousands of Prophets as is sometimes claimed, or whether Jesus Christ was the last and only Messiah or Muhammad the last Prophet is all immaterial and insignificant when eternity and Reality are under consideration. It matters very little to dispute whether there have been ten or twenty-six or a million *Avatars*. The truth is that the *Avatar* is always one and the same, and that the five *Sadgurus* bring about the advent of the *Avatar* on earth. This has been going on cycle after cycle, and millions of such cycles must have passed by and will continue to pass by without affecting eternity in the least."

29 Gnosis of the Seventh Plane (159)

Meher Baba describes the gnosis of "I am God" * of the seventh plane, belonging to a *Majzoob*, an *Azad-e-Mutlaq*, a *Qutub*, and the *Rasool* respectively as follows:—

---

* After disembodiment (physical death) the gnosis of all of them continues endlessly to remain "I am God."

I   *MAJZOOB* (*Brahmi Bhoot*)
    Anal Haqq—This means "I am God" (endlessly).

II *AZAD-E-MUTLAQ* (*Jivanmukta*)
    Anal Haqq, with
    Hama ba man ast—This means "Everything is with Me."

III *QUTUB* (*Sadguru*)
    Anal Haqq, simultaneously with
    Hama man am—This means "Everything is Me."
    Hama dar man ast—This means "Everything is in Me."
    Hama az man ast—This means "Everything is from Me."

IV *SAHEB-E-ZAMAN* . (*Avatar*) *
    Anal Haqq, simultaneously with
    Man hama am—This means "I am everything."
    Man dar hama am—This means "I am in everything."
    Hama az man ast—This means "Everything is from Me."
    Hama dar man ast—This means "Everything is in Me."

30   The *Avatar* **and the** *Sadguru* **(160)**

The sense Meher Baba wishes to convey is: "When a *Sadguru* is said to be in good health or ill, all this is said and seen and felt by ordinary human beings. The underlying truth from the point of view of the *Sadguru* is that neither good health nor illness nor anything whatsoever affects (touches) his being (infinity) in the least, because he is perfectly conscious (fully aware) of Illusion as illusory and is thus fully aware that health and illness are both illusory (*i.e.,* they are the outcome of the Nothing).

"How could the Nothing ever affect him? The *Sadguru* has overcome the impressions of Nothing through the process of evolution, reincarnation and involution, and he has realized

---

* [Pointing out the subtle difference between the gnosis of the *Qutub* and the *Saheb-e-Zaman* (*Avatar*), Meher Baba further explained:

Qutub's gnosis is "I am God and God is Everything," whereas gnosis of *Saheb-e-Zaman* is "I am God and I am Everything." Ed.]

that he is the Everything (which, of course, includes the Nothing). Even though the *Sadguru* remains within the law of Creation, the law itself does not touch him.

" '*Sadguru*' means that man has become God. Therefore, when man has **become** God he can no longer **be** man, and if he has to live as man he has to act, behave or appear like a man by spontaneously putting into action, that is, demonstrating all the natural tendencies of man.

"Being a Perfect Master, the *Sadguru* enacts the part (or plays the role, or lives through the role) so perfectly on all levels and in all planes that, under all circumstances and in all other respects, he **appears** to ordinary human beings as if he were a man amongst men of the gross world. He also **appears** as if he were one of the men in the subtle planes for those who are in the subtle planes, and to those who are in the mental planes he appears as if he were one of them.

"The *Sadguru* is simultaneously on the level of the lowest and of the highest. On one hand he is established in infinity (Reality) and on the other hand he is the master of Illusion. Thus the *Sadguru* has under his sway the two extremes, and reconcilement between the two extremes could only be established and maintained throughout all intermediary stages and states by the *Sadguru* **acting** on all planes and on all levels simultaneously.

"In the case of the *Avatar*, the story is quite different. All the difference is contained in the fact that *Sadguru* means man becoming God, while *Avatar* means God becoming man. It is very difficult to grasp the entire meaning of the word '*Avatar*'. For mankind it is easy and simple to declare that the *Avatar* is God and that it means that God becomes man. But this is not all that the word '*Avatar*' means or conveys.

"It would be more appropriate to say that the *Avatar* is God and that God becomes man for all mankind and simultaneously God also becomes a sparrow for all sparrows in Creation, an ant for all ants in Creation, a pig for all pigs in Creation, a particle of dust for all dusts in Creation, a particle of air for all airs in Creation, etc., for each and everything that is in Creation.

"When the five *Sadgurus* effect the presentation of the Divinity of God into Illusion, this Divinity pervades the Illusion in effect and presents Itself in innumerable varieties of forms— gross, subtle and mental. Consequently in *Avataric* periods God mingles with mankind as man and with the world of ants as an ant, etc. But the man of the world cannot perceive this and hence simply says that God has become man and remains satisfied with this understanding in his own world of mankind.

"Whatever be the understanding of man, the fact remains that the *Avatar* **becomes** and the *Sadguru* **acts.**

"The *Avatar's* illness has nothing to do with the taking on of *karma* of individuals. As the *Avatar* is God Who has become man in all respects, there is no reason why He should not be susceptible to all the natural tendencies of a human being. After all, God has become man and He **is** man indeed. But although the *Avatar* actually becomes ill, as a man who falls ill, it must be remembered that He also has simultaneously the background of His infinite power, knowledge and bliss.

"The *Avatar* never takes on the *karma* of individuals but His Godhood functions universally."

31 Action and Inaction (161)

I. In the Beyond-Beyond state of God there is unconscious inaction.

II. In the state of God-realization there is conscious inaction. This is the state of perfection but **not** of the Perfect Master.

III. In the intermediate state (between I and II) there is conscious action.

Actions promote *sanskaras* (impressions). *Sanskaras* in turn breed more actions and create bindings. In this state there is bondage.

IV. In the state of the *Majzoob* of the seventh plane there is unconscious action.

V. In the state of Perfect Masters there is conscious **active** inaction.

Perfect Masters are free of *sanskaras*. They have no impressions. As such, there cannot be room for actions of their own. Their lives are of inaction, but made active because of the prevailing environmental circumstances. Actions of Perfect Masters are prompted by the environment—by whatever atmosphere prevails then.

EXAMPLES:

I. The Beyond-Beyond state of God may be compared with a child fast asleep in a cradle. It is an example of unconscious inaction.

II. The state of the God-realized person (not a Perfect Master) may be compared with a child wide awake but still in the cradle. This is an example of conscious inaction.

III. The state in between I and II may be compared with a child awake and out of the cradle. It is an example of conscious action.

IV. The state of the *Majzoob* of the seventh plane may be compared with a somnambulist. The somnambulist walks about or performs other actions in sleep and is not aware of what he does in this state. Similarly the *Majzoob* of the seventh plane does actions and is not conscious of them. His is unconscious action: he eats, drinks, speaks, etc. But all this is his unconscious action.

V. The state of a Perfect Master may be compared with a child wide awake but inside the cradle that is continuously rocked by mankind. It is conscious **active** inaction. Inaction is being inside the cradle and active inaction is the rocking of the cradle by others.

32   Meher Baba on the Hierarchy (161)

Meher Baba says, "In each cycle of time,* which ranges from 700 to 1400 years, there are eleven ages of 65 to 125 years each. From the beginning to the end of each cycle, there are altogether 55 Perfect Masters and that means each age * has only five (5) Perfect Masters. In the last, the eleventh age of each cycle, the *Avatar* (*Saheb-e-Zaman*) is also present. Besides the 55 Perfect Masters and the *Avatar* there are also 56 *Majzoobs-e-Kamil* in each cycle. These *Majzoobs*, who experience the state of *fana-fillah*, are the 'sleeping' or 'inactive' partners in the conduct of the divine sport (*lila*) of Creation."

	PERFECT MASTERS (*Sadgurus*)	PERFECT ONES (*Majzoobs-e-Kamil*)	
1st age	5	7	(of which 4 leave the body immediately after Realization)
2nd age	5	3	
3rd age	5	7	(of which 4 leave the body immediately after Realization)
4th age	5	3	
5th age	5	7	(of which 4 leave the body immediately after Realization)
6th age	5	3	
7th age	5	7	(of which 4 leave the body immediately after Realization)
8th age	5	3	
9th age	5	7	(of which 4 leave the body immediately after Realization)
10th age	5	3	
11th age	5	6	(of which 3 leave the body immediately after Realization)
Avatar	1		
	56	56	

* In Vedanta a cycle of time is called *yuga*, and an age is called *kal;* the Sufis call a cycle *daor* or *zaman* and an age *waqt*.

In studying this table we should remember that:—

(1) One cycle lasts for about 700 to about 1400 years and is made up of 11 ages. Each age lasts for about 65 to 125 years, its length, like the length of a cycle, depending on material, spiritual and universal circumstances.

(2) In each age the functioning hierarchy consists of 7,000 spiritual beings (either advanced or perfect). The advanced beings are on or between the first through sixth planes and the Perfect Ones are either *Sadgurus* or *Majzoobs*. In each of the ages one to ten inclusive there are five *Sadgurus* (*Qutubs*), one of whom is the *Qutub-e-Irshad*.

(3) In the eleventh and last age of a cycle the *Qutub-e-Irshad* ceases to function as such as soon as the *Avatar* (*Saheb-e-Zaman* or Saviour) in person assumes His own office of Christhood (*muqam-e-Muhammadi*). Thus the number of five *Sadgurus* in each age remains constant.

(4) The Perfect *Majzoobs* alternate in number in each successive age, there being seven in the first age, three in the second, seven in the third, and so on. In the eleventh age, however, there are six *Majzoobs-e-Kamil*.

In those ages where there are more than three *Majzoobs, i.e.,* the first, third, fifth, seventh, ninth and eleventh ages, the extra ones leave the body **immediately** after becoming realized (*Majzoob-e-Kamil*). This means that in the first, third, fifth, seventh and ninth ages, four out of the seven *Majzoobs* die at once after Realization, and that in the eleventh and final age, in which there are six perfect *Majzoobs,* three die at once after Realization.

The result is that in any given age **only** three *Majzoobs* remain in the body. Thus from the point of view of the **functioning** hierarchy there are really only three *Majzoobs* in each age.

Meher Baba distributes the 7,000 members of the **functioning** hierarchy for a particular age in and between the seven spiritual planes as follows:

In the first plane, and also between 1st and 2nd, between 2nd and 3rd, between 3rd and 4th, between 4th and 5th, between 5th and 6th and between

6th and 7th	5,600
In the second plane	666
In the third plane	558
In the fourth plane	56
In the fifth plane	56
In the sixth plane	56
In the seventh plane (*i.e., Majzoobs* in the body)	3
Perfect Masters (*Sadgurus*)	5
	7,000

The *Avatar,* in the eleventh age of each cycle, brings the number to 7,001

There are always, at all times and in all ages, fifty-six God-realized souls or *Shiv-Atmas* in human form on earth; and out of these fifty-six only eight have public recognition and function as active members of the **functioning** spiritual hierarchy, consisting of 7,000 members, who do the assigned spiritual duties on various planes of consciousness according to their spiritual advancement or perfection.

The remaining forty-eight God-realized ones are not amongst the functioning spiritual hierarchy of 7,000 members. They remain aloof and people are not cognizant of their divinity, though all forty-eight have the same experience and enjoy the same divine state of "I am God" as the other eight. These forty-eight are, as it were, on the waiting list ready to help in any spiritual contingency cropping up through one or more of the functioning members dropping the body.

Out of the eight God-realized souls who are at the head of the functioning spiritual hierarchy of 7,000 members, five are Perfect Masters who, besides having a wide public recognition, have a duty to perform in the rendering of spiritual service and benefit to the whole of mankind. The remaining three are *Majzoobs* who, in spite of having achieved Godhood and remaining in the physical body, have no spiritual duty to perform towards mankind. Yet they are the source of spiritual benefit to all who come into contact with them.

So it could be said that whereas the five Perfect Masters render spiritual service to humanity as a whole, the **few** who come into contact with and serve the three *Maizoobs* draw spiritual benefit from them, while the forty-eight God-realized ones keep aloof from recognition and function, until a gap is created in the functioning hierarchy by one or more of the eight God-realized ones dropping the physical body.

33 Advent of God as *Avatar* (162)

The universe has come out of God. God has not come out of the universe. Illusion has come out of Reality. Reality has not come out of Illusion. God alone is real; the universe by itself is illusion.

God's life lived in Illusion, as the *Avatar* and as Perfect Masters, is not illusory; whereas God's life lived in Creation as all animate and inanimate beings is both real and illusory. Illusion, illusory life and God's life in Illusion, are not and cannot be one and the same. Illusion has no life and can have no life. Illusion is illusion and is nothing by itself. Illusory life means life in Illusion, with Illusion, surrounded by Illusion, and though it is life (as experienced by the soul in Creation) it is illusory life. But God's life lived in Illusion is not illusory, because in spite of living the illusory life God remains conscious of His own Reality.

God is absolutely independent, and the universe is entirely dependent upon God. Yet when the Perfect Masters effect the descent of God on earth as the *Avatar*, they make Reality and Illusion interdependent, each upon the other. And thus it is that His infinite mercy and unbounded love are eternally drawn upon by those who are immersed in Illusion.

Between God and the universe, infinite mercy and unbounded love act as a prominent link which is eternally made use of by men who become God (*Sadgurus,* Perfect Masters or *Qutubs*), and by God who becomes man (*Avatar,* Christ or *Rasool*), and so the universe becomes the eternal playmate of God. Through this prominent link the *Avatar* not only established life in his divine play, but also established law in Illusion. And this law, being established by the God-Man or *Avatar,* is the law of the lawless Infinite and it is eternally real and at the same time illusory. It is this law that governs the universe—all its ups and downs. Construction and devastation are guided by this law.

At the cyclic period, God's independent Absoluteness is made to work upon this law by the God-Man as God's will, and this means that anything and everything that the *Avatar* wills is ordained by God.

34 *Tauhid*
or The Unitary State of God (170)

The principle involving *tauhid,* or the unitary state of God, is indisputable. It is the basic foundation of all known religions and the goal of spiritual discipline in both Sufism and Vedanta. To accept *tauhid* in theory is the privilege of the masses, but to indulge in research thereof is the specialty of the select few. It is both easy and difficult. *Tauhid* is seemingly so easy that it is talked about universally on pulpit and platform and yet it is so difficult of achievement that the best of efforts therein yield nothing but stupefaction and bewilderment.

The unity of God, in its transcendent aspect, is the *tauhid-e-tanzihi* (Absolute Oneness) of Sufism, and the *advaita* of Vedanta. The problem of *tauhid* presents multifarious aspects, as is exemplified by the old story of several blind people examining an elephant. Each touched a different part of the creature and formed a different opinion. Individual approach to the subject is relatively quite true and unchallengeable, and yet

the elephant as a whole is something quite different and ununder-
standable for the blind. The following are a few utterances of
eminent Sufis concerning *tauhid* and the aspects thereof which
appeal to them: *

"*Tauhid* is that reality in which the impressions (*nuqush*)
are wiped out, and knowledge appears and God remains as immaculate and pure as He was before."

—Junayd of Baghdad

"*Tauhid* is the knowledge of God and this knowledge enables the gnostic to differentiate between the original (*qadim*)
and the contingent (*hadas*) being. The transcendent state of
tauhid involves the denial of *tauhid*."

—Junayd of Baghdad

"*Tauhid* is the effacement of the lover in the attributes of
the beloved."

—Jehangir Samnani

---

* The apparent contradictions in the words of Sufis are merely due to
limitations of the means to express the experienced truths and to describe the
realized Truth in different contexts, under different circumstances and from
different points of view that always go together in a single experience or
realization as a whole. Meher Baba says that such wordy differences do not
contradict but complement the expressions of experienced and realized truths
which underlie such contradictions. Explanations in this respect such as have
already been given in preceding pages should therefore be always borne in
mind, *viz:*

Page 206: The approach to Truth is individual, and so in the matter of details
much depends upon one's spiritual tendency, physical aptitude and external
circumstances.

Page 210: A thousand seekers may be enjoying as many experiences, yet the
Path of Gnosis is only one.

Page 221: In spite of the different aspects of the experiences of the Experience,
all the aspects are experienced together at the same time.

Page 243: On the one hand, more details confuse one more, and less details
explain things less. This gives rise to a variety of terms and expressions for
use from different viewpoints and in different contexts. In the absence of actual
experience, descriptions of the same one thing often sound contradictory. But
in the light of relative experiences or the final realization of Truth, these very
contradictions prove to be really complementary expressions about the same
one truth.

Tauhid has two aspects: one is the state and the other is the description of it. The descriptive aspect of *tauhid* belongs to the worldly mission of the Prophets, and the state thereof involves the infinite and boundless ocean. The descriptive aspect depends on the instrumentality of speech, sight, hearing and cognition, and all of these require separate confirmation. To confirm on the basis of extraneous proofs is to suggest duality, and *tauhid* is free of all tinge of duality. Faith in a man walks through the crowded thoroughfare of duality, and this stage cannot altogether be dispensed with.

Descriptive *tauhid* is like a lamp, while *tauhid* in itself and by itself is the sun. When the sun appears, the light of the lamp vanishes into nothingness. Descriptive *tauhid* is changeable, while the state of *tauhid* is immutable and eternal. The words uttered by the tongue are overruled by the heart. When one on the spiritual journey occupies the station of the heart the tongue becomes defunct and mute. Later on the heart, too, is over-ridden by the spirit (*jan*), and at this stage the wayfarer talks to Him. This talk is not in relation to the essence, but in relation to its attribute. The attribute changes and not the essence (*ayn*). The sun warms up the water, whereby the attribute is changed but not the water. Thus, "the very attempt to affirm *tauhid* is to deteriorate the pristine purity of *tauhid*" ('*Aṣbat ut-tauḥīd, fāsidūn fīt-tauḥīd*).

Tauhid veils for the unitarian (*mawahid*) the beauty of Absolute Oneness (*jamal-e-ahadiyat*). *Tauhid* on that account is suspect, because you desire it from yourself.

"One who writes about *tauhid* is a *mulhid* (rationalist); one who points towards it is a dualist; one who infers it is an idolator; one who talks about it is irresponsible; one who is silent about it is ignorant; one who thinks that he has realized it, is self-deluded; one who imagines its nearness, is distant from it; one who weighs it with intellect, and forms ideas thereof, is indulging in make-believe; and the one who finds it without seeking is the lost one."

—Abu Bakr Shibli

"*Tauhid*, if spoken of in relation to absolutism (*tanzeeh*) is to qualify it, and to refer to it as qualified (*tashbeeh*) is to make it limited and finite. To equilibrate the two extremes is, however, perfect and just what is desirable."

—Muhyuddin Ibn Arabi

"*Tauhid* is essentially forgetfulness of *tauhid*. Those returning to normal consciousness must needs have some work on the material plane. Hence *tauhid* may be likened to a creditor that can never be adequately and fully paid off in life."

—Quduntul-Kubra

Tauhid, the unitarian stage of God, therefore admits of no language, as in that transcendent state there is none to whom to address oneself.

The Sufis have classified *tauhid* into five main categories, in keeping with or connoting the different stages of man's spiritual unfoldment. They are known as:

(a) *Tauhid-e-aqwali*—the verbal unity of God.
(b) *Tauhid-e-afa'ali*—the active unity of God.
(c) *Tauhid-e-ahwali*—the feeling unity of God.
(d) *Tauhid-e-sifati*—unity of God in attributes.
(e) *Tauhid-e-zati*—unity of God in essence.

(a) *Tauhid-e-aqwali* belongs to the majority of mankind who believe in any one Prophet (*Avatar*) and have faith in His message. At this stage mere verbal acceptance of God or the unity of God, and the performance of duties pertaining thereto enjoined by the lawgiver, are considered enough as a preparation for the forthcoming stages of spiritual life. This is also known as *tauhid-e-shariat*.

(b) *Tauhid-e-afa'ali* concerns those who have actually been initiated into the Path. The expression of the unity of God with such initiates of the subtle sphere (*alam-e-malakut*) simulates intrinsically the life of the pure souls, the angels.

At this stage the spiritual conviction engendered within is that behind everything, good or bad, is the motivating power of God.

(c) *Tauhid-e-ahwali* dawns on those advanced souls of the fifth plane in the mental sphere. At this stage the soul finds itself invested with direct radiation of Divinity and consciously or unconsciously gives immense help to others in the subtle and gross spheres.

(d) *Tauhid-e-sifati* belongs to the sixth plane in the same sphere (mental). All the aspects of materiality from the gross and subtlety from the subtle planes, still clinging to the soul, are completely removed and dissolved, like the lustre of stars getting dissipated before the sun. Both (c) and (d) *tauhid* belong to the same mental sphere (*alam-e-jabrut*) and all the three (b), (c) and (d) are also collectively known as *tauhid-e-tariqat*.

(e) *Tauhid-e-zati* is God-realization in the fifth Real sphere of *haqiqat*, which includes the different stages or aspects of the *marefat-e-haqiqat*, viz., *halat-e-Muhammadi* in the stage of *lahut*, and *haqiqat-e-Muhammadi* in the stage of *hahut* of the sphere of Reality.

The Sufis are unanimous on the point that amongst the various aspects inherent in the realization or *tauhid-e-zati,* the most perfect one is the accentuation of the difference of *ubudiyat* (servantship) between man and God. This spiritual fact the church has misconstrued and misapplied, in adducing that man is man and God is God, and that man can never become God nor can God ever devolve into man. The truth underlying the situation, however, is that after the realization of *tauhid-e-zati* the emphasis on *ubudiyat* (servantship) connotes the third journey of the *Saliks* called *seyr-e-ma Allah,* the return to normal consciousness **with** God.

The varying stages and aspects of *tauhid* as discussed above are given below in tabular form:—

Stages	Aspects	Spheres
Tauhid-e-Zati	1) *Ashiq-o-Mashuq* (lover and beloved in one) 2) *Ashiq* (lover) and *Mashuq* (beloved) simultaneously	1) *Alam-e-Lahut* 2) *Alam-e-Hahut* (Fifth Sphere)
Tauhid-e-Sifati	*Ashiq* (lover)	*Alam-e-Jabrut*
Tauhid-e-Ahwali	*Arif* (knower)	(Third Sphere)
Tauhid-e-Afa'ali	*Wasif* (praiser)	*Alam-e-Malakut* (Second Sphere)
Tauhid-e-Aqwali	*Waqif* (gross-conscious)	*Alam-e-Nasut* (First Sphere)

Wujudiyyah AND *Shuhudiyyah*

Amongst the various types of unitarians (*ahl-e-tauhid*), the most important and controversial are the two schools of thought known as *Wujudiyyah* and *Shuhudiyyah*.

Muhyuddin Ibn Arabi is the greatest advocate of the *Wujudiyyah* school, upholding *wahdat-ul-wujud* (unity of existence), which in Vedanta is Advaitism, upheld by its greatest exponent Sankaracharya. According to Ghazur-e-Ilahi, Ibn Arabi held that existence (*wujud*) is not more than one, and is the very same, is manifest to itself by itself, like water which is manifest to itself in the form of ice by way of limitation. When in the state of *fana*, the limitation (the form) disappears, the Absolute remains and becomes *Hu Hu* (He, He).

Sheikh Shahabuddin Suhrawardi, one of the chief sponsors of the *Shuhudiyyah* school, characterizing its philosophy as *wahdat-ul-shuhud* (apparentism), the *Vishistadvaita* of Vedanta, maintains that in *fana*, *bandah* (the limited) becomes *kaanahu Hu* (like Him) and not *Hu Hu* (He, He), as iron in the fire, which becomes like fire but not fire itself—the reality of iron being quite different from that of fire. The *Shuhudiyyahs* define two different existences (*zat*) and two distinct things in view—iron and fire. The iron becomes fire temporarily and then iron is iron and fire is fire.

Mirza Jan Janan says that the relationship between the unmanifest aspect of God and the manifest aspect of God is that which exists between the ocean, the waves and the bubbles. And this multiplicity does not in any way affect or interfere with the Oneness of Reality. This is *wahdat-ul-wujud* (Identityism). In contrast with this, the other position determining the relationship between God and the created, as that of the original and its shadow or the sun and its rays, is *wahdat-ul-shuhud* (apparentism).

Wahdat-ul-wujud of Muhyuddin Ibn Arabi is from the heights of *ahadiyat* (conscious unity), and the gnosis pertaining to this stage is, therefore, *"Hama ust"* (Everything is He.)

Wahdat-ul-shuhud of Sheikh Shahabuddin Suhrawardi, also known as *Mujaddid,* is from the same heights of Reality (*haqiqat*), but the gnosis expressed is *"Hama az ust"* (everything is from Him).

The two doctrines and the resultant controversies are a later development at the beginning of the present *daor-e-qalandari* (cycle of mastery), and so did not arise during the lifetime of the Arabian Prophet. The doctrine of the *Wujudiyyahs* is based on experience plus reason and the *Shuhudiyyahs* base it on experience and the Quranic aspects of common interest.

Ibn Arabi denies transcendence and immanence, which imply duality. He maintains that God is one and it is He alone Who exists. All else that appear to exist are His manifestations or *tajalliyat*. Hence God is identical with *sifat* (attributes), and all divine names are identical with the named, which is *Allah*. The saints who belong to the *Wujudiyyah* school of thought have their eyes on the oneness of existence (*wahid-ul-wujud*), the first *tajalli* (manifestation) of God, from the stage of *ahadiyat;* and therefore the later devolutions (*viz.* mental, subtle and gross worlds) are like a shadow (*zil*) which is nothing and as such constitutes an adumbration on *zat* (divine essence). The shadow (*zil*), however, owes its existence to and is dependent upon God, Who is infinite and eternal. Thus the shadow also **is** in the sense that the *Wujudiyyahs* look upon everything as God, even the shadows (mental, subtle and gross worlds) which have no independent existence.

The *Shuhudiyyahs*, as said before, hold two *zats*, the one of reality and the other of non-reality, the one of God and the other of *bandah*. The *zat* of *bandah* is zero (*adum*) and this *adum* (nothingness) is relational (*izafi*), and is not real (*haqiqi*). If nothing (*adum*) is to be considered as an essence (Reality), then there will be two *zats*, which results in dualism. The *adum-e-izafi* is only relatively an *adum* (nothing). It is mere zero. If any number of zeroes are added to a zero the value of the number does not change. Thus *adum* is therefore a symbol in the knowledge of God. Since perfection appertains to *zat*, God is Perfection itself. Imperfection relates to *adum* and hence "evil" is the manifestation of *adum* (non-existent existence). The *Mujaddid* only reaffirmed and reemphasized the doctrine of *wahdat-ul-shuhud* (apparentism), originally founded by Abdul Karim al-Jili, the author of *Al-Insan-ul-Kamil*.

The spiritual fact, however, is that *Wujudiyyah* philosophy is of a loftier kind and admits of no considerations of convenience or compromise. The gnosis of Meher Baba is equally applicable to both these approaches to Truth and in order to follow it as given in the "Ten States of God" some familiarity with the Sufi way of delineating the *tanazzulat*—the devolutions of the Absolute—through successive stages of manifestations known as *khamsa wujudat* (Five Existences) of the Sufi world would be of help to the seeker.

The Gnosis of all Perfect Sufis implies that God in the Beyond the Beyond state is unknowable and undefinable. In comprehending this state of God (*Wara-ul-Wara*) which is Beyond the Beyond, the wings of thought and imagination are paralyzed. In the Beyond the Beyond state, the Absolute God (*Wujud-e-Mutlaq*) **is.**

The Sufis have described this transcendent state of God in many ways, such as:

Ghaib-ul-Ghaib (the Hidden of the Hidden).

Majhul-un-Nat (the Unknowable and the Undefinable). It is in this state that there is no knowledge of Itself for *zat*.

Munqata-ul-Izharat (the state in relation to which all indications are dropped).

Al Ama (the Dark Mist) which implies a state of latent potentiality of God in relation to its inward aspect of Beyond the Beyond, and in its outward aspect of *ahadiyat* (conscious Oneness) in which *zat* is aware of its transcendent Unity.

Meher Baba explains that although God from the Beyond state (conscious Oneness) cannot return to the Beyond the Beyond state, He knows that He **was** and **is** Infinite Existence, Infinite Knowledge and Infinite Bliss and from that knows that His original state was the Beyond-Beyond state (*Zat-al-Baht*).

However, with a view to making the subject intelligible to the seekers, the Sufis have treated the Divine Theme in terms of devolutions or manifestations of five different types, thus:—

Khamsa Wujudat OR FIVE KINDS OF EXISTENCE

(1) *Wahid-ul-wujud* (Unitary Existence) is the first manifestation or *tajalli-e-avval* in the *alam-e-lahut* of the Real Sphere and comprises the stage of *ahadiyat* (conscious Oneness).

(2) *Arif-ul-wujud* (Knowing Existence) is the stage associated with *haqiqat-e-Muhammadi* (Reality of Muhammad) or *nur-e-Muhammadi* (Light of Muhammad),* the stage of *hahut* in the Sphere of Reality. This is the stage of *wahdiyat* conscious of *wahidiyat* (conscious Oneness conscious of Oneness-in-manyness). It is the second manifestation, the *tajalli-e-dovvom*.

(3) *Mumtan-ul-wujud* (Negative Existence) is the third stage of manifestation (*tajalli-e-sevvom*). This is *alam-e-jabrut*

---

* *Haqiqat-e-Muhammadi:* God's original Word realized.
Nur-e-Muhammadi: God's original Word expressed.
Haqiqat-e-Muhammadi includes *nur-e-Muhammadi,* but *nur-e-Muhammadi* does **not** include *haqiqat-e-Muhammadi.*

(the mental sphere) at which point the stage of *wahidiyat* (Oneness in manyness) begins.

(4) *Mumkin-ul-wujud* (Possible Existence) amongst other things comprises the world of angels and spirits, and is known as *alam-e-malakut* (the subtle sphere), which is the sphere of Energy. This represents *tajalli-e-chaharom*, the fourth stage of manifestation.

(5) *Wajib-ul-wujud* (Necessary Existence) comprises everything relating to gross existence. It is known to the Sufis as *alam-e-nasut* (the gross sphere), the fifth aspect of manifestation, the *tajalli-e-panjom*.

These represent the five devolutions of God from the Beyond state, known as *tajalliyat-e-khamsa* (five manifestations) or *khamsa wujudat* (five existences).

Now we shall treat each one of them in the ascending series beginning with *wajib-ul-wujud* (Necessary Existence) and ending with *wahid-ul-wujud* (Unitary Existence).

In the domain of *shariat* (law), *wajib-ul-wujud* (Necessary Existence) means to the theologian the Absolute God from Whom all grades of existence derive their being. The Sufis on the other hand use the term to denote everything that is gross and material. Here *wujud* means body, since the evolving soul in stone, vegetable, animal and human form cannot be said to evolve without the gross mediums composed of five elements. This gross existence in the stage of *wajib-ul-wujud* is a great boon conferred by God, as without it the achievement of the stages of Perfection, sainthood and leadership would be unthinkable.

The gross body is a wonderful and unique mechanism which has in it all the other four relative and real existences, the subtle, mental and sub-supramental and God Himself. Hence the human body is called by the Sufis as *alam-e-saghir* (Microcosm) which is the epitome of *alam-e-kabir* (Macrocosm) which comprises all the five existences, the mystery of which no one can unravel without the help of the universal mind of a Perfect

Master or the Saviour.

Wajib-ul-wujud (Necessary Existence, or gross sphere) derives its existence from or is the reflection of *mumkin-ul-wujud* (subtle sphere). The relationship between God and Creation at this stage is that of the lord and the slave. The evolving consciousness or mind of this stage is called *nafs-e-ammara* (evil self) and it has the natural tendency to enjoy anything that is gross. Here the idea of God's relation to man is known as *tauhid-e-aqwali* (verbal unity of God) which acknowledges the existence of God orally.

Mumkin-ul-wujud (Possible Existence, or subtle sphere) derives its existence from *mumtan-ul-wujud* (mental sphere). Herein the relationship between God and His manifested attributes is of the sort that exists between father and children. Here God is kind, merciful and vigilant towards His children who are carefree, with no thoughts of punishment or reward, no desire for knowledge and no craving for spiritual attainments. And such entities are commonly known as angels. The consciousness of this sphere (*alam-e-malakut*) is styled as *nafs-e-lawaama* (reproachful self) and the cognition of God at this stage is called *tauhid-e-afa'ali* (unity of action), which means the entities of this world are exclusively busy with their appointed task of remembering God.

Mumtan-ul-wujud (Negative Existence, or mental sphere) contains the fifth and sixth planes of the Path which at this stage reaches *wahidiyat* (Oneness in manyness). *Wahidiyat* begins from the fifth and reaches its zenith in the sixth plane and has explicit in it all the details of Creation comprising the subtle and the gross planes. This is the *alam-e-jabrut* which derives its existence from and is the reflection of *arif-ul-wujud* (the stage of *haqiqat-e-Muhammadi*). It is called *mumtan-ul-wujud*, or Negative Existence, for the simple reason that *mumtana* means that which is non-existent, and *wujud* means the form or body of existence. Thus, the word *mumtan-ul-wujud* signifies that the form is non-existent therein. This stage is akin to the seed which contains within it the potential for the roots and the branches of the tree, which, when fully evolved and manifest, go to represent the subtle and the gross planes. The Sufis know this as *la makan* in which all ideas of time and space converge to a point.

The consciousness of the mental sphere is called by the Sufis *nafs-e-mutmainna,* meaning beatified or satisfied self, in the fifth plane, and *nafs-e-mulhima,* meaning inspired self, in the sixth plane. Herein the relationship between God and Creation is that of Beloved and the lover, and the idea of God in these stages is known to the Sufis as *tauhid-e-ahwali* (unity of feeling). This is the stage known as *haqiqat-e-insani* (Reality of man) wherein man comes face to face with God, but has not yet shed his ego and is still in the domain of duality.

Wahid-ul-wujud (Unitary Existence) in the stage of *alam-e-lahut* of the Sphere of Reality, is the state in which God first became conscious of His *ahadiyat* (conscious Oneness), and *arif-ul-wujud* in the stage of *alam-e-hahut* of the same sphere of Reality is the state of *wahdiyat-e-wahidiyat* (conscious Oneness of Oneness-in-manyness) also called *haqiqat-e-Muhammadi.*

In the state of *Wara-ul-Wara,* God, according to the Sufis, was a hidden treasure and wanted to be known. No sooner did "the hidden treasure" express a desire to know itself, than it became aware of itself as Light (*nur*), or *nur-e-Muhammadi,* which has implicit and latent in it the existence of all the Creation and the manifest world; and it is in relation to this that Prophet Muhammad has said, "God created my light first, and from my light the universe came into being." This is the aspect of *jamal* (beauty) in the knowledge of God included in *tauhid-e-zati* (Unity of Essence). Here, the relationship existing between God and the Creation is that existing between the Lover and the beloved. Here the Lover is God and Muhammad is the beloved. God here possesses complete awareness of both Himself and Creation.

Wahid-ul-wujud (Unity of Existence) is the first limitation of God in the Beyond-Beyond state and is one of the stages of the fifth sphere known as *lahut.* This is the stage of conscious Absolutism which, when used by the *arif-ul-wujud* (Knowing

Existence) gives him the experience of both *fana* and *baqa*. This stage, like all other stages of the Path, is beyond mind and intellect and cannot be encompassed in words, and includes *tajalli-e-jamali* (epiphany of beauty) and *tajalli-e-jalali* (epiphany of beatitude). *Tajalli-e-jalali* is that which confers on a soul the experience of *fana* (complete annihilation), and *tajalli-e-jamali* endows him once again with the consciousness of normality, known to the Sufis as *baqa* (permanency). *Tajalli-e-jalali* is also *ashqiyyat* wherein God is the Beloved and man is the lover; and *tajalli-e-jamali* is *mashuqīyat* wherein God is the Lover and man is the beloved. This latter is the highest spiritual manifestation, known as *faqr* or *faqiri*.

Thus in *alam-e-lahut* and *alam-e-hahut* of the fifth, the Real Sphere, are the stages of Perfection in the respective aspects of *ashiq-o-mashuq* (Lover and the Beloved in One) and *ashiq* (Lover) and *mashuq* (Beloved) simultaneously. In *alam-e-jabrut* (mental sphere) are the stages of *ashiq* (lover) and *arif* (gnostic), in *malakut* (subtle sphere) is the stage of enumerator of attributes, and in *nasut* (the gross sphere) is the stage of *waqif* (gross-conscious one). Describing these stages in the ascending order, when *waqif*, the conscious one, becomes more conscious, he enters the stage of *wasif* (attributes). And from *wasif* he arrives at the stage of *irfan* (gnosis) and from *irfan* he reaches the domain of the mysteries of God (*maarif*). From the stage of *maarif* he is presented with the sight of God which confers upon him the status of a lover, and when he ultimately becomes LOVE, he finds that he himself was the end-all and be-all of everything. In this stage of *Huyat*, everything is dissolved in the "I am God" state of God.

35 *Maya* * (180)

The force that keeps a man spiritually blind, deaf, etc., is his own ignorance which is governed by the principle of cosmic

---

* [Meher Baba, "Maya," as quoted in *In Quest of Truth*, Irene Conybeare (Kakinada, A.P., India: Swami Satya Prakash Udaseen), pp. 274–275. Ed.]

ignorance generally known as *Maya*.*

To understand *Maya* is to understand the universe. All false values and false beliefs are due to the grip of *Maya*. Intellect in particular plays into the hands of *Maya*, for intellect is not capable of that consciousness which realizes that God is Truth. Truth can only be known after one transcends the cosmic illusion which appears as real owing to *Maya*.

Maya, the principle of ignorance, can only be transcended when the spiritual aspirant is able to realize that *Maya* is God's shadow and as such is nothing. The enigma of *Maya* solves itself only after Self-realization.

36   Meher Baba Says: (202)

A. SPIRITUAL PARADOX

"Unless and until ignorance is removed and Knowledge is gained (the Knowledge whereby the divine life is experienced and lived) everything pertaining to the spiritual seems paradoxical—God, whom we do not see, we say is real; and the world, which we do see, we say is unreal. In experience, what exists for us does not really exist; and what does not exist for us, really exists.

"We must lose ourselves in order to find ourselves; thus loss itself is gain. We must die to self to live in God; thus death means life. We must become completely void inside to be completely possessed by God; thus complete emptiness means absolute fullness. We must become naked of selfhood by being nothing, so as to be absorbed in the infinity of God; thus nothing means Everything."

B. EXISTENCE IS SUBSTANCE
AND LIFE IS SHADOW

"Existence is eternal, whereas life is perishable.

"Comparatively, Existence is what his body is to man, and life is as the cloth that covers the body. The same body changes

---

* [See also: Meher Baba, "Maya," *Discourses*, 3: 137–159. Ed.]

clothes according to the seasons, time and circumstances, just as the one and eternal Existence is always there throughout the countless and varied aspects of life.

"Shrouded beyond recognition by the cloak of life with its multifarious folds and colours, is Existence unchangeable. It is the garb of life with its veils of mind, energy and gross forms that 'shadows' and superimposes on Existence, presenting the eternal, indivisible and unchangeable Existence as transient, varied and ever-changing.

"Existence is all-pervading, and is the underlying essence of all things, whether animate or inanimate, real or unreal, varied in species or uniform in forms, collective or individual, abstract or substantial.

"In the eternity of Existence there is no time. There is no past and no future; only the everlasting present. In eternity nothing has ever happened and nothing will ever happen. Everything is happening in the unending NOW.

"Existence is God; whereas, life is illusion.

"Existence is Reality; whereas, life is imagination.

"Existence is everlasting; whereas, life is ephemeral.

"Existence is unchangeable; whereas, life is ever-changing.

"Existence is freedom; whereas, life is a binding.

"Existence is indivisible; whereas life is multiple.

"Existence is imperceptible; whereas, life is deceptive.

"Existence is independent; whereas, life is dependent upon mind, energy and gross forms.

"Existence **is;** whereas, life appears to be.

"Existence, therefore, is not life.

"Birth and death do not mark the beginning or end of life. Whereas the numerous stages and states of life which constitute the so-called births and deaths are governed by the laws of evolution and reincarnation, life comes into being **only once,** with the advent of the first dim rays of limited consciousness, and succumbs to death **only once** on attaining the unlimited consciousness of infinite Existence.

"Existence, all-knowing, all-powerful, all-present God, is

beyond cause and effect, beyond time and space, beyond all actions.

"Existence touches all, all things and all shadows. Nothing can ever touch Existence. Even the very fact of its being does not touch Existence.

"To realize Existence, life must be shed. It is life that endows limitations to the unlimited Self. Life of the limited self is sustained by the mind creating impressions; by energy supplying the impetus to accumulate and dissipate these impressions through expressions; and by gross forms and bodies functioning as the instruments through which these impressions are spent, reinforced and eventually exhausted, through **actions.**

"Life is thickly linked with actions. Life is lived through actions. Life is valued through actions. Life's survival depends on actions. Life cognizant is actions—actions opposite in nature, actions affirmative and negative, actions constructive and destructive.

"Therefore, to let life succumb to its ultimate death is to let all actions end. When actions end completely, life of the limited self spontaneously experiences itself as Existence of the unlimited Self. Existence being realized, evolution and involution of consciousness is complete, illusion vanishes, and the law of reincarnation no longer binds.

"Simply to desist from committing actions will never put an end to actions. It would merely mean putting into action yet another action—that of inactivity.

"To escape from actions is not the remedy for the uprooting of actions. Rather, this would give scope to the limited self to get more involved in the very act of escaping, thus creating more actions. Actions, both good and bad, are like knots in the tangled thread of life. The more persistent the efforts to undo the knots of action, the firmer become the knots and the greater the entanglement.

"Only actions can nullify actions, in the same way that poison can counteract the effects of poison. A deeply embedded thorn may be extricated by the use of another thorn or any sharp object resembling it, such as a needle, used with skill and precaution. Similarly, actions are totally uprooted by other actions —when they are committed by some activating agent other than the 'self.'

"*Karma yoga, dnyan yoga, raj yoga,* and *bhakti yoga* serve the purpose of being prominent signposts on the path of Truth, directing the seeker toward the goal of eternal Existence. But the hold of life, fed by actions, is so tight on the aspirant that even with the help of these inspiring signposts, he fails to be guided in the right direction. As long as the Self is bound by actions, the aspirant, or even the pilgrim on the path toward Truth, is sure to go astray through self-deception.

"Throughout all ages, *sadhus* and seekers, sages and saints, *munis* and monks, *tapasavis* and *sanyasis,* yogis, Sufis and *talibs,* have struggled during their lifetimes, undergoing untold hardships in their efforts to extricate themselves from the maze of actions and to realize the eternal Existence by overcoming life.

"They fail in their attempts because the more they struggle with their 'selves,' the firmer the selves become gripped by life, through actions intensified by austerities and penances, by seclusions and pilgrimages, by meditation and concentration, by assertive utterances and silent contemplation, by intense activity and inactivity, by silence and verbosity, by *japas* and *tapas,* and by all types of *yogas* and *chillas.*

"Emancipation from the grip of life and freedom from the labyrinths of actions are made possible for all and attained by a few, when a Perfect Master, *Sadguru* or *Qutub* is approached and his grace and guidance are invoked. The Perfect Master's invariable counsel is complete surrender to him. Those few who do surrender their all—mind, body, possessions—so that with their complete surrender they also surrender consciously their own 'selves' to the Perfect Master, still have their very being left conscious to commit actions which are now activated only by the dictates of the Master.

"Such actions, after the surrender of one's 'self,' are no longer one's own actions. Therefore, these actions are capable of uprooting all other actions which feed and sustain life. Life then becomes gradually lifeless and eventually succumbs, by the grace of the Perfect Master, to its final death. Life, which once debarred the persevering aspirant from realizing perpetual Existence, can now no longer work its own deception.

"I have emphasized in the past, I tell you now, and I shall age after age forevermore repeat that you shed your cloak of life and realize Existence which is eternally yours.

"To realize this truth of unchangeable, indivisible, all-pervading Existence, the simplest way is to surrender to me completely; so completely that you are not even conscious of your surrender, conscious only to obey me and to act as and when I order you.

"If you seek to live perpetually, then crave for the death of your deceptive self at the hands of complete surrender to me. This *yoga* is the essence of all *yogas* in one."

C. THE FOUR JOURNEYS

"God is infinite and His shadow is also infinite. The shadow of God is the infinite space that accommodates the infinite gross sphere which, with its occurrences of millions of universes, within and without the range of men's knowledge, is the Creation that issued from the point of finiteness in the infinite Existence that is God.

"In these millions of universes are many systems with planets. Some are in gaseous states, some in states of solidification, some of stone and metal, some which also have vegetation. Some have also developed life forms such as worms, some also fish, some also birds, some also animals, and a few also have human beings.

"Thus it is that throughout the myriads of universes there are planets on which the seven kingdoms of evolution are manifested, and the evolution of consciousness and forms is completed.

"But only on the planet Earth do human beings reincarnate and begin the involutionary path to Self-realization.

"Earth is the centre of this infinite gross sphere of millions of universes inasmuch as it is the Point to which all human-conscious souls must migrate in order to begin the involutionary path.

"This involutionary path has seven stations and arrival at the seventh station completes the first journey to God.

"Although the completion of this journey is the Goal of all human souls, only a very few at any given moment embark upon it. The arrival at the end of this journey is the drowning of individuality in the Ocean of infinite consciousness, and the journey's completion is the soul's absorption in the state of 'I am God' with full consciousness, and, as God, it experiences infinite Power, Knowledge and Bliss.

"Out of all the souls who complete the first journey, a very few enter the second journey. This journey has no stations. It is an instantaneous journey—the journey of infinite consciousness being shaken from its absorption in 'I am God' to abiding in God as God. In this state individuality is regained, but individuality is now infinite, and this infinity includes gross consciousness, and so as man and God it experiences infinite Power, Knowledge and Bliss in the midst of most-finiteness—the unlimited Soul knows Its unlimitedness in the midst of limitation.

"The third journey is undertaken only by those who have accomplished the second journey, and whose lot it is to bear the burden of the exercise of infinite Power, Knowledge and Bliss and so live God's life both as man and God simultaneously.

"There are only five such masters living on the earth at any given moment, and they control the movement of the universes and the affairs of the worlds of men. Only when one of these five Perfect Masters drops his body can one of those who are abiding in God as God move onwards and complete the third journey to fill the vacant office.

"It is the duty of these five Perfect Masters to precipitate the advent of the Ancient One (*Avatar*) and to hand over to Him the charge of His own Creation.

"All those who live God's life on earth and all those who

abide in God as God on earth, when they drop their bodies, also shed forever their subtle and mental vehicles and pass away utterly as God, retaining infinite individuality and experiencing infinite Power, Knowledge and Bliss. This is the fourth journey.

"In reality these four journeys are never journeyed, for God has nowhere to journey. He is without beginning and without end. And everything, which has the appearance of being, appeared from That which has no beginning and passes back into That which has no ending."

37 The World of the Astral (247)

There is no astral world as such. The astral world is not a portion of the subtle world. However, in between the gross and the subtle worlds there are seven sheaths which form the so-called world of the astral, and this serves as a link between these two worlds.

A gross-conscious soul may be said to have an astral body which links the gross with the subtle. The astral may be called the imprint of the subtle over the gross, which imprint is neither gross nor subtle.

In sleep, in the ordinary dream state, one experiences the impressions of the gross world with the subtle body subconsciously, and not with the astral body. All experiences in the world of the astral, experienced through the medium of the astral body are as insignificant as dreams.

After disembodiment the soul experiences the world of the astral in the astral body. This may be said to be the astral journey of the soul. When the soul gets embodied, the astral body is shed and with the new gross body it gets a fresh astral body; but as long as it does not get embodied, its subtle and mental bodies undergo the experiences of the state of heaven or hell through the medium of the astral body, in accordance with the impressions that were accumulated while it was in an embodied state.

The spiritual Path begins only with the involution of consciousness when the soul begins to experience the first plane of the subtle world, and not when it just has access to the astral phenomena from the gross world. At the stage when the soul experiences fully the first plane of the subtle world, the astral sheath that linked the subtle with the gross is snapped for good.

GOD-REALIZATION BY MAN

(Man becoming God eternally)

The Sphere of Reality

The gnosis of "I am God" is common to each one and does not end on physical death.

Term	Status	State	Stage or Aspect	Gnosis
Sufi	Majzoob-e-Kamil	Jam or Halat-e-Muhammadi	Alam-e-Lahut	Anal Haqq
Vedantic *	Brahmi Bhoot	Nirvikalpa Samadhi	Vidnyan	Aham Brahmasmi
Mystic	Perfect One	God-merged	Super-consciousness	I am God
Sufi	Majzoob-Salik or Salik-Majzoob	Jam alternately with or without Farq	Fana-ma-al-Baqa	"Anal Haqq" alternately with or without "Hama ba man ast"
Vedantic	Paramhansa	Nirvikalpa Samadhi alternately with or without the consciousness of Tribhuvan	Turiya Avastha	Shivoham alternately with or without Jivoham
Mystic	Divine Super-Man	God-consciousness alternately with or without Creation-consciousness	Divine Junction	"I am God" alternately with or without "Everything is with Me"

Sufi	*Azad-e-Mutlaq* or *Saheb-e-Jamo-Farq*	*Jam with Farq*	*Fana-ma-al-Baqa*	*"Anal Haqq"* with *"Hama ba man ast"*
Vedantic	*Jivanmukta*	*Sahaj Samadhi* with the consciousness of *Tribhuvan*	*Turiya Avastha*	*Shivoham* with *Jivoham*
Mystic	Liberated Incarnate	God-consciousness with Creation-consciousness	Divine Junction	"I am God" with "Everything is with Me"
Sufi	*Qutub*	*Jam-ul-Jam* or *Baqa-Billah* or *Farq-ba-dul-Jam*	*Muqam-e-Muhammadi*	*"Anal Haqq," "Hama man am," "Hama dar man ast,"* and *"Hama az man ast"* simultaneously
Vedantic	*Sadguru*	*Sahaj Samadhi* or *Atmapratisthapana* with the duty of *Tribhuvan*	*Vidnyan Bhumika*	*Shivoham* and *Sarvoham* simultaneously
Mystic	Perfect Master	Man-God	God-consciousness and Creation-consciousness simultaneously	"I am God" and "Everything is Me, in Me and from Me" simultaneously

NOTE: *Jam* is consciousness of union with God.
Farq is consciousness of separateness from God. *Farq* therefore implies the consciousness of any or all of the three spheres—gross, subtle, mental.
Hal (the inner experience of relative existence) obtains only in the planes in and up through the sixth. There is no *hal* in the seventh plane.

* Vedantic and near-Vedantic terms.

Epilogue

God is everywhere and **does** everything.
God is within us and **knows** everything.
God is without us and **sees** everything.
God is beyond us and **IS** everything.
God alone **IS.**

Glossary

This glossary is a collection of terms used by Meher Baba in dictating *God Speaks*. The non-English terms originate, for the most part, in the Sufi or Vedantic traditions. Nearly all of them come from the Arabic, Persian, or Sanskrit languages. While dictating *God Speaks* on the alphabet board in his silence, Meher Baba would use words from as many as four different languages in one sentence, to save time in conveying his precise meaning. On the other hand, he would sometimes use a word in a somewhat different sense than, say, the precise meaning which that word carries in the Vedanta teaching. In such case, he would define it by the context in which he used it.

The definitions in this glossary are for the sense in which the word is used by Meher Baba. The letter (S) after a word means that it is of Sufi origin and comes from the Arabic or Persian languages. The letter (V) means that it is a Sanskrit word, usually but not always defined as used in the Vedanta tradition. Those words that originate in other languages (*e.g.,* Hindi, Marathi) are so marked. English words are not italicized.

The spelling of all non-English words in the text of *God Speaks* is in accordance with usage among Meher Baba and his *mandali*. They are listed in the glossary according to that spelling. Fortunately for us, before he dropped the body, Meher Baba went over and approved this glossary after I mailed it to him.

Following each word in the glossary is the transliteration

into English letters using the system of the U.S. Library of Congress. This is described in their Cataloging Service Bulletin 64, dated February 1964.

Ludwig H. Dimpfl, April 5, 1971.

* * *

abdal (S): (abdāl) A master who has the characteristic that he can and does exchange one of his physical bodies for another at will.

abrar (S): (abrār) A saint of the fifth plane. V: *mahapurush* (*sant*).

Adam: The first soul who completed the cycle of evolution (from stone to man), and involution (from man back to God). Traditionally, the first man. Also, the first *Avatar*.

adhyatma marga (V): (adhyātmamārga) The spiritual Path. S: *tariqat, rah-e-tariqat.*

adhyatmic marga (V): (adhyātmikamārga) = *adhyatma marga.*

adum (S): ('adam) Nothingness.

advaita (V): (advaita) Absolute Oneness. One without a second. S: *tauhid-e-tanzihi.*

Advaitism: The "non-dualist" school of Vedanta founded by Sankaracharya. Comparable views are held by the Sufi *Wujudiyyah.*

afrad (S): (afrād) An adept pilgrim on the sixth plane. V: *satpurush.*

Afridgar (S): (āfrīdgār) The Creator. V: *Brahma.*

ahadiyat (S): (aḥadīyat) Lit., Oneness. Conscious Unity. The highest consciousness. S: *halat-e-Muhammadi.* V: *vidnyan.*

Aham Brahmasmi (V): (ahambrahmāsmi) "I am God." S: *Anal Haqq.*

ahl-e-tauhid (S): (ahl-i tauḥīd) Members of mystic schools concerned with *tauhid,* the unity of God. *Wujudiyyah* and *Shuhudiyyah.*

Ahuramazda (Zoroastrian): Almighty God. S: *Allah.* V: *Paramatma.*

aikya (V): (aikya) Union. S: *haqiqat, vasl.*

ain-ul-yaqin: See: *yaqin.*

akhyar (S): (a<u>kh</u>yār) An advanced pilgrim on the Path. V: *mahatma.*

Akmal (S): (akmal) A Most Perfect One. A rare type of God-realized *Salik* in *baqa-billah* who has duty in Duality, but no circle of disciples. Also called *Salik-e-Akmal.*

al-: (The Arabic article is not alphabetized.)

alam-e-hahut (S): ('ālam-i hāhūt) The sphere of Mastery. The aspect of the fifth (Real) sphere from which the *Qutub* and *Avatar* direct the universe. V: *vidnyan bhumika.*

alam-e-jabrut (S): ('ālam-i jabrūt) The mental sphere, comprising the fifth and sixth planes of consciousness. V: *mano bhuvan.*

alam-e-kabir (S): ('ālam-i kabīr) The macrocosm, comprising the five kinds of existence, *khamsa wujudat.*

alam-e-lahut (S): ('ālam-i lāhūt) The sphere of Perfection. V: *vidnyan.*

alam-e-malakut (S): ('ālam-i malakūt) The subtle sphere, which comprises the first through the fourth planes of consciousness. V: *pran bhuvan.*

alam-e-nasut (S): ('ālam-i nāsūt) The gross sphere. The world of matter, of which most human beings are exclusively conscious. V: *anna bhuvan.*

alam-e-saghir (S): ('ālam-i ṣa<u>gh</u>īr) The microcosm. The human body.

Allah (S): (allāh) God in the Beyond state. Almighty God. V: *Paramatma.* Zoroastrian: *Ahuramazda, Yezdan.*

al Ama (S): (al-a'mā) The Dark Mist. A designation of the Beyond-Beyond state of God.

Anal Haqq (S): (anālḥaqq) "I am God." V: *Aham Brahmasmi.*

anand (V): (ānanda) Bliss. S: *musarrat.*

anant (V): (ananta) Infinite. S: *la mahdood.*

anna (Hindi): (ānā) A small coin, one sixteenth of a rupee.

anna bhumi (V): (annabhūmi) The gross world. S: *alam-e-nasut.*

anna bhumika (V): (annabhūmikā) The gross plane.

anna bhuvan (V): (annabhuvana) The gross sphere. S: *alam-e-nasut.*

antar drishti (V): (antardṛṣṭi) Lit., inner "seeing" (seeing God). Conviction by sight. S: *ain-ul-yaqin.* See: *yaqin.*

anwar (S): (anvār) pl. of *nur, q.v.* See also under *tajalli.*

aql-e-kull (S): ('aql-i kull) The Universal Mind. Acquired by Perfect Masters. V: *sarvabhaumic manas.*

arif (S): ('ārif) Lit., knower. A soul on the fifth plane of consciousness.

arif-ul-wujud: See: *wujud.*

arsh-e-ala (S): ('arsh-i 'alā) Lit., the high throne. The highest spiritual state, *i.e.,* of *Avatar* and Perfect Masters. V: *vidnyan bhumika.*

asan (V): (āsana) Posture, as for meditation.

asar (S): (aṣar) The influence (of God experienced by the recipient of *hal*).

ashiq (S): ('āshiq) Lit., lover. A soul on the sixth plane of consciousness.

ashiq-o-mashuq (S): ('āshiq o ma'shūq) Lover and the Beloved in One, the aspect of God in the sphere of Perfection, *alam-e-lahut.*

ashqiyyat (S): ('ashqiyyat) The state of being a lover. The epiphany of glory in the first manifestation, wherein God is the Beloved and man the lover.

asman (S): (āsmān) Plane. V: *bhumika.*

atma (V): (ātmā) (also, *atman:* ātman) The soul. S: *jan* or *ruh.*

atmapratisthapana (V): (ātmapratiṣṭhāpana) = *sahaj samadhi.* See: *baqa-billah.*

Attar, Sheikh Fariduddin. Of Nishapur. Author of *Mantiq-ut-Tayr (Conference of the Birds).* Killed in the Mongol sack of Nishapur in 1229 A.D.

Avatar (V): (avatāra) The Christ, the Saviour, the Ancient One. S: *Rasool, Saheb-e-Zaman.*

awagawan (Hindi): (āvāgavan) See: *rij'at.*

Awarif-ul-Maarif (S): ('avārifulma'ārif) *The Gifts of Gnosis,* treatise by the thirteenth century Sufi, Sheikh Suhrawardi.

ayn (S): ('ain) (or *ain*) The Essence, synonymous with *zat*. Also, the eye, or sight.

Azad-e-Mutlaq (S): (āzād-i muṭlaq) The Liberated Incarnate. God in the ninth state. V: *Jivanmukta*.

Azl-ul-Azal (S): (azalulazāl) The Eternity of eternities. A designation of the Beyond-Beyond state of God.

bandah (S): (bandah) Lit., slave; servant. The limited soul bound in illusion.

baqa (S): (baqā') Abiding. See: *fana-baqa.*

baqa-billah (S): (baqā' billāh) Abiding in God at the end of the Second Divine Journey. V: *atmapratisthapana, sahaj samadhi.*

baqa-ul-baqa (S): (baqā'lbaqā') The state of God becoming God-Man (God's knowing Himself as *Avatar*).

ba sifat ba surat (S): (bā ṣifat bā ṣūrat) Qualitied and manifest in form. V: *saguna sakar.*

bhav (V): (bhāva) Ecstasy. Form of devotion (in relation to the Diety). Trance. S: *hal.*

bhumika (V): (bhūmikā) Plane. Stage. S: *asman.*

bihoshi (S): (bī hūshī) Lit., unconsciousness. An involuntary loss of interest in the world caused by setbacks or personal tragedy. Of little spiritual value.

bikhudi (S): (bī khvudī) Forgetfulness of self. Among the first steps on the Path.

Brahma (V): (brahmā) The Creator. S: *Afridgar.*

Brahman (V): (brahman) Reality. S: *Haqq.*

brahmand (V): (brahmāṇḍa) The cosmos. The illusory universe.

Brahmi Bhoot (V): (brahmībhūta) The God-merged soul. God in State VIII. S: *Majzoob-e-Kamil.*

Buddha: The *Avatar* whose teachings come to us through the Buddhist religion. He was born in Magadha (Bihar, India) around 568 B.C. and died about 477 B.C.

chilla (S): (cillah) The period of forty days (of austerities).

chilla-nashini (S - Hindi): (cillah-naśīnī) The undertaking of forty days' austerities.

chit (V): (cit) Divine Knowledge. S: *marefat*.

crore (Hindi): (karoṛa) 100 *lakhs*. Ten million (10,000,000).

daor (S): (daur) = *zaman:* A cycle of time, of 700 to 1400 years, which begins whenever the *Avatar* appears. V: *yuga*.

daor-e-Qalandari (S): (daur-i qalandarī) The cycle of Mastery.

darshan (V): (darśana) Lit., seeing, audience. The appearance of the Master on some occasion, to bestow blessings on devotees, sometimes in the form of *prasad* (*q.v.*).

dharma shastra (V): (dharmaśāstra) The exoteric path. Orthodoxy. S: *shariat*.

Discourses: A collection of articles authored by Meher Baba from 1938 to 1944.

divan (S): (divān) One of the principal styles of Persian poetry. Many poets have written in this style. A collection of poems by one author in this style is called his *Divan*. See: Hafiz.

Examples of other important styles are *masnavi* (*q.v.*), and *rubaiyyat*.

Divine Theme: The outline by Meher Baba of the subject matter in *God Speaks,* first published in 1943. It is now reprinted as Supplement 14 in *God Speaks*.

dnyan (V): (jñāna) Gnosis. S: *irfan*.

do alam (S): (do 'ālam) Two spheres; *viz.,* the gross (*duniya*) and the subtle/mental (*uqba*), and including the fourth (composite) sphere also. V: *tribhuvan*.

Donkin, Dr. William: (1911–1969) British doctor, longtime disciple of Meher Baba. First met in London in 1933. Author of *The Wayfarers*.

duniya (S): (dunyā) See: *do alam*.

Everything, the: God the Infinite. The Everything, being everything, includes the Nothing.

fana, the final (S): (fanā') Annihilation of the Mind (self). V: *manonash* (*nirvana*).

fana-baqa (S): (fanā' baqā') May refer to one of three types of annihilation-abiding experiences between which parallels may be drawn: 1) the going to sleep, and reawakening each day of the ordinary human, 2) the annihilation (*fana*) of some aspect of the false self which precedes entering each plane of the Path, and living the life (*baqa*) in that plane, and 3) the real *fana-fillah* of the *Majzoob-e-Kamil,* and *baqa-billah* of the *Jivanmukta* and *Sadguru.*

fana-fillah (S): (fanā' fīllāh) The "I am God" state of the Perfect One. V: *nirvikalpa samadhi.*

Fanakar (S): (fanākār) The Destroyer. V: *Shiva, Mahesh.*

fana-ma-al-baqa (S): (fanā' m'ahulbaqā') The ninth state of God at the Divine Junction. V: *turiya avastha.*

fana-ul-fana (S): (fanā'lfanā') The state of God becoming man (direct descent of God on earth as *Avatar*).

faqiri (S): (faqīrī) Lit., poverty. The life of a dervish. Also: The highest spiritual manifestation. Perfection.

faqr (S): (faqr) = *faqiri.*

farq (S): (farq) Conscious separateness from God.

farq-ba-dul-jam (S): (farq badūljam') = *baqa-billah, q.v.*

Al-Futuhat-al-Makkiyya (S): (al-futūhātulmakkiyyah) See: Ibn Arabi.

Ghaib-ul-Ghaib (S): (ghaibulghaib) The hidden of the hidden. A designation of the Beyond-Beyond state of God.

ghair (S): (ghair) Lit., the other. Duality.

Ghazali, Imam Muhammad: Prominent Islamic theologian and writer on Sufism. Born in Tus (Khorasan) ca. 1059 A.D. Died 1111 A.D.

ghunghat (Hindi): (ghūṅghaṭa) Lit., a woman's veil. Symbolically, the veil of Ignorance.

God-Man: The Christ. The Messiah. S: *Rasool.* V: *Avatar.*

Gulshan-e-Raz (S): (gulshan-i rāz) *The Rose Garden Mystery,* a thirteenth century Sufi poem by Maulana Shabistari.

guna (V): (guṇa) See: *sifat.*

hadas (S): (ḥadas̱) That which is contingent, or derived. Compare *qadim*.

Hafiz, Shamsuddin Muhammad: Fourteenth century Perfect Master of Shiraz. Noted for his *Divan*. Meher Baba's favorite poet.

hahut (S): (hāhūt) Mastery.

hairat (S): (ḥairat) Enchantment.

hal (S): (ḥāl) A spiritual trance bringing ecstasy, experienced on entering a new station or plane. V: *bhav*.

halat-e-Muhammadi (S): (ḥālat-i muḥammadī) = *ahadiyat*: The conscious unity of God-realized souls.

hama az man ast (S): (hamah az man ast) Everything is from Me.

hama az ust (S): (hamah az ūst) Everything is from Him.

hama ba man ast (S): (hamah bah man ast) Everything is with Me.

hama ba ust (S): (hamah bah ūst) Everything is with Him.

hama dar man ast (S): (hamah dar man ast) Everything is in Me.

hama dar ust (S): (hamah dar ūst) Everything is in Him.

hama man am (S): (hamah manam) Everything is Me.

hama ust (S): (hamah ūst) Everything is He.

haqiqat (S): (ḥaqīqat) Truth. Reality.

haqiqat-e-insani (S): (ḥaqīqat-i insānī) The Reality of man. The state of the sixth plane saint who sees God face to face.

haqiqat-e-Muhammadi (S): (ḥaqīqat-i muḥammadī) The Reality of Muhammad. Perfect Masterhood. The tenth state of God.

haqiqi (S): (ḥaqīqī) Real. Compare *izafi*.

Haqq (S): (ḥaqq) Lit., truth. Reality. God. V: *Brahman*.

Haqq-ul-yaqin: See: *yaqin*.

Hu (S): (hū) Lit., He. God.

Hujwiri, Ali ben Uthman: Author of *Kashf-al-Mahjub* (*Unveiling of the Mystery*). Born in Ghazna ca. 1000 A.D. Died ca. 1075 A.D.

Huwal akher (S): (huvalāk̲h̲ir) He is the last.

Huwal awwal (S): (huvalavval) He is the first.

Huwal batin (S): (huvalbāṭin) He is the internal.

Huwal zaher (S): (huvaẓẓāhir) He is the external.

Huyat (S): (huvīyat) Lit., He-ness. God knowing himself as Himself. Godhood.

Ibn Arabi, Muhyuddin: Perfect Master, born in Spain, July 1165; died Damascus, October 1240. His exposition of Sufism is in his principal work, *Al-Futuhat-al-Makkiya.*

Ignorance: Knowledge of Illusion, without higher spiritual knowledge. The state of knowledge of the gross-conscious soul.

Illusion: The creation of *Maya,* the universes, which the gross-conscious soul mistakes for Reality.

ilm-ul-yaqin: See: *yaqin.*

insan (S): (insān) Human. The individual. V: *manava.*

Insan-e-Kamil (S): (insān-i kāmil) The Perfect (*i.e.,* God-realized) Man. V: *Shiv-Atma.*

Al-Insan-ul-Kamil (S): (al-insānalkāmil) *The Perfect Man,* a treatise by the fourteenth century Sufi, Abdul Karim al-Jili.

Iqbal, Dr. Muhammad: Pakistani poet and philosopher, born 1873 at Sialkot, Punjab.

irfan (S): ('irfān) Gnosis. The knowledge of the *arif;* also the knowledge of those on the sixth and seventh planes. V: *dnyan.*

irteqa (S): (irtiqā') Evolution. V: *utkranti.*

Israfeel (S): (isrāfīl) The archangel Raphael.

izafi (S): (iẓāfī) Relational, or relative. Compare *haqiqi.*

Izraeel (S): ('izrā'īl) The archangel Israel.

jalal (S): (jalāl) Glory. Beatitude.

Jalaluddin Rumi, Maulana: The thirteenth century Perfect Master. Founder of the Mevlevi ("whirling") dervishes. Author of the *Masnavi.*

jam (S): (jam') Lit., cup. Conscious union with God. God-realization.

jamal (S): (jamāl) Beauty.

jamal-e-ahadiyat (S): (jamāl-i aḥadīyat) The beauty of Absolute Oneness.

jam-ul-jam (S): (jam'uljam') = *baqa-billah, q.v.*

jan (S): (jān) The soul. V: *atma,* or *atman.*

jan-e-jismi (S): (jān-i jismī) See: *jiv-atma.*

janan (S): (jānān) The Beloved.

japas (V): (japa - singular) Repetitions, generally of *mantras* or prayers.

Jesus: Of Nazareth, the Christ.

Jibraeel (S): (Persian: jibrā'īl; *Koran:* jibrīl.) The archangel Gabriel.

al-Jili, Abdul Karim: Author of *Al-Insan-ul-Kamil (The Perfect Man),* and founder of the Sufi school of Apparentism (*wahdat-ul-shuhud*). Died ca. 1408 A.D.

jism-e-altaf (S): (jism-i alṭaf) The mental body. V: *karan sharir.*

jism-e-kasif (S): (jism-i kaṣīf) The gross body. V: *sthul sharir.*

jism-e-latif (S): (jism-i laṭīf) The subtle body. V: *sukshma sharir.*

Jivanmukta (V): (jīvanmukta) A Perfect One. S: *Azad-e-Mutlaq, Saheb-e-jamo-farq, Salik-e-Kamil.* See also: *Mukta.*

jivanmukti: See: *mukti.*

jiv-atma (V): (jīvātmā) The embodied soul. The individual. S: *jan-e-jismi.*

jivoham (V): (jīvo'ham) "I am individual."

Junayd of Baghdad: The celebrated ninth century Sufi Sheikh. Died ca. 910 A.D.

kaanahu Hu (S): (kā'nnahu hū) Lit., exactly He. Like Him. Description by the *Shuhudiyyah* school of what the soul becomes at final *fana.*

Kabir: The fourteenth century Perfect Master of Benares, 1435–1518 A.D.

kal (V): (kāla) An age of about 65 to 125 years duration. There are eleven ages in each cycle. S: *waqt.*

Kamil (S): (kāmil) = *Salik-e-Kamil:* See: *Salik.*

karamat (S): (karāmat) (pl. *karamaat:* karāmāt) A miracle performed by those on the fifth and sixth planes.

karan sharir (V): (karaṇaśarīra) The mental body. S: *jism-e-altaf*.

karma (V): (karma) Lit., action. Fate. The natural and necessary happenings in one's lifetime, preconditioned by one's past lives.

karma kanda (V): (karmakāṇḍa) See: *shariat*.

kasb (S): (kasb) An acquisition, as by buying or trading. Compare *maohib*.

Kashf-al-Mahjub (S): (kashfalmaḥjūb) See: Hujwiri.

khamsa wujudat (S): (k̲h̲amsah vujūdāt) The five kinds of existence. The five devolutions of God in the Beyond-Beyond state into man. See: *wujud*.

khudi (S): (k̲h̲vudī) The false ego.

Krishna: The *Avatar* whose history is told in the Hindu epic poem, the *Mahabharata*. His discourse to the warrior Arjuna just before battle is known as the *Bhagavad Gita*.

lahar (Hindi, Marathi): (lahara) Lit., ripple, wave, fancy, whim. The Whim of God, which caused the Creation.

lahut (S): (lāhūt) Perfection.

lakh (Hindi): (lākh) 100,000. V: *laksha*.

la mahdood (S): (lā maḥdūd) Infinite. V: *anant*.

la makan (S): (lā makān) Lit., placeless; "no" point. The "seed" in the mental sphere where all ideas of time and space converge to a point, and from which the subtle and gross worlds emanate.

la sifat la surat (S): (lā ṣifat lā ṣūrat) Attributeless and formless. V: *nirguna nirakar*.

lila (V): (līlā) The "Divine Sport" of Creation. The "game" which God plays, which manifests the Universe.

maarif (S): (ma'ārif) The domain of the mysteries of God (the domain of Divine Knowledge).

mahachaitanya (V): (mahācaitanya) Super-consciousness. Full consciousness fully involved as conscious Consciousness.

mahakarana sharir (V): (mahākaraṇaśarīra) The Universal Body.

mahapralaya (V): (mahāpralaya) A great dissolution of the universe at the end of a cosmic age. S: *qiamat*.

mahapurush (V): (mahāpuruṣa) A fifth plane saint. S: *wali, abrar*.

mahatma (V): (mahātmā) A great soul. S: *akhyar*.

mahayogi (V): (mahāyogī) A fourth plane *yogi*.

Mahesh (V): (maheśa) = *Shiva:* the Destroyer. S: *Fanakar*.

Majhul-un-Nat (S): (majhūlnna't) The unknowable and undefinable. A designation of the Beyond-Beyond state of God.

majzoob (S): (majẓūb) Lit., absorbed in. One who is absorbed in a plane of involving consciousness.

Majzoob-e-Kamil (S): (majẓūb-i kamil) The God-merged soul (of the seventh plane). V: *Brahmi Bhoot*.

majzoobiyat (S): (majẓūbīyat) The eighth state of God, that of the *Majzoob-e-Kamil*.

Majzoob-Salik (S): (majẓūb salik) A Perfect One whose *Majzoob*-like qualities are dominant. V: *Paramhansa*.

man dar hama am (S): (man dar hamah am) I am in everything.

Man-God: A Perfect Master. S: *Qutub*. V: *Sadguru*. See also: God-Man.

man hama am (S): (man hamah am) I am everything.

mana (Marathi or Hindi): (mana) Lit., mind, also the mental body. S: *jism-e-altaf*. V: *manas*.

manava (V): (mānava) See: *insan*.

mandali (Hindi): (maṇḍalī) The members of Meher Baba's circle. V: *mandala* = circle.

mano bhumi (V): (manobhūmi) The mental world. S: *alam-e-jabrut*.

mano bhumika (V): (manobhūmikā) The mental plane.

mano bhuvan (V): (manobhuvana) The mental sphere. S: *alam-e-jabrut*.

manonash (V): (manonāśa) Annihilation of the Mind (self). S: the final *fana*.

Mantiq-ut-Tayr (S): (manṭiquttair) *The Conference of the*

Birds, an allegorical tale by the eleventh-twelfth century Sufi, Sheikh Fariduddin Attar.

mantra (V): (mantra) A sacred name or phrase given by a master to his disciple as a spiritual discipline. S: *wazifa.*

maohib (S): (maohib) Given; a gift. Compare *kasb.*

marefat (S): (ma'rifat) Divine Knowledge. V: *chit, dnyan.*

marefat-e-haqiqat (S): (ma'rifat-i ḥaqīqat) The Gnosis of Reality. The gnosis of the Perfect Master or *Avatar,* who has duty in Duality. V: *satyanubhuti.*

mashuq (S): (ma'shūq) Beloved.

mashuqiyat (S): (ma'shūqīyat) Lit., the state of being the beloved. The epiphany of beauty in the first manifestation (*tajalli-e-avval*), wherein God is the Lover and man the beloved.

Masnavi, The (S): (maṡnavī) The major literary work of Jalaluddin Rumi. See also, *divan.*

mast (S): (mast) A God-intoxicated soul on the Path.

masti (S): (mastī) See: *suluk.*

mawahid (S): (muvaḥḥid) A unitarian; one of the *ahl-e-tauhid.*

Maya (V): (māyā) Lit., illusion. False attachment. That which makes the Nothing appear as everything. The root of Ignorance. Shadow of God. S: *mejaz.*

mejaz (S): (majāz) = *Maya.*

Mevlevi (S): (molavī) See: Jalaluddin Rumi.

Mikaeel (S): (mīkā'īl) The archangel Michael.

mojeza (S): (mu'jizah) (pl. *mojezat:* mu'jizāt) A miracle performed by the *Avatar* or *Qutub.*

moksha (V): (mokṣa) See: *mukti.*

Muhammad: (muḥammad) The Prophet, 570–632 A.D.

Muhasibi of Basra, Abdullah Haris: Early writer on *hal* and *muqam.* Died 857 A.D.

mujaddid (S): (mujaddid) Apparentists. Adherents of the doctrine of *wahdat-ul-shuhud.*

mujahida (S): (mujāhadah) Practice; striving; endeavor. V: *sadhana.*

Mukammil (S): (mukammil) The Supremely Perfect One. The

Perfect Master. Also called *Salik-e-Mukammil, Qutub.* V: *Sadguru.*

Mukta (V): (mukta) One who is Liberated (from the cycle of rebirth).

Videh Mukta: (videhamukta) The God-merged soul = *Brahmi Bhoot.* S: *Majzoob-e-Kamil.*

Jivanmukta: (jīvanmukta) The Liberated Incarnate. S: *Azad-e-Mutlaq, Salik-e-Kamil.*

Param Mukta: (paramamukta) The Perfect Master = *Sadguru.* S: *Qutub, Salik-e-Mukammil.*

mukti (V): (mukti) Liberation. Release from the cycle of births and deaths (*i.e.,* reincarnation).

ordinary *mukti:* = *moksha.* The liberation achieved by most souls. S: *najat.*

videh mukti: (videhamukti) "I am God" state without consciousness of duality.

jivanmukti: (jīvanmukti) "I am God" state with consciousness of duality.

param mukti: (paramamukti) "I am God" state with God-consciousness and Creation-consciousness simultaneously.

mulhid (S): (mulḥid) Atheist. V: *nastik.*

mumkin-ul-wujud: See: *wujud.*

mumtan-ul-wujud: See: *wujud.*

munis (V): (muni - singular) Lit., one who practices silence. A holy man, hermit, ascetic.

Munqata-ul-Izharat (S): (munqaṭa'uliẓhārāt) The state in relation to which all indications are dropped. A designation of the Beyond-Beyond state of God.

Munsiff, Dr. Abdul Ghani: Longtime disciple of Meher Baba. Died August 20, 1951.

muqaddar (S): (muqaddar) See: *prarabdha.*

muqam (S): (maqām) (pl. *muqamat:* maqāmat) A station, or plane, on the Path.

muqam-e-furutat (S): (maqām-i furūtat) The Divine Junction. V: *turiya avastha.*

muqam-e-hairat (S): (maqām-i ḥairat) The Place of Enchantment. A station on the Path intermediate between the third and fourth planes, where the aspirant can get long delayed in his spiritual advancement.

muqam-e-Muhammadi (S): (maqām-i muḥammadī) State of God-consciousness and Creation-consciousness simultaneously. V: *vidnyan bhumika.*

musarrat (S): (masarrat) Bliss. V: *anand.*

mutawassit (S): (mutavassiṭ) Advanced soul. V: *sadhu.*

nad (V): (nāda) Sound. The celestial music. The original WORD.

nafs (S): (nafs) The self; the false ego.

nafs-e-ammara (S): (nafs-i ammārah) The lustful self. The consciousness of the gross world or sphere.

nafs-e-lawaama (S): (nafs-i lavāmah) The reproachful self. The consciousness of the subtle sphere.

nafs-e-mulhima (S): (nafs-i mulhimah) The inspired self. The consciousness of the soul on the sixth plane.

nafs-e-mutmainna (S): (nafs-i muṭmā'innah) The beatified self. The consciousness of the soul on the fifth plane.

najat (S): (najāt) Liberation. V: ordinary *mukti, q.v.*

nastik (V): (nāstika) Atheist. S: *mulhid.*

nirakar (V): (nirākāra) Without form. S: *la surat.*

nirguna (V): (nirguṇa) Attributeless. S: *la sifat.*

nirvana (V): (nirvāṇa) The first stage of the Real *fana.* In some cases it is followed immediately by the second stage, the *fana-fillah.*

nirvikalpa samadhi: See: *samadhi.*

Nothing, the: The infinite shadow of God, Who is the Everything.

nuqush-e-amal (S): (nuqūsh-i āmāl) Lit., the impressions of actions. V: *sanskaras, q.v.*

nur (S): (nūr) (pl. *anwar*) Effulgence.

nur-e-Muhammadi (S): (nūr-i muḥammadī) The light of which God first became aware as a consequence of the desire (the Whim) to know Himself.

Om (V): (aum) God. Also, the first Word, the primal sound at the beginning of the Beginning of Creation. See also, *nad.*

Paramatma (V): (paramātmā) (or *Paramatman*) Almighty God. S: *Allah*. Zoroastrian: *Ahuramazda, Yezdan*.

Paramhansa (V): (paramahaṃsa) A Perfect One, who is sometimes "drowned" in God, in which case he is called a *Majzoob-Salik;* and sometimes also conscious of Creation, in which case he is called a *Salik-Majzoob*.

Param Mukta: See: *Mukta*.

param mukti: See: *mukti*.

Paratpar Parabrahma (V): (parātparaparabrahma) The Beyond-Beyond (first) state of God. S: *Wara-ul-Wara, Ghaib-ul-Ghaib*.

Parvardigar (S): (parvardigār) The Preserver or Sustainer. V: *Vishnu*.

pir (S): (pīr) A sixth plane master. V: *satpurush*.

pran (V): (prāṇa) Lit., vital energy. The subtle body. Also, Breath of all life.

pran bhumi (V): (prāṇabhūmi) The subtle world. S: *alam-e-malakut*.

pran bhumika (V): (prāṇabhūmikā) The subtle plane.

pran bhuvan (V): (prāṇabhuvana) The subtle sphere. S: *alam-e-malakut*.

prarabdha (V): (prārabdha) The *sanskaric* links which not only determine the length of time one remains in the body, but also determine the very course of life. Inevitable destiny. S: *muqaddar*.

prasad (V): (prasāda) A small gift, usually edible, given by the Master as a concrete expression of his love. When swallowed it acts as a seed that will eventually grow into full-blown love. A gracious gift of the Master.

punar janma (V): (punarjanma) Reincarnation. S: *rij'at*.

Puratan Purush (V): (purātana puruṣa) Lit., The Ancient One. S: *Saheb-e-Zaman*.

qadim (S): (qadīm) That which is original (ancient). Compare *hadas*.

qiamat (S): (qiyāmat) The great (final) dissolution of the universe. V: *mahapralaya.*

qudrat (S): (qudrat) Divine Power. V: *sat.*

qurbat (S): (qurbat) Lit., nearness. Relationship to God.

qurb-e-farayiz (S): (qurb-i farā'iẓ) Involuntary (necessary) nearness: the relationship of the *Avatar* to God.

qurb-e-nawafil (S): (qurb-i navāfil) Voluntary nearness: the relationship of the Perfect Master to God.

Qutub (S): (quṭb) Lit., the hub or axis. A Perfect Master. V: *Sadguru.*

Qutub-e-Irshad (S): (quṭb-i irshād) The head of the five living *Qutubs* who directs the affairs of the universe. In an *Avataric* age this office is filled by the *Avatar.*

qutubiyat (S): (quṭubīyat) Perfect Masterhood. The tenth state of God.

rah-e-tariqat (S): (rāh-i ṭarīqat) See: *tariqat.*

rahrav (S): (rahrev) One who traverses the Path. V: *sadhak.*

Rama: The *Avatar* whose life is the subject of the Hindu epic, the *Ramayana.*

Rasool (S): (rasūl) The Saviour, the Christ. V: *Avatar.*

rij'at (S): (rij'at) Reincarnation. V: *punar janma, awagawan.*

ruh (S): (rūḥ) = *jan.* Soul. V: *atma.*

Sadguru (V): (sadguru) A Perfect Master. S: *Qutub.*

sadhak (V): (sādhaka) One who traverses the Path. S: *rahrav.*

sadhana (V): (sādhana) See: *mujahida.*

sadhu (V): (sādhu) A pilgrim. An advanced soul. S: *mutawassit.*

sadrat-ul-muntaha (S): (sadratulmuntahā) The last limit. The point in the fourth (composite) sphere beyond which no unembodied soul (such as angel or archangel) can go to approach God.

saguna (V): (saguṇa) With attributes, qualitied. S: *ba sifat.*

sahaj samadhi: See: *samadhi.*

sahavas (Hindi): A gathering held by the Master so that his devotees may enjoy his company, *i.e.,* his physical presence.

Saheb-e-jamo-farq (S): (ṣāḥib-i jam' o farq) = *Azad-e-Mutlaq:* The Liberated Incarnate; a Perfect One. A soul in the ninth state of God. V: *Jivanmukta.*

Saheb-e-Zaman (S): (ṣāḥib-i zamān) = *Rasool, q.v.*

sakar (V): (sākāra) With form. S: *ba surat.*

salb-e-wilayat (S): (salb-i vilāyat) The snatching away of miraculous powers from a soul on one of the first four planes by a Perfect Master or *Avatar.*

Salik (S): (sālik) One who consciously has divine experience of any of the six planes. Real *Salik* = Man as God experiencing the state of *baqa-billah.*

Salik-e-Akmal (S): (sālik-i akmal) A Most Perfect One.

Salik-e-Kamil (S): (sālik-i kāmil) A Perfect One. V: *Jivanmukta.*

Salik-e-Mukammil (S): (sālik-i mukammil) A Supremely Perfect One = *Qutub.* V: *Sadguru.*

Salik-Majzoob (S): (sālik majẕūb) See: *Paramhansa.*

samadhi (V): (samādhi) Trance, induced by spiritual meditation.

nirvikalpa samadhi: (nirvikalpasamādhi) The "I am God" state of the Perfect One. Divinity in expression. S: *fanafillah.*

sahaj samadhi: (sahajsamādhi) The effortless and continual state of Perfection of the Perfect Master and *Avatar.* Divinity in action. S: *baqa-billah.*

Sankaracharya: Hindu Perfect Master, founder of the *Advaita* school of Vedanta. 686–718 A.D.

sanskaras (V): (saṃskāra - singular) Impressions. Also impressions which are left on the soul as memories from former lives, and which determine one's desires and actions in the present lifetime. S: *nuqush-e-amal.*

sant (Hindi): (santa) Saint. S: *abrar, wali.* V: *mahapurush.*

sanyasis (V): (saṃnyāsī - singular) Those who have renounced the world.

sarvabhaumic manas (V): (sārvabhaumika manas) The Universal Mind. S: *aql-e-kull.*

Sarvoham (V): (sarvo'ham) "I am All." S: *hama man am.*

sat (V): (sat) Divine Power. S: *qudrat.*

satpurush (V): (satpuruṣa) A sixth plane saint. S: *pir, afrad.*

satyanubhuti (V): (satyānubhūti) The Gnosis of Reality. S: *marefat-e-haqiqat.*

seyr-e-ma Allah (S): (sair-i m'ahullāh) Lit., excursion with God. The Third Divine Journey.

Shabistari, Maulana Mahmud: The thirteenth century Sufi author of *Gulshan-e-Raz.*

shakti (V): (śakti) Power.

Shamsi Tabriz: Perfect Master, wandering dervish and spiritual master of Jalaluddin Rumi. Died 1246 A.D.

shariat (S): (sharī'at) The exoteric path; orthodoxy. V: *dharma shastra, karma kanda.*

sharir (V): (śarīra) Lit., body. The gross body.

Shibli, Abu Bakr: A disciple of Junayd of Baghdad. Died 946 A.D.

Shiva (V): (śiva) = *Mahesh:* the Destroyer. Also, God. S: *Fanakar.*

Shiv-Atma (V): (śivātman) (Also *Shivatman.*) A perfect, God-realized soul. S: *Insan-e-Kamil.*

Shivoham (V): (śivo'ham) "I am God." *Aham Brahmasmi.* S: *Anal Haqq.*

shobada (S): (shu'badah) A display of powers by those on the first through the third planes.

Shuhudiyyah (S): (shuhūdiyyah) The Apparentist school of Sufism. The corresponding Vedantic school is *Vishistadvaita.*

siddhis (V): (siddhi - singular) Divine Powers, also occult powers. S: *tajalliyat.*

sifat (S): (ṣifat) The attributes of God, as contrasted to His divine essence (*zat*). V: *guna.*

sthan (V): (sthāna) A station. S: *muqam.*

sthul sharir (V): (sthūlaśarīra) The gross body. S: *jism-e-kasif.*

Sufis (S): (ṣufī - singular) The mystics whose origins lie in the Middle East. Their beginnings are lost in antiquity. They existed at the time of Zoroaster and were revitalized by Muhammad. They exist today in all parts of the world.

Suhrawardi, Sheikh Shahabuddin: 1145–1234 A.D. Author of *Awarif-ul-Maarif*. Exponent of Apparentism (*wahdat-ul-shuhud*).

sukshma sharir (V): (sūkṣmaśarīra) The subtle body. S: *jism-e-latif*.

suluk (S): (sulūk) As opposed to *masti*. The return to normal (Creation-) consciousness after God-realization, truly experienced by the Real *Saliks* in *baqa-billah*.

sulukiyat (S): (sulūkīyat) The final *sulukiyat* is the state of the Real *Salik* in *baqa-billah*.

tajalli (S): (tajallī) (pl. *tajalliyat:* tajalliyāt) Lit., manifestation. The Glory of God as experienced by the aspirant on the spiritual Path.

1) The manifestation of God as His illusory Creation.

2) Powers of the first three planes of the subtle world.

3) Divine powers of the fourth plane (*anwar-o-tajalliyat*).

tajalli-e-avval (S): (tajalli-yi avval) The first manifestation, *wahid-ul-wujud*.

tajalli-e-chaharom (S): (tajalli-yi cahārum) The fourth manifestation, *mumkin-ul-wujud*.

tajalli-e-dovvom (S): (tajalli-yi duvvum) The second manifestation, *arif-ul-wujud*.

tajalli-e-jalali (S): (tajalli-yi jalālī) The epiphany, or manifestation, of glory, which confers on the soul the experience of *fana, ashqiyyat*.

tajalli-e-jamali (S): (tajalli-yi jamālī) The epiphany, or manifestation, of beauty, which again endows the God-realized soul with consciousness of normality, *mashuqiyyat*.

tajalli-e-panjom (S): (tajalli-yi panjum) The fifth manifestation, *wajib-ul-wujud*.

tajalli-e-sevvom (S): (tajalli-yi sivvum) The third manifestation, *mumtan-ul-wujud*.

tajalliyat (S): pl. of *tajalli, q.v.*

tajalliyat-e-khamsa (S): (tajalliyāt-i khamsah) The five manifestations = *khamsa wujudat*, the five kinds of existence. See: *wujud*.

talib (S): (ṭālib) A seeker.

tanazzulat (S): (tanazzulat) The devolutions of the Absolute through the five kinds of existence.

tantriks (V): (tantrika - singular) Those who have become adept in occult powers through *tantrik* exercises. *Tantrik* exercises are based on scriptures known as *tantras*. The *tantras* prescribe practices (in legend, originally written down by Lord Shiva) which lead to such powers.

tanzeeh (S): (tanzīh) Absolute. Transcendent.

tapas (V): (tapa - singular) Austerities.

tapasavis (V): (tapasavī - singular) Ascetics.

tariqat (S): (ṭarīqat) The spiritual Path. The esoteric path of spiritual advancement. V: *adhyatmic marga*.

tasawwuf (S): (taṣavvuf) The spiritual Wisdom.

tashbeeh (S): (tashbīh) Similar. Qualified. Likened. Compared.

tauba (S): (taubah) Repentance. A turning away from the life of the senses toward God, arising from a spontaneous longing. The first of the spiritual stages, or *muqamat*.

tauhid (S): (tauhīd) The unitary state of God.

tauhid-e-afa'ali (S): (tauhīd-i afa'ālī) The active unity of God; the unification achieved by a soul on the subtle planes.

tauhid-e-ahwali (S): (tauhīd-i ahvālī) The feeling unity of God; the unification achieved by a soul on the fifth plane.

tauhid-e-aqwali (S): (tauhīd-i aqvālī) The verbal unity of God; the unification achievable by the majority of mankind, who have not yet entered the Path.

tauhid-e-shariat (S): (tauhīd-i sharī'at) The unification of law = *tauhid-e-aqwali*.

tauhid-e-sifati (S): (tauhīd-i sifātī) The unity of God in attributes; the unification achieved by a soul on the sixth plane.

tauhid-e-tanzihi (S): (tauhīd-i tanzīhī) Absolute Oneness. V: *advaita*.

tauhid-e-tariqat (S): (tauḥīd-i ṭarīqat) The unification of those on the spiritual Path. Comprises *tauhid-e-afa'ali, ahwali,* and *sifati.*

tauhid-e-zati (S): (tauḥīd-i ẓātī) The unity of God in essence. The *tauhid* of the God-realized soul.

tawajjoh (S): (tavajjuh) Lit., influence. The tearing away of veils from the inner eye of an aspirant by a *wali* gazing into the physical eyes of the aspirant.

tribhuvan (V): (tribhuvana) The triple sphere. The created universe, consisting of the gross, subtle, and mental spheres, and including the fourth (composite) sphere. S: *do alam* (*duniya* and *uqba*).

turiya avastha (V): (turīyāvasthā) The state of Divine Junction. S: *fana-ma-al-baqa* at *muqam-e-furutat.*

ubudiyat (S): ('ubūdīyat) Servantship. The role of Real *Saliks* who have returned to normal consciousness to benefit humanity in bondage.

uqba (S): ('uqbā) See: *do alam.*

urf-ul-yaqin: See: *yaqin.*

utkranti (V): (utkrānti) Evolution. S: *irteqa.*

vairagya (V): (vairāgya) Permanent (irrevocable) renunciation.

vaitag (Marathi): Temporary renunciation through frustration.

vasl (S): (vaṣl) See: *aikya.*

Vedantists (V): (vedānta) Those who practice the philosophy of Vedanta which is based not only on the essence of the four Vedas but also on sacred books written after the Vedas, including the Upanishads.

Videh Mukta: See: *Mukta.*

videh mukti: See: *mukti.*

vidnyan (V): (vijñāna) Conscious unity. The highest divine consciousness. S: *ahadiyat.*

The super-conscious stage of the Perfect One. S: *alam-e-lahut.*

vidnyan bhumika (V): (vijñānabhūmikā) State of God-consciousness and Creation-consciousness simultaneously: the consciousness of Perfect Masters. (*Majzoob-e-Kamil* is only God-conscious in *vidnyan bhumika*.) S: *muqam-e-Muhammadi*.

Vishistadvaita (V): (viśiṣṭādvaita) The Vedantic school which holds views comparable to *Shuhudiyyah*. Apparentists.

Vishnu (V): (viṣṇu) The Preserver. S: *Parvardigar*.

wahdat-ul-shuhud (S): (vaḥdatushshuhūd) Lit., unity of witness. Apparentism.

wahdat-ul-wujud (S): (vaḥdatulvujūd) Lit., unity of existence. Identityism.

wahdiyat (S): (vaḥdīyat) Conscious Oneness.

wahdiyat-e-wahidiyat (S): (vaḥdīyat-i vaḥidīyat) Conscious Oneness conscious of Oneness-in-Manyness. This is the consciousness of *haqiqat-e-Muhammadi* in the *alam-e-hahut* (sphere of Mastery).

wahidiyat (S): (vaḥidīyat) Oneness conscious of manyness. The *tauhid* of Illusion.

wahid-ul-wujud: See: *wujud*.

wajib-ul-wujud: See: *wujud*.

wali (S): (valī) Lit., friend. One who has *wilayat, q.v.* Frequently used in a more restricted sense to mean a saint on the fifth plane. V: *mahapurush*.

wali Allah (S): (valī allāh) Lit., a friend of God. A *wali*.

waqif (S): (vāqif) Lit., one who knows. A gross-conscious soul.

waqt (S): (vaqt) An age of 65–125 years duration. There are eleven ages in each cycle. V: *kal*.

Wara-ul-Wara (S): (varā'ulvarā') God in State I. The Beyond-Beyond state of God. V: *Paratpar Parabrahma*.

wasif (S): (vāsif) Lit., praiser. A subtle-conscious soul.

Wayfarers, The: A book by William Donkin, describing Meher Baba's work with *masts*. Published 1948 by Adi K. Irani, in India.

wazifa (S): (vazīfah) A *mantra, q.v.*

wilayat (S): (vilāyat) Lit., friendship (with God). The state of a soul on the fifth and sixth planes.

wujud (S): (vujūd) Lit., existence.

> *arif-ul-wujud:* ('ārifulvujūd) Knower of existence (knowing existence), descriptive of the *Qutub* in the sphere of Mastery (*alam-e-hahut*). Corresponds to the second manifestation (*tajalli-e-dovvom*).
>
> *mumkin-ul-wujud:* (mumkinulvujūd) Possible existence, of a soul in the subtle sphere (*alam-e-malakut*). Corresponds to the fourth manifestation (*tajalli-e-chaharom*).
>
> *mumtan-ul-wujud:* (mumtana'lvujūd) Negative existence, of a soul in the mental sphere (*alam-e-jabrut*). Corresponds to the third manifestation (*tajalli-e-sevvom*).
>
> *wahid-ul-wujud:* (vahidulvujūd) Unitary existence, the conscious oneness (*ahadiyat*) experienced by the *Majzoob* in the sphere of perfection (*alam-e-lahut*). Corresponds to the first manifestation (*tajalli-e-avval*).
>
> *wajib-ul-wujud:* (vājibulvujūd) Necessary existence, of the normal gross-conscious individual in the gross sphere (*alam-e-nasut*). Corresponds to the fifth manifestation (*tajalli-e-panjom*).

Wujud-e-Mutlaq (S): (vujūd-i muṭlaq) The Absolute Existence.

wujudat (S): (vujūdāt) Existence.

> *khamsa wujudat:* (khamsah vujūdāt) The five kinds of existence. See: *wujud.*

Wujudiyyah (S): (vujūdiyyah) The Sufi school of Identityism, whose views are comparable to the *Advaita* school of Vedanta.

yaqin (S): (yaqīn) Certainty. Conviction.

> *ain-ul-yaqin:* ('ainulyaqīn) The conviction by sight, which comes by seeing God face to face on the sixth plane. V: *antar drishti.*
>
> *Haqq-ul-yaqin:* (ḥaqqulyaqīn) The certainty of Realization.
>
> *ilm-ul-yaqin:* ('ilmulyaqīn) Intellectual conviction based on rock-like faith.
>
> *urf-ul-yaqin:* ('urfulyaqīn) The certainty of Gnosis, of the *Avatar* and Perfect Masters, who use their Knowledge to

help souls in bondage.

yaqin-ul-yaqin: (yaqīnulyaqīn) Conviction of souls on the first through the fifth plane.

Yezdan (Zoroastrian): Almighty God. V: *Paramatma.* S: *Allah.*

yoga (V): (yoga) Lit., union. The state of an individual when his life of action and thought is totally in harmony with the very source of his being.

There are varieties of *yoga,* such as:

bhakti yoga: (bhaktiyoga) The *yoga* of love or devotion.

dnyan yoga: (jñānayoga) The *yoga* of knowledge.

karma yoga: (karmayoga) The *yoga* of action.

raj yoga: (rājayoga) *Yoga* by means of meditation and contemplation.

yogi (V): (yogī) = *sadhak:* One who traverses the Path. S: *rahrav.*

yuga (V): (yuga) A cycle of time, of about 700 to 1400 years duration, which begins whenever the *Avatar* appears. S: *daor, zaman.*

zaman (S): (zamān) = *yuga.*

zat (S): (zāt) God's divine essence.

Zat-al-Baht (S): (zātalbaht) The pure essence. A designation of the Beyond-Beyond state of God.

zil (S): (zill) Lit., footnote; appendix, tail. God's illusory manifestation.

Zoroaster: (also, Zarathustra) The ancient *Avatar* who lived in Iran, one of the earliest of whom we have records.

Index